*The*

# WILDLIFE

## OF SOUTHERN AFRICA

*A field guide to
the animals and plants
of the region*

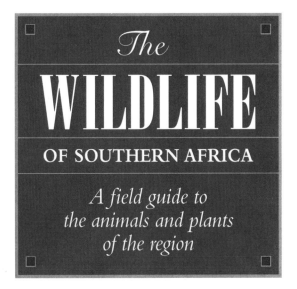

# The
# WILDLIFE
## OF SOUTHERN AFRICA

*A field guide to
the animals and plants
of the region*

Edited by
**Vincent Carruthers**

Struik Publishers
(a division of New Holland Publishing (South Africa) (Pty) Ltd)
Cornelis Struik House
80 McKenzie Street
Cape Town 8001
South Africa

New Holland Publishing is a member of Johnnic Communications Ltd.
Visit us at www.struik.co.za

www.imagesofafrica.co.za

IMAGES OF AFRICA
PHOTO    LIBRARY

First published by Southern Book Publishers (Pty) Ltd 1997
This edition published by Struik Publishers 2000

14  16  18  20  19  17  15

Cover design: Alix Gracie
Concept design: Alix Gracie
Editing and Proofreading: Marina Pearson
Illustrations: Penny Meakin, Ken Newman, Elsa Pooley,
Elizabeth Tarr, Michael Thayer and Dave Voorvelt

Typesetting: Gerhardt van Rooyen
Printed and bound by Paarl Print, Oosterland Street, Paarl, South Africa

ISBN: 1 86872 451 4

# CONTRIBUTORS

## Authors

Peter Apps
Bill Branch
Vincent Carruthers
Astri Leroy
Michael Musgrave
Ken Newman
Elsa Pooley
Christine Read
Paul Skelton

## Illustrators

Penny Meakin
Ken Newman
Elsa Pooley
Elizabeth Tarr
Michael Thayer
Dave Voorvelt

# ACKNOWLEDGEMENTS

Compiling a guide of this nature has required an unusually wide range of expertise and the editors, authors and artists have drawn on many different people and sources for assistance. We are extremely grateful to the following for their invaluable contributions:

Louise Grantham, Reneé Ferreira, Marina Pearson, Kate Rogan and Kim Sharp provided essential publishing, editorial and proofreading expertise. Jane Carruthers suggested excellent editorial improvements as well as giving continuous encouragement throughout the book's development.

Valuable advice on moths was received from Neville Duke. Rosemary Peter assisted the artist with the illustrations of ticks.

Astri Leroy thanks Ansie Dippenaar-Schoeman and Annette van den Berg of the Plant Protection Research Institute of the Agricultural Research Council who helped with the identification of spiders, as well as all those who assisted on field trips, especially her husband, John Leroy.

Bill Branch would like to thank Dove.

Frances Perryer meticulously edited the chapter on freshwater fishes.

The writing and illustrating of the botanical chapters were greatly assisted by Guy Berry, Neil Crouch, Tansa Clare, Di Dold, Judy and Humphrey Hollis, Geoff Nichols, Nic Stamatis, Rosemary Williams, the Natal Herbarium, and the Wildlife and Environment Society (Natal Branch). The author of these chapters is especially indebted to her family, Tony, Simon, Justin and Thomas Pooley.

# CONTENTS

# INTRODUCTION

This book has been written for all who enjoy nature and seek to learn about it. Its primary purpose is to enable readers to identify and name the wild plants and animals that they are most likely to find in southern Africa. The enormous wealth and diversity of wildlife in this subcontinent have long fascinated naturalists and scientists, and the national parks and nature reserves of the region have become internationally renowned. In the past, the reputation of these conserved areas rested mainly on the big game species but today many people are aware of — and more interested in — the entire diversity of nature and the complex plant and animal communities that constitute the ecosystem.

Literature on the wildlife of southern Africa is extensive and field guides are available for almost every group of plants or animals. However, a trip to the bush or a backpacking hike needs to be accompanied by a small library of publications if one is to study the tremendous variety of nature that might be encountered.

*The Wildlife of Southern Africa* attempts to resolve this problem by providing holiday-makers and visitors from abroad with a simple, single-volume field guide to species they might see. People with particular interests, such as birding, will doubtless use their specialist field guides, while this book will throw light on the myriad of other life forms that are inevitably exposed. For serious naturalists and even professional scientists it is hoped that the book will serve as an elementary field reference for observations that can be substantiated later in more formal works. For gardeners, farmers, teachers and hikers this book is intended to enhance their knowledge and enjoyment of their surroundings.

## Scope and comprehensiveness

Comprehensive coverage of all the tens of thousands of species in southern Africa is clearly impossible. However, *The Wildlife of Southern Africa* is intended to ensure that all life forms that are likely to be encountered will be identifiable and that descriptions are precise enough for confident identification. To achieve this aim several techniques and principles have been adopted:

- The following life forms are excluded from the definition of southern African wildlife:
  - marine and aquatic life except freshwater fishes and marine mammals
  - microscopic plants and animals
  - internal parasites
  - rare or very insignificant species or groups
  - species that occur only at the periphery of the southern African region.
  A more detailed explanation of the coverage of each section is given in the introductory remarks to each chapter. In this way it is hoped that readers will be aware of the probability of positive identification.

- Text has been kept single-mindedly on features which aid identification. Peripheral information has been sacrificed in favour of more comprehensive coverage.
- Where more than one similar species or group occurs, one is illustrated and described in full and the others are identified by providing very brief diagnostic features by which they can be separated reliably.
- In the case of invertebrates, the unit of description is generally the family, rather than individual species. The latter would be impractical because of the large numbers involved and the difficulty of identification in the field. Exceptions to this principle do occur and these are explained in the introductory sections to each chapter.
- Other devices to keep the book compact yet comprehensive are the use of a concise language style, abbreviations and a small typeface.

## Arrangement of contents

The book is divided more or less into halves, one dealing with animals and the other with plants.

Animals are dealt with in accordance with zoological classification, the basic unit of which is the species.

A **species** is a group of individuals evolved from common ancestral stock and capable of breeding with one another to produce fertile offspring.

A **genus** is a group of species with certain common characteristics and believed to have a relatively recent common evolutionary line.

A **family** is a group of genera with common characteristics.

An **order** is a combination of families with common characteristics.

A **class** is the broad category of classification, e.g. birds, mammals, reptiles. In this book each of the animal chapters, except chapter 1, deals with a single class.

A **phylum** is the largest unit of classification. There are 25 phyla in the animal kingdom, only five of which are of relevance to this book.

The accompanying table shows how the animal chapters are arranged to accommodate the systematic classification.

| Phylum | Class | Chapter |
| --- | --- | --- |
| 20 phyla of lower animals: mostly marine, microscopic or internal parasites | — | Not covered by the book but listed in the chapter on lower invertebrates |
| Molluscs | Gastropods | Lower invertebrates (certain terrestrial snails) |
| Annelids | Oligochaeta | Lower invertebrates (earthworms) |
| | Hirudinae | Lower invertebrates (leeches) |
| Onychophora | Peripatus | Lower invertebrates (velvet worms) |
| Arthropods | Myriapods | Lower invertebrates (centipedes and millipedes) |
| | Crustaceans | Lower invertebrates (freshwater crabs and wood lice) |
| | Arachnids | Spiders and other arachnids |
| | Insects | Insects |
| Chordata (vertebrates) | Fishes | Freshwater fishes |
| | Amphibians | Frogs |
| | Reptiles | Reptiles |
| | Birds | Birds |
| | Mammals | Mammals |

In botany the basic unit of classification is — as in the case of animals — the species. At higher levels of grouping, however, scientific classification is a less useful basis for arranging the plant section of the book. Chapters are therefore arranged in non-systematic groups which are more easily observed in the field: Grasses, sedges, ferns and fungi (although completely different visually and systematically, these are placed in one chapter because the section on each is relatively brief); wild flowers; and trees.

## The southern African region

The area covered by *The Wildlife of Southern Africa* is that part of the African continent south of the Cunene and Zambezi rivers. It includes all or part of seven countries:

- Namibia
- Botswana
- South Africa
- Zimbabwe
- Mozambique
- Swaziland
- Lesotho

The region includes widely different habitats, climates and topography, with a consequent diversity of plant and animal species.

**Natural habitats in southern Africa**

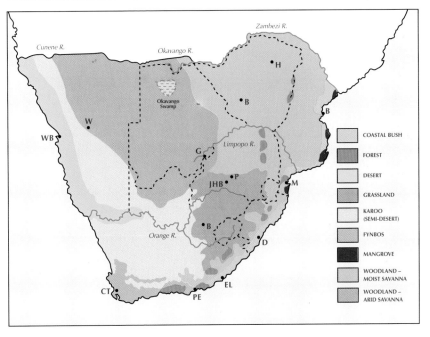

## Habitats

- **Coastal bush**. This consists of dense evergreen vegetation with thick undergrowth and some tall trees. It grows on sandy soils along a narrow strip along the east and south coast.
- **Forest**. The indigenous forests of southern Africa, comprising large trees that form a closed canopy, occur only in patches in high rainfall areas along the south coast and eastern escarpment at various altitudes.
- **Woodland** (savanna, bushveld, mopaniveld, miombo). This is an extensive and variable region of open woodland with trees that are spaced sufficiently apart so that there is an understorey of grass and no closed canopy. Moist savanna, in the north-eastern, higher rainfall areas, has a predominance of broadleaved, often deciduous, trees. Arid savanna, in the north-western parts, is dominated by acacia species and is generally more open.
- **Grassland**. Open, undulating grassland is typical across the central highveld regions and on mountain slopes. Under natural conditions it would be lacking in all but a few indigenous trees, but copses of introduced species are now common.
- **Karoo** (semi-desert). The arid south-central and west-central areas are stony with low, flat-topped koppies and sparse scrub vegetation.

- **Desert**. The extremely dry Namib desert along the coast of Namibia varies from sandy flats to mountains and is characterised by very sparse, highly specialised plants and animals. The only regular source of moisture is the coastal fog. The Kalahari desert lies further inland and is less arid.
- **Fynbos**. This unique and strikingly diverse floral kingdom lies in the winter rainfall area of the southern and south-western Cape. It includes mountains and coastal lowlands.
- **Mangroves**. Confined to isolated pockets on the north-east and east coast, these specialised communities of estuarine and intertidal fauna and flora are dominated by mangrove trees.

## Aquatic ecoregions of southern Africa

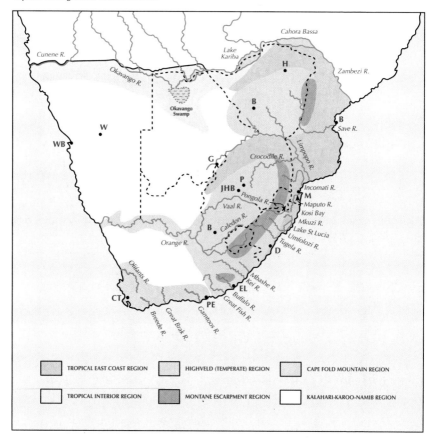

TROPICAL EAST COAST REGION    HIGHVELD (TEMPERATE) REGION    CAPE FOLD MOUNTAIN REGION

TROPICAL INTERIOR REGION    MONTANE ESCARPMENT REGION    KALAHARI-KAROO-NAMIB REGION

- **Tropical east coast region** (including the Zambezi and Limpopo valleys). The rivers are generally low-gradient mature systems with floodplain reaches. Other water bodies include coastal lakes, swamps and temporary, rain-filled pans.
- **Tropical interior region** (upper Zambezi-Okavango-Caprivi). This includes relatively large, well-watered catchments with a distinct annual flood regime in response to seasonal rainfall, mature stretches with extensive floodplain and swamp reaches.
- **Highveld (temperate) region**: (a) the interior plateau of Zimbabwe, with comparatively higher numbers of tropical species as a result of connections to the Zambezi systems; (b) South African highveld, extending to the south-east coast, and west along the Orange River valley.
- **Montane escarpment region** (Drakensberg and eastern Zimbabwe). Generally high-gradient streams with cool temperatures.
- **Cape fold mountain region**. Cool, generally clear waters.
- **Kalahari-Karoo-Namib region**. Intermittent rivers and temporary pans; isolated springs and sinkholes.

## Rainfall of southern Africa

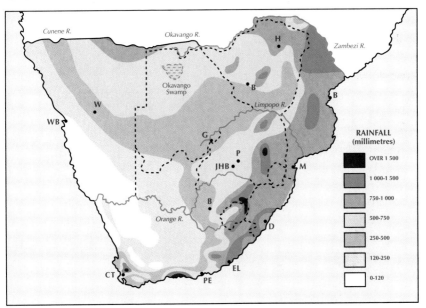

RAINFALL (millimetres)

- OVER 1 500
- 1 000-1 500
- 750-1 000
- 500-750
- 250-500
- 120-250
- 0-120

## Topography of southern Africa

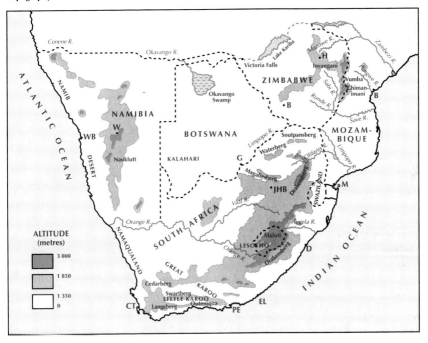

ALTITUDE (metres)

- 3 000
- 1 850
- 1 350
- 0

## Distribution

Distribution of plants and animals within the southern African region will be greatly influenced by the factors depicted in the rainfall and habitat maps. The distribution information provided with each description in the book is, of necessity, very limited. Its precision is greatly improved if read in conjunction with the habitat information given.

Abbreviations used in the distribution information include:

| | | | | | |
|---|---|---|---|---|---|
| N | = | north | n | = | northern |
| S | = | south | s | = | southern |
| E | - | east | e | = | eastern |
| W | = | west | w | = | western |
| NE | = | northeast | nw | = | northwestern, etc. |

The application of these terms is shown on the distribution notation map. References to the provinces of South Africa have deliberately been avoided because at the time of going to press some of the names and borders may still be subject to change.

**Distribution notation**

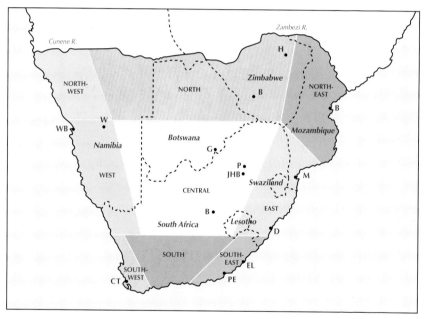

## Terminology

For every plant or animal described, the scientific name and the English name (if there is one) are given. Where there has been a recent change in the scientific name, the earlier name is given in brackets. Scientific nomenclature is associated with the system of classification (see Arrangement of contents above). The scientific name of a species of animal or plant always includes the genus (spelt with a capital letter) and the species (spelt without a capital), both written in italics, e.g. *Passer melanurus,* Cape sparrow.

Names of families, orders and classes are not written in italics even though they are Latinised, e.g. Ploceidae, the family to which sparrows, weavers and others belong.

English common names exist for most familiar plants and animals and many people find these easier to remember than scientific names. The widely used names also tend to remain unchanged whereas scientific ones are constantly under revision as our understanding of taxonomic relationships expands. However, common names are subject to the whims of their users and different local names for a single species often occur.

Technical biological terms have been kept to a minimum in this book but are sometimes unavoidable if accuracy and brevity are to be maintained simultaneously. The glossary on p. 282 and the morphological diagrams at the beginning of chapters should allow readers to understand any unfamiliar words.

## How to use this book

The objective is to identify a plant or animal that has been observed.

*Step 1*

Become familiar with the sections of the book in advance. In particular, learn which characteristics to look out for by reading the introduction to each chapter.

*Step 2*

Scan the illustrations until one is found that resembles the specimen to be identified.

*Step 3*

Read the text and ensure that all the characteristics are present. Pay particular attention to statements in **bold** type.

*Step 4*

Consider the habitat information. Most forms of wildlife have preferred habitats and this should be helpful. However, exceptions are not infrequent and habitat is not a rigid diagnostic feature.

*Step 5*

Consider the locality information. Only broad indications of range are given, but there ought not to be gross differences between the given distribution and the locality of the specimen being identified.

*Step 6*

If the specimen fits most but not all of the description, scan the alternatives under the heading **Similar** to find a match. If this proves unsuccessful, it may be necessary to refer to a specialist field guide or other work. Note that the size or distribution of species under the **Similar** heading is given only if this differs significantly from that of the main species with which it is being compared.

*Step 7*

Identifying and naming wildlife is only the start of an interesting process which becomes possible now that the specimen is known. At the back of this book is a list of references for further reading about each chapter. The behaviour, ecology and biology of the specimen will all be fascinating areas to explore further.

# LOWER INVERTEBRATES

The great majority of animal species are invertebrates, i.e. lacking a spinal supporting axis.
They range from microscopic, single-cell protozoa to highly complex animals such as insects and
spiders. The more advanced animals are loosely called "higher" invertebrates and the less
biologically complex ones "lower" invertebrates.

Of the 23 major divisions (phyla) of invertebrates, only four have members that can be regarded as southern African wildlife:

- Molluscs: snails and slugs (most of the 45 000 species of molluscs worldwide are marine animals and account for the millions of seashells found on beaches)
- Annelids: earthworms and leeches
- Onychophora: velvet worms
- Arthropods: invertebrates with jointed limbs

## Scope of this chapter

This chapter deals with those invertebrates that are likely to be encountered by the naturalist and are not included in the chapters on insects and spiders. These include the commonly found terrestrial snails, both earthworms and leeches, the velvet worm or *Peripatus*, and the important terrestrial arthropods (other than spiders and insects, which are described in subsequent chapters). Crustaceans, millipedes and centipedes are also included in this chapter. The main orders within each class are described.

All other invertebrates fall outside the scope of this book. However, some are of medical or economic importance and for the sake of comprehensiveness, the remaining invertebrate phyla are listed below:

Protozoa:            single-cell animals
Mesozoa:             minute parasitic worms
Porifera:            sponges
Coelenterata:        jellyfish, sea anemones, corals
Ctenophera:          comb jellies
Platyhelminthes:     tapeworms and flukes, such as bilharzia *(Schistosoma)*
Nemertinea:          ribbon worms
Entoprocta:          minute stalk-like tubes
Aschelminthes:       parasitic roundworms such as *Ascaris* worm in humans

| | |
|---|---|
| Acanthocephala: | spiny-headed worms |
| Bryozoa: | moss animals |
| Phoronidea: | mud-tube worms |
| Brachiopoda: | lamp shells |
| Sipunculoidea: | peanut worms |
| Echiuroidea: | sausage-like marine worms |
| Chaetognatha: | arrow worms |
| Echinodermata: | starfish, sea urchins |
| Pogonophora: | beard worms |
| Hemichordata: | tongue worms |

## Biology and habits

The lower invertebrates are so widely diverse that few aspects of their biology are common to the group as a whole.

**Slugs and snails** are confined to moist habitats and nocturnal activity or to periods of relatively high humidity. They move by means of undulating contractions of the muscular foot. Mucus is laid down to lubricate their passage.

Although hermaphrodite, pairs of individuals crossfertilise by simultaneously transferring sperm into each other. Eggs are deposited in damp hollows and hatch into fully formed miniature adults. As the snail grows, the shell is enlarged by adding to the spiral.

**Earthworms** move through the soil by consuming it and squeezing it in waves of contraction through the body. Organic food is ingested in the process.

Although hermaphrodite, individuals come to the surface to crossfertilise, each partner coming halfway out of its burrow. They position themselves side by side, their heads pointing in opposite directions, and secrete a mucous sheath that binds them together for as long as three or four hours. In this position sperm is exchanged via grooves that run along the surface of each worm's body. After they separate, each worm secretes a mucous ring which slides over the body. As it passes over the openings of the sperm receptacles it receives sperm. Fertilisation thus takes place within the mucous ring, which, when it eventually slips off the head of the worm, forms a "cocoon" and is left amid leaf litter on the surface of the ground. Typically, not all the eggs in a cocoon hatch and those that do not are absorbed by the few young worms that do develop. There are no larval stages and the young worms resemble miniature adults.

**Leeches** move over surfaces by attaching the rear sucker, extending the body, attaching the front sucker and then releasing the rear and contracting the body again. They swim by undulating their flattened bodies. The parasitic leeches attach themselves to their hosts and suck blood and body fluids from them. Some remain permanently attached to their hosts, others drop off after feeding. Scavenging and predatory forms have a proboscis which they can wrap around food such as a small worm, and so pull it into the mouth. Some leeches are able to tide over the dry winter months in protective cocoons.

Leeches are hermaphrodites but because their male and female reproductive systems are active at different times, crossfertilisation occurs after a brief mating in the warm months. Eggs are laid in a cocoon and buried in the mud or attached to submerged vegetation. Some attach the cocoon to themselves or to the animals they parasitise. Certain species even brood the eggs and young, which in all species hatch as miniature leeches and grow by moulting.

**Velvet worms** (genus *Peripatus*) feed on wood lice and other arthropods on the forest floor. They defend themselves by ejecting two fine jets of sticky fluid which form an entanglement of threads for about 20 cm in front of the worm. This effectively wards off attacks by aggressive predators and may help to immobilise prey. Velvet worms have remained unchanged for 500 million years and may have been the first creatures to venture from the sea onto land.

Mating is unique in the animal kingdom. Males deposit adhesive sperm packets randomly on the skin of the female. The skin ruptures and the sperm enters the body and finds its way to the ovaries. The young are born after a gestation period of about 13 months.

**Terrestrial crustaceans** include two very different forms, freshwater crabs and wood lice.

**Freshwater crabs** are common along rocky streams and ponds, but move far from water during wet weather. They have a strong sense of smell with which they both scavenge and hunt for food.

They mate "face to face" and the eggs, which are fertilised internally, are carried by the female on specially modified appendages on her second to fifth abdominal segments. Female crabs carrying eggs are said to be "in berry" and may be encountered in the warm months. Unlike most of their marine relatives, freshwater crabs have no larval stage and the young which hatch are miniature adults. The young crabs fend for themselves and grow by progressive moults in which the hard outer layer of the body is shed, allowing the animal to increase its body size.

♀ 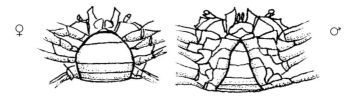 ♂

VENTRAL ASPECT OF FRESHWATER CRABS

**Wood lice**, in adapting to terrestrial life, have had to economise on water use. They lack the waxy skin covering present on most other land-living arthropods and therefore select cool, damp areas and are mostly active at night. They breathe principally by means of gills which they must keep moist. To do this, some species have developed a special technique of squeezing water out of damp vegetation by pressing their backs against it. Their habit of rolling up into a tight ball, although functional for defence, is also thought to cut down on evaporative water loss by reducing the exposed surface area.

After mating, usually in the warm months, the females carry the batch of small spherical eggs with them in a special brood pouch or marsupium, formed by flat projections on the underside of the body. After hatching, the young grow by successively shedding the toughened external skeleton.

**Centipedes** are solitary predators, immobilising their prey with formidable poison claws. They move with a snake-like motion and are capable of running relatively fast. If molested, they wriggle violently in an attempt to shake off the attacker. Some types have the last pair of walking legs modified into stout pincer-like appendages with which to defend themselves as they retreat into a hiding place.

Breeding generally occurs in spring and early summer. Courtship is very brief and simple and mating consists only of the male attaching a small spermatophore to the female. Fertilisation takes place at a later stage and eggs are laid in a hollow. In many species, the mother curls around them protectively.

**Millipedes** are entirely vegetarian and lack poison appendages for attack or defence. In defence they coil themselves up and secrete offensive fluids from spiracles along the midline of the body.

Mating pairs intertwine to allow the male to deposit a spermatophore onto the female. In pill millipedes the male creates a squealing sound by stridulation to induce the female to uncoil and accept the spermatophore. After mating, eggs are laid in the soil, deposited in capsules amid humus. Some species make receptacles out of regurgitated material or dig a nest chamber in which the spherical white eggs are left. Newly hatched millipedes have only eight segments and three pairs of legs and grow by moulting the skin and adding segments with legs to the rear end of the body immediately in front of the final segment.

## Dimensions

Dimensions given with the illustrations in this chapter refer to body length, from head to final segment. Soft-bodied animals such as leeches are measured in a natural, extended position.

## 1   GARDEN SNAIL                    *Helix aspersa*

**Two pairs of tentacles**, one pair long with eyes at tips, one pair short. Body light grey to cream. **Shell light brown with dark brown streaks and spots.** Mouthparts (radula) used to scrape away leaf tissue. Snails are hermaphrodites but mate to exchange sperm. Eggs are deposited in the soil and young hatch during wet season. Introduced from Europe. Common in gardens in moist areas.
**Similar**
**HERBIVOROUS SNAILS  Genus *Sheldonia***
Smaller (about 10 mm). Body darker, black in parts.

20-30 mm

## 2   CARNIVOROUS SNAIL               *Natalina cafra*

One pair of tentacles bearing the eyes. Fleshy palp present either side of mouth. **Shell large, olive-green to brown with fine ridges crossing the whorls. Body colour light yellow.** Feeds on other snails, earthworms. Pulls snail out of shell, eats it and absorbs some of the calcium from the shell for strengthening its own shell. Hermaphrodite but mates to exchange sperm. Lays several white, pea-sized eggs. Eggs hatch after several weeks. Coastal strip from SW to s Mozambique, never more than 250 km inland.
**Similar**
**LESSER CARNIVOROUS SNAIL  *Nata vernicosa***
Smaller (about 10 mm). Shell pale brown.

50-100 mm

## 3   PANTHER AGATE SNAIL            *Achatina immaculata*

Two pairs of tentacles, larger pair bearing eyes at tips. Smaller pair located either side of mouth. **Shell conical, cream or pale yellow with dark brown stripes.** The largest land snail. Dead shells often seen in veld. Feeds on plant matter, carrion. May eat whitewash off walls to obtain calcium for shell construction. Lays several hundred pea-sized yellow eggs which hatch after a few days. Warm, low-lying areas.

150-200 mm

## 4   SLUGS                     Genus *Stylommatophora*

**Two pairs of tentacles, one pair longer. Eyes at tips of longer pair.** Body flattened on top. Moist, slimy, with small bumps along upper surface. **Breathing hole sometimes clearly visible.** Found only in moist, dark habitats under stones or leaf litter. Feeds on fresh plant material. Absence of shell is thought to be an adaptation to low levels of calcium available on land. Hermaphrodite but mates to exchange sperm. Moist forest habitats throughout South Africa.

Radula: mouthparts of snail

40-80 mm

**1**

100 mm

**2**

10-40 mm

**3**

50-80 mm

**4**

60-120 mm

**5**

10-20 mm

### 1   COMMON EARTHWORM     *Lumbricus terrestris*

Body cylindrical. Outer surface smooth, moist. **Slightly swollen band encircles body about one third of the way from head.** Pale brown. Juveniles occur near surface, adults from surface to several metres down. Constructs burrows by eating soil and plastering digested material against walls. Introduced. Widespread except in dry areas.

**Similar**

There are numerous indigenous species, often with very local distribution. Some reach several metres in length.

### 2   LEECHES     Class Hirudinea

**Body flattened on top and below, tapering towards head. Suckers present at head and tail.** Sucker at head is smaller. Body smooth, glossy black. In shallow, vegetated, calm water. Attaches to fish and mammals, sucks blood. Anticoagulant is secreted to prevent clotting at site of attachment, causing excessive bleeding when leech is removed. Swells to many times original size while feeding. Hermaphrodite but mates to exchange sperm. Warmer parts of s Africa.

### 3   VELVET WORMS (PERIPATUS)     Phylum Onychophora

Short antennae easily visible. **Body covered in small bumps** which detect wind and touch. **Large number of fleshy legs tipped with claws. Pinkish-brown.** Found under logs, stones or along stream banks. Feeds on snails, insects, earthworms. Confined to moist forests along E coast. Represents evolutionary link between earthworms and arthropods.

### 4   FRESHWATER CRABS     Order Decapoda

No antennae. **Eyes on stalks.** Body brown. **Five pairs of limbs: four pairs of legs, one pair of pincers.** Inhabits streams and shallow fresh water. Burrows into banks and forages from there, feeding on detritus. Male and female mate facing each other. Female carries eggs until they hatch. Throughout s Africa.

### 5   WOOD LICE     Order Isopoda

No antennae. **Body flattened top and bottom.** Seven pairs of legs. Dull to dark grey. Avoids light, seeks out humid habitats under stones and in leaf litter to reduce water loss. Feeds on algae, fungi, moss, decaying plant matter. Eggs brood in water-filled cavity in female. Throughout s Africa, particularly in moist areas.

**Similar**

**SAND HOPPERS   Order Amphipoda**

Body flattened laterally. Legs of unequal length.

**1   WORM-LIKE MILLIPEDES**            Order Juliformia

Antennae short. **Head tucked in, pointing downwards.** 40–60 segments. Glossy black or with alternating yellow and black bands. **Up to 120 pairs of legs.** Feeds on decaying plant material and fungi. Female lays several hundred pinhead-sized eggs. Young hatch with three pairs of legs, acquiring more at each moult. Throughout s Africa, less common in dry areas.
**Similar**
**KEELED MILLIPEDES  Order Polydesmoidea**
About 20 segments. Keels on sides, concealed legs.

**2   PILL MILLIPEDES**            Order Oniscomorpha

**Antennae easily visible. 12 segments which are smooth, shiny.** 21 pairs of legs covered by lateral extensions of segments. Rolls into sphere when disturbed. Feeds on decaying plant matter, lichens, moss. Female lays about 20 eggs. Young hatch with three pairs of legs, acquiring more at each moult. Confined to moist forests.

**3   LARGE CENTIPEDES**            Order Scolopendromorpha

Antennae one quarter body length. **25 pairs of legs, equal in length to width of body, last pair long with conspicuous spines at tips.** Often bright red or orange. Active at dawn and dusk or on cloudy days. Aggressive predator. Prey includes frogs, small birds. Bite painful but not dangerous. Female cares for offspring. Throughout s Africa.

**4   EARTH CENTIPEDES**            Order Geophilomorpha

Antennae short with 14 segments. **Body long, worm-like. Legs shorter than body width.** Last pair of legs long, similar to antennae. Lives in burrows in loose soil and compost heaps. No eyes. Head difficult to distinguish from rear. Moves backwards and forwards with equal speed and agility. Feeds on earthworms. Digests food externally, sucking up liquid residue. Some species capable of producing light. Female cares for offspring. Moist soils throughout s Africa.

**5   STONE CENTIPEDES**            Order Lithobiomorpha

Antennae roughly one third body length. **Legs longer than body width. Body shiny, light to dark reddish-brown.** 15 pairs of legs. Hides under stones, bark. Sheds legs to aid escape from predators; they regrow. Squirts sticky fluid from rear to trap predators such as ants, spiders, earwigs. Feeds on flies, gnats, other insects. Female does not care for offspring. Throughout s Africa.
**Similar**
**HOUSE CENTIPEDES  Order Scutigeromorpha**
Antennae longer than body. Legs long, delicate.

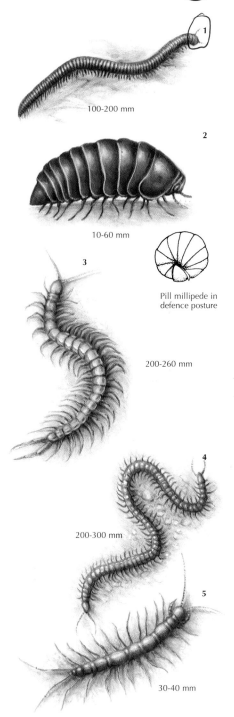

100-200 mm

10-60 mm

Pill millipede in defence posture

200-260 mm

200-300 mm

30-40 mm

# SPIDERS AND OTHER ARACHNIDS

Arachnids are a class of arthropods with four pairs of legs. There are no antennae as in insects and the body is in two principal sections, the cephalothorax (combined head and thorax) and the abdomen.

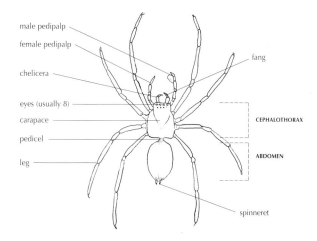

male pedipalp

female pedipalp

fang

chelicera

eyes (usually 8)

carapace

CEPHALOTHORAX

pedicel

ABDOMEN

leg

spinneret

The cephalothorax bears the eight legs as well as a pair of jaws (chelicerae) containing the fangs, and a pair of appendages (pedipalps) which are leg-like in female spiders, have swollen tips in male spiders and are developed into pincers in scorpions. In certain spiders such as baboon and trapdoor spiders the chelicerae are directed forwards and the spider strikes downwards with its fangs. In all other spiders the fangs close with a pincer motion. Generally, eight simple eyes are located towards the front of the cephalothorax.

The abdomen is not segmented as in insects. It contains the reproductive organs and in spiders the silk glands or spinnerets which issue strands of silk.

## Scope of this chapter

There are 11 orders of arachnids, of which the following occur in the southern African region:

- Spiders (Araneae)
- Solifuges (Solifugae)
- Harvestmen (Opiliones)
- Whip scorpions (Amblypygi)
- Book scorpions (Pseudoscorpiones)
- Scorpions (Scorpiones)
- Ticks and mites (Acari)

More than 3 000 spider species are thought to exist in southern Africa. They are divided into 65 families, all but the most insignificant of which are covered in this chapter. In many instances particularly conspicuous genera and even individual species are described.

One example of the solifuges, the red roman spider, is described. There are about 200 species known from southern Africa, mostly from the arid western areas and Namibia. All can be recognised by their enormous jaws. They fall into two broad categories: the diurnal forms which are generally darkly patterned like the red roman spider, and the nocturnal forms which are larger and are uniformly pale.

One example of harvestmen is described. Most of the known species resemble the illustrated example but a small group are nocturnal and have shorter legs and sluggish movements.

Whip scorpions are widespread in the tropics, but only the illustrated species *Damon variegatus* is commonly found in southern Africa.

The known species of book scorpions show little variation in size or appearance from the example illustrated, but they are distributed in a wide variety of habitats throughout the region.

Of the approximately 600 known species of scorpions throughout the world more than 160 occur in southern Africa. All of the important genera are covered in the text, including specific descriptions of two members of the dangerous *Parabuthus* genus.

Only the three most common of the many species of ticks are illustrated. For more detailed treatment of this group readers will need to refer to more specialised works.

Of the thousands of species of mites, only the velvet mite is described because its colour and open, sandy habitat make it particularly conspicuous. Most other mites are minute, often microscopic, and fall outside the scope of this book.

## Distribution

The distribution of most arachnids is not well known and the indication of distribution given in the text is only approximate.

## Reproduction and development

Courtship and breeding take many forms: male hunting spiders locate their mates by finding and following the draglines laid down by the female. Males of the web-spinning spiders announce their approach by plucking the strands of the female's web. The jumping spiders and wolf spiders have excellent vision and use leg signals and movement in their courtship. Prior to mating, males fill the ends of their pedipalps with sperm and after courtship insert them into the female. Later the female lays her eggs into a protective silk egg sac.

Courtship in scorpions is an elaborate affair. The male clasps the female's pincers with his own and leads her back and forth in a ritualistic dance. During the dance he deposits a stalked package of sperm (spermatophore) on the ground and leads her over it. As her genital aperture passes over the spermatophore, it bursts, impregnating her with its contents. Gestation may last for more than a year, after which live young are born and transported on the back of the female during their infancy.

## Silk and webs

The diversity of purposes for which spiders use silk is remarkable. Most spiders make silk egg sacs. Some use silk to build nurseries for their young. Many hide in silk-lined burrows with trapdoors that are constructed from and hinged with silk. The young of several species extrude a fine line of silk which is caught by the wind, wafting the spider over long distances to new habitats. Draglines are laid down to enable spiders to retrace their steps and to act as guides for potential mates. Silk is used as a snare and to bind entrapped prey; one group uses silk as a casting net, and another constructs a silken bolas, which it uses as a club. But the most conspicuous use of silk is for the construction of webs. Four broad categories of webs are identified by Filmer (1991):

- **Sheet webs**: These are closely woven and spread over the substrate. In the case of funnel-web spiders, the edge of the sheet enters a tube-like retreat. Other sheet-web builders hang suspended under the sheet awaiting prey.
- **Scaffold webs**: These are complex, three-dimensional structures, often with a retreat of silk. These "cobwebs" frequently gather dust and debris. Button spiders are typical builders of these webs, as are daddy long legs.
- **Tunnel webs**: Many species construct tubes or cocoons in tunnel crevices, under rocks or in cracks in bark. Often a system of trip lines is rigged at the entrance to warn the spider of approaching prey.
- **Orb webs**: These are the classic spider webs which are spun across the flight path of insects. There are many variations. Usually the spider waits at the hub of the web, or in adjacent foliage.

The structure of a simple orb web is shown in the accompanying illustration (after Filmer 1991). The web is constructed as follows:

1  An initial bridge is established by allowing a light thread to be blown from one anchor point to the other or by carrying it overland. This is reinforced into a foundation line by laying down additional threads.
2  A frame of tough thread is anchored to points around the perimeter of the web.
3  Radial threads are set up from the hub to points around the frame.

**4** The hub may be reinforced or some species leave it open.
**5** Non-sticky silk is used to construct the inner circle of the web.
**6** A space is left between the dry inner circle and the adhesive catch web.
**7** Starting from the outer circumference, viscid thread is laid in a close spiral.
**8** Some species build a line from the hub to an adjacent retreat. This transmits vibrations from trapped prey to the hidden spider and it also gives the spider quick access to the web.
**9** Certain species spin a zigzag stabilimentum of thick silk across the web. This may be to strengthen the web or to alert birds and other animals to the presence of the web so that they do not break it.

## Venom

All spiders except feather-legged spiders (Uloboridae) subdue their prey with venom injected through their fangs. However, very few spiders have fangs large enough to penetrate human skin. Of those that are capable of biting humans, only the following are known to deliver anything more than a painful bite:

- **Black button spiders**: Neurotoxic venom causes pain at the site of the bite, muscular dysfunction, heart palpitations, abdominal pain, difficulty in breathing, vomiting and extreme anxiety. Death may follow in untreated cases, but is rare. Medical attention should be sought. Other species of button spiders have less toxic venom.
- **Violin spiders, sac spiders and six-eyed desert crab spiders**: Cytotoxic venom causes little discomfort initially but later severe ulceration and necrosis develop around the site. A bite from certain species of six-eyed desert crab spiders may cause death.
- **All scorpions** possess tails with venomous stings with which they immobilise prey and defend themselves. Stings from all species are painful but only those of the buthid family (thick-tailed scorpions) are potentially dangerous and can be lethal if not treated. Some buthid species can also spray venom into the eyes of victims. The symptoms are severe pain at the site followed within 24 hours by high temperature, speech and respiration difficulty, convulsions, abdominal pain and vomiting. Children and the aged are particularly vulnerable. Medical attention should be sought without delay.

## Dimensions

The dimensions given in this chapter for arachnids other than scorpions refer to body length from the head to the end of the abdomen, unless otherwise stated.

Scorpion dimensions refer to the total length of the animal, including the tail.

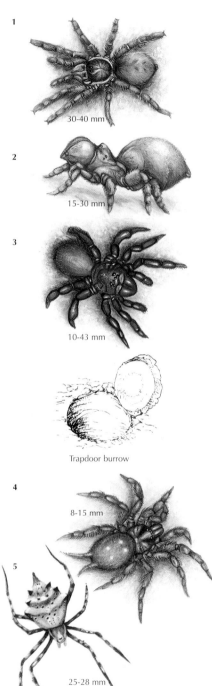

1

30-40 mm

2

15-30 mm

3

10-43 mm

Trapdoor burrow

4

8-15 mm

5

25-28 mm

**1  COMMON BABOON SPIDERS**    Genus *Harpactira*
Heavily built. Hairy. Thick legs, pedipalps long and leg-like. Dark brown to black. Spinnerets protrude beyond abdomen. Lives in silk-lined burrow.
**Similar**
**GOLDEN-BROWN BABOON SPIDERS  Genus *Pterinochilus***
Golden-brown, orange or pinkish-brown.
**HORNED BABOON SPIDERS  Genus *Ceratogyrus***
Silvery-grey with dark markings. "Horn" in centre of carapace.
**LESSER BABOON SPIDERS  Genus *Harpactirella***
Smaller (under 30 mm). Brown.

**2  AFRICAN PURSE-WEB SPIDERS**    Genus *Calommata*
Large fang bases. Legs short, hindlegs thick. Eyes elevated. Lives in burrow with crater-shaped silk covering.

**3  TRAPDOOR SPIDERS**    Family Ctenizidae
Robust, slow-moving. Head shiny, hairless. Fang bases massive. Spiny "rake" on sides of jaws for digging. Dark brown. Burrow has cork-like trapdoor lid. Waits for prey at night at mouth of burrow, legs just protruding under door.
**LESSER TRAPDOOR SPIDERS  Family Cyrtaucheniidae**
Burrow has multiple openings with flap-like doors.
**FRONT-EYED TRAPDOOR SPIDERS  Family Idiopidae**
Burrows with thin or thick doors. Some plug burrow with hardened abdomen.

**4  FUNNEL-WEB MYGALOMORPHS**    Family Dipluridae
Slender. Spinnerets very long. Dark brown. Large, closely woven sheet web with open-ended funnel-shaped retreat in crevices or tree forks.

**5  BLACK-AND-YELLOW GARDEN SPIDER**    *Argiope australis*
Head silvery grey, abdomen and legs striped black and yellow. Lobed abdomen. Hangs head down in web with two back and two front legs together. Web generally less than 1 m from ground with stabilimentum (zigzag of thick silk).
**Similar**
**BANDED GARDEN SPIDER  *A. trifasciata***
Smaller with narrow bands, unlobed abdomen. Often near water.
**RED-LEGGED GARDEN SPIDER  *A. aurocincta***
Cream with silver-yellow and brown bands. Red legs.
**SAINT ANDREW'S CROSS SPIDER  *A. flavipalpis***
Cream with thin black lines. X-shaped stabilimentum.
**GRASS ORB-WEB SPIDERS  Genus *Larinia***
Under 10 mm. Long, fawn-coloured abdomen.
**PYJAMA SPIDERS  Genus *Singa***
Under 6 mm. Shiny, striped abdomen.
**LADYBIRD SPIDERS  Genus *Paraplectana***
3–8 mm. Black spots on yellow or red abdomen. Looks like ladybird.

**1 HAIRY FIELD SPIDERS** Genera *Neoscona* and *Araneus*
Fawn, brown, grey or greenish. Abdomen oval, high in front,
overhanging head region. Orb webs of fine silk. Hangs head
down at hub of web or monitors vibrations from nearby retreat
with one foot on silk line.

**2 BARK SPIDERS** Genus *Caerostris*
Abdomen has thorny or wart-like projections. Coloration imitates
bark and lichen. Hangs head down at hub of orb web. Most are
nocturnal and remove web at dawn. Rests perfectly camouflaged
against bark by day.
**Similar**
**BIRD-DROPPING SPIDERS** *Genus Aethriscus*
10–15 mm. Black and grey body looks like bird dropping. Nocturnal.

**3 GARBAGE-LINE SPIDERS** Genus *Cyclosa*
Mottled silver, black and grey. Long, lumpy abdomen, pointed
towards rear. Head tucked under front of abdomen. Legs short.
Small orb web with line of debris and egg cases down centre. Spider waits in middle of garbage line.

**4 STONE NEST SPIDERS** Genus *Nemoscolus*
Dark with white markings on cylindrical abdomen. Head tucked
under abdomen. Horizontal orb web drawn up at hub to conical
retreat made from sand and other debris, where spider hides.

**5 TROPICAL TENT-WEB SPIDERS** Genus *Cyrtophora*
Dull-coloured with white markings. Abdomen has paired tubercles. Fine-meshed, tent-shaped web surrounded by trip lines; line
of egg cases and other debris down centre. Spider hides in debris
line. Webs often close together among aloes, bushes.

**6 HEDGEHOG SPIDERS** Genus *Pycnacantha*
Golden brown with darker markings and spine-like protruber-
ances on abdomen. Front legs robust, armed with spines. Nocturnal. Hangs by back legs from silk trapeze, catches moths with
front legs. May emit pheromone lure. Sits immobile in vegetation
by day.

**7 AFRICAN BOLAS SPIDERS** Genus *Cladomelea*
Creamy-yellow. Abdomen has pimple-like, yellow protuberances.
Line of dark spines between eyes. Nocturnal. Hangs sideways
from silk trapeze, swings "bolas" of silk tipped with sticky glob
ule to catch moths. Grassland on e escarpment.

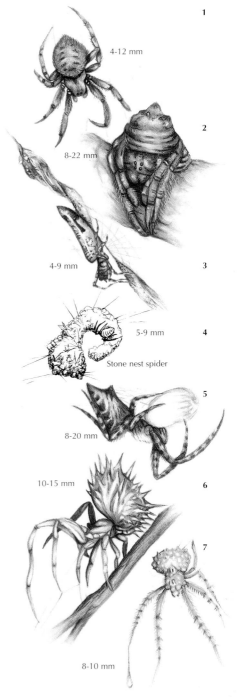

1

4-12 mm

2

8-22 mm

3

4-9 mm

4

5-9 mm

Stone nest spider

5

8-20 mm

6

10-15 mm

7

8-10 mm

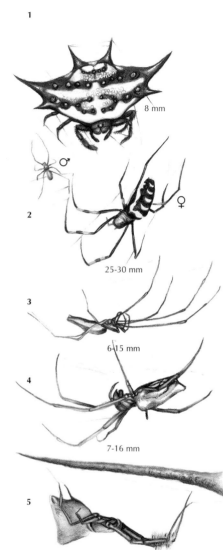

8 mm

♂

♀

25-30 mm

6-15 mm

7-16 mm

under 6 mm

3-8 mm

**1   KITE SPIDER**                                      Genus *Gasteracantha*
Abdomen shiny, hard, rather flattened with spiny projections. Yellow or white with black markings, especially at tips of projections. Legs short. Symmetrical orb web in tree.
**Similar**
**BOX KITE SPIDERS  Genus *Isoxya***
Squarish abdomen, subdued colouring. Orb web.

**2   BANDED-LEGGED GOLDEN ORB-WEB SPIDER  *Nephila senegalensis***
Abdomen cylindrical, black with yellow markings. Carapace brown with silvery hair. Legs banded black and yellow with "hair" tufts on three pairs. Hangs in large web of golden silk surrounded by trip lines. Small males often present in web.
**Similar**
**BLACK-LEGGED GOLDEN ORB-WEB SPIDER  *N. pilipes***
Abdomen yellow with blue marbling. Legs tufted, unbanded.
**RED-LEGGED GOLDEN ORB-WEB SPIDER  *N. inaurata***
Larger (35 mm). Silvery with yellow, grey and rufous markings. Legs reddish, banded, untufted. Ne and E coast.
**HERMIT SPIDER  *N. cruentata***
Abdomen rounded. Black with yellow along sides. Legs banded, untufted. Hides in retreats. White web silk. N and E.

**3   LONG-JAWED WATER SPIDERS**              Genus *Tetragnatha*
Fawn or brown. Abdomen long, cylindrical, pointed towards rear. Jaws very large; palps of male extend beyond jaws. Forelegs long, slender. Horizontal orb web near water. Hides by stretching out along grass stem.
**Similar**
**THICK-JAWED SPIDERS  Genus *Pachygnatha***
Abdomen shorter. Jaws thick but not as long. Legs shorter.

**4   SILVER VLEI SPIDERS**                         Genus *Leucauge*
Abdomen cylindrical, truncated at rear. Silver, gold, red or green with fringe on hindlegs. Jaws fairly thick. Orb web horizontally inclined; quite low in vegetation.
**Similar**
**CAVE ORB-WEB SPIDERS  Genus *Meta***
More spherical abdomen. Drab colouring. Prefers dark places.

**5   FEATHER-LEGGED SPIDERS**                 Genus *Uloborus*
Long, humped abdomen. Grey or brown. Front legs long with hair tufts. Horizontal web with fluffy silk. No venom glands. Rests at hub of web with legs stretched forward.
**Similar**
**SINGLE-LINE-WEB SPIDERS  Genus *Miagrammopes***
Snare is single line of fluffy silk. Nocturnal.
**TRIANGLE-WEB SPIDERS  Genus *Hyptiotes***
Snare is triangular segment of orb web. Fluffy silk.

**6   HACKLE-WEB SPIDERS**                      Family Dictynidae
Small spiders but recognisable from irregular fluffy silk web network over dry terminal twigs of plants.

**1  BLACK BUTTON SPIDERS**  *Latrodectus renivulvatus,
L. indistinctus, L. cinctus*
Abdomen globular, black with dull red dot or stripe dorsally.
Sometimes indistinct creamy stripes towards front of abdomen.
Nocturnal. Cobweb with snare threads leading to ground and to
refuge under rock or other hiding place. Venom neurotoxic, dan-
gerous. Egg sac smooth, spherical, cream, pea-sized.
**Similar**
**KAROO BUTTON SPIDER  *L. karrooensis***
Red T outlined in cream on abdomen. Faint red mark on under-
side. Web well above ground. Pebble "roof" over retreat. Only in
Karoo.

**2  BROWN BUTTON SPIDER**  *Latrodectus geometricus*
Cream to black. Pale specimens have geometrical white to orange
markings above with darker centres and borders. Hourglass-
shaped orange-red marking below. Legs long, tapered. Cobweb
with threads leading to opaque, tunnel-shaped silk refuge. Egg
sac spherical, covered in silk spikes. Venom less dangerous than
of black button spiders.
**Similar**
**RHODESIAN BUTTON SPIDER  *L. rhodesiensis***
Egg sac fluffy, three times larger than in other species. From
Johannesburg northwards.

**3  FALSE HOUSE BUTTON SPIDERS**  **Genus *Theridion***
Abdomen globular, mottled brown or grey. Legs long, tapered.
Stiff hairs on back legs. Web consists of horizontal runway sec-
tion, scaffolding and attachment threads, with retreat either to
side or in centre, sometimes incorporating curled leaf or debris.
In sheltered places outdoors or in houses. Egg cases spherical,
brownish.
**Similar**
**DEW-DROP SPIDERS  Genus *Argyrodes***
Smaller (3–5 mm). Metallic silver abdomen, often conical. Lives
in webs of other spiders, feeds on their prey.
**FALSE BUTTON SPIDERS  Genus *Steatoda***
Larger (5–15 mm). Black with white band towards front of
abdomen.

**4  HAMMOCK-WEB SPIDERS**  **Family Linyphiidae**
Dark with thin tapered legs. Abdomen a rounded oblong with
white markings. Hangs below filmy dome web in low vegetation.

**5  DADDY LONG LEGS SPIDERS**  **Family Pholcidae**
Very long, thin legs up to 30 mm span. Grey-brown, cylindrical
abdomen with darker markings. Hangs inverted under irregular
cobweb. Shakes rapidly if disturbed. Eggs held in female's jaws till
they hatch.

1

8-15 mm

2

7-10 mm

3

6 mm

4

1-4 mm

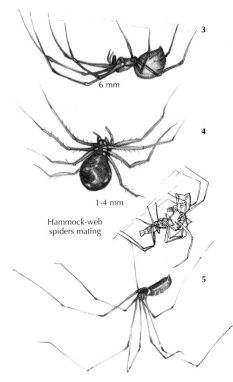

Hammock-web
spiders mating

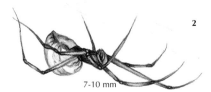

5

8-15 mm

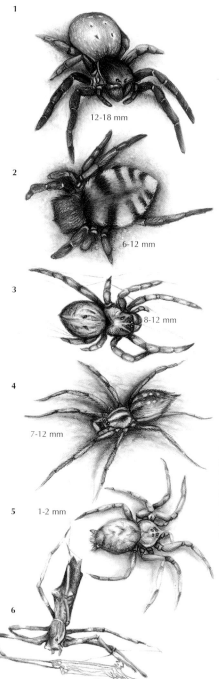

**1**

12-18 mm

**2**

6-12 mm

**3**

8-12 mm

**4**

7-12 mm

**5**    1-2 mm

**6**

15-20 mm

**1    VELVET SPIDERS    Genera *Gandanameno* and *Dresserus***
Dark grey, brown or reddish. Covered in short velvety hair. Corpulent, oval abdomen. Legs short, robust. Front of head blunt. Lurks under flat web of dry-looking silk in rock crevices, loose bark, masonry and under stones on ground.
**Similar**
**DECORATED VELVET SPIDERS  Genus *Adonea***
Smaller (20–30 mm). Strikingly marked black and white.

**2    BUCKSPOOR SPIDERS    Genus *Seothyra***
Brown, corpulent, oval abdomen. Males often have orange, cream and silvery markings or may mimic ants, wasps. Short legs. Front of head blunt. Flat, lobed web on sandy soil resembles antelope spoor. Silk-lined tunnel leads from centre of web into ground. Dry, sandy areas.

**3    COMMUNITY NEST SPIDERS    Genus *Stegodyphus***
Pale grey with dark markings. Corpulent. Short legs. Two dark triangles on blunt "face". Numerous spiders of all ages nest together in spherical web. Nest becomes cardboard-like and debris-littered over time. Catching webs of fluffy elastic silk sheets extend for several square metres around nest.

**4    GRASS FUNNEL-WEB SPIDERS    Family Agelenidae**
Abdomen long, tapering, dark brown with paired pale dots. Long spinnerets. Soft, opaque sheet webs near ground with funnel-shaped retreat to one side. Egg cases resemble bottles of sand and are hung under rocks. Common in grassland.

**5    DWARF ROUND-HEADED HOUSE SPIDERS    Genus *Oecobius***
Overall impression grey but markings visible under magnification. Flat sheet web 10 mm in diameter on wall; noticeable when numerous. Preys on small ants. Found in human habitations. Probably introduced.
**Similar**
**DWARF ROUND-HEADED ROCK SPIDERS  Genus *Uroecobius***
Sheet webs outdoors against rocks and tree trunks.
**ROUND-HEADED DESERT SPIDERS  Genus *Uroctea***
Larger (6–10 mm). Sheet webs incorporate sand grains in dry rocky areas.

**6    OGRE-FACED NET-CASTING SPIDERS    Genus *Deinopis***
Very long body and legs. Large eyes. Nocturnal. Hangs from silk strands in low vegetation holding elastic silk snare between front two pairs of legs. Throws snare over prey. Immobile, twig-like by day. In thick vegetation and forests.
**Similar**
**HUMPBACKED NET-CASTING SPIDERS  Genus *Menneus***
Female has asymmetrical hump on abdomen. Widespread.
**CAMEL-BACKED SPIDERS  Genus *Avellopsis***
Symmetrically humped abdomen. Reddish-brown. Sw Cape.

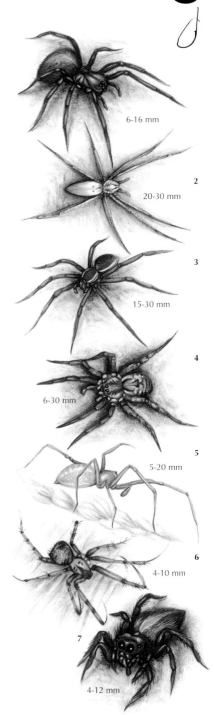

**1  LIGHT-EYED CRIBELLATE SPIDERS  Family Amaurobiidae**

Velvety, dark, sometimes with green or rufous tinge. Abdomen oval, some with vague markings. Light eyes. Long legs. Net-like sheet web in dark places with retreat into crevice or under stones. Nocturnal.

6-16 mm

**2  NURSERY-WEB SPIDERS  Genera *Euprosthenops* and *Chiasmopes***

Abdomen long, tapering. Front two pairs of legs and back two pairs held together, span up to 50 mm. Brown with symmetrical leaf-shaped pattern on abdomen. Domed sheet web slopes to silk tunnel in base of tree or similar hole. Female carries egg sac under body until young ready to emerge, then spins a nursery around them and guards them.
**Similar**
**Genera *Cispius, Rothus* and *Perenthis***
Smaller (15–30 mm). No webs; free-running hunters.

2

20-30 mm

**3  FISHING SPIDERS  Genus *Thalassius***

Robust, fast-moving. Dark with various colours and patterns. White band often present around edge of carapace. Legs held widespread and equally spaced. Moves fast on water surface or aquatic vegetation. Preys on insects, tadpoles, small frogs, fish. Female carries egg sac and guards young.

3

15-30 mm

**4  WOLF SPIDERS  Family Lycosidae**

Brown or grey with symmetrical markings on abdomen, sometimes black beneath. Radiating pattern on head. One pair of eyes very large. Most are free roaming; others build trapdoor tunnels. One genus, *Hippasa*, builds a funnel web. Male's palps decorated with tufts of hair. Female carries egg sac attached to spinnerets until young hatch, then they ride on mother's back.
**Similar**
**WANDERING SPIDERS  Family Ctenidae**
Very similar. Different eye patterns visible under microscope.

4

6-30 mm

**5  LYNX SPIDERS  Family Oxyopidae**

Most common species green with pink markings; others fawn or golden yellow. Abdomen pointed towards rear. Legs long with spines. Front of head squared off. Active hunter on vegetation. Leaps considerable distances.

5

5-20 mm

**6  PIRATE SPIDERS  Family Mimetidae**

Shiny, golden brown with darker markings. Globular abdomen. Front two pairs of legs long with curved spines, hindpairs shorter. Slow-moving, crepuscular. Invades webs and preys on other spiders. Remains immobile in vegetation by day. Widespread but seldom seen.

6

4-10 mm

**7  JUMPING SPIDERS  Family Salticidae**

Many species with varied colouring, often hairy. Head truncated at front, generally larger than abdomen. Abdomen pointed or oval, often hairy. Some species mimic ants. One pair of eyes very large. Eyesight acute. Builds opaque silk retreat but moves freely by day. Leaps on prey after securing a silk line to substrate. Male waves palps (often decorated) to communicate.

7

4-12 mm

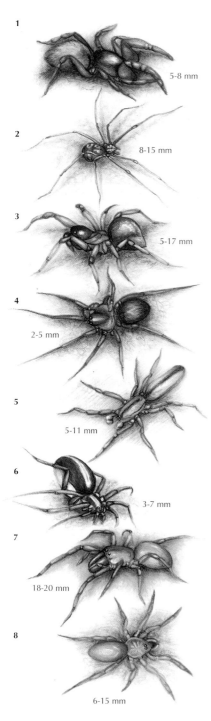

1

5-8 mm

2

8-15 mm

3

5-17 mm

4

2-5 mm

5

5-11 mm

6

3-7 mm

7

18-20 mm

8

6-15 mm

**1   PALP-FOOTED SPIDERS**                       Family Palpimanidae
Dark reddish-brown. Head and front legs dark and shiny, oval abdomen usually paler, more hairy. Front pair of legs large, robust. Nocturnal hunter. Lives in tube of sticky silk under rocks, logs, etc. Egg case attached to wall of tube. Young remain for a while in tube after hatching.

**2   VIOLIN SPIDERS**                               Family Loxoscelidae
Carapace flat, abdomen oval. Legs long, slender. Colour red-brown with darker markings. Venom can cause severe necrosis. Nocturnal hunter. Hides by day in dark places.
**Similar**
**SPITTING SPIDERS  Family Scytodidae**
Smaller (5–15 mm). Domed carapace. Ejects sticky fluid to pin down prey.
**LEAF LITTER SPIDERS  Family Drymusidae**
Hangs under loose, domed web in sheltered place. Sw Cape.

**3   BURROWING ARMOURED SPIDERS**                    Subfamilies
                              Cyriocteinae, Storeninae and Cydrelinae
High carapace and rounded or oval abdomen, often higher towards rear. Pale with sepia markings. Builds silk-lined tunnel or pocket-like retreat. Members of subfamily Cydrelinae "swim" in loose sand with specially adapted legs.

**4   ANT-EATING ARMOURED SPIDERS** Subfamily Zodariinae
Pale orange-red, light brown or yellow, with brown and sepia markings. Abdomen oval. Lives on ground under stones, rocks, near ant and termite nests. Some make "igloos" of sand grains held together with silk. Preys on termites and ants.

**5   LONG-BODIED ARMOURED SPIDERS**                  Subfamily
                                            Storenomorphinae
Carapace and legs usually yellow, abdomen grey with paler markings or grey with longitudinal brown and fawn stripes. Eyes in tight cluster. Long-bodied, abdomen cylindrical. Lives in vegetation. Some "sew" grass leaves together for retreat.

**6   SAND DIVERS**                               Genus *Ammoxenus*
Abdomen round, reddish with pale longitudinal markings. Legs backswept, long and slender with flexible ends. Preys on termites which are bound in silk and buried. Moves fast over surface of sand and dives into it if disturbed, flipping upside down as it burrows. Cup-shaped egg sacs are also buried.

**7   LONG-JAWED INTERTIDAL SPIDERS**           Family Desidae
Carapace, fang bases and legs reddish-brown. Abdomen grey. Large fang bases project forward one third body length. Found in intertidal zone along rocky shores. Builds silk retreat in empty limpet shell or rock crevice, which traps air during high tide. Air is also trapped in body hairs. Preys on intertidal arthropods. W and S coast.
**Similar**
**SEASHORE SPIDERS  Family Anyphaenidae**
Smaller (13–17 mm). Grey with lighter markings. Fang bases not as large.

**8   ORANGE SPIDERS**                           Family Caponiidae
Carapace and legs orange. Abdomen grey-brown or yellowish. Carapace smooth, abdomen hairy. Eyes in tight cluster at front of carapace. Nocturnal, free-ranging hunter. Hides under rocks, loose bark.

**1   SIX-EYED TUNNEL SPIDERS      Family Segestriidae**
Dark brown or black. Abdomen long, oval. Carapace shiny. Three
front pairs of legs directed forwards. Silk tube, some with trip
lines radiating from mouth, is built in crack or crevice of stone,
log, etc. Nocturnal. Waits at mouth of tunnel with three front
pairs of legs ready for passing prey.

**2   SCORPION SPIDERS            Family Trochanteriidae**
Shiny, red-brown or black. Some have pale marks on abdomen.
Legs paler than body. Large, widely diverging fang bases. Body
extremely flattened. Often folds a pair of legs back over body.
Nocturnal. Hides in crevices and under bark.

**3   SAC SPIDERS        Genera Cheiracanthium and Clubiona**
Pale grey, cream, pinkish or yellowish. Dark fang bases and leg
tips contrast with pale body. Legs long. Venom of *Cheiracanthium
furculatum* causes necrosis. Nocturnal, often indoors. Runs swift-
ly; jumps if alarmed. Builds silk sacs in corners, curtain folds,
under bark or in curled leaves.
**Similar**
**ANT-LIKE SAC SPIDERS  Family Corinnidae**
Imitates ants and wingless wasps.
**MOUSE SPIDERS  Family Gnaphosidae**
Darker. Pair of spinnerets extend beyond end of abdomen.

**4   LONG-SPINNERED SPIDERS          Genera Hersilia**
**and Tama**
Marbled greys and browns. Flattish. Carapace raised towards
front, eyes easily visible in two rows. Spinnerets protrude well
beyond abdomen. Third pair of legs short. Waits head down,
motionless, well camouflaged on trees or rocks. One species,
*Tama arida*, constructs inverted circular curtain-like retreat incorporating pebbles under rocks.

**5   WALL SPIDERS                Family Selenopidae**
Mottled greys and browns. Flat-bodied. Abdomen heart-shaped.
Legs held sideways, crab-like. Builds flat, papery egg cases on
walls, poles or under bark. Moves quickly to run down prey. Conspicuous on plain walls. Hides in cracks.

**6   RAIN SPIDERS                   Genus Palystes**
Greyish with slightly darker markings on abdomen. Legs banded
yellow and dark brown underneath. Builds tennis-ball-sized egg
nests of dried leaves in vegetation. Nocturnal, free-ranging hunter.
Curls legs against body at rest. Often comes indoors.
**Similar**
**ROCK RAIN SPIDERS  Genus Olios**
Pearl-coloured. Dark fang bases. Nests under rocks.
**GRASS RAIN SPIDERS  Genus Pseudomicrommata**
Smaller. Reddish longitudinal stripes. Restricted to grassland.

**7   WHITE LADY SPIDERS         Genera Leucorchestris**
**and Carparachne**
Whitish. Lives in deep trapdoor tunnel in loose sand. Some *Carparachne* cartwheel down dunes to avoid predatory wasps. Only
in sandy desert habitats.

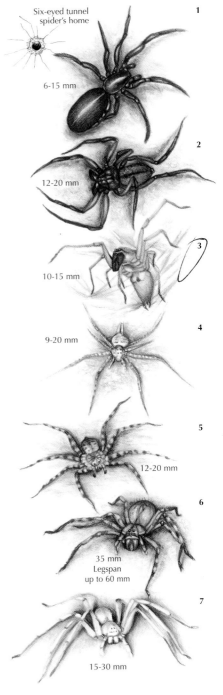

Six-eyed tunnel
spider's home

6-15 mm

12-20 mm

10-15 mm

9-20 mm

12-20 mm

35 mm
Legspan
up to 60 mm

15-30 mm

**1**

8-15 mm

**2**

4-15 mm

**3**

5-15 mm    ♂

♀

**4**

20-50 mm

**5**

4-6 mm
Legspan
50 mm

**6**

10-25 mm

**7**

1-5 mm

**1   SIX-EYED DESERT CRAB SPIDERS        Family Sicariidae**

Takes on colour of habitat because sand particles adhere to body. Sturdy legs held sideways. Venom possibly life-threatening. Buries itself by flicking sand over body with front legs. Remains immobile for long periods under sand but can move fast. Favours rock overhangs with sandy floors. Restricted to hot, sandy areas.

**2   SMALL WANDERING SPIDERS        Genus *Tibellus***

Elongated body; legs more or less equal in length. Yellow, brown or straw-coloured. Lies in wait for prey on grass.

**3   CRAB SPIDERS        Family Thomisidae**

Legs directed sideways, first two pairs long, robust, armed with spines. Colours blend with background, often bright to match flowers. Some species change colour to suit background. Waits on plants to ambush prey which is often larger than itself. No webs.

**4   RED ROMAN SPIDERS        Order Solifugae**

Not spiders. Not venomous. Brown, yellow or reddish, some with dark markings. Hairy body in two parts: massive, hard head with formidable toothed jaws, and soft, segmented abdomen. Leg-like palps and front pair of legs held off ground. Swift, voracious hunter; kills prey without venom and digests internally. Digs burrows. Widespread in hot, dry areas.

**5   HARVESTMEN        Order Opiliones**

Not spiders. Not venomous. Head and abdomen fused into one unit. Eight slender legs up to 50 mm span. Palps sometimes large. Odiferous glands often present. Eyes sometimes on turrets. Most species are predators; some feed on carrion or plant juices.

**6   TAILLESS WHIP SCORPIONS        Order Amblypygi**

Not scorpions. Not venomous. Dusty black. Flattened body with wide head, no tail. Segmented abdomen. Front legs extremely long, whip-like. Nocturnal. Preys on insects. Found under loose bark, stones, leaf litter. Female carries eggs in transparent chamber below abdomen. Hatched young transfer to mother's back.

**7   BOOK SCORPIONS        Order Pseudoscorpiones**

Minute scorpion-like animal without tail. Venom glands at tips of pincers. Pincers covered in tactile hairs and held out in front as sensors. Small insects are paralysed by pincers and eaten. Spins silk nest in which young develop. Under bark, stones or leaf litter throughout s Africa.

**1   BLACK ROCK SCORPIONS**          **Genus *Hadogenes***

Blackish-brown, flattened, medium-sized pincers, long thin tail. Venom not dangerous. Nocturnal. In crevices in rocky areas in N and W.
**Similar**
**BURROWING ISCHNURIDS  Genus *Cheloctonus***
Not flattened. Digs vertical burrow. E areas.
**CAPE ROCK SCORPIONS  Genus *Opisthacanthus***
Not as flattened. Cape fold mountains.

**2   SMOOTH-HEAD DIGGING SCORPIONS          Genus *Opisthophthalmus***

Robust. Large pincers, short tail. Brown or yellow with pale legs. Sting painful but not deadly. Builds complex, spiral burrow. Throughout s Africa.

**3   TRANSVAAL THICK-TAILED SCORPION          *Parabuthus transvaalicus***

Dark brown or black. Pincers thin, tail thick. Base tail segment rough. Sting segment as wide as tail. Stings and sprays venom. Dangerous. Nocturnal. Rests in shallow burrow under rocks by day. N areas excluding those with high rainfall.
**Similar**
**HAIRY THICK-TAILED SCORPION  *P. villosus***
More hairy. Not strictly nocturnal. More westerly distribution.

**4   WESTERN GRANULATED THICK-TAILED SCORPION          *Parabuthus granulatus***

Light brown. Pincers thin, tail thick, sting segment narrower than tail. Dangerous. Found in scrapes and burrows. Widespread in western and central parts of the region.
**Similar**
**Genera *Hottentotta, Karasbergia, Pseudolychas* and *Uroplectes***
Smaller (35–50 mm). Most are pale yellow or greenish.

**5   CATTLE and DOG TICKS          Family Ixodidae**

**Red-brown flattened body with hard shield.** Protruding mouthparts. Female grey when engorged. Six-legged larvae (pepper ticks) and eight-legged nymphs and adults transmit human and animal diseases. Widespread.
**Similar**
**SOUTH AFRICAN TORTOISE TICK  *Amblyomma marmoretum***
Found on tortoises; occasionally snakes, leguaans.

**6   SOUTH AFRICAN BONT TICK          *Amblyomma hebraeum***

Brown, yellow and black. Mouthparts extend one third body length.

**7   TAMPAN          *Ornithodorus moubata***

**Body grey, leathery, slightly fiddle-shaped. Mouthparts hidden from above.** Inhabits cracks in walls of human dwellings. N areas.

**8   VELVET MITES          Genus *Dinothrombium***

Bright red; looks like velvet cushion. Appears in sandy areas after rain. Preys on other invertebrates.

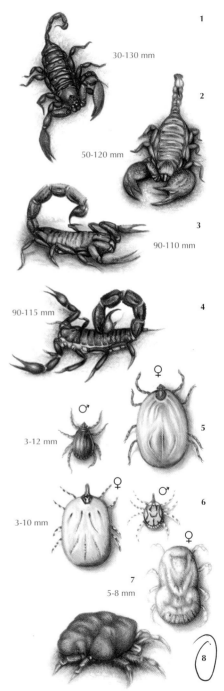

1

30-130 mm

2

50-120 mm

3

90-110 mm

4

90-115 mm

♂

♀

5

3-12 mm

♀

♂

6

3-10 mm

♀

7

5-8 mm

8

5 mm

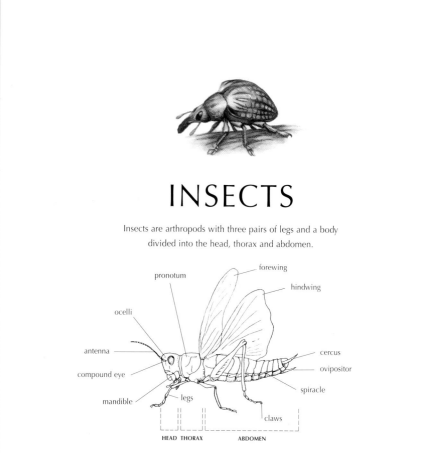

# INSECTS

Insects are arthropods with three pairs of legs and a body
divided into the head, thorax and abdomen.

The head bears two large compound eyes, and two or three small simple eyes (ocelli) are usually present.

Antennae, sensory organs that vary greatly in length and shape, are usually located on the front of the head below the ocelli.

Mouthparts are situated on the underside of the head or project forwards from it. They may be modified for either chewing or sucking. Chewing mouthparts have mandibles that move sideways. In sucking mouthparts, the mandibles are either absent or modified to form a beak (proboscis) which is used to suck up food. In some insects, e.g. bees, both types of mouthparts are present.

The thorax consists of three segments. In many insects the pronotum, which forms part of the front segment, forms a large shield-like plate covering the upper surface of the thorax between the head and the base of the wings. Each segment bears a pair of legs and usually the middle and rear segments each bear a pair of wings. Flies have only one pair of wings.

The abdomen typically consists of 11 segments but fewer segments may be visible due to fusion. The last segment usually takes the form of appendages, the most obvious being a pair of cerci (singular cercus) located on the top and to the sides of the tip of the abdomen. The reproductive organs occur at the tip of the abdomen. In the female of some species, a specialised egg-laying tube, the ovipositor, extends backwards from the terminal segments of the abdomen.

## Scope of this chapter

More than three quarters of all known animal species are insects — about a million described species world-wide, and probably ten times that number as yet undescribed. In southern Africa about 80 000 species have been recorded and new species are being discovered continually. They are divided into 63 orders, all of which are covered in this chapter. In most insect groups the identification of species requires a detailed knowledge of insect anatomy and specialised techniques for preparing specimens. This chapter therefore identifies insects by order; in the larger and more varied orders the families are described individually.

Butterflies have been treated differently from the other insects because of their conspicuousness, the higher level of interest that they arouse, and the ability of many to be identified at species level without special equipment or scientific training. About 100 of the more commonly seen species are described.

## Reproduction and development

Mating between male and female insects involves internal fertilisation. Fertilised eggs are deposited in a wide variety of situations: some are buried, others are parasitic and are deposited on or in the host species, and yet others have special adhesive devices that secure them in safe situations. Very few insects demonstrate any form of parental care. Once hatched, the insects develop through a process of metamorphosis into the adult form. Metamorphosis can be divided into three basic types:

- **Holometabolous** development involves four stages: egg, larva, pupa and adult. The larval stage bears no resemblance at all to the adult. There are four basic types of larva (after Scholtz and Holm 1985):

protopod larva

Protopod larvae are underdeveloped embryos and exist in, and are nourished by, the body fluids of parasitised hosts. Examples are parasitic wasp larvae.

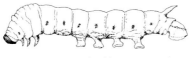

polypod larva

Polypod larvae are caterpillars with three jointed legs in the thoracic region and a number of fleshy prolegs supporting the length of the body. They are often protected by poisonous hairs or other defensive devices. Examples are the larvae of butterflies and moths.

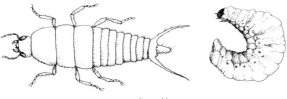

oligopod larvae

Oligopod larvae have three pairs of legs on the thorax only, and no prolegs on the rest of the body. Examples are the "cut worm" larvae of many beetles, and antlion larvae.

apodous larva

Apodous larvae lack any form of legs and are typified by the maggots of most fly species.

pupa

The pupal stage is usually dormant and, with a few exceptions, feeding does not take place. In most species the pupa is encased in some form of cocoon which protects the animal during this inactive and vulnerable stage in its life cycle.

The adult emerges from the pupa at the start of the breeding season. In most parts of southern Africa this coincides with the first summer rainfall.

- **Hemimetabolous** insects hatch from eggs into nymphs. As the nymphs grow they moult their exoskeletons periodically, eventually attaining adult size and sexual maturity. Each successive nymphal stage is called an instar. The most conspicuous difference between the early instars and the adult is the development of wings, which are generally absent or mere buds in the first stages. Other differences may be adaptations to habitat such as in dragonflies, which have aquatic nymphs that feed and breathe under water. Mayflies, stoneflies and aphids are other examples.

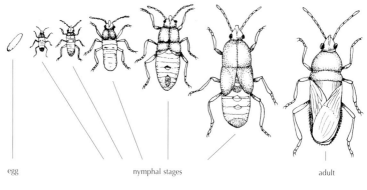

egg       nymphal stages       adult

**HEMIMETABOLISM**

- **Ametabolous** development occurs in primitive insects such as fishmoths and bristletails. The nymphs are identical to the adults in all obvious respects, except size and sexual development.

## Dimensions

The dimensions given for insects other than moths and butterflies in this chapter refer to the longest dimension illustrated. In most cases this is the body length from head to the end of the abdomen, excluding appendages such as antennae or cerci. If the folded wings extend beyond the abdomen, the measurement includes the wings. In the case of butterflies and moths the wingspan measurement is given.

**1   FISHMOTHS**                    Order Thysanura

Body flattened, covered in fine scales. **Silvery grey.** Long antennae and **three tail-like structures or cerci.** Common household species found among clothes, books. Accidentally introduced from Europe. Native species live in ant and termite nests, under leaf litter and stones. Never drinks water, absorbs moisture from the air. Around human habitation throughout s Africa.
**Similar**
**BRISTLETAILS  Order Archaeognatha**
Humpbacked appearance.

**2   MAYFLIES**                    Order Ephemeroptera

**Wings transparent, held vertically above body.** Body plain brown, grey or speckled. **Three, sometimes two, tail-like filaments or cerci.** Adults short-lived, do not feed, often appear suddenly in large numbers near water. Eggs laid into water, larvae aquatic. In clear, unpolluted streams throughout s Africa.

**3   SKIMMER DRAGONFLIES**          Family Libellulidae

**Wings held out horizontally when at rest. Hindwings broad.** Large compound eyes **touch at the top.** Wings and body may be brightly coloured, but **not metallic.** Females **lack ovipositor.** Strong, fast flyers. Libellulidae is the most common family of dragonflies. Feeds on other insects. **Mating takes place on the wing.** Female skims surface of water to lay eggs. Larvae aquatic and predatory. Throughout s Africa.
**Similar**
**CORDULID DRAGONFLIES  Family Corduliidae**
Larger (35-65 mm). Metallic red, blue or green. Found in thicket or forest. Females with ovipositor.
**CLUBTAIL DRAGONFLIES  Family Gomphidae**
Larger (30-55 mm). Compound eyes do not touch at the top. Green or yellow with black markings. Tail tip distended.

**4   DARNER DRAGONFLIES**           Family Aeschnidae

**Wings held out horizontally when at rest.** Largest s African dragonflies (wingspan up to 140 mm). Large compound eyes **touch at the top.** Aggressive predators, may feed on other dragonflies. **Mating takes place while perched.** Females have **well-developed ovipositor** which is used to lay eggs into plant tissue just below water. Widely distributed. Some species migrate through Africa to Europe and Asia.

**5   DAMSELFLIES**                  Suborder Zygoptera

**Wings folded above abdomen at rest. Fore- and hindwings similarly shaped.** Compound eyes bulbous, widely separate. **Light-bodied and delicate.** Brightly coloured green, blue or red. Adult may be found far from water avoiding predators. Mates on the wing. Eggs laid directly into water or into plant tissue below water. Larvae aquatic, prefers clean water. Throughout s Africa.

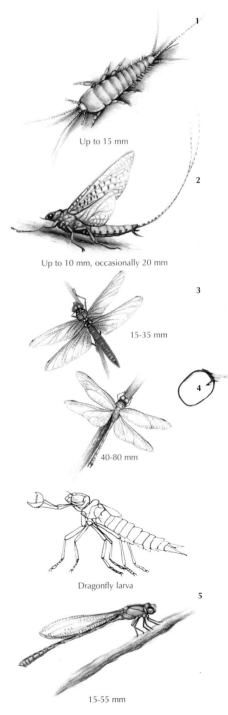

Up to 15 mm

Up to 10 mm, occasionally 20 mm

15-35 mm

40-80 mm

Dragonfly larva

15-55 mm

♀

4-10 mm

♀

6 mm

13 mm

Macrotermes          Harvester termite

Odontotermes        Trinervitermes
**Termite nests**

15-40 mm

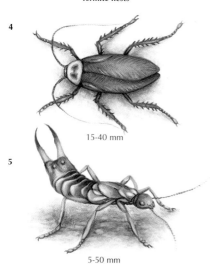

5-50 mm

## 1, 2 & 3  COMMON TERMITES          Family Termitidae
**Head reddish-brown, abdomen pale, soft-bodied.** Colonies include reproductives (imagoes) (3), a queen, workers and soldiers. Mouthparts large, pincer-like in soldiers (1), smaller in workers. Eyes not visible. Imagoes have compound eyes and wings.

Three genera are recognisable examples of this family:

*Macrotermes:* One species builds low, extensive mounds partly covered in vegetation including substantial trees. Fungus is cultivated underground to render cellulose fibre digestible. Another semitropical species builds pinnacles up to 3 m high.

*Odontotermes:* Builds chimneys at surface to ventilate underground nests. Fungus cultivation often emerges at surface. May nest under houses.

*Trinervitermes:* Builds bald hemispherical mounds about 30 cm high. Does not cultivate fungus. Soldiers are adapted to squirt toxic fluid at attackers from a snout (2).

Species not cultivating fungi have gut bacteria which secrete enzymes to digest fibre. Winged imagoes ("flying ants") emerge after rains, fly short distances, shed their wings and attract a mate by pheromones. Female digs a chamber 25 mm below the surface and becomes queen of a new colony. Eventually becomes too large to move and lays up to 20 000 eggs per day for the rest of her life. Majority of eggs develop into workers, others into soldiers or imagoes. Workers collect food, remove and store eggs, repair the mound and feed the queen. Soldiers defend the nest against attack mostly from ants. Termites distributed worldwide but Africa has widest diversity.

**Similar**

**HARVESTER TERMITES  Family Hodotermitidae**
Does not build mounds. Nests completely underground. Collects grass by night and on cool days, transports it underground.

**DRY WOOD TERMITES  Family Kalotermitidae**
Nests in dry wood without contact with soil.

**MOIST WOOD TERMITES  Family Termopsidae**
Nests in dead stumps rooted in soil. Confined to extreme S and SW.

**RHINO TERMITES  Family Rhinotermitidae**
Soldier has pincers and tubular "horn" which exudes fluid.

## 4  COCKROACHES          Order Blattodea
Easily recognisable **flattened shape, long antennae and dark coloration.** Fast, scurrying movements. Head is bent down beneath thorax, not easily visible from above. Some species common in houses but majority found under rocks, logs and in decaying vegetation. Omnivorous. Eggs laid in cigar-shaped egg case or retained inside female until hatching. Widely distributed throughout the world.

## 5  EARWIGS          Order Dermaptera
Compound eyes visible, antennae roughly half of body length. **Elongated body** with very short wings or no wings. **Pair of pincer-like structures at rear end** highly distinctive. Mostly scavenges on rotting plant matter; some species are predators. Pincers used for defence, harmless to humans. Female cares for eggs until young hatch.

**1   STONEFLIES**                                    **Order Plecoptera**

Elongated body with long membranous wings. **Inner wings folded fan-like under outer wings.** Female has two tail-like cerci projecting from abdomen. Pale greenish-brown. Generally seen resting on stones or plants on stream banks.

**Similar**

**WEBSPINNERS   Order Embiidina**

Confined to web tunnels under stones. Forelegs swollen with silk glands. Cerci squat. Only male has wings.

**2   GRASSHOPPERS**                                  **Family Acrididae**

Large compound eyes, **short antennae. Wings at least body length**, held roof-like over abdomen. **Wings often brightly coloured in flight. Large hindlegs.** Body coloration usually drab. Male makes shrill buzzing sound. Feeds on living plant material. Female lays eggs under soil in egg case using hard ovipositor at end of abdomen. Young hatch a month later. This family includes the locusts that gather in swarms.

**Similar**

**PYGMY GRASSHOPPERS   Family Tetrigidae**

Much smaller (under 15 mm). Hard shield covers body and wings.

**PINE HOPPERS   Families Euschmidtiidae and Thericleidae**

Much smaller (under 20 mm). Body narrow. Feeds on pines and ferns. Hindlegs very large.

**KAROO GRASSHOPPERS   Family Charilaidae**

Smaller (35 mm). Double keel over thorax. Arid grassland.

**DESERT STONE GRASSHOPPERS   Family Lathiceridae**

Wingless and stone-like. Namib desert.

**FOREST GRASSHOPPERS   Family Lentulidae**

Sluggish. Wingless. Feeds on forest floor or in trees.

**3   BLADDER GRASSHOPPERS**                          **Family Pneumoridae**

Large compound eyes, short antennae. Thorax large and crested. Male has a pair of wings, female wingless. Hindlegs similar size as other legs. **Abdomen distended with air, body bright grass green.** Call: a loud, long, resonant croak reminiscent of a large frog. Male calls at night to attract female. Restricted to forested areas.

**4   BUSH CRICKETS, 5 KATYDIDS &**         **Family Tettigoniidae**
**6 ARMOURED GROUND CRICKETS**

Green or brown. **Antennae longer than body**, thin, delicate. Head bent down towards thorax. Forewings hard, leathery. Wings rudimentary and used only for stridulation in armoured ground crickets. Hindlegs large. **Tibia of front legs have hearing organs on inside. Legs long in proportion to slim, elongated body.** Call: wings are rubbed together to produce sounds which range from loud rasping in some species to a continuous trill in others. Most species nocturnal. Found mainly on trees and bushes, sometimes in grass. Feeds mostly on living plant matter but some species are omnivorous, also eating other insects. Eggs laid in living plant tissue. Bush crickets and katydids throughout s Africa, especially in areas with high rainfall. Armoured ground crickets endemic to s Africa, mostly in arid areas.

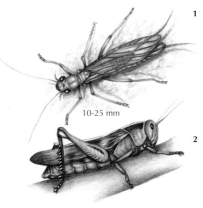

**1**

10-25 mm

**2**

10-60 mm

**3**

45 mm

**4**

38 mm

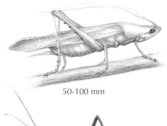

**5**

50-100 mm

**6**

20-80 mm

**1**

20-50 mm

**2**

20-70 mm

**3**

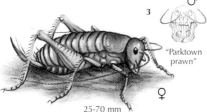

♂

"Parktown prawn"

♀

25-70 mm

**4**

20-75 mm

**5**

21 mm

**6**

30-40 mm

**1  PYRGOMORPHID GRASSHOPPERS**  Family Pyrgomorphidae

Antennae short, head bent down towards thorax. **Bright combinations of black, red, green or blue.** Hindlegs modified for jumping. Longitudinal furrow on forehead. Makes no sound. Slow-moving. Colours warn predators that it is poisonous. Produces foul-smelling foam if disturbed.

**2  TOAD GRASSHOPPERS**  Family Pamphagidae

Short, **sword-shaped antennae.** Longitudinal furrow on forehead. Thorax may be crested or flattened, sometimes bark-like. Smaller species **remarkably toad-like. Coloration generally drab.** Call: buzzing or rasping, day or night. Male sits in tree calling, female remains on ground. Mostly in arid areas.

**3  KING CRICKETS ("PARKTOWN PRAWN")**  Family Stenopelmatidae

Antennae longer than body. Male has large mandibles. Female (illustrated) has scimitar-shaped ovipositor. Hindlegs very large. **Wingless. Cricket-like but much larger.** Brown to black. Call: a cricket-like chirping at night. Mostly omnivorous. Nocturnal. Produces foul-smelling faecal matter if disturbed. Gardens and beaches in warmer regions.
Similar
DUNE CRICKETS  Family Schizodactylidae
Colourless. Feet have projections for gripping sand. W Cape.
CAMEL CRICKETS  Family Rhaphidophoridae
Wingless. Long legs and antennae. Only on Table Mountain.

**4 & 5  CRICKETS**  Family Gryllidae

Antennae longer than body. **Feet always have three joints. Hearing organs on front legs.** Wings or wingless. Female has long ovipositor. Call: repetitive chirping at night. Garden crickets (subfamily Grillinae) black and brown. Tree crickets (subfamily Oecanthinae) (5) pale and slender; male amplifies its call by spreading its wings against a leaf as resonator.

**6  MOLE CRICKETS**  Family Gryllotalpidae

Antennae shorter than body. **Front legs enlarged, specialised for digging.** Dark brown, furry. **Forewings shorter than abdomen. Folded hindwings protrude like spikes.** Call: constant whirring at night from burrows in damp soil not more than 1 m below ground. Feeds mainly on roots underground or on the surface. Throughout Africa.
Similar
PYGMY MOLE CRICKETS  Family Tridactylidae
Smaller (10 mm). Folded hindwings very long. Short, powerful forelegs.

**1  PLANT HOPPERS (SPITTLE BUGS)**  **Superfamily Cercopoidea**

Antennae not visible. **Head and thorax form triangle.** Outer wings stiff, held roof-like over abdomen. Adult jumps long distances. Mostly dull but may be red, yellow, black. Immature (spittle bug) enclosed in protective spittle-like foam of water and wax on plant stems. Some species construct calcareous tubes containing froth.

**Similar**

**LEAFHOPPERS  Family Cicadellidae**

Head not smaller than thorax, does not form triangle.

**TREEHOPPERS  Family Membracidae**

Smaller (5 mm). Shell over thorax mimics thorns or bark.

**2  CICADAS**  **Family Cicadidae**

Short antennae. **Sucking mouthparts folded beneath body. Transparent wings.** Large compound eyes, **three simple eyes between them.** Call: familiar, loud zinging sound on hot days and evenings. Feeds on plant sap with sucking mouthparts. Female lays eggs in slits in tree bark. Life cycle of African species unknown. American species take 13 years to mature from nymph to adult. Mainly in warm regions.

**3  SCALE INSECTS**  **Superfamily Coccoidea**

Adult sedentary within **dark encrusted scales, white waxy mass or woolly specks** on twigs, fruit or leaves. Young disperse by crawling or blown by wind. Male in some species covered with hard oval scales, in others has visible head, thorax and abdomen. Waxy scales provide protection from dehydration and predators.

**4  APHIDS**  **Family Aphididae**

Winged or wingless. **Two tubular structures from rear of abdomen visible under magnification.** Soft, fleshy body. Familiar garden pest, feeds on plant sap. Often in large numbers on stems and leaves. Produces eggs in late summer; live young emerge the following season. Throughout s Africa, many species introduced. Two exotic aphid families have also been introduced: Adelgidae (on pine trees only) and Phylloxeridae (on grape vines and oaks).

**Similar**

**WHITEFLIES  Family Aleyrodidae**

Covered in white powdery wax.

**JUMPING PLANT LICE  Family Psyllidae**

Hindlegs developed for jumping.

**BOOKLICE  Order Psocoptera**

Large compound eyes. Long antennae reaching to end of wings.

**5  ASSASSIN BUGS**  **Family Reduviidae**

Antennae roughly half body length. **Mouthparts long, proboscis-like, with three segments.** Usually yellow, red and black. **Forewings hard with membranous tips.** Preys on other insects and millipedes. Injects saliva to paralyse prey, then sucks out body fluids. Inflicts painful bite if handled. Soft clicking sometimes audible.

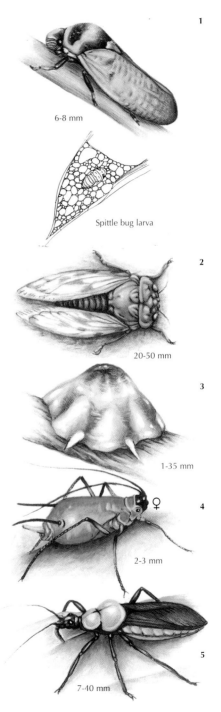

1

6-8 mm

Spittle bug larva

2

20-50 mm

3

1-35 mm

♀  4

2-3 mm

5

7-40 mm

**1**

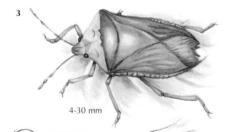

5-40 mm

**2**

6-20 mm

**3**

4-30 mm

**4**

5-20 mm

**5**

20-40 mm

**6**

4-12 mm

**1   TWIG WILTER BUGS**                    Family Coreidae

Proboscis-like mouthparts. Thorax often has pointed projections. **Forewings leathery with membranous tips. Hindlegs enlarged with inward-pointing spur.** Drab brown. Produces foul-smelling secretion as defence. Feeds on sap in twigs, causing wilting. Eggs laid on stems of plants.

**2   SHIELD-BACKED BUGS**            Family Scutelleridae

**Beetle-like in appearance, with green or blue metallic covering over upper surface of abdomen. Sucking mouthparts folded beneath body.** Feeds on plants, but details of life cycle unknown. Mainly in warm areas.

**3   STINK BUGS**                         Family Pentatomidae

**Antennae roughly half body length.** Colour variable: brown, green, red, blue. **Forewings leathery with membranous tips. Emits foul odour if handled.** Feeds on plant sap. Eggs laid on the host plant, young feed immediately on hatching. Some species are eaten by humans.

**4   WATER STRIDERS**                      Family Gerridae

**Antennae roughly half body length. Middle and hindlegs used to skate on water surface.** Detects vibrations of insects that fall into water, attacks them and sucks out body fluids. Ripples water surface to communicate.
Similar
**HYDROMETRIDS  Family Hydrometridae**
Remains out of water in thick vegetation.

**5   WATER SCORPIONS**                     Family Nepidae

**Antennae not visible. Front legs claw-like. Long tail-like breathing tube.** Waits on bottom of ponds for tadpoles, mosquito larvae and other prey. Can inflict painful bite. Eggs laid in slits in water plants.
Similar
**GIANT WATER BUGS  Family Belastomatidae**
Larger (up to 75 mm). No scorpion-like tail.
**SMALL WATER BUGS  Family Naucoridae**
Smaller (under 15 mm). No tail.

**6   BACKSWIMMERS**                   Family Notonectidae

**Antennae not visible. Eyes large. Long hindlegs with hairy fringes for swimming. Swims upside down.** Attacks prey from below, sucks out body fluids. Traps air bubble on abdomen for breathing, giving silvery appearance. In stagnant water throughout s Africa.
Similar
**WATER BOATMEN  Family Corixidae**
Middle **and** hindlegs used for swimming. Swims right way up.
**MINIATURE BACKSWIMMERS  Family Pleidae**
Smaller (under 3 mm). Rounded back.

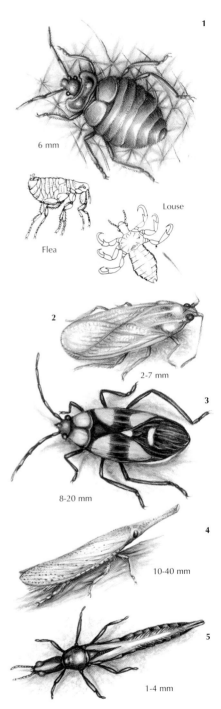

6 mm

Flea

Louse

2-7 mm

8-20 mm

10-40 mm

1-4 mm

**1   BED BUGS**            **Family Cimicidae**

Wingless, flattened oval body. Reddish-brown. Parasitic on humans, bats and birds. Nocturnal, retreating into crevices during day. Can survive without food for several months.

**Similar**

**BAT BUGS  Family Polyctenidae**

Much smaller (2 mm). Long back legs. No eyes. Only on bats.

**PIRATE BUGS  Family Anthocoridae**

Smaller (3 mm). Winged. Parasitises insects but bites humans occasionally.

**FLEAS  Order Siphonaptera**

Much smaller (2 mm). Narrow, oval body. Reddish-brown.

**LICE  Order Phthiraptera**

Flat, blind, whitish with hooked legs.

**RAT LICE  Order Hemimerina**

Larger (10 mm). Only on rats. Fast-moving.

**2   LACE BUGS**            **Family Tingidae**

**Flat lace-like projecting margins to thorax and abdomen.** Shield over thorax has triangular backward point. Feeds on the underside of leaves causing characteristic curling and white spots on upper surface.

**Similar**

**BARK BUGS  Family Aradidae**

Deeply etched wing pattern. Feeds on fungus under loose bark.

**3   COTTON STAINER BUGS**       **Family Pyrrhocoridae**

Robust elongated or oval body. **Red or orange and black.** Feeds on plant sap of low-growing vegetation. Mating pairs often seen tail-to-tail. Named for fungal discoloration of cotton plants eaten by it.

**Similar**

**SEED BUGS  Family Lygaeidae**

Feeds on plant seeds.

**4   LANTERN FLIES**       **Superfamily Fulgoroidea**

Head elongated into long tube in some species. **Inner wings have many cross veins towards rear.** Brown or green. Adult and immature exude delicate tails of wax filaments.

**5   THRIPS**            **Order Thysanoptera**

Elongated body. **Wings feather-like if present. Feet terminate in bulbs which can be inflated** when walking on slippery surfaces. Brown or yellow.

40-85 mm
♀

1a

1b

2

5-60 mm

3

10-250 mm

4

10-45 mm

Lacewing eggs
Stalk 8 mm

Antlion
larva

5

20-30 mm

**1  PRAYING MANTIDS**                     Order Mantodea

Large compound eyes. **Head distinct from thorax, highly mobile. Chewing mouthparts visible. Front legs held in a "praying" manner.** Two pairs of wings. Colour and pattern highly variable. Predators of other insects. Female chews off head of male during mating. Eggs laid in frothy egg case from which young hatch. Young look like large ants with abdomen curved upwards. Four families: Hymenopodidae (eye-like spirals on wings) (1a), Amorphoscelidae (bark-like), Mantidae (common green or brown mantids) (1b) and Empusidae (bizarre appendages to enhance camouflage).
**Similar**
**MANTIDFLIES  Family Mantispidae**
Much smaller (15 mm). Wings transparent. Absent from arid W.

**2  CADDIS FLIES**                     Order Trichoptera

Compound eyes clearly visible. Two pairs of hairy wings held roof-like over body. Brown to grey. **Moth-like in appearance but lacks proboscis-like mouthparts.** Adult nocturnal near fresh water. Larva builds elaborate case from stones, sand or twigs and moves about like hermit crab. Throughout s Africa.

**3  STICK INSECTS**                     Order Phasmatodea

**Resembles grass blade or dead twig.** Legs long and delicate, sometimes with small hooks and spines to improve resemblance. Green, brown or mottled grey. Feeds on plant material. Nocturnal. Most species cannot fly. Relies on camouflage to escape predators. May raise wings threateningly or drop to the ground and feign death if disturbed. Two families: Phylliidae (resemble leaves) and Phasmatidae (resemble twigs or grass).

**4  ANTLIONS and LACEWINGS**                     Order Neuroptera

**Adult appears similar to damselfly but wings longer than body. Antennae present (unlike damselfly) and often thickened at ends in the shape of a club.** Wings up to 80 mm, clear or patterned, sometimes iridescent. Threadwings (family Nemopteridae) have hindwings modified into long trailing ribbons. Green lacewings (family Chrysopidae) lay eggs on 8 mm stalks. Antlion larvae (family Myrmeleontidae) construct conical pits in soft sand and wait at bottom for prey to fall in. Prey taken in strong jaws and sucked dry.
**Similar**
**ALDERFLIES  Order Megaloptera**
Wings opaque. Relict populations in mountainous areas.

**5  HANGINGFLIES**                     Order Mecoptera

**Antennae thin, fragile.** Compound eyes clearly visible. Snout-shaped mouthparts. **Legs long, thin, fragile. Two pairs of wings. Body yellowish-brown.** Hangs by front legs waiting to pounce on prey. Little known about habits. Male keeps female occupied with gift of food during mating to avoid being eaten. Most species in wooded areas.

*✱ BLACK TIP DRAGON FLY*

# 1 GROUND BEETLES          Family Carabidae

**Large jaws projecting forward.** Moves fast on long legs. **Black, sometimes with yellow.** Fierce diurnal predator. Some spray formic acid from rear in defence.

# 2 WHIRLIGIG BEETLES          Family Gyrinidae

Antennae not visible. **Body shiny black oval. Legs seldom visible when swimming rapidly on water surface.** May dive if alarmed. Cannot walk. Flies to new ponds when necessary.

### Similar
**DIVING BEETLES Family Dytiscidae**
Swims beneath surface. Hindlegs visible when swimming.
**WATER BEETLES Families Haliplidae and Hydrophilidae**
Crawls on underwater vegetation or shelters under stones.

# 3 DUNG BEETLES          Subfamilies Scarabaeinae and Aphodiinae

Usually black but some iridescent metallic. **Antennae end in three flattened fan-like segments.** Utilises dung as both food and nursery. Front legs adapted for manipulating dung. Some species construct a dung ball which is rolled away and buried with eggs inside; others breed in dung heap or in soil beneath it.

### Similar
**TROX BEETLES Family Trogidae**
Rough, grey, deeply pitted. Found in carrion.
**CERATOCANTHUS BEETLES Family Ceratocanthidae**
Folds up into enclosed, spherical shell when disturbed.
**HISTERID BEETLES Family Histeridae**
Shiny black or brightly coloured. Found in carrion.

# 4 LEAF CHAFERS (ROSE BEETLES)          Subfamilies Rutelinae and Melolonthinae

Bronze, yellow or black nocturnal species, brightly coloured diurnal species. **Body slightly furry.** Causes severe damage to cultivated plants.

# 5 FRUIT CHAFERS          Subfamily Cetoniinae

Body robust, **slightly flat and square.** No hairs. Black and yellow or red. **Upper wings immobile when flying.** Damages fruit crops throughout s Africa.

# 6 RHINOCEROS BEETLES          Subfamily Dynastinae

Antennae not visible from above. Male has **large horn for fighting. Shiny dark brown to black.** Adult never feeds, but larva eats fresh and decaying plant matter.

### Similar
**STAG BEETLES Family Lucanidae**
Antler-like processes from jaws.
**CLUBBED BEETLES Family Geotrupidae**
Head armed with bizarre processes. Antennae club-shaped.

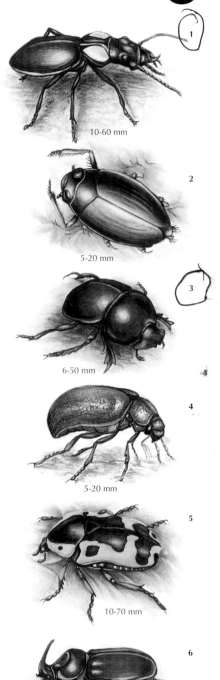

10-60 mm

5-20 mm

6-50 mm

5-20 mm

10-70 mm

♂ 10-45 mm

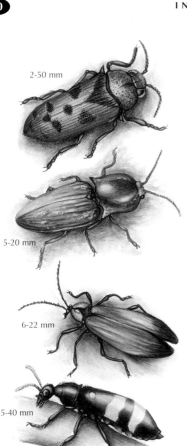

2-50 mm

5-20 mm

6-22 mm

5-40 mm

**5a**  ♀

10-25 mm

**5b**

♂

1-10 mm

**1   BUPRESTID BEETLES**                   **Family Buprestidae**
Antennae short but visible. **Body elongated, streamlined,** metallic red, blue, yellow or green. Flies fast. Active on hot days. Attracted to fire. Larva bores **oval tunnels** in dead wood.
**Similar**
**SHOT-HOLE BORERS  Superfamily Bostrychoidea**
Never brightly coloured. Larva bores circular tunnels.

**2   CLICK BEETLES**                          **Family Elateridae**
Body elongated, **black or brown. Back edge of thorax has two pointed angles.** Nocturnal plant feeder. Mechanism under body used to right insect when on its back; creates a powerful click. Click apparatus only effective in this family.
**Similar**
**TUMBLING BEETLES  Family Mordellidae**
Head tucked under body. Tumble about if captured.

**3   NET-WINGED BEETLES**                    **Family Lycidae**
Antennae serrated on inside edge. **Body flat, almost leaf-shaped. Wings black and orange, ridged.** Feeds on plants. Mimicked by other insects. Mostly in savanna.

**4   BLISTER BEETLES**                        **Family Meloidae**
**Body narrow, boat-shaped. Head separated from thorax by a "neck".** Claws divided in two. Body often hairy, **usually yellow, red or blue with black markings.** Feeds on flowers. Secretes cantharidin which can blister the skin. Larva of some species parasitises bees, others grasshopper eggs.
**Similar**
**FLOWER BEETLES  Family Melyridae**
Smaller (2–7 mm). Body flattened. Does not secrete cantharidin.

**5   GLOW-WORMS and FIREFLIES**          **Family Lampyridae**
Head hidden under thorax shield. **Light-producing organ at abdomen tip attracts mates.** Both sexes of fireflies (subfamily Luciolinae) are winged (5b). In glow-worms (subfamily Lampyrinae) female (5a) is wingless, larva-like and transmits light while crawling on vegetation. Larva preys on snails but adult does not feed. Throughout s Africa near water.
**Similar**
**ROVE BEETLES  Family Staphylinidae**
Similar to glow-worm females but no light emission. Can fly. Outer wings cover less than half of abdomen. Inner wings folded.

**6   LADYBIRD BEETLES**                   **Family Coccinellidae**
Antennae barely visible. Head sunken into thorax. **Body almost hemispherical.** Colours bright, often spotted red or yellow on black. Feeds on scale insects and aphids. Secretes toxic yellow fluid if harassed. Forms large aggregations in winter under rocks or other shelter. Throughout s Africa.

## 1 TENEBRIONID BEETLES (TOK-TOKKIES)  Family Tenebrionidae

Very varied family including many highly adapted desert dwellers. The well-known "tok-tokkies" have **head slightly sunken and pointed downwards. Body well rounded, elevated on relatively long legs.** Brown to black. Taps abdomen on hard surfaces to attract mate. Omnivorous. Mostly in arid areas.

## 2 TIGER BEETLES  Family Cicindelidae

Antennae roughly half body length. **Eyes large, slightly bulbous. Biting mouthparts clearly visible. Legs well adapted for running.** Some species black, others brightly coloured, metallic. Aggressive predator, running extremely fast after prey or to escape enemies. Most species can also fly. Most active during heat of day. Larva lives in burrow and attacks other insects that pass by entrance. Especially common in sandy, windswept areas.

## 3 LONG-HORN BEETLES  Family Cerambycidae

Antennae longer than body, stout, highly manoeuvrable. Head usually points downwards. One or more spines on thorax. Feet of many species have flattened pads. Brown, black or often strikingly coloured, sometimes metallic. Faint squeaking audible when handled. Larva is wood borer. Eggs laid in deep cracks in dead wood. Adult feeds on wood, bark, sap or fruit. Some species active by day, others nocturnal. Throughout s Africa.
**Similar**
**CANTHARID BEETLES  Family Cantharidae**
Antennae roughly half body length. Body hairy.

## 4 LEAF BEETLES (TORTOISE BEETLES)  Family Chrysomelidae

Members of this family differ widely. Many are brightly coloured and poisonous from ingesting toxic foodplants. Tortoise beetles (subfamily Cassidinae) are broad and flat, entirely protected by outer wings and shield over thorax. Flea beetles (subfamily Alticinae) jump long distances. Black and yellow or red. Larva of some flea beetles used by Kalahari San to poison arrowheads. Throughout s Africa.

## 5 WEEVILS  Superfamily Curculionoidea

**Antennae short, sharply elbowed, bulbous at tips. Head elongated to form snout.** Feet often have flattened pads. **Body covering extremely hard, surface pitted or lined.** Feigns death if disturbed. Female uses mouthparts to bore holes in plants to lay eggs. Largest animal family: 45 000 species worldwide, unknown number in s Africa.

## 6 ANTS' NEST BEETLES  Family Paussidae

**Antennae short, flat, wide.** Abdomen straight-sided. Brown to reddish-brown. Normally survives only in ants' nests, often attracted to light at night. Produces secretion licked by ants, in return ants feed the beetle. Some species produce defensive chemical which can burn human eyes or skin.

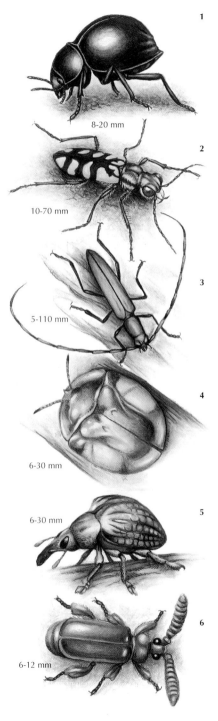

1

8-20 mm

2

10-70 mm

3

5-110 mm

4

6-30 mm

5

6-30 mm

6

6-12 mm

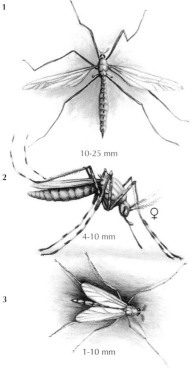

10-25 mm

♀

4-10 mm

1-10 mm

10-25 mm

3-40 mm

5-20 mm

**1   CRANE FLIES**          Families Tipulidae, Ptychopteridae and Tanyderinae

**Legs long, delicate. One pair of wings.** Yellowish-brown. **Resembles large mosquito.** Some species never feed, others feed on nectar. Male moves body or one limb to attract female. Larva inhabits moist soil, feeding on decaying plants. Common among lush vegetation.

**2   MOSQUITOES**          Family Culicidae

Antennae short, feathery in males. **Proboscis clearly visible.** One pair of wings. **Rests with hindlegs raised.** Feeds on plant fluids. Female sucks blood for egg development. One genus, *Anopheles*, transmits malaria; body points downwards at rest, all others horizontal as illustrated. Larva hangs suspended in water.
**Similar**
**MOUNTAIN MIDGES  Family Blephariciridae**
Hindlegs on surface at rest. Proboscis very small.

**3   MIDGES**          Family Chironomidae

Antennae short, feathery. **Proboscis not clearly visible.** Appearance mosquito-like, **but rests with front legs raised. Often occurs in small, dense swarms** of mostly males, perhaps to attract females. Eggs laid in static water. Larvae red, the only insects with haemoglobin in the blood. Haemoglobin assists oxygen absorption.
**Similar**
**BITING MIDGES  Family Ceratopogonidae**
Does not swarm.
**MOTH FLIES  Family Psychodidae**
Very hairy. Wings broad and moth-like.

**4   HORSEFLIES**          Family Tabanidae

Short, simple antennae. **Eyes iridescent, occupying most of head. Body heavily built.** One pair of wings, longer than abdomen. Feeds on nectar; female also sucks blood. Bite causes brief, intense pain. Can transmit diseases such as anthrax. Larva preys on insects.

**5   ROBBER FLIES**          Family Asilidae

Antennae short. **Eyes have deep groove between them at top of head. Short, sharp proboscis.** Legs long. One wing folds under the other. Predator: adult takes prey in flight. Bites painfully if handled. Maggot-like larva feeds on rotting plant matter.

**6   HOVER FLIES**          Family Syrphidae

Very short antennae. **Eyes occupy almost entire head. Appears bee-like, but only one pair of wings.** Feeds on nectar and pollen. Hovers motionless for long periods. Larvae of some species prey on aphids, others live in water and breathe through tail-like tube.
**Similar**
**BEE FLIES  Family Bombyliidae**
Wings held horizontally at rest. Long proboscis. Cannot sting.

**1 STALK-EYED FLIES**     **Family Diopsidae**
**Antennae and eyes at end of stalks.** Function of stalks unknown.
One pair of wings. Reddish-brown to black. Feeds on nectar or
rotting plants. Slow, clumsy flyer. Larva bores into rice, maize and
sugar cane stems. Restricted to low-lying, subtropical areas.

**2 TSETSE FLIES**     **Family Glossinidae**
Antennae not clearly visible. **Proboscis points slightly upwards
and forwards from bottom of head.** Yellowish-grey. Thorax has
black stripes. One wing folded under the other. Feeds on mammal
blood. Transmits nagana in animals, sleeping sickness in humans.
Larva matures inside female, exits, pupates and hatches later as
adult. Restricted to hot, subtropical areas. Now eradicated from
most of former range.

**3 FRUIT FLIES**     **Family Tephritidae**
**One pair of wings, usually with dark spots and stripes.** Body yel-
lowish to black. Tilts each wing slowly to signal to mate. Maggot-
like larva burrows into fruit, dropping into soil to pupate.
**Similar**
**VINEGAR FLIES Family Drosophilidae**
Smaller (under 2 mm). Eyes red.

**4 HOUSE FLIES**     **Family Muscidae**
Antennae not visible, eyes large, reddish. **Single pair of wings, do
not overlap at rest.** Grey to black. Associated with humans. Adult
feeds on moist food. Transmits numerous diseases by transferring
bacteria adhering to its feet. Often rubs front legs together in
grooming action. Breeds in human or animal faeces. Common
throughout the world.
**Similar**
**FANNID FLIES Family Fanniidae**
Smaller (5 mm); wing venation differs.

**5 BLOW FLIES**     **Family Calliphoridae**
**Similar in appearance to house fly but metallic blue or green.**
Breeds in rotting meat and faeces. Larvae are maggots commonly
associated with putrefaction. One species, Putsi fly, lays eggs on
clothes; larvae hatch, bore into skin causing boil-like swelling.
**Similar**
**RED-HEADED FLIES Family Platystomatidae**
Larger (20 mm). Metallic blue with large red head.
**TACHINID FLIES Family Tachinidae**
Yellow with bristle-covered abdomen and thorax.

**6 FLESH FLIES**     **Family Sarcophagidae**
**Thorax grey with black stripes. Similar to house fly but may be
larger.** Most species feed on carrion or rotting plants; may infest
human wounds. Larva hatches inside female, then deposited on
suitable food source. Other species parasitise bees and wasps.

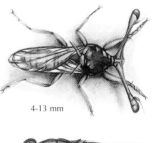

1

4-13 mm

2

8-10 mm

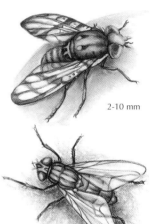

3

2-10 mm

4

6-10 mm

5

5-15 mm

6

5-15 mm

**1**

10-25 mm

♀

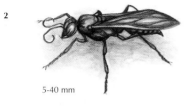

**2**

5-40 mm

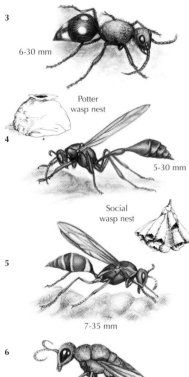

**3**

6-30 mm

Potter
wasp nest

**4**

5-30 mm

Social
wasp nest

**5**

7-35 mm

**6**

5-20 mm

**1  ICHNEUMONID WASPS    Superfamily Ichneumonoidea**
Abdomen joined to thorax by slender "waist". **Hindlegs larger than others. Antennae, legs often banded.** Orange, brown, black or yellow. Female has long tail-like ovipositor. Lays eggs on caterpillars and other insects. When larvae hatch they eat host alive.
**Similar**
**ENSIGN WASPS  Family Evaniidae**
Smaller (6–10 mm). Short, stout thorax. Abdomen joined to top of thorax.
**BRACONID WASPS  Family Braconidae**
Smaller (under 12 mm). Female's ovipositor short.
**CHALCIDOID WASPS  Superfamily Chalcidoidea**
Much smaller (under 4 mm). Black, metallic. Wings lack network of veins.

**2  SPIDER WASPS                              Family Pompilidae**
Antennae curled. Legs long, especially hindlegs. Black, sometimes with orange. Wings opaque black. Quick, jerky movements on ground. Paralyses spider, transports it to burrow and lays single egg. Larva feeds on spider.
**Similar**
**BURROWING WASPS  Families Scoliidae and Tiphiidae**
Robust, shiny black with white or yellow bands. Feeds on nectar. Burrows into soil to parasitise beetle larvae.

**3  VELVET ANTS                                Family Mutillidae**
**Abdomen black with white spots. Thorax rusty red, pitted.** Female ant-like, male winged. Active on hot, sunny days. Parasitises wasps, ants, bees, flies. Eggs laid on host. Larvae bore into host and consume it.

**4  POTTER WASPS                             Family Eumenidae**
**Long jaws cross over at rest. Forewings fold lengthwise.** Body black with yellow, orange or white markings. Builds pot or tubular mud nest for eggs and food for larvae.
**Similar**
**MASARID WASPS  Family Masaridae**
Builds "chimney-pot" walls at entrance to underground burrows.
**SPHECID WASPS  Family Sphecidae**
Builds burrows or communal mud nests under shelter.

**5  SOCIAL WASPS                              Family Vespidae**
**Forewings fold lengthwise. Brown with yellow or white markings on abdomen. Female builds communal paper nest for eggs.** Larvae fed on chewed caterpillars. Cells are capped while larvae pupate.

**6  CUCKOO WASPS                          Family Chrysididae**
Antennae short. Eyes large. **Metallic green. Head, thorax pitted.** Legs short. Adult lays eggs in nest of bees or other wasps. Larva parasitises host larva or steals its food.

**1   CARPENTER BEES**                          Subfamily Xylocopinae

**Body hairy, black with yellow or white bands on thorax and abdomen.** Wings darkly opaque. Bores into dry wood and lays an egg in each hole on deposit of pollen and nectar. Larva consumes food, pupates and emerges as new adult. Can sting.

**2   SOCIAL BEES**                             Family Apidae

**Abdomen banded black and yellow.** Legs modified to collect pollen. Social structure comprises queen, workers and drones. Honey bees (subfamily Apinae) nest in holes and construct wax comb with cells for larvae and honey. Information conveyed by means of "dancing". Indigenous subspecies displace domestic bees. Stingless bees (subfamily Meliponinae) build sticky tubular entrance to their nest.
**Similar**
**MINING BEES  Family Halictidae**
Dark, banded abdomen. Nests in holes but no social structure.
**ANTHOPHORID BEES  Family Anthophoridae**
Lacks pollen-collecting hairs on legs.
**LEAF-CUTTER BEES  Family Megachilidae**
Yellow tuft under abdomen. Some line nest with cut leaves.

**3   MYRMICINE ANTS**                          Subfamily Myrmicinae

**Head, thorax reddish-brown, abdomen black. Worker possesses sting.** Does not follow scent trails. Guards aphids and scale insects, receives honeydew in return. Common species: small brown house ant (**nests in shallow soil under stones**), harvester ant (**leaves seed husks at nest entrance**) and cocktail ant (**triangular abdomen erected in anger**).

**4   DRIVER ANTS (RED ANTS)**                  Subfamily Dorylinae

Male winged, stingless (illustrated). Worker has sting, 3–8 mm. Swarms of workers periodically move about in dense masses devouring any prey unable to escape.

**5   FORMICINE ANTS**                          Subfamily Formicinae

**Legs long in proportion to body, capable of swift running.** Many spray formic acid in defence. Protects aphids and scale insects in return for honeydew. Species include the 3 mm black ants which trail around dwellings, brown sugar ants (**brown with sparse hairs covering the abdomen**) and tailor ants (**bind leaves together to form nest in tree**).
**Similar**
**ARGENTINE ANT  Subfamily Dolichoderinae**
Brown. Thorax more elongated, flattened than in black ant.

**6   PONERINE ANTS**                           Subfamily Ponerinae

Large, black, stinging ant. **Abdomen constricted about one third of way down.** Matabele ant raids termitaria in military-like columns a few centimetres wide and several metres long. Stridulation can be heard as they move.

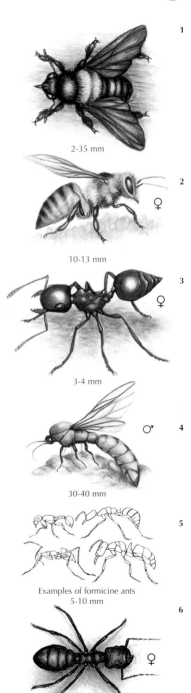

2-35 mm

10-13 mm ♀

3-4 mm ♀

30-40 mm ♂

Examples of formicine ants
5-10 mm

8-20 mm ♀

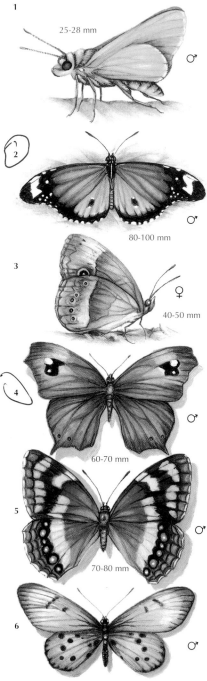

25-28 mm ♂

80-100 mm ♂

40-50 mm ♀

60-70 mm ♂

70-80 mm ♂

45-50 mm ♂

**1  LATREILLE'S SKIPPER**                    *Gegenes hottentota*
Antennae slightly curved outwards at tips. Male **straw-coloured**, darker near wing tips. Indistinct **dark spot near bottom of forewing.** Female darker brown, **small white patches on forewing.** Flies fast. Perches briefly, then flies off again. Drives intruders out of territory. Open bushveld. Common in n and e Zimbabwe.
**Similar**
About 20 small, brown, fast-flying species.

**2  AFRICAN MONARCH**                    *Danaus chrysippus*
Narrow body. **Thorax black above, spotted white below.** Wings **orange-brown**, apex of forewing black with white patches. **Hindwings have three or four black spots.** Larva feeds on milkweeds, absorbing poison to deter predators. Mimicked by other species. Throughout Africa.
**Similar**
**COMMON DIADEM** *Hypolimnas misippus*
Only one black spot on front margin of hindwing.

**3  COMMON BUSH BROWN**                    *Bicyclus safitza*
Wings, body brown. **Small brown eye spot with white centre near apex of forewing. Larger eye spot below.** Folded wings look like dead leaf. Weak, floppy flight. If disturbed flies for short distance then settles. Attracted to rotting fruit. Common along E coast.
**Similar**
**OTHER BUSH BROWNS** Genera *Bicyclus* and *Henotesia*
Spots on upper hindwing.

**4  TWILIGHT BROWN**                    *Melanitis leda*
Small body in proportion to wings. **Wings brown. Apex of forewing has two white spots in black patch surrounded by diffused golden brown area. Veins at base of forewing large.** Flies mainly at dusk, with slow flapping. Rests by day among fallen leaves. Forests in E.
**Similar**
**VIOLET-EYED EVENING BROWN** *M. libya*
White spots surrounded by purple on forewing.

**5  TABLE MOUNTAIN BEAUTY**                    *Aeropetes tulbaghia*
Body, wings dark brown. **Light orange bands across both wings. White eye spots surrounded by purple and black rings** along outer margin of hindwing. December to March. Mountainous areas.

**6  GARDEN ACRAEA**                    *Acraea horta*
Body black. Wings reddish-orange. **Forewings have translucent tips.** Hindwings spotted black. Flight slow, floppy. Secretes distasteful fluid when attacked. Throughout s Africa except arid NW.
**Similar**
**TREE-TOP ACRAEA** *Hyalites cerasa*
Both hind- and forewings have translucent tips.
**DUSKY-VEINED ACRAEA** *Hyalites igola*
Black band along outer margin of hindwing.

**1   PEARL CHARAXES**                   *Charaxes varanes*

Body light grey. **Wings white near body, remainder orange with brown patches and flecks. Pointed tail on each hindwing.** Flies fast, all year. Attracted to rotting fruit, dung. Common in forests in E.

**Similar**

**POINTED PEARL CHARAXES  C. acuminatus**

Darkly speckled brown, less orange. Only in e Zimbabwe.

**2   PEARL-SPOTTED CHARAXES**            *Charaxes jahlusa*

Stout body. **Upperside of wings orange with black patches and margins. Two short tails on each hindwing. Underside of wings pinkish with black spots on forewing, pearl spots on hindwing.** Flies all year, commonest in summer. Males fly around selected trees and congregate on hilltops. S Karoo to e Cape and along E coast.

**3   BUSHVELD CHARAXES**                *Charaxes achaemenes*

Body stout, light brown. Wings light brown near body, bisected by **band of white patches (yellow in female)** and dark brown along outer margins. **Hindwing edged with silver-grey patches and blue flecks.** Two tails on each hindwing. Flies all year. Drives intruders out of territory. N of Tugela into Zimbabwe and Namibia.

**Similar**

**BLUE-SPANGLED CHARAXES  C. guderiana**

Female difficult to distinguish. Zimbabwe and Mozambique.

**4   GREEN-VEINED CHARAXES**            *Charaxes candiope*

Body tan. **Wings pale orange near body, darker with dark brown patches along outer margin. Veins near body distinct, raised, light green.** Two tails on each hindwing. Drives intruders out of territory. Attracted to rotting fruit, dung. Forests, bushveld throughout s Africa, except cool highveld and Cape provinces.

**Similar**

**WILD-BAMBOO CHARAXES  C. macclounii**

Wings dark orange near body. Lacks green veins.

**5   FOXY CHARAXES**                     *Charaxes jasius*

Body stout, brown. **Wings brown near body; wide yellow band across both wings;** brown band spotted with orange along outer wing margins. Two tails on each hindwing. Male defends territory from hilltop vantage point. Attracted to rotting fruit, dung, damp soil. Warm savanna areas in e South Africa, Zimbabwe and Botswana.

**6   WHITE-BARRED CHARAXES**            *Charaxes brutus*

Body stout, black. Wings black with **white band across both wings, broadening from top to bottom. Small orange spots along outer margin of forewing,** hindwing edged dull white. Two short tails on each hindwing. Flies all year, fast and high above trees. Attracted to sap oozing from wounds in trees. From E coast of South Africa into interior.

**Similar**

**LITTLE CHARAXES  C. baumanni**

Band of white does not taper in width.

80-100 mm  ♂

45-60 mm  ♂

55-65 mm  ♂

83-100 mm  ♂

80-105 mm  ♀

60-80 mm  ♀

**1** · 55-75 mm · ♂

**2** · 45-50 mm · ♂

**3** · 60-70 mm · ♂

**4** · 60-70 mm · ♀

**5** · 35-40 mm · ♀

**6** · 45-55 mm · ♂

### 1  GOLD-BANDED FORESTER        *Euphaedra neophron*

Antennae tipped white. **Body, hindwings and central part of forewings brilliant metallic blue. Two black bands enclosing gold band diagonally across forewing.** Rapid gliding flight. Flies off quickly when disturbed. Attracted to fermenting fruit, sugary plant secretions. Dense, shady forests; occasionally basks in sunny patches with wings held flat. Tropical forests in NE.

### 2  SMALL-SPOTTED SAILOR        *Neptis saclava*

Grey-brown. **Three white patches near apex of forewing, two white patches lower on forewing.** White band diagonally from outer to inner margin of hindwing. Both wings edged with small patches of black and brown in three parallel rows. Flight characterised by long periods of gliding. Attracted to sap exuding from trees. E half of region.
**Similar**
About 10 other species of *Neptis,* all difficult to distinguish.

### 3 & 4 COMMON DIADEM        *Hypolimnas misippus*

**Male black with two large purple-ringed white spots on forewing and one on hindwing (3). Female mimics African monarch but has only one black spot on hindwing (4).** Flies fast, all year. Defends territory against intruders. Shy, difficult to approach. Open wooded country throughout Africa except dry areas.
**Similar**
**FALSE MONARCH  *Pseudacraea poggei***
Mimics African monarch. Only in n Namibia.

### 5  BOISDUVAL'S TREE NYMPH        *Sallya boisduvali*

Body and wings dull tan. Row of small dark brown spots on hindwing. Female has dull orange patches near apex of forewing. Abundant at times. Appears to hatch in large numbers at one locality and disperse from there. Flies all year. E half of region.
**Similar**
**NATAL TREE NYMPH  *S. natalensis***
Diffuse black areas near apex of forewing.

### 6  AFRICAN JOKER        *Byblia anvatara*

Body black. **Wings deep orange, edged black.** Black band along front margin of forewing. Central black band extends outwards from body over both wings. Orange spots along margin of hindwing. Often seen drinking at patches of damp soil. Attracted to rotting fruit, dung. Very common in open country. Flies all year, commonest in wet season. Mainly in E.
**Similar**
**COMMON JOKER  *B. ilithyia***
Small black spots in row diagonally across centre of hindwing. Widespread.

**1   COMMON MOTHER-OF-PEARL**          *Protogoniomorpha*
                                        *parhassus*

**Wings shiny greenish-white with purple, red and black spots.
Tips of forewings black.** Short tail projects from each hindwing.
Drinks from patches of damp soil. When disturbed flies quickly
into upper canopy. Coastal and inland forests and along stream
banks throughout s Africa.
**Similar**
**CLOUDED MOTHER-OF-PEARL**  *P. anacardii*
Whiter; has more black on forewings.

**2   GAUDY COMMODORE**                      *Precis octavia*

Body black. **Wings metallic blue.** Two white spots near apex of
forewing. **Bands of black and one band of red run parallel with
margin of both wings.** Female and wet season forms are orange
with rows of black spots parallel to margin of wings. **Margin of
hindwing scalloped.** Cluster together in holes in banks during
cold weather. Attracted to hilltops. Gardens, open grassland in E.
**Similar**
**DARKER COMMODORE** *P. antilope*
Margin of hindwing smooth.

**3 & 4 GARDEN COMMODORE**                   *Precis archesia*

**Dull brown body, wings.** Dry season form (3): **red band with
small white spots across both pairs of wings**; forewing has blue
patches on inner and outer margin and two white patches below
apex; both pairs of wings edged white. Wet season form (4):
**bright yellow band with small brown spots,** forming Y at front
margin of forewing; both pairs of wings spotted with white along
margins. Active during heat of day, attracted to flowers in gardens,
on grassy hilltops, rocky slopes. Common in n interior and E.
**Similar**
**MARSH COMMODORE**  *P. ceryne*
Similar to wet season form (4) but with yellow patches on wings.

**5   BLUE PANSY**                           *Junonia oenone*

**Antennae white, body and wings black.** Forewing has patches of
white and two brick-red eye spots near outer margin. **Hindwing
has prominent blue spot in centre,** is edged white and has eye
spot on lower margin. Male defends territory against other males.
Attracted to hilltops during warmth of day. Often settles on
ground with wings flat, making identification easy. Woodland and
bushveld throughout s Africa except dry W.

**6   YELLOW PANSY**                         *Junonia hierta*

Body black. Centre of wings yellow, becoming orange, then black
nearer margins. **Large purple spot near front margin of hindwing.**
Male defends territory against other males. Suns itself on ground.
Flight characteristic: flaps wings a few times then glides short distance. Feeds on flowers. Flies all year. Open grassy areas or open
woodland throughout s Africa except dry areas and SW.

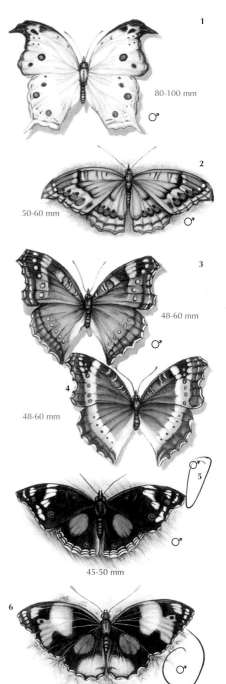

1

80-100 mm     ♂

2

50-60 mm     ♂

3

48-60 mm     ♂

4

48-60 mm

♂
5

45-50 mm     ♂

6

45-50 mm     ♂

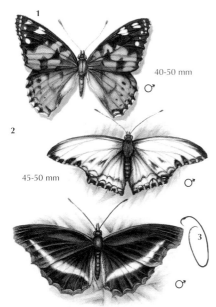

40-50 mm ♂

45-50 mm ♂

3

45-50 mm ♂

♂

50-60 mm

5

40-50 mm ♂

6

40-45 mm ♂

**1   PAINTED LADY**                    *Vanessa cardui*

Body dirty brown. **Wings orange with black patches and spots, grey near body.** Apex of forewing spotted white. Flies fast, low along ground, often resting on sunny patch. Flies all year. Common throughout the world, widespread in s Africa.
**Similar**
**COMMON JOKER** *Byblia ilithyia*
Similar pattern of orange and black but no white on forewing.

**2   BATTLING GLIDER**                *Cymothoe alcimeda*

Body greyish-black. **Wings white, outer margin black with small orange spots.** Settles with wings held flat. Edges of moist forest. Subspecies *C.a. alcimeda* has black bar near front of forewing. Occurs in w Cape. *C.a. trimeni* in e South Africa and interior further N.
**Similar**
**BLONDE GLIDER** *C. coranus*
Larger (wingspan 58 mm), no orange spots along wing margin.

**3   PIED PIPER**                      *Eurytela hiarbas*

Body, wings black. **White band from middle of forewing to inner margin of hindwing.** Defends territory. Flies with long periods of gliding. Escapes quickly if approached. Forests along e escarpment.

**4   PIRATE**                        *Catacroptera cloanthe*

Body grey. **Wings orange**, grey near body. Forewing has black bars along front margin and purple and black eye spot. **Similar eye spots in row on hindwing.** Flies close to ground, wary when approached. Open grass, vleis. Throughout s Africa except dry W.
**Similar**
**BLOTCHED LEOPARD** *Lachnoptera ayersii*
Lacks eye spots on wings.

**5   LONG-TAILED ADMIRAL**          *Antanartia schaeneia*

Body, wings dark brown. **Orange band from front of forewing to bottom corner and down outer margin of hindwing.** Apex of forewing black with small white spots. Hindwing has **two purple-centred eye spots and two tails** of unequal length. Flies low. Forests in E.
**Similar**
**SHORT-TAILED ADMIRAL** *A. hippomene*
Tails shorter, orange band on hindwing broader.

**6   AFRICAN LEOPARD**                *Phalanta phalanta*

**Body, wings orange.** Forewing has fine black patches. **Row of small black spots and scalloped black pattern along wing margins.** Infrequently stops flying to rest, slowly opening and closing wings. Feeds on *Lantana* flowers. Open woodland throughout Africa except dry areas.
**Similar**
**BLOTCHED LEOPARD** *Lachnoptera ayresii*
Lacks pattern of black spots along wing margins.

**1   COMMON BLUE**                    *Leptotes pirithous*
**Upperside of wings plain light blue, edged white.** Underside
mottled black and white with **two eye spots near base of hindwing.** Hindwing has single delicate tail near eye spots. Rests with
antennae hidden. Slowly opens and closes wings. Common
throughout s Africa.
**Similar**
Four other species of *Leptotes*, difficult to distinguish.

**2   BOLAND SKOLLY**                  *Thestor protumnus*
Body light brown. **Wings dusky orange** edged with broad black
band. Brown and white fringe of hairs along wing margins. **Mottled black patches on each wing.** Lives in colonies and often seen
on bare ground. Flies off with jerky, rapid flight, quickly returning
to same spot. October to December. SW and Karoo.
**Similar**
Nine other species of *Thestor*, difficult to distinguish.

**3   BROWN PLAYBOY**                  *Deudorix antalus*
**Body and wings near body dusty blue, fading to greyish-brown.**
Outer margin fringed with fine white hairs. Hindwing has single
eye spot and delicate tail. Fast flyer, often on hilltops or basking
on shrubs. More common in summer. Bushveld in N and along
entire coast.
**Similar**
**VAN SON'S PLAYBOY** *Viracloa vansoni*
Smaller (wingspan 24 mm). NE of South Africa and into Zimbab-
we.

**4   FIG-TREE BLUE**                  *Myrina silenus*
Body greyish-black. **Wings brilliant metallic blue. Apex of
forewing tipped reddish-brown**, separated from blue by black
band. Margin of hindwing reddish-brown with **single, long, twisted tail.** Flies fast and straight, seldom resting. Perches with wings
half open. Associated with fig trees throughout s Africa.
**Similar**
**LESSER FIG-TREE BLUE** *M. dermaptera*
Apex of forewing black, not reddish-brown.

**5 & 6   SOUTHERN SAPPHIRE**          *Iolaus silas*
Body greyish-black. **Upperside of wings brilliant metallic blue.**
Apex of forewing, outer margin of hindwing black (5). **Two tails
of different length and single red spot on lower margin of hindwing.** Underside of wings brilliant white (6). Lower margin of hindwing has
black eye spot surrounded by red. Fine black bars along bottom
of hindwing. Perches high on shrubs in full sun with wings closed.
Wide variety of habitats from coastal forest to dry savanna wood-
and. From w Cape northwards along E coast.
**Similar**
Three other species of *Iolaus*. Black band on margin of hindwing narrower.

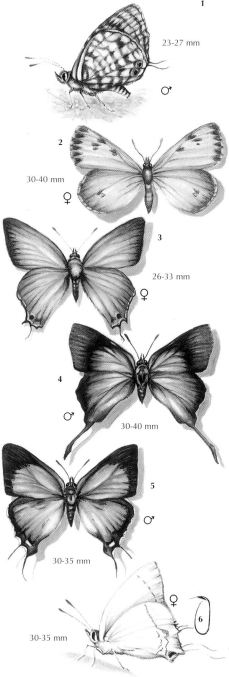

1        23-27 mm        ♂

2        30-40 mm        ♀

3        26-33 mm        ♀

4        30-40 mm        ♂

5        30-35 mm        ♂

6        30-35 mm        ♀

1

20-25 mm

♂

2

20-30 mm

♀

3

35-40 mm

♂

4

25-35 mm

♀

5

25-30 mm

♂

6

15-20 mm

♂

**1  COMMON SCARLET**　　　　　*Axiocerses tjoane*

Body black with reddish hairs. **Wings red. Apex of forewing black. Hindwings thinly edged black. Single short tail on hindwing.** Fast, alert flyer. Moves wings and tails slowly when perched to deceive predators. E coast of South Africa into interior further N.
**Similar**
**BUSH SCARLET  A. amanga**
Wings reddish-orange. Black on forewing apex less extensive.

**2  CAPE BLACK-EYE**　　　　　*Leptomyrina lara*

Body, wings light brown. Brown and white fringe of hairs along wing margins. Two black eye spots surrounded by white on forewing and hindwing. Flies fast at about knee height, settling often. Rocky areas from sea level to high mountains throughout central areas and SW.
**Similar**
**HENNING'S BLACK-EYE  L. henningi**
Wings golden brown.
**COMMON BLACK-EYE  L. gorgias**
Larger (wingspan 28 mm), wings slightly pearly grey.

**3  KING COPPER**　　　　　*Tylopaedia sardonyx*

Body black with orange hairs. **Wings orange with fine white hairs along margins.** Forewing has patches of black, **one black spot** and black margin. Hindwing has black margin. Flies rapidly over rocky slopes. Male defends territory. Arid scrubland in S.
**Similar**
**LARGE SILVER-SPOTTED COPPER  Argyraspodes argyraspis**
No black in central forewing.

**4  PALE HAIRTAIL**　　　　　*Anthene butleri*

Body dark grey. **Wings light blue surrounded by light brown,** outer margins fringed with white hairs. **Hindwing has black eye spot on margin with orange semicircle and two tails.** Frequents acacia trees and hilltops. Open, hilly country throughout s Africa except n Cape.
**Similar**
Six species of Anthene. Eye spot less distinct.

**5  LUCERNE BLUE**　　　　　*Lampides boeticus*

Body dark grey. **Wings light blue with silvery sheen,** edged with light brown and fringe of white hairs. **Two black spots and single delicate tail on hindwing.** Common throughout Africa and Europe.

**6  GAIKA BLUE**　　　　　*Zizula hylax*

Antennae finely barred black and white. **Wings light blue surrounded by brown,** fringed with white hairs. Flies weakly, close to ground. May be seen at muddy patches of soil. Throughout s Africa except Karoo.
**Similar**
Five other species. Brown border along forewing margin narrower

**1  ZEBRA WHITE**  *Pinacopteryx eriphia*
Body black. Wings yellow, edged with black and yellow patches; **black band across each wing.** Open country, often congregating in large numbers. Throughout s Africa except Karoo.

**2  AFRICAN MIGRANT**  *Catopsilia florella*
Body greyish-white. Wings white in male, yellow with tan margins in female. **Single black spot near front margin of forewing.** May feed singly on flowers or congregate in large numbers to migrate in Ne direction. Throughout s Africa except dry areas.
**Similar**
**AUTUMN-LEAF VAGRANT**  *Eronia leda*
Similar to female African migrant but lacks spot on forewing.

**3  BROAD-BORDERED GRASS YELLOW**  *Eurema brigitta*
Body black. Wings bright yellow, broad black margin on each wing. Inside edge of black band on forewing curves smoothly. Flies weakly, close to ground. When perched hangs by one leg to imitate dead leaf. Throughout s Africa except arid W.
**Similar**
**COMMON GRASS YELLOW**  *E. hecabe*
Inside edge of black band on forewing uneven, wavy.
**ANGLED GRASS YELLOW**  *E. desjardinsii*
Hindwing squared off, but this is difficult to see in the field.

**4  VINE-LEAF VAGRANT**  *Eronia cleodora*
Body black. Upperside of wings white with broad black borders. **Two white spots at apex of forewing. Underside mottled yellow, brown and black resembling dead leaf.** Feeds on flowers at forest edges. Fast flyer. Warm areas in E.
**Similar**
**LARGE VAGRANT**  *Nepheronia argia*
No black on hindwings.

**5  BROWN-VEINED WHITE**  *Belenois aurota*
Body black. Upperside of wings white with apex of forewing and margin of hindwing brown. **Brown arc from front margin of forewing into centre. Underside of wings white to light yellow with brown veins,** brown rings along margins. Flies rapidly. Millions migrate, usually towards NE, each year. Open woodland and grassland throughout s Africa.
**Similar**
**FOREST WHITE**  *B. zochalia*
White spots on forewing apex. Hindwing has black patches.

**6  LARGE VAGRANT**  *Nepheronia argia*
Body black. Wings white with black apex in male. Female has orange patch at base of forewing and variable amounts of yellow on hindwing. Black markings variable in female. Swift, erratic flight. Forest and forest margins along e escarpment and coastal areas.

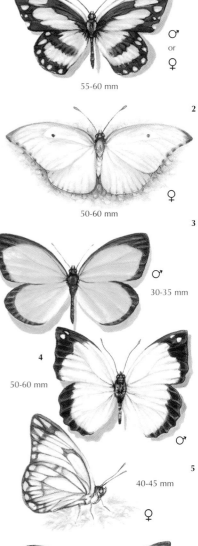

1

♂
or
♀
55-60 mm

2

♀
50-60 mm

3

♂
30-35 mm

4

50-60 mm

♂

5

40-45 mm

♀

6

♀
55-70 mm

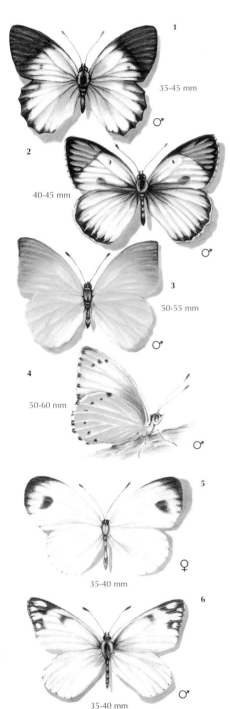

1
35-45 mm
♂

2
40-45 mm
♂

3
50-55 mm
♂

4
50-60 mm
♂

5
35-40 mm
♀

6
35-40 mm
♂

**1  SCARLET TIP**                                      *Colotis danae*

Body charcoal. Wings white, grey near body with **red apex.** Hindwings edged black. Flies low and fast in open areas, settling frequently and moving off quickly when approached. Dry savanna, woodlands in N and NE.
**Similar**
**PURPLE TIPS  C. regina, C. ione, C. erone**
Tips of forewings purple.

**2  RED TIP**                                          *Colotis antevippe*

Body grey. **Wings white with orange-red tips. Black band extends horizontally from body.** Outer margins of wings black. **Black spot in centre of forewing.** Flies fast, low on ground. Bush, open bushveld from w Cape along E coast into n interior.
**Similar**
**ORANGE TIP  C. evenina**
No black spot on forewing. E and w bushveld into Namibia.
**SPECKLED SULPHUR TIP  C. agoye**
Wings lightly speckled with grey. No black markings.

**3  AUTUMN-LEAF VAGRANT**                              *Eronia leda*

Body dark grey. **Wings bright yellow with apex of forewing orange.** Flight swift and straight, stopping occasionally to feed at flowers. Coastal bush to open woodland and bushveld in e South Africa, Mozambique, Zimbabwe, n Botswana and Namibia.

**4  FALSE DOTTED BORDER**                              *Belenois thysa*

Wet season form: upperside of wings white with pinkish forewing base, orange hindwing base; **underside of hindwing and forewing tips yellow; red patch under base of forewing.** Dry season form: lemon yellow with margins of forewing bordered black; **black spots along outer margin of hindwing.** Flies slowly, stopping frequently to feed on flowers. E coast forests.
**Similar**
**STREAKED DOTTED BORDER  Mylothris rubricosta**
Red patches on underside **and** upperside of forewing.

**5  AFRICAN WOOD WHITE**                               *Leptosia alcesta*

Body, wings white. **Apex of forewing black with single black spot beneath.** Flight slow, cumbersome, gliding as far as possible, flapping infrequently. Shady areas near dense, wet forests from NE coast through Swaziland and e escarpment into Zimbabwe.

**6  MEADOW WHITE**                                     *Pontia helice*

Body black. **Wings white** except **apex of forewing which has black patches, single black patch below apical area.** Flies slowly but will increase speed if chased. Open habitat such as old fields. Congregates on surrounding hilltops. Common throughout s Africa.

**1   CITRUS SWALLOWTAIL**                   *Papilio demodocus*
**Body, wings charcoal.** Body striped yellow beneath. **Band of yellow patches and spots through centre and along outer margin of fore- and hindwings.** Two russet and blue eye spots on each hindwing. **No tails on hindwings.** Common throughout s Africa, especially in wet season.

**2   GREENBANDED SWALLOWTAIL**              *Papilio nireus*
Body, wings black. **Turquoise band through fore- and hindwings, turquoise spots along wing margins.** Short tails on hindwing. Common during wet season. Woodland and forest edges throughout s Africa.
**Similar**
**LARGE STRIPED SWORDTAIL   Graphium antheus**
Turquoise patches pale, longish tails on hindwing.

**3   EMPEROR SWALLOWTAIL**                 *Papilio ophidicephalus*
Body black. Wings black with **two lines of yellow patches along margins of fore- and hindwings. Yellow bar diagonally across hindwing. Hindwing has two purple, black and orange eye spots and long lobed tail.** Largest butterfly in s Africa. Flies in open glades in forests of e Cape, along e escarpment to Zimbabwe.
**Similar**
**CONSTANTINE'S SWALLOWTAIL   P. constantinus**
Lacks eye spots on hindwing.

**4   SMALL STRIPED SWORDTAIL**             *Graphium policenes*
Body, wings black. **Large turquoise patches dominate central portion of wings with straight bars along front of forewing.** Red spot and **long tail on hindwing.** Fast flyer, difficult to approach. Coastal bush and e escarpment forests.
**Similar**
**LARGE STRIPED SWORDTAIL   G. antheus**
Bars on forewing wavy, not straight.

**5   MOCKER SWALLOWTAIL**                   *Papilio dardanus*
Body charcoal. **Colours highly variable. Male (5a): wings yellow with black forewing apex area containing single yellow spot; hindwing has irregular black markings and lobed tail.** Female **(5b): lacks tails;** forewing black with variable yellow or cream spots; hindwing may be russet, yellow or cream with wide black margins containing row of pale dots. Forest edges in e Cape, along e escarpment to Zimbabwe.

**6   VEINED SWORDTAIL**                     *Graphium leonidas*
Body black. **Wings black with pale blue patches on forewing** and smaller pale blue spots along margins of fore- and hindwings. **Central portion of hindwing whitish with black veins.** Wary when approached, fast flying. Open woodland in e Cape and along e escarpment.
**Similar**
**WHITE LADY SWORDTAIL   G. morania**
White area on hindwing extends into forewing.

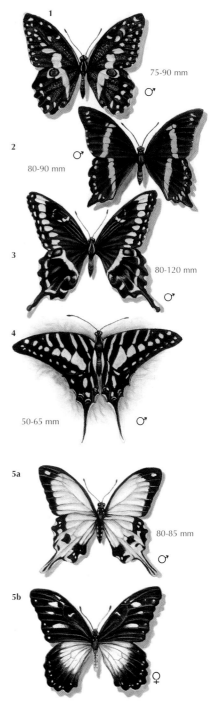

1

75-90 mm
♂

2

80-90 mm
♂

3

80-120 mm
♂

4

50-65 mm
♂

5a

80-85 mm
♂

6

75-80 mm
♂

5b

♀

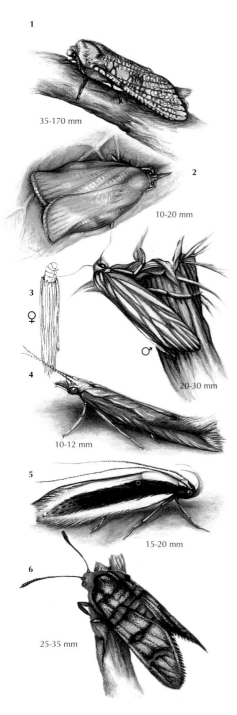

35–170 mm

10–20 mm

♀

♂

20–30 mm

10–12 mm

15–20 mm

25–35 mm

### 1   GOAT MOTHS                    Family Cossidae

Antennae roughly one quarter body length, comb-like. **Large with stout, heavy body. Forewings long, narrow, mottled dull grey or brown.** Larva bores into living plants, never feeds on dead wood. Resin oozing from borer holes said to smell like male goat. Eggs laid in cracks in bark at night, larvae burrow into stem. Pest of quince, apple, pear trees. Common throughout s Africa except dry areas.

**Similar**

**BAGWORMS Family Psychidae**

Some goat moth larvae construct cases similar to bagworms.

### 2   LEAF ROLLERS                  Family Tortricidae

Antennae roughly same length as body. **Both wings broad, forewings square at tips.** Dull brown or grey. **Hindwings fringed with short hairs.** Flies at dusk with rapid, darting flight. Larva of some species feeds on fruit. Larva rolls up in leaf on which it feeds. Here it pupates to emerge as adult. Throughout s Africa except dry areas.

**Similar**

**CODLIN MOTHS Family Olethreutidae**

Can only be distinguished by wing venation.

### 3   BAGWORMS                     Family Psychidae

Antennae half body length. Body covered with rough hairs. **Larva constructs distinctive bag of twigs, thorns, leaves or grass in which it lives and pupates, finally emerging as adult.** Male adult: wings transparent without scales; drab coloration; does not feed, is short-lived, seldom seen. Female: wingless, maggot-like; remains in bag for life. Throughout s Africa.

### 4   CABBAGE MOTHS                Family Plutellidae

Antennae roughly one third body length, **held pointed forward at rest.** Wings dull brown or grey. Body small. Larva a major pest of plants in cabbage family. Other species feed on leaves of other plants or are stem borers. Adult holds wings rolled tightly closed at rest. Throughout Africa.

**Similar**

**WEB SPINNERS Family Yponomeutidae**

Larvae often gregarious. Lives in silk web draped over plants.

### 5   TUBER MOTHS                  Family Gelechiidae

Antennae as long as body. **Wings narrow, pointed. Hindwings fringed with long hair-like cilia.** Wings held tightly rolled against body at rest. Colour greyish to brown, some species striped black and white. Larvae attack potatoes, cotton, tobacco and cereal crops. Some species "mine" leaves, eating worm-shaped tunnels through leaf tissue. Common throughout the world.

### 6   BURNETS                      Family Zygaenidae

**Antennae thickened at tips**, half body length. Eyes prominent. **Wings, body often brightly coloured metallic green, orange, red or yellow.** Bright colours are warning to predators: some species contain cyanide. Flies during daytime, feeding on flowers. Flight slow, heavy. Moist areas. Colour and diurnal behaviour may cause it to be mistaken for a butterfly.

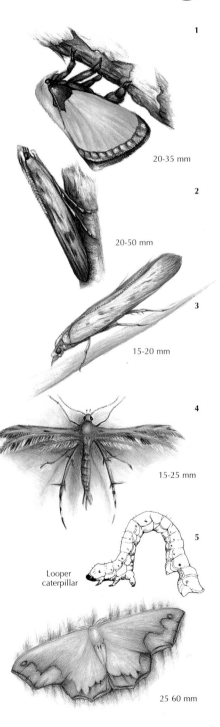

## 1   SLUG MOTHS            Family Limacodidae

Antennae short, less than half body length, comb-shaped. **Body thick, heavy, hairy.** Forewings green or mottled drab brown. **Both pairs of wings rounded at tips.** Larva slug-like, covered in sharp spines. Inflicts severe pain if handled. Feeds on leaves of fruit trees. Eggs overlap like roof tiles. Moist areas.
**Similar**
**GOLD FRINGED MOTHS  Family Chrysopolomidae**
Forewings broad. Body short, squat.

20-35 mm

## 2   PYRALID MOTHS            Family Pyralidae

**Antennae half body length, simple, thread-like.** Thorax hairy, body medium in length. **Forewings taper sharply from narrow base to broad tips.** Dull grey or brown with darker markings. Habits vary widely. Larva feeds in leaves tied together, stems, flowers or fruit. Often a pest in stored foods like grain. One species introduced from South America to control prickly pear. Throughout s Africa.
**Similar**
**WAX MOTHS  Family Galleriidae**
Larva feeds on wax in beehives. Not commonly encountered.

20-50 mm

## 3   GRASS MOTHS            Family Crambidae

Antennae thin, thread-like, held tightly along side of body at rest. Mouthparts held pointed forward. Cream, light yellow or streaked brown. Adult often flushed from tall grass. Rests longitudinally along grass stem with wings tightly folded around body for camouflage. Larva constructs silk gallery in grasses on which it lives and feeds. Throughout s Africa except dry W.
**Similar**
**PHYCITID MOTHS  Family Phycitidae**
Conspicuous row of hairs along margin of forewing.

15-20 mm

## 4   PLUME MOTHS            Family Pterophoridae

Antennae simple. **Fore- and hindwings divided into two to four feathery plumes.** Colour cream to light brown. **Legs long, slender, often with prominent spurs projecting outwards.** Fragile, delicate appearance. Weak flyer. Rests with wings and legs spread out. May be mistaken for mosquito when perched. Larva mostly feeds on flowers or leaves of daisy plant family. Throughout s Africa.
**Similar**
**FEATHER MOTHS  Family Alucitidae**
Wings divided into six or seven plumes. Lacks spurs on legs.

15-25 mm

## 5   LOOPERS            Family Geometridae

Antennae roughly half body length, varying from thin to broad and comb-like. **Thorax often hairy. Abdomen slender. Wings broad, generally dull, mottled pale grey to brown or sometimes greenish.** Adult has slow, floppy flight. Usually presses wings flat against surface of perch, but some species hold wings above body like butterflies. Larva lacks support in middle of body necessitating characteristic "looping" gait. Larva camouflaged to look like twig, usually very difficult to detect unless moving. Common throughout s Africa.

Looper caterpillar

25  60 mm

90-150 mm

30-120 mm

20-35 mm

20-80 mm

40-60 mm

250 mm

**1 & 2  EMPEROR MOTHS**                    Family Saturniidae

Antennae roughly one third body length. **Antennae broad, fan-like in male, simple in female.** Body small in proportion to wings. Colours variable but usually has **large eye spots on fore- or hindwings or both.** Wings sometimes have long tails (2). Adult has no mouthparts, unable to feed, hence only lives two to three days. Flight slow, ponderous. Larvae often congregate in large numbers, cause considerable damage to food plants. Larvae of one species (Mopane worms) collected in large numbers for food. Other species are pests in pine plantations. Cocoons of pupae are used as rattles on the legs and arms in African traditional dress. Restricted to moist e edge of s Africa and into n interior.

**3  MONKEY MOTHS**                    Family Eupterotidae

Antennae roughly one third body length, **comb-like but with slender appearance.** Wings rounded, broad, fringed with hairs along margins, usually dull with cryptic patterns for camouflage. **Body large, heavy, with thick covering of hairs.** Adult flies slowly. Rests on tree trunks during day. Larva covered with long, soft hairs often swept backwards, hence common name. Habits poorly known. Some larvae feed on grasses. Most species in moist S and E.

**4  EGGAR MOTHS**                    Family Lasiocampidae

**Antennae roughly one quarter body length,** comb-like. **Forewings narrow, elongate, hindwings rounded. Body stout, hairy.** Larvae often cluster together in silk webs on food plants. Caterpillars of many species have sparse hairs. Hairs become embedded in skin if touched and cause severe irritation. Some species incorporate these hairs into cocoon to protect pupa inside. Common throughout s Africa.

**5  PROMINENTS**                    Family Notodontidae

**Antennae roughly one quarter to one third body length,** simple or finely comb-like. **Head, eyes small in relation to large stout body.** Common name derived from **prominent tuft of hairs projecting from middle of forewing above the body when at rest.** Adult shams death, dropping to ground if disturbed. Larvae have many peculiar shapes and structures designed to scare off predators. Throughout s Africa.

**6  FALSE TIGER MOTHS**                    Family Agaristidae

Antennae half body length, simple, **thickened towards end, tips finely pointed. Wings brightly coloured in combinations of red, yellow or black.** Adult active during day with rapid, powerful flight. Bright colours warn predators of toxicity. Male of some species produces sound by rubbing legs against wings. Larva brighly marked in warning colours of black, yellow or orange. Throughout s Africa except dry areas.

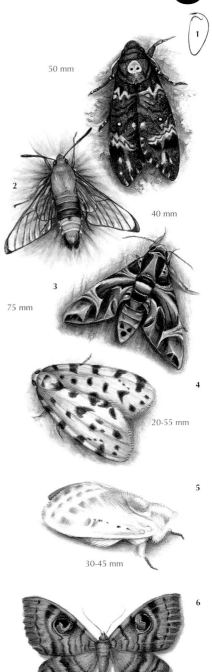

**1, 2 & 3  HAWK MOTHS**  　　　　　Family Sphingidae

Antennae short, roughly one third body length, **simple, relatively thick, sometimes slightly hooked at tips.** Eyes large, prominent. **Wings held delta-shape,** elongated, narrow. Hindwings small relative to forewings. Wing colour highly variable. Body large, streamlined, thorax often covered in dense hair. Abdomen frequently banded with circular rings. Swift, strong flyer, can reach 50 km/h. Fore- and hindwings linked together in flight by special coupling mechanism. Most species nocturnal but some, **hummingbird hawk moths** (2), diurnal. Mouthparts consist of long proboscis used to suck nectar from flowers. Proboscis of some species longer than body. **Death's head moth** (1) uses strong proboscis to pierce wax cells of beehives and suck out honey. Some species can squeak in protest when handled. Larva highly characteristic with large horn on last segment of abdomen, its function unknown. Common throughout s Africa.

**4  TIGER MOTHS**  　　　　　　Family Arctiidae

Antennae half body length, comb-like in male, simple in female. Stout-bodied. **Both pairs of wings long, moderately broad, often brightly coloured and spotted in yellow, black, red.** Adult active during day. Many species poisonous to predators. Larva covered in dense layer of woolly hairs, feeds on poisonous plants and incorporates toxins into body as defence against predators. Throughout s Africa except dry areas.

**Similar**

**SNOUTED TIGERS  Family Hypsidae**

Projecting mouthparts give snouted appearance.
May also be mistaken for a butterfly.

**5  TUSSOCKS**  　　　　　　Family Lymantriidae

Antennae one third body length, comb-like in male, simple in female. Forewings broad, hindwings rounded. **Usually white, cream or yellow. Abdomen of female ends in thick, blunt tuft.** Adult does not feed, mouthparts poorly developed. Some species exude yellow poisonous fluid from thorax when handled. Larva has tuft of hair on back, hence common name. Common throughout s Africa except dry areas.

**6  OWL MOTHS**  　　　　　　Family Noctuidae

Antennae roughly one third body length, **simple, thread-like. Wing colour generally drab grey or brown, forewing darker than hindwing, occasionally with owl-like eye spots as illustrated.** Adult active at night and most species look very similar. Difficult to separate in the field. Larvae are among the worst crop pests of all Lepidoptera. Cut worms, army worms and stalk borers are all members of this family. Very common throughout s Africa and the world.

50 mm

40 mm

75 mm

20-55 mm

30-45 mm

25-60 mm

# FRESHWATER FISHES

Fishes are ectothermic vertebrates, living in water, breathing by means of gills and having fins for stability and movement. Most of those described in this chapter are confined to inland waters; however, the eels *(Anguilla)* breed in the ocean and the young migrate into rivers to mature.

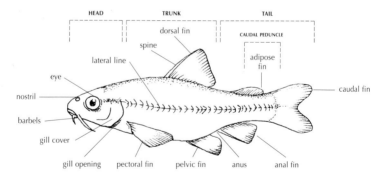

The body of a fish consists of a head, trunk and tail. The head, which bears the eyes, nostrils, mouth and gills, is measured from the snout to the end of the gill covers. The trunk comprises the body from behind the head to the anus or the start of the anal fin. The tail region is taken from the anal fin to the end of the caudal fin. The caudal peduncle is the flexible region from the hind end of the anal fin to the base of the caudal fin.

Mucus is secreted from the skin to provide a friction-reducing layer, for protection against diseases and parasites, for initial healing of wounds and, in many cases, as toxic secretions for defence against predators.

Scales consist of a bony plate covered by a thin layer of skin. They protect the body and sometimes have an ornamental function. Bony scales increase in size by adding concentric outer layers. The pattern of these growth rings indicates the age of a fish. There are different kinds of scales: cycloid scales are simple and round or ovoid in shape; ctenoid scales have fine teeth on the free edge.

Fins are either paired (pectoral and pelvic fins) or lie in the midline (dorsal, caudal and anal fin). Fins are supported by spines and soft rays. Spines may have barbs along the edges. The spines of many catfishes can be held erect by means of a locking mechanism, and form an effective defence. Soft rays are divided into two halves and are segmented; they may be simple or branched.

Many fishes have a second dorsal fin, the adipose fin, which may be small and lobate like that of a trout, or large and firm like that of the vundu. Fins perform a variety of functions: producing and controlling movement, defence, display and communication. Their shape, size and position are important identifying characters.

In many fishes the upper and lower jaws can both be moved and the mouth actively protruded during feeding. The lips indicate the feeding style of the species. Fishes that scrape their food from firm surfaces have firm sharp lips, grubbers have large soft lips, predators have thin lips that may cushion the teeth but allow them to be exposed when feeding. Some fishes, e.g. the yellowfishes which have a wide range of feeding habits, are able to develop different forms of lip, depending on the circumstances.

The lateral line is a system of sensory organs that detect water currents and moving bodies close to the fish. It is prominent in actively swimming and schooling fishes and may be absent from more sedentary species.

## Scope of this chapter

About 245 species of fishes have been recorded in the inland waters of southern Africa, excluding several marine species that have been found sporadically in the lower reaches of rivers. This chapter deals with about 150 species, representing the main groups likely to be encountered.

## Distribution

The inland waters of southern Africa can be subdivided into aquatic ecoregions (see map on p. 4), each with a typical fish fauna. The river systems mentioned in the species descriptions in this chapter are also shown on the map:

- **Tropical east coast region**. A diverse range of fishes occur here, including large species such as the cornish jack and lungfish, barbs and labeos, the tigerfish and imberi, annual killifishes, several important cichlid species such as the Mozambique tilapia, and climbing perch species. Eels are also present.
- **Tropical interior region**. The fishes of this region are the most diverse in southern Africa but there are several notable species absent or excluded by waterfalls such as the Victoria Falls. Characteristic fishes include groups of catfishes such as squeakers and air-breathing catfishes. There are also a number of large cichlids including largemouth breams, tilapias, riverine dwarf breams, robbers and the tigerfish. The African pike is a noteworthy species of the area. The bulldog and similar species are most common here. Notable species that do not occur are the lungfish, eels, the cornish jack, the electric catfish and the vundu.
- **Highveld (temperate) region**. The fish fauna of this region is relatively poor, with a few yellowfish species and one or two minnow and labeo species predominating. The more tropical fishes are either absent or represented by one or two species only. Carp is the most prominent alien species in the region.
- **Montane escarpment region**. Smaller flowing-water species such as mountain catfishes, suckermouth catfishes, eels, a few barbs and knerias are characteristic of these waters.
- **Cape fold mountain region**. Redfin minnows, the Cape galaxias, Cape kurper and in certain rivers larger cyprinids such as the sawfin and whitefish are characteristic.
- **Kalahari-Karoo-Namib region**. A few hardy species tolerant of fluctuating environments are found here, e.g. the sharptooth catfish, smallmouth yellowfish, moggel and chubbyhead barb. Carp also occur in most rivers.

## Reproduction and development

Males of some species, especially the cichlids (breams, tilapias and others), acquire bright colours during the breeding season and use these together with ritual movements to attract females. Eggs are laid by the female and the male deposits sperm over them. Several species clear nesting depressions in the bottom sediments, and guard the territory and eggs from intruders. Females of the mouthbrooding species scoop their eggs into the mouth for safekeeping, once they are fertilised.

Annual killifishes have adapted to live in temporary pans. During the wet season, eggs hatch and mature into adulthood in a matter of weeks. The adults lay new eggs and die when the pan dries up. The eggs remain dormant until the pan refills the following year.

Eels breed at sea and the leaf-like larvae metamorphose into transparent "glass eels" and move into estuaries. After some time they change again into elvers and migrate further upstream. Here they remain and mature for 10 or 20 years before returning to the sea to breed.

## Dimensions

The dimensions given with the illustrations of fishes refer to the total length from the front of the head to the end of the tail.

30-60 cm

50-120 cm

15-30 cm

Up to 1,2 m

15-30 cm

**1  LUNGFISH**                    *Protopterus annectens*
Greyish-brown with dark brown spots and blotches. **Body elongated, tapered to a point, pectoral and pelvic fins slender, tapered.** Airbreathing lung enables it to live in poorly oxygenated pans, swamps. During drought burrow is formed in soft sediments and mucous cocoon secreted in which it lies dormant, breathing through a small opening. Middle Zambezi valley, Mozambique coastal plains southwards to Incomati River.

**2  CORNISH JACK**              *Mormyrops anguilloides*
Grey above, silvery white below, often with bronze or yellow sheen. Head and body elongated, **dorsal and anal fins set well back**, dorsal shorter than anal. Prefers deep, quiet water. Middle and lower Zambezi, Buzi and Pungwe rivers.

**3  BULLDOG**              *Marcusenius macrolepidotus*
Light golden brown to dark olive and grey with bronze flecks and dark brown blotches. Dorsal and anal fins set well back, **prominent lobe on lower jaw.** Shoals in margins of rivers, floodplains. Cunene, Okavango and Zambezi systems, also E coast to Umhlatuzi River.
**Similar**
SLENDER STONEBASHER *Hippopotamyrus ansorgii*
Smaller. Dark brown or black, vertical bar from dorsal origin. Cunene, upper Zambezi, Okavango, Buzi, Pungwe.
ZAMBEZI PARROTFISH *H. discorhynchus*
Greyish-brown to nearly black. Cunene, Okavango, Zambezi, Buzi, Pungwe.

**4  LONGFIN EEL**                  *Anguilla mossambica*
**Long, smooth-skinned, snake-like form.** Dorsal fin begins ahead of anal fin. Olive-brown or grey, lighter below; on maturity, prior to entering sea, colour changes to dark bronze above and light yellow below. E coast rivers to Cape Agulhas.
**Similar**
SHORTFIN EEL *A. bicolor bicolor*
Dark olive-brown above, pale below; mature adult changes to bronzy silver. Beginning of dorsal/anal fins opposite.
AFRICAN MOTTLED EEL *A. bengalensis labiata*
Yellowish-brown, mottled with dark brown or black. Uncommon S of Save River.
GIANT MOTTLED EEL *A. marmorata*
Mottled yellow and dark brown or black. More common S of Limpopo River.

**5  LONGTAIL SPINY EEL**    *Aethiomastacembelus frenatus*
Brown; pattern of fine markings may form "eye-spots" on tail. **Short spines along back.** Vegetation along margins of flowing rivers; also rocky crevices. Upper Zambezi, Okavango.
**Similar**
OCELLATED SPINY EEL *A. vanderwaali*
Mottled dark brown and yellow. Larger head.

## 1   BREEDE RIVER REDFIN   *Pseudobarbus burchelli*

Juvenile and young adult olive-brown with scattered spots and blotches, an irregular stripe expanding into triangle at base of tail. Breeding adult deepens to dark olive-brown, lighter underneath, with **scarlet patches at base of fins**. Pools and deeper-flowing stretches of Breede River and adjacent systems.
**Similar**
Six more species, five from Cape fold mountains and one from Drakensberg, 7-13 cm, recognisable by their scarlet fin bases. All are threatened: two endangered, two critically endangered.

6-13,5 cm

## 2   CHUBBYHEAD BARB   *Barbus anoplus*

**Breeding male golden in summer**; female and non-breeding male greyish-green above with small dot at base of caudal fin. Prefers cooler waters in various habitats from small streams to large lakes; often in cover of fallen logs or marginal vegetation. Highveld Limpopo through E to SW (east of fold mountains), middle and upper Orange basin and Karoo.
**Similar**
**REDTAIL BARB  *B. gurneyi***
E, from Umtamvuna to Amatikulu.
**MARICO BARB  *B. motebensis***
S highveld tributaries of Limpopo.
**AMATOLA BARB  *B. amatolicus***
Kei and Mbashe systems.

9-12 cm

## 3   BROADSTRIPED BARB   *Barbus annectens*

Translucent olive-brown with either **three spots or broad dark band along body**, dark spot at base of anal fin. Favours slow-flowing streams with vegetation. E coast rivers from Zambezi system to Mkuze, lowveld S of Limpopo.
**Similar**
**BAROTSE BARB  *B. barotseensis***
Cunene and Okavango systems.

5-7,5 cm

## 4   LINE-SPOTTED BARB   *Barbus lineomaculatus*

Translucent brown with variable dark spots along body, **lateral line scales with prominent chevron bars**. Small streams to large rivers. Spawns upstream in flooded grassy areas. Cunene, Okavango, Zambezi, Limpopo systems.

## 5   GOLDIE BARB   *Barbus pallidus*

Translucent light brown above, silvery on sides and below; **breeding male turns bright golden**. Favours pools in clear, rocky streams with emergent vegetation. Coastal streams of SE from Great Fish to Krom; tributaries of Vaal, Limpopo, Tugela, Pongolo.
**Similar**
**SHORTFIN BARB  *B. brevipinnis***
Dashes or stripe along midbody. Sabie-Incomati and Steelpoort-Limpopo systems.
**SIDESPOT BARB  *B. neefi***
Large dark spots along body. Tributaries of Steelpoort-Limpopo.

5-7,5 cm

5-7,5 cm

**1**

8-14 cm

**2**

5-7 cm

**3**

3 cm

**4**

4-6 cm

**5**

10-15 cm

**6**

6-8 cm

**1  LONGBEARD BARB**          *Barbus unitaeniatus*

Translucent brown with silvery white below, **dark lateral stripe and chevron markings on lateral line.** Two pairs of long barbels. Flowing and standing waters, thrives in dams and lakes. Cunene, Okavango and Zambezi southwards to Pongolo.
**Similar**
**BEIRA BARB  *B. radiatus***
Stripe passes through eye, barbels short.

**2  HYPHEN BARB**          *Barbus bifrenatus*

Translucent brown, silvery white on sides and below. **Black stripe from tip of snout through eye to end of caudal peduncle, lateral line marked by black.** Floodplains, pools, shallow streams with vegetation. Cunene, upper Zambezi, Okavango, Limpopo systems and St Lucia.
**Similar**
**BOWSTRIPE BARB  *B. viviparus***
Black stripe from behind head ends in spot at base of tail. E coastal rivers and lakes southwards to Vungu River.
**BLACKBACK BARB  *B. barnardi***
Irregular black spots along midline of back. Cunene, upper Zambezi, Kafue, Okavango systems.
**EAST COAST BARB  *B. toppini***
Smaller (3-4 cm). E coast southwards to Mkuze system.
**BROADBAND BARB  *B. macrotaenia***
Smaller (3-4 cm). Lower Zambezi, Pungwe River.

**3  SICKLE-FIN BARB**          *Barbus haasianus*

Translucent brown to rosy red (breeding male). **Sickle-shape anal fin in mature male.** Swamps and floodplains of Okavango, upper and lower Zambezi, Pungwe.

**4  RED BARB**          *Barbus fasciolatus*

**Light rose to red,** silvery below; 10-15 black vertical bars on body. Favours well-oxygenated floodplain river channels and lagoons. Cunene, Okavango, upper and middle Zambezi.

**5  THREESPOT BARB**          *Barbus trimaculatus*

Silvery, tinged with gold when in breeding condition; usually three clear black spots on body and base of tail. **Spine in dorsal fin.** Hardy, common. E coast southwards to Umvoti, also Orange, Cunene systems.
**Similar**
**DASHTAIL BARB  *B. poechii***
Oblong black dash at base of tail. Cunene, Okavango.

**6  CLANWILLIAM REDFIN**          *Barbus calidus*

Brown above, silvery white below, with broad dark band along body, irregular dark blotches along back. **Serrated spine in dorsal fin.** Large, deep pools in clear streams. Tributaries of Clanwilliam Olifants in SW. Endangered.
**Similar**
**TWEE RIVER REDFIN  *B. erubescens***
Breeding male turns red. Twee River in SW. Critically endangered.

**1 STRAIGHTFIN BARB** *Barbus paludinosus*

Plain olive-grey or silvery in turbid waters. **Dorsal fin with serrated spine**, hind margin vertical; two pairs short barbels. Prefers quiet, well-vegetated waters. E coast rivers southwards to Vungu. Also Cunene, Okavango, Orange.

**Similar**

**NAMAQUA BARB** *B. hospes*

Pale silvery or white. Orange River below Augrabies Falls.

**BORDER BARB** *B. trevelyani*

Translucent grey-brown. Keiskamma and Buffalo systems in SE. Critically endangered.

**YELLOW BARB** *B. manicensis*

Plain silvery. Pungwe, Buzi and lower Zambezi in Mozambique.

**2 SPOTTAIL BARB** *Barbus afrovernayi*

Translucent grey-brown with iridescent lilac-yellow stripe along body, silvery below; **large black spot on caudal peduncle**. Quiet, well-vegetated water. Cunene, upper Zambezi, Okavango.

**3 ORANGEFIN BARB** *Barbus eutaenia*

Olive above, silvery white below, fins yellow or orange; **broad black band runs from snout through mid-caudal fin**. Prefers clear-flowing waters with rocky habitats. Cunene, Okavango, E coast systems southwards to Incomati.

**Similar**

**ZIGZAG BARB** *B. miolepis*

Deeper body, more robust head, smaller eye. Okavango.

**COPPERSTRIPE BARB** *B. multilineatus*

Breeding male has copper stripe along body through tail. Cunene, Okavango, upper and middle Zambezi.

**REDSPOT BARB** *B. kerstenii*

Yellow, orange or red spot on gill covers. Cunene, Okavango, upper and lower Zambezi, Save and Runde systems.

**4 PAPERMOUTH** *Barbus mattozi*

**Silvery with orange fins.** Large pools in perennial rivers, also thrives in dams. Larger individuals are valued angling targets. Limpopo system, headwaters of Gwai (Zimbabwe), Cunene.

**Similar**

**ROSEFIN BARB** *B. argenteus*

Fins orange-red. Incomati and Pongolo.

**PLUMP BARB** *B. afrohamiltoni*

Silvery. Lowveld reaches of E coast rivers southwards to Pongolo.

**5 WHITEFISH** *Barbus andrewi*

Deep olive above, sides golden, cream below. **Long, pointed snout**, two pairs barbels. Favours deep, rocky pools of larger tributaries and mainstreams; does well in dams. Occasionally caught by anglers. Status declining since introduction of bass. Berg, Breede rivers in SW.

**Similar**

**SAWFIN** *B. serra*

Olifants system in SW. Endangered.

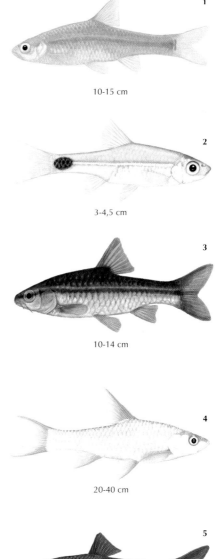

1

10-15 cm

2

3-4,5 cm

3

10-14 cm

4

20-40 cm

5

40-60 cm

**1**

20-32 cm

**2**

30-50 cm

**3**

30-40 cm

**4**

15-30 cm

**1 INCOMATI CHISELMOUTH** *Varicorhinus nelspruitensis*
Dark olive above, light olive-yellow to creamy white below. **Straight, hard-edged lower jaw**, one pair short barbels. Cool, rocky, flowing water in schools of 50-100. Escarpment streams of Incomati and Pongolo systems.
**Similar**
**SHORTSNOUT CHISELMOUTH** *V. nasutus*
Middle and lower Zambezi, Pungwe River.
**PUNGWE CHISELMOUTH** *V. pungweensis*
Pungwe and Buzi rivers in Mozambique.

**2 MOGGEL** *Labeo umbratus*
**Mouth underhanging, soft, fleshy.** Greyish with iridescent pink and cream mottling, off-white below, scales small. Standing or gently flowing water; thrives in dams. Orange-Vaal system, river systems in S and SE.
**Similar**
**ORANGE RIVER MUDFISH** *L. capensis*
Grey. Orange-Vaal system.
**TUGELA LABEO** *L. rubromaculatus*
Tugela system.
**CLANWILLIAM SANDFISH** *L. seeberi*
Very small scales. Clanwilliam-Olifants system in SW. Critically endangered.

**3 MANYAME LABEO** *Labeo altivelis*
Body deep, dorsal fin large. Iridescent pinkish scales on bright green base; bright green band behind gill cover, fins deep bluish-grey. **Bright red tubercles on snout.** Large rivers, lakes, dams. Middle, lower Zambezi southwards to Save River.
**Similar**
**REDNOSE LABEO** *L. rosae*
Snout with red tubercles. Lowveld reaches of Limpopo, Incomati, Pongolo.
**SILVER LABEO** *L. ruddi*
Plain silvery. Cunene, also lowveld reaches of Limpopo, Incomati.

**4 REDEYE LABEO** *Labeo cylindricus*
Body cylindrical or tubular, snout with prominent tubercles. Olive to yellow-green with darker band along body, **eye red above**. Rocky habitats, usually in running water. Okavango and Zambezi southwards to Pongolo.
**Similar**
**PURPLE LABEO** *L. congoro*
Greenish-grey with purple sheen. Dorsal fin high. Lowveld reaches of middle and lower Zambezi, E coast rivers southwards to Pongolo.
**LEADEN LABEO** *L. molybdinus*
Middle and lower Zambezi southwards to Tugela.
**UPPER ZAMBEZI LABEO** *L. lunatus*
Dorsal fin high, crescent-shaped. Okavango.
**CUNENE LABEO** *L. ansorgii*
Cunene River.

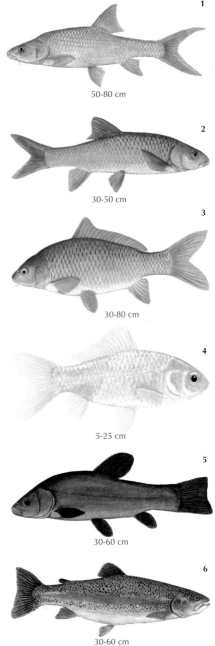

**1  LARGEMOUTH YELLOWFISH**    *Barbus kimberleyensis*
**Silvery olive-grey**, anal fin light orange in adult. Largest indigenous scale-bearing species. Renowned angling fish. Prefers flowing water in deep channels or below rapids, does well in dams. Mainstream and larger tributaries of Orange-Vaal system. Vulnerable.

50-80 cm

**2  SMALLMOUTH YELLOWFISH**    *Barbus aeneus*
**Olive-bronze above, cream below.** Lips variable, from thin to fleshy. Clear-flowing waters of large rivers, dams. Important angling species. Orange-Vaal system, translocated to Limpopo and larger rivers in S.
**Similar**
**SCALY  *B. natalensis***
30-60 cm. Widespread from Mkuze southwards to Umtamvuna.
**SMALLSCALE YELLOWFISH  *B. polylepis***
30-46 cm. Limpopo, Incomati, Pongolo systems.
**CLANWILLIAM YELLOWFISH  *B. capensis***
30-90 cm. Clanwilliam-Olifants system in SW. Vulnerable.
**LARGESCALE YELLOWFISH  *B. marequensis***
30-47 cm. Middle, lower Zambezi southwards to Pongolo system.
**UPPER ZAMBEZI YELLOWFISH  *B. codringtonii***
20-39 cm. Upper Zambezi, Okavango.

30-50 cm

**3  CARP**    *Cyprinus carpio*
Olive-brown to rich gold, fins grey. **Serrated spine in dorsal and anal fins.** May be partly naked with scattered scales, or without scales. Favours large water bodies with slow-flowing or standing water. Introduced, now widespread in all but mountain and tropical areas.
**Similar**
Grass carp and silver carp have been introduced to farm dams and hatcheries.

30-80 cm

**4  GOLDFISH**    *Carassius auratus*
Body shape, fin form and colour variable; wild colour metallic olive-bronze. **No barbels.** Prefers quiet, weedy habitat. Feral populations around larger towns.

**5  TENCH**    *Tinca tinca*
Olive-green or coppery brown to almost black, **deep yellow underneath, fins black**. Minute scales. Prefers deep, vegetated water in vleis, swamps. Introduced. Breede River, isolated farm dams in SW, SE and E.

5-25 cm

**6  RAINBOW TROUT**    *Oncorhynchus mykiss*
Streamlined body with very small scales. Sharp teeth. Lower jaw of mature male enlarged and hooked. Silvery or light golden with small black spots, **lilac-mauve band from head to tail**. Renowned angling species Introduced. Dams and streams; cold water necessary for breeding (Jun-Sept).
**Similar**
**BROWN TROUT  *Salmo trutta***
Large brown and red spots on upper half. Introduced.

30-60 cm

30-60 cm

**1**

40-50 cm

**2**

4,5 cm

**3**

50-70 cm

**4**

15-18 cm

**5**

40-47 cm

**1   CHESSA** *Distichodus shenga*

Silvery olive with sooty dorsal, caudal and anal fins, pectorals and pelvics yellowish. **Fin bases covered by scales with fine teeth on free edge.** Body rises steeply from behind pointed head. Large rivers, shoals over rock and sand. Middle and lower Zambezi, Buzi and Pungwe.
**Similar**
**NKUPE** *D. mossambicus*
Deep olive, almost black.

**2   MULTIBAR CITHARINE** *Hemigrammocharax multifasciatus*

Slender body. Translucent light olive, with **16-25 dark vertical bars** and a prominent spot at base of caudal fin. Vegetated margins of rivers and oxbow lagoons or shallow lakes. Cunene, Okavango, upper Zambezi, Kafue.
**Similar**
**DWARF CITHARINE** *H. machadoi*
Caudal fin with prominent dark "eye" spot and two or three vertical bands. No adipose fin.
**BROADBAR CITHARINE** *Nannocharax macropterus*
Light olive above, white below, with irregular broad dark lateral band.

**3   TIGERFISH** *Hydrocynus vittatus*

Silvery, with bluish sheen on back and series of parallel longitudinal black stripes. **Adipose fin black, other fins yellow-red.** Schools in warm, well-oxygenated water in larger rivers and lakes, tending to frequent surface layers. Okavango, Zambezi and lowveld reaches of E coast rivers southwards to Pongolo. Major angling gamefish.

**4   IMBERI** *Brycinus imberi*

Silvery with yellowish fins, adipose fin orange, top half of eye orange. **Black spot behind head, dash on caudal peduncle.** Shoals in wide variety of habitats including larger rivers, pans, lagoons. E coast rivers southwards to Pongolo.
**Similar**
**STRIPED ROBBER** *B. lateralis*
Prominent black caudal dash surrounded by yellow. Cunene, upper Zambezi, Okavango, Buzi rivers and St Lucia.
**SILVER ROBBER** *Micralestes acutidens*
Black tip to dorsal fin. Cunene, Okavango, Zambezi and E coast rivers southwards to Pongolo.
**SLENDER ROBBER** *Rhabdalestes maunensis*
Bluish-green iridescent band along body, black band along base of anal fin. Cunene, upper Zambezi, Okavango.
**BARNARD'S ROBBER** *Hemigrammopetersius barnardi*
Black band passes across anal fin. Lower Zambezi, Pungwe, Buzi systems.

**5   AFRICAN PIKE** *Hepsetus odoe*

Rich brassy olive with dark brown blotches and cream underparts, adipose fin orange with black spots, three brown bands radiate behind eye. Jaws pointed, with sharp irregular teeth. Quiet, deep water, as in channels and lagoons of large floodplains. Breeding pairs guard floating foam nest in shelter of marginal vegetation. Cunene, upper Zambezi, Kafue, Okavango.

**1   ROCK CATFISH**                    *Austroglanis sclateri*

Olive-brown with scattered spots, lips fleshy, **three pairs short barbels**. Rocky habitats in flowing water, favours rapids. Orange-Vaal system.
**Similar**
**ZAMBEZI GRUNTER** *Parauchenoglanis ngamensis*
Larger (30-38 cm), 5-7 vertical lines of black spots. Upper Zambezi and Okavango.
**BUZI GRUNTER** *Amarginops hildae*
Smaller (9-11 cm). Olive-grey. Lower Buzi.
**SPOTTED ROCK CATFISH** *Austroglanis barnardi*
Smaller (6-12 cm). Golden brown with dark brown blotches. Tributaries of Clanwilliam-Olifants system.
**CLANWILLIAM ROCK CATFISH** *Austroglanis gilli*
Smaller (6-12 cm). Greyish to yellowish-brown, usually without prominent markings. Tributaries of Clanwilliam-Olifants system.

**2   COMMON MOUNTAIN CATFISH** *Amphilius uranoscopus*

Yellowish/greyish-brown, mottled or with dark shadows or blotches. **No spines in fins**. Eyes on top of head. Clear flowing water in rocky habitats. Young easily mistaken for tadpoles. Okavango, Zambezi systems, E coast rivers southwards to Mkuze.
**Similar**
**NATAL MOUNTAIN CATFISH** *A. natalensis*
Escarpment streams from Eastern Highlands of Zimbabwe to Drakensberg (Umkomaas system).
**SPOTTED SAND CATLET** *Leptoglanis rotundiceps*
Across N of region from Cunene to Save.

**3   SILVER CATFISH**                    *Schilbe intermedius*

Light olive or silvery grey with yellow edges; dark chocolate mottling in clear waters. Head flattened, four pairs barbels. **Anal fin long-based.** Shoals in standing or slowly flowing open water with emergent or submerged vegetation. Cunene, Okavango, Zambezi systems southwards to Pongolo.

**4   SHARPTOOTH CATFISH**                    *Clarias gariepinus*

Varies from almost black to light brown, often marbled in shades of olive-green or grey; underparts white. **Head large, heavy boned and flattened**, jaws with bands of fine, pointed teeth, four pairs long barbels. Most widely distributed fish in Africa, naturally found as far S as Orange River system and Umtamvuna (E coast), translocated to certain rivers in S. Favours floodplains, large sluggish rivers, lakes, dams. Can move overland, crawling on extended pectoral spines.
**Similar**
Six species difficult to identify accurately, widely distributed N of Orange River.

**5   VUNDU**                    *Heterobranchus longifilis*

**Adipose fin large.** Olive-grey or reddish-brown, head and abdomen white below. Barbels reach beyond head. Within mainstream in large deep rivers, or deep pools/lakes. Largest freshwater fish in region, up to 55 kg. Important angling species. Middle and lower Zambezi.

**1**

20-30 cm

**2**

10-17 cm

**3**

20-30 cm

**4**

Up to 1,4 m

**5**

Up to 1,2 m

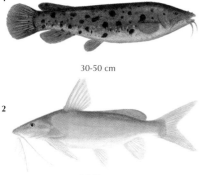

30-50 cm

20-43 cm

4-6,5 cm

3-4 cm

3-5 cm

3-5 cm

2-3,5 cm

## 1 ELECTRIC CATFISH *Malapterurus electricus*

Grey above, off-white below, irregular black blotches. **Head and body rounded, fleshy.** Sluggish water among rocks or roots. Active at night, feeding mainly on fish stunned by electric shocks of 300-400 volts. Forms pairs, breeds in excavated cavities or holes. Middle and lower Zambezi, Pungwe, lower Save.

## 2 BROWN SQUEAKER *Synodontis zambezensis*

Plain olive-brown or grey. Bony skull, long, branched barbels. Common name comes from sound it makes on being removed from the water. **Large sharp dorsal and well-barbed pectoral fin spines** can be locked in place to form defence mechanism. Sandy stretches of flowing rivers. Middle, lower Zambezi southwards to Pongolo system.

**Similar**

The cloudy squeaker *(S. nebulosus)*, with large brown or yellowish blotches, occurs in same area. Seven further species, difficult to identify accurately, occur in Cunene/upper Zambezi/Okavango area.

## 3 SHORTSPINE SUCKERMOUTH *Chiloglanis pretoriae*

Dark brown with small lighter patches, series of vertical spots along body. Sharp spines in dorsal and pectoral fins. **Mouth forms sucker disc,** used to cling onto rocks or plants. Fast-flowing rocky streams or rapids and rocky stretches in larger rivers. Incomati, Limpopo, middle and lower Zambezi, Pungwe, Buzi.

**Similar**

Seven further species, difficult to identify accurately: five in Pongolo/Incomati/Limpopo, one in Okavango, one in Cunene, Zambezi, Pungwe and Buzi.

## 4 CAPE GALAXIAS *Galaxias zebratus*

Translucent pale brown with or without darker blotches or bars, **internal organs visible** in living specimens. Hardy, favours gentle currents within shelter of banks. Coastal streams and rivers from S coast to Clanwilliam-Olifants system.

## 5 SLENDER TOPMINNOW *Aplocheilichthys johnstoni*

Translucent yellowish-green with silvery blue iridescence, **iris of eye silvery blue.** Inshore well-vegetated habitats, often in very shallow water, small shoals near surface. Cunene, Okavango, Zambezi, Limpopo.

**Similar**

**NATAL TOPMINNOW *A. myaposae***

Maputaland, Kosi to Umlazi.

## 6 STRIPED TOPMINNOW *Aplocheilichthys katangae*

**Zigzag black band along body**, white below, scattered midbody scales iridescent blue-turquoise. Dense marginal vegetation of streams and rivers. Cunene, Okavango, Zambezi, Maputaland.

## 7 MESHSCALED TOPMINNOW *Aplocheilichthys hutereaui*

Translucent yellowish, iris of eye turquoise. **Sooty pigment on scale edges gives mesh effect.** Restricted to swamps and floodplains. Upper Zambezi, Okavango, Buzi, Pungwe.

**1 SPOTTED KILLIFISH** _Nothobranchius orthonotus_

Female plain fleshy brown, male brightly patterned red or blue; **red spots on head.** Temporary rainpools or riverine floodplains. Life cycle is completed within a year. Eggs can endure drying out, and hatch the following rainy season. E coastal plain southwards to Mkuze River.

**Similar**

**BEIRA KILLIFISH** _N. kuhntae_
Floodplains of the Pungwe near Beira.

**TURQUOISE KILLIFISH** _N. furzeri_
Pans in Gona-re-Zhou Game Reserve, Zimbabwe.

**RAINBOW KILLIFISH** _N. rachovii_
Marshes on coastal plain near Beira, pans in Kruger NP.

5-10 cm

**2 LARGEMOUTH BASS** _Micropterus salmoides_

Olive-green above, light green on flanks, series of dark olive-green bars forming band along body, two or three stripes radiate behind eye. **End of jaw extends behind eye.** Clear standing or slow-flowing water, thrives in farm dams. Popular gamefish. Widely introduced throughout region.

**Similar**

**SMALLMOUTH BASS** _M. dolomieu_
Narrow vertical bars on body. Jaw ends below eye.

**SPOTTED BASS** _M. punctulatus_
Diamond-shaped bars along midbody, spotted below midline.

40-60 cm

**3 BLUEGILL** _Lepomis macrochirus_

Iridescent green-blue with vague vertical bands along body. Chest orange in breeding male. **Blunt black projection on gill cover.** Quiet well-vegetated waters. Male constructs nest and guards eggs. Introduced to coastal drainages in S, midlands in E, less common further N.

**4 SOUTHERN MOUTHBROODER** _Pseudocrenilabrus philander_

Female light brown with black vertical bars and light yellowish fins. Male body a mesh of iridescent light blue and yellow with oblique bar through eye and iridescent blue lower jaw. Anal fin with orange tip. **Caudal fin rounded.** Wide variety of habitats from flowing water to lakes, isolated sinkholes. Breeds early spring to late summer. Male defends territory and constructs nest. Eggs are mouthbrooded by female. Orange River and E coast northwards throughout region.

**Similar**

**CUNENE DWARF BREAM** _Schwetzochromis machadoi_
Dark bars from eye to mouth and from eye across top of gill cover. Cunene system.

**EASTERN BREAM** _Astatotilapia calliptera_
Olive-green with 8-9 olive vertical bars, dark bar from eye to corner of mouth, red "egg-spots" on anal fin. Lower Zambezi to lower Save system.

10-20 cm

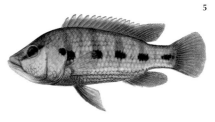

7-13 cm

**5 BANDED JEWELFISH** _Hemichromis elongatus_

Body green above, red below, 4-5 black vertical bars. **Two enlarged conical teeth in front of upper jaw.** Near shores in rivers, permanent floodplain lagoons with clear water. Upper Zambezi and Okavango.

15-20 cm

**1**

15-20 cm

**2**

30-48 cm

**3**

30-45 cm

**4**

20-31 cm

**1   CANARY KURPER**　　　　　*Chetia flaviventris*

Olive-brown above, scales with orange-red base, **mature male with bright yellow chest**, membranes of dorsal and caudal fins with rows of dark brown spots, anal fin with orange "egg-spots". Standing or slow-flowing pools. Female mouthbroods young. Tributaries of Limpopo.

**Similar**

**ORANGE-FRINGED LARGEMOUTH  C. brevis**

Dorsal fin with orange spots and tips, anal fin of male with two rows of large orange spots. Komati-Incomati system.

**ZAMBEZI BREAM  Pharyngochromis acuticeps**

Okavango, upper and middle Zambezi, upper Save.

**2   PINK BREAM**　　　　　　*Sargochromis giardi*

**Robust body and head.** Greyish-green head and back, flanks and underparts creamy yellow, fins dark grey with red margins and dark red spots, anal fin with rows of bright yellow orange-centred "egg-spots" along membranes. Deep river channels, floodplain lagoons. Female mouthbroods young. Cunene, upper Zambezi, Okavango.

**Similar**

**RAINBOW BREAM  S. carlottae**

Concave head profile. Upper Zambezi, Okavango.

**GREEN BREAM  S. codringtoni**

Green colour distinctive. Upper Zambezi, Okavango.

**DEEPCHEEK BREAM  S. greenwoodi**

Deep cheek distinctive. Upper Zambezi, Okavango.

**3   NEMBWE**　　　　　　*Serranochromis robustus*

**Large mouth with conical teeth.** Olive to bright green, with deep olive band along midbody, anal fin of male with small orange "egg-spots", orange margin to dorsal and caudal fins. Channels and lagoons. Breeds in summer, nesting along vegetated edges of mainstreams, female mouthbroods young. Upper Zambezi and Okavango; translocated to Swaziland and southwards.

**Similar**

**PURPLEFACE LARGEMOUTH  S. macrocephalus**

Anal fin of male with large orange "egg-spots". Cunene, Okavango.

**BROWNSPOT LARGEMOUTH  S. thumbergi**

Blue margin to dorsal and caudal fins. Cunene, upper Zambezi, Okavango.

**4   LOWVELD LARGEMOUTH  Serranochromis meridianus**

Olive-brown to yellow, **fins yellowish with dark red spots**. Male dorsal fin edged with yellow, anal fin with numerous "egg-spots". Prefers standing or slow-flowing pools with marginal vegetation. Male clears a nest, female mouthbroods young. Sabie-Sand tributary of Incomati, coastal lakes of Maputaland and southern Mozambique.

**Similar**

**HUMPBACK LARGEMOUTH  S. altus**

Olive-brown. Upper Zambezi, Okavango.

**THINFACE LARGEMOUTH  S. angusticeps**

Head with red spots. Cunene, upper Zambezi, Okavango.

**1　BANDED TILAPIA**　　　　　　　*Tilapia sparrmanii*
Deep olive-green with 8-9 vertical bars on body and two bars between the eyes. **"Tilapia spot" on soft dorsal fin.** Prefers quiet or standing waters. Male constructs a nest in which eggs are guarded by both parents. Orange River northwards and E; widely translocated S of Orange.
**Similar**
**OKAVANGO TILAPIA　*T. ruweti***
Dorsal, caudal and anal fins spotted, margin of dorsal a thin blue, white and red band. Upper Zambezi, Okavango.
**REDBREAST TILAPIA　*T. rendalli***
Bright red throat and chest. Cunene, Okavango, Zambezi southwards to Pongolo. Widely introduced in KwaZulu-Natal.

10-23 cm

**2　MOZAMBIQUE TILAPIA**　　*Oreochromis mossambicus*
Silvery olive to deep blue-grey, dorsal and caudal fins with red margins. **Breeding male turns grey-black with white lower head and throat.** Occurs in all but fast-flowing waters. Male constructs saucer-shaped nest, female mouthbroods. E coast rivers from lower Zambezi system to Bushmans system in SE. Widely dispersed inland, S and SW.
**Similar**
**BLACK TILAPIA　*O. placidus***
Frequently occurs with Mozambique tilapia in N. Deeper bodied, breeding male sooty grey with black throat and fins, black head markings.

20-40 cm

**3　CAPE KURPER**　　　　　　　*Sandelia capensis*
Yellow or golden brown with black spots and wavy bands, head with **black stripes radiating from eyes.** Hardy, prefers slow-flowing water with plant or root cover. Male defends breeding territory and guards the scattered eggs. S coastal rivers from Algoa Bay to Verlorenvlei.
**Similar**
**EASTERN CAPE ROCKY　*S. bainsii***
Olive or grey-brown. Nahoon, Buffalo, Keiskamma, Great Fish and Kowie systems in SE.

10-20 cm

**4　MANYSPINED CLIMBING PERCH　*Ctenopoma multispine***
**Spines on edge of gill cover.** Brown with irregular dark bars and spots. Vegetated backwaters, floodplain lagoons, swamps. Can endure warm, stagnant water; air-breathing organ enables it to leave the water and move overland during wet weather or at night. Okavango, lower Zambezi, ne coastal plain southwards to Maputaland.

10-13,5 cm

**5　KAPENTA**　　　　　　　　　*Limnothrissa miodon*
Transparent with silvery band from head to tail. Large shoals rise in water column and disperse at night, congregating and descending during day. Introduced to Lake Kariba, where it is an important commercial catch; also present in Lake Cahora Bassa.

3-5 cm

**6　SOUTHERN KNERIA**　　　　　*Kneria auriculata*
Translucent brown with flecks and blotches on upper body, scales minute. Shoals in pools of small, clear rocky streams. Upland streams of lower Zambezi, Pungwe, Buzi, Save; also in Crocodile River (Incomati system).

4-7 cm

# FROGS

The class Amphibia has three orders, only one of which, the Anura (frogs), occurs
in southern Africa. The other two orders are the Caudata (salamanders and newts of the northern
hemisphere) and the Apoda (legless caecilians confined to tropical forests). Amphibians are distinguished
by having two stages to their life: the larval or tadpole stage, which in most species is aquatic
and vegetarian, and the terrestrial, four-legged, carnivorous adult.

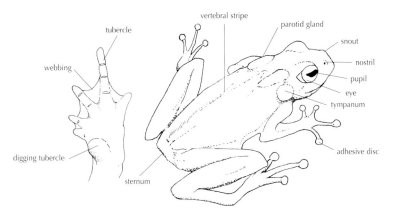

The terms frog and toad are confusing. The Anura include more than a dozen families each with its own distinctive characteristics. One of these families, the Bufonidae, which is characterised by laying its eggs in strings, was identified as toads by early naturalists. It is more correct to refer to all the Anura as frogs, regarding toads as simply one family of frogs.

The skin of frogs is permeable to water, and if unprotected in dry conditions, the animal soon desiccates. Most species therefore hide in dark, humid retreats during the day. The skin is glandular and secretes fluids. The secretions of the parotid glands on the necks of some species are toxic or distasteful to predators. Other secretions keep the skin moist to allow the absorption of oxygen.

Frog mouths are generally wide to allow large prey items to be swallowed whole. In all species except the platanna, which feeds underwater, the tongue is hinged at the front of the mouth and flipped forward and out to pick up food items. Most species have no teeth. The two bullfrog species have two tooth-like projections in the lower jaw which are used to fasten onto prey and to bite attackers. The giant bullfrog feeds on other frogs, small mammals, reptiles and large insects.

In most species the eyes are large and well developed for nocturnal activity. The tympanum or eardrum is usually large because calling, and therefore hearing, is of considerable importance to their biology.

Toes and feet are adapted to suit the habitat in which the species occurs and are often useful means of identification. Species that frequently enter water have webbed feet. Digging species have hardened tubercles on the heels. Climbing species have adhesive pads on the toe tips, and the desert rain frog has thickly webbed feet to aid movement on loose desert sand.

## Scope of this chapter

About 130 species of frogs have been recorded in southern Africa, of which 95 are covered in this chapter. Those that have been omitted are confined to the extremities of the region or are rarely seen.

## Distribution

Frog species in southern Africa can be divided into three broad geographic groups:

- Tropical species (33% of all species) are found in the north and north-west of southern Africa. The ranges of most of these species extend northwards into equatorial Africa and few are found south of the Orange or Tugela rivers.
- Transitional species (47% of all species) are located mostly in the eastern high rainfall areas.
- Cape species (20% of all species) are endemic to the southern part of the area, especially the south-west.

Some species have extremely limited ranges, while others are widely dispersed in a variety of localities and climatic regions. However, most species are fairly restricted in the type of habitat they prefer, especially in their choice of breeding site, and this is a useful guide to their identification.

## Frog calls

The mating call of male frogs is essential to the survival of frogs because in each species it is unique and is the signal by which the females recognise partners of their own kind. It follows that the most reliable way to identify species of frogs is by learning their calls. Other sounds produced less frequently by frogs are used to alarm predators, to keep males spaced apart at the breeding site and to summon other males to the chorus. The female has her own particular release call to terminate mating.

Frogs produce their calls by passing air back and forth from the lungs to the mouth cavity over the vocal cords. The mouth is kept closed and the sound is intensified by resonance in the vocal sac, a highly elastic skin pouch under the throat. Male advertisement calls are often made in chorus and may continue incessantly from sunset until well past midnight.

## Reproduction and development

Once the females are attracted to the breeding site, mating takes place. Fertilisation is external and the male clasps the female, depositing sperm onto the eggs as they are laid. The eggs have no shells and most species breed in water to avoid desiccation. However, several species have developed specialised egg-laying strategies: foam-nest frogs climb into trees overhanging water and create a ball of froth around the eggs as they are laid. The foam insulates the eggs and protects them from predation. The tadpoles fall into the water below. Leaf-folding frogs protect their eggs underwater by enclosing them in a folded and glued leaf. Rainfrogs lay their eggs in moist cavities underground. The emergent tadpoles remain in the cavity, nourished by the egg-yolk, until they emerge as fully formed miniature frogs.

The tadpole or larval stage is also very vulnerable. With the exception of rainfrogs and a few other species that have also developed terrestrial breeding, tadpoles are aquatic. In temperate high rainfall areas many species have a larval stage that lasts for several months or even a year. In more erratic climates, metamorphosis of the tadpoles is rapid and they emerge and disperse as immature froglets before the breeding site dries up.

## Dimensions

The dimensions given with the illustrations of frogs refer to the total body length from the snout to the sternum. Limbs are excluded.

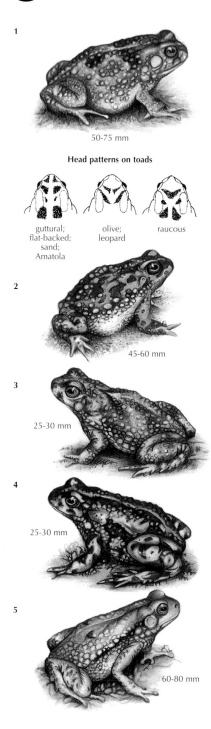

50-75 mm

**Head patterns on toads**

guttural;
flat-backed;
sand;
Amatola

olive;
leopard

raucous

45-60 mm

25-30 mm

25-30 mm

60-80 mm

**1   GUTTURAL TOAD**                     *Bufo gutturalis*

Skin has rough, lumpy elevations. Elongated swelling on each shoulder. Brown or grey. Pairs of dark, irregular dorsal patches: **one pair on snout, another over eyes. Red tincture on thighs.** Belly granular off-white. Male has dark throat. Call: vibrant snores usually in large choruses. Eggs laid in jelly strings in shallow water. Bushveld and grassland N of Orange River.
**Similar**
**SAND TOAD   *B. angusticeps***
No red on legs. W Cape.
**AMATOLA TOAD   *B. amatolica***
No red on legs. Amatola mountains, e Cape.
**FLAT-BACKED TOAD   *B. maculatus***
No red on legs. Lowveld.
**OLIVE TOAD   *B. garmani***
Red on legs. No snout patches. N of Vaal and Tugela rivers.
**LEOPARD TOAD   *B. pardalis***
No red on legs. No patches on snout. E and w Cape.
**RAUCOUS TOAD   *B. rangeri***
No red on legs. No patches on snout. Dark bar between eyes.

**2   KAROO TOAD**                       *Bufo gariepensis*

Skin covered with rounded lumps. Large swelling on each shoulder. Dull brown, often with irregular darker patches. Belly granular, sometimes spotted. **Thick ridge of skin on inside edge of foot.** Call: rasping squawks alternating between males. Jelly strings of eggs laid in streams or rain pools in Karoo scrub or grassland. Central and s interior.

**3   NORTHERN PYGMY TOAD**              *Bufo fenoulheti*

Skin rough, leathery. Mottled dark patches on back, **pale patch between shoulders.** Belly granular, sometimes spotted. Male has yellow throat. Call: short, quick nasal rasping. Eggs laid in exposed rain pools in rocky, barren areas. N and e South Africa and Zimbabwe.
**Similar**
**SOUTHERN PYGMY TOAD   *B. vertebralis***
Central interior grassland and Karoo.

**4   ROSE'S TOADLET**                   *Capensibufo rosei*

Skin smooth with blister-like elevations. Irregular patterns with pale vertebral stripe and bar between eyes. **Rufous on flanks.** Glandular lumps on shoulders **and lower legs.** Belly has dark marbling. Call unheard. Breeds in shallow depressions in mountain fynbos. SW of Tulbagh.
**Similar**
**TRADOUW TOADLET   *C. tradouwi***
Mountains E of Tulbagh. Squeaky call.

**5   RED TOAD**                         *Schismaderma carens*

Skin leathery. **Russet with one or two pairs of spots. Dark glandular line separates russet back** from grey-mottled flanks. Belly granular with grey flecks. Call: deep, protracted boom often in choruses. Breeds in permanent deep water in grassland. N of Vaal and Tugela rivers.

**1  BUSH SQUEAKER**          *Arthroleptis wahlbergi*

**Distinct hourglass pattern on back.** Belly granular with grey flecking. Call: long, thin, mournful squeak repeated continuously from concealed position in undergrowth. Eggs laid among decaying vegetation away from water. Tadpoles develop in jelly capsule. S and e coastal belt.
**Similar**
**SHOVEL-FOOTED SQUEAKER  A. stenodactylus**
Large digging tubercle on heel.

25-30 mm

**2  MOTTLED SHOVEL-NOSED FROG  Hemisus marmoratus**

Rotund body. Hard, sharp snout. Small eyes, **vertical pupils.** Mottled grey and brown. Belly smooth, pinkish-white. Male dark under jaw. Call: incessant buzzing from mud banks, easily mistaken for mole cricket. Eggs laid underground where tadpoles develop. E lowveld.
**Similar**
**SPOTTED SHOVEL-NOSED FROG   H. guttatus**
Yellow spots on brown background.

35-40 mm

**3  CAPE RAIN FROG**          *Breviceps gibbosus*

Rotund, inflatable body. Flattened snout. Small eyes, horizontal pupils. Granular grey-brown and cream skin. Mottled brown and cream. **Large digging tubercle on heel.** Call: burred squawk repeated at short intervals. Eggs laid underground where tadpoles develop. Sw Cape.
**Similar**
**STRAWBERRY RAIN FROG  B. acutirostris**
Pink skin with black granules. Sw Cape forests.
**PLAIN RAIN FROG  B. fuscus**
Charcoal to brown skin, black granules. S forests.
**PLAINTIVE RAIN FROG  B. verrucosus**
Indistinct broad vertebral band. E forests.

60 mm

**4  BUSHVELD RAIN FROG**          *Breviceps adspersus*

Body toad-like, inflated when threatened. Horizontal pupil. Dark brown with orange-brown patches. Belly smooth, whitish. Male has dark throat. **Large digging tubercle on heel.** Call: short burred whistle, usually in small, widely spaced choruses. Eggs laid underground. Bushveld and woodland NE of Vaal River.
**Similar**
**CAPE MOUNTAIN RAIN FROG  B. montanus**
Stony hillsides in sw Cape.
**SAND RAIN FROG  B. rosei**
Sandveld and dunes in sw Cape.

Digging tubercle on Cape rain frog

**DESERT RAIN FROG**          *Breviceps macrops*

Rotund inflatable body. Blunt snout. Large eyes, horizontal pupils. Smooth cream and tan skin. Belly smooth, translucent. **Spatulate hindfeet.** Call: protracted clear whistle. Nw Namaqualand coastal dunes.
**Similar**
**NAMAQUA RAIN FROG  B. namaquensis**
Rock outcrops in Namaqualand.

25-35 mm

40 mm

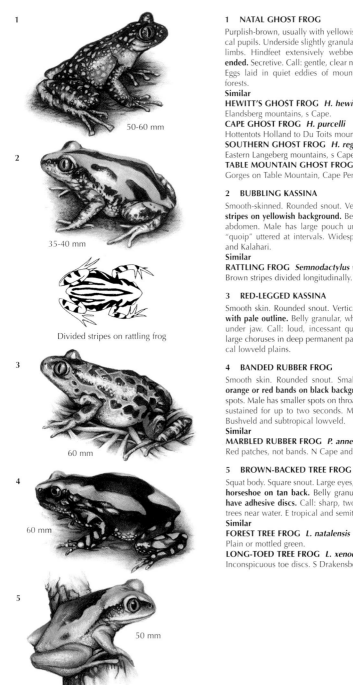

50-60 mm

35-40 mm

Divided stripes on rattling frog

60 mm

60 mm

50 mm

**1　NATAL GHOST FROG**　　　*Heleophryne natalensis*
Purplish-brown, usually with yellowish patches. Large eyes, vertical pupils. Underside slightly granular, whitish, flesh-coloured on limbs. Hindfeet extensively webbed. **Toes expanded, square-ended.** Secretive. Call: gentle, clear note, about twice per second. Eggs laid in quiet eddies of mountain torrents. E escarpment forests.
**Similar**
**HEWITT'S GHOST FROG** *H. hewitti*
Elandsberg mountains, s Cape.
**CAPE GHOST FROG** *H. purcelli*
Hottentots Holland to Du Toits mountains, sw Cape.
**SOUTHERN GHOST FROG** *H. regis*
Eastern Langeberg mountains, s Cape.
**TABLE MOUNTAIN GHOST FROG** *H. rosei*
Gorges on Table Mountain, Cape Peninsula.

**2　BUBBLING KASSINA**　　　*Kassina senegalensis*
Smooth-skinned. Rounded snout. Vertical pupil. **Bold chocolate stripes on yellowish background.** Belly white, granular on lower abdomen. Male has large pouch under jaw. Call: loud, liquid "quoip" uttered at intervals. Widespread except n and w Cape and Kalahari.
**Similar**
**RATTLING FROG** *Semnodactylus wealii*
Brown stripes divided longitudinally.

**3　RED-LEGGED KASSINA**　　　*Kassina maculata*
Smooth skin. Rounded snout. Vertical pupil. **Large brown spots with pale outline.** Belly granular, white. Male has yellow pouch under jaw. Call: loud, incessant quacking once per second in large choruses in deep permanent pans. E tropical and semitropical lowveld plains.

**4　BANDED RUBBER FROG**　　　*Phrynomantis bifasciatus*
Smooth skin. Rounded snout. Small eyes, round pupils. **Bold orange or red bands on black background.** Belly grey with white spots. Male has smaller spots on throat. Call: loud, melodious trill sustained for up to two seconds. Males call on banks of pans. Bushveld and subtropical lowveld.
**Similar**
**MARBLED RUBBER FROG** *P. annectens*
Red patches, not bands. N Cape and Namibia.

**5　BROWN-BACKED TREE FROG**　　*Leptopelis mossambicus*
Squat body. Square snout. Large eyes, vertical pupils. **Dark brown horseshoe on tan back.** Belly granular, beige. **Fingers and toes have adhesive discs.** Call: sharp, two syllables "yack-yack" from trees near water. E tropical and semitropical lowveld plains.
**Similar**
**FOREST TREE FROG** *L. natalensis*
Plain or mottled green.
**LONG-TOED TREE FROG** *L. xenodactylus*
Inconspicuous toe discs. S Drakensberg foothills only.

**1, 2 & 3  PAINTED REED FROG**   *Hyperolius marmoratus*

Yellow, black and orange striped (1) N of Swaziland; plain tan specimens (2) throughout range; spotted (3) in e Cape; variable colour patterns in between. Horizontal pupils. Belly whitish, dark pink on limbs. Toes have adhesive discs. Call: short, loud, piercing whistle. Reedbeds at water's edge. E below escarpment as far S as Port Elizabeth.

**Similar**

**ARUM LILY FROG  H. horstocki**
Cream or tan. S coastal plain from Cape Town to Port Elizabeth.

**TINKER REED FROG  H. tuberilinguis**
Plain green, yellow or brown. Ne semitropical coastal plain.

**4  YELLOW-STRIPED REED FROG**   *Hyperolius semidiscus*

Green or brown. Yellow side stripes with **thin black outline**. Horizontal pupils. Belly cream or yellow. Toes have adhesive discs. Call: harsh creak uttered from reeds along rivers, pans. E grassland and temperate coastal plains from Swaziland to e Cape.

**Similar**

**ARGUS REED FROG  H. argus**
Thick black border to stripes. Stripes often broken or absent.

**PICKERSGILL'S REED FROG (MALE)  H. pickersgilli**
Smaller (25 mm or less). Blunt snout. Only male has stripes.

**LONG REED FROG (MALE)  H. nasutus**
Smaller (25 mm or less). Long, pointed snout. Only male has stripes.

**5  WATERLILY FROG**   *Hyperolius pusilus*

**Translucent green**, occasionally with very faint dark spots or stripes. Rounded snout. Horizontal pupils. Belly transparent. Call: blurred tick as when clicking the tongue on roof of mouth. E semitropical lowveld and coastal plain.

**Similar**

**PICKERSGILL'S REED FROG (FEMALE)  H. pickersgilli**
Plain **opaque green** or brown.

**LONG REED FROG (FEMALE)  H. nasutus**
Long, pointed snout.

**6  GOLDEN LEAF-FOLDING FROG**   *Afrixalus aureus*

Elongated body. Golden yellow with occasional brown markings. Brown flanks with white spots. **Vertical pupils**. Belly yellow or white, slightly granular. Call: short, repeated buzz. Calls from emergent vegetation in pans. Eggs laid along leaves folded into tubes. E semitropical lowveld and coastal plain.

**Similar**

**DELICATE LEAF-FOLDING FROG  A. delicatus**
Almost indistinguishable. Call: a short "zip" and sustained trill.

**NATAL LEAF-FOLDING FROG  A. spinifrons**
Dark mid-dorsal band. Black asperities concentrated on snout.

**KNYSNA LEAF-FOLDING FROG  A. knysnae**
Asperities cover body in male. E Cape seaboard only.

**GREATER LEAF-FOLDING FROG  A. fornasinii**
Larger (40 mm). Broad mid-dorsal band.

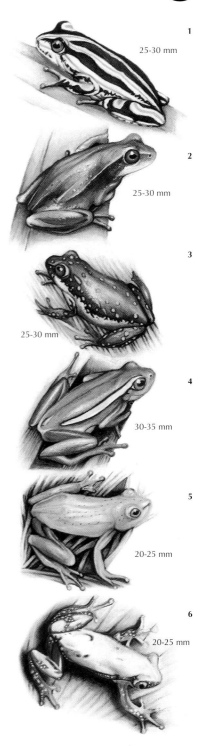

1    25-30 mm

2    25-30 mm

3    25-30 mm

4    30-35 mm

5    20-25 mm

6    20-25 mm

20 mm

30 mm

20-25 mm

**Ventral pattern on cacos**

Common caco        Bronze caco

30-35 mm

25-30 mm

**1   HOGSBACK FROG**              *Anhydrophryne rattrayi*
Colour varies from black to brown and copper. With or without dorsal stripes. Horizontal pupils. Dark facial mask. **Male has calloused snout for digging.** Underside smooth, mottled white and grey. Feet without webbing. Call: clear melodious cheeps repeated, about four per second. Calls from wet banks adjacent to forest streams. Eggs laid in underground nests. Confined to forests in the Amatola mountains, e Cape.
**Similar**
**NATAL CHIRPING FROG** *Arthroleptella hewitti*
Wet banks in riverine forest. Drakensberg and e midlands.
**CAPE CHIRPING FROG** *Arthroleptella lightfooti*
Mossy banks of streams and seepage. Sw Cape only.
**MIST-BELT CHIRPING FROG** *Arthroleptella ngongoniensis*
Rank vegetation in grassland. KwaZulu-Natal midlands.
**MICRO FROG** *Microbatrachella capensis*
Smaller (15 mm). Pans in coastal fynbos near Kleinmond and Hermanus.

**2   CAPE CACO**                    *Cacosternum capense*
Orange patches on tan background. **Large bean-like glands on rump and flanks.** Horizontal pupils. Underside smooth, white with large irregularly shaped dark areas. Feet without webbing. Call: harsh creak repeated, about two per second. Vleis and depressions in sw Cape coastal fynbos.

**3   COMMON CACO**                 *Cacosternum boettgeri*
Colour varies from dark brown to green or red. With or without stripes. Horizontal pupils. Dark facial mask. **Underside smooth, white with grey spots with indistinct edges.** Feet without webbing. Call: brisk bursts of explosive ticks. Inhabits any marshy area or inundated grassland.
**Similar**
**BRONZE CACO** *C. nanum*
Underside has clear dark spots. Call: short chirp.
**NAMAQUA CACO** *C. namaquensis*
Underside has large dark areas. Nw Namaqualand only.

**4   KLOOF FROG**              *Natalobatrachus bonebergi*
Brown or grey with pale vertebral stripe. Pointed snout with **pale triangular patch.** Horizontal pupils. **Fingers T-shaped at tips.** Belly white with dark flecks. Call: soft clicks at intervals. Eggs laid over water in kloofs on KwaZulu-Natal S coast.

**5   SNORING PUDDLE FROG**      *Phrynobatrachus natalensis*
Squat-bodied. Colour, skin texture variable. With or without dorsal stripes. Horizontal pupils. Belly plain whitish. **Male has skin folds along jaw line.** Feet webbed. Call: continuous snoring, two or three per second, often in choruses. Pools or marshland throughout e half of region.
**Similar**
**EAST AFRICAN PUDDLE FROG** *P. acridoides*
Chevron-shaped gland on shoulders. N Maputaland only.
**DWARF PUDDLE FROG** *P. mababiensis*
Smaller (15 mm). Call: insect-like buzzing.
**MARSH FROG** *Poyntonia paludicola*
Raised glandular patch behind each eye. Sw Cape mountains.

**1   ORNATE FROG**                    *Hildebrandtia ornata*

Variable, bold symmetrical patterns in green, orange, brown, white. Horizontal pupils. Throat black with pair of broad white Y-shaped stripes. Call: long nasal quacks about one every two seconds. Breeds in shallow pans in Kruger National Park area, Zimbabwe and s Mozambique.

**2   PLAIN GRASS FROG**              *Ptychadena anchietae*

Six or more longitudinal ridges down back. **Plain russet or brown, occasionally with dark flecks.** Sharp snout with distinct pale triangle. Belly smooth, white. Large, muscular legs. **Patches on posterior of thigh form elongated pattern.** Call: high-pitched trills, about three per second. Calls from open banks of rivers, dams. Subtropical lowveld and bushveld.
**Similar**
**SHARP-NOSED GRASS FROG  *P. oxyrhynchus***
Dark spots on back. Posterior of thigh irregularly mottled.

**3   BROAD-BANDED GRASS FROG** *Ptychadena mossambica*

Six or more longitudinal ridges down back. **Broad, light vertebral stripe down back.** Snout lacks any distinct pale triangle. Belly smooth, white. Large, muscular legs. Call: nasal, duck-like quacking repeated, about two per second. Calls from concealed positions on banks of vleis, pans. Subtropical lowveld and bushveld.
**Similar**
**MASCARENE GRASS FROG  *P. mascareniensis***
Length from heel to toe greater than length of lower leg.
**DWARF GRASS FROG  *P. pumilio***
Smaller (under 35 mm). Longitudinal stripes on posterior of thigh.

**4   STRIPED GRASS FROG**            *Ptychadena porosissima*

Six or more longitudinal ridges down back. **Three light stripes on back.**Snout lacks any distinct pale triangle. Belly smooth, white. Large, muscular legs. Indistinct white spots on posterior of thigh. Call: short low-pitched rasping sounds, about two per second. Marshy areas, pans along temperate and subtropical e escarpment and coast.

**5   COMMON RIVER FROG**             *Rana angolensis*

Green or brown with dark spots. Often a light stripe down back. Sharp snout. Belly smooth, white, sometimes with dark mottling. Large, muscular legs. Call: sharp rattle followed by short croak. Common near most perennial waters except in arid w areas and sw Cape.
**Similar**
**DRAKENSBERG RIVER FROG  *R. dracomontana***
Only at summit of Drakensberg where (5) is absent.
**CAPE RIVER FROG  *R. fuscigula***
Blunt snout. S and w Cape as well as central highveld.

**6   AQUATIC RIVER FROG**            *Rana vertebralis*

Dark mottled greenish-grey. Broad, flat head. Rounded snout. Belly with dark vermiculation. Feet extensively webbed. Call: hollow knocking followed by low-pitched groan. Generally remains immersed. Can survive under sheets of surface ice. Restricted to high-altitude Drakensberg streams.

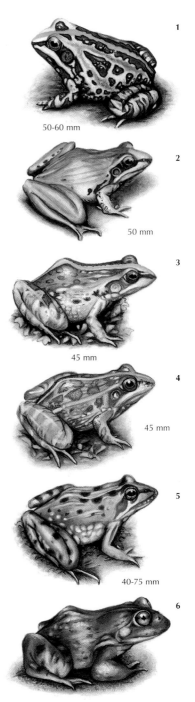

1

50-60 mm

2

50 mm

3

45 mm

4

45 mm

5

40-75 mm

6

50-90 mm

**1    BANDED STREAM FROG**      *Strongylopus bonaspei*

Brown and orange stripes on back, sometimes broken or fused. Horizontal pupils. Belly white. Male has yellow throat. **Dark bars across legs.** Toes extremely long. Call: short, harsh squawks followed by rapid cackle. Breeds in marshy areas and seepage in sw Cape.

**2    STRIPED STREAM FROG**      *Strongylopus fasciatus*

Parallel yellow, tan and brown stripes on back. Horizontal pupils. Belly white. Male has yellow throat. **Longitudinal dark stripes along legs.** Toes extremely long. Call: sharp piercing "pip" uttered singly or in quick series of three or four. In long grass alongside water. S and e coastal regions, e escarpment and high rainfall areas of highveld.

**3    CLICKING STREAM FROG**      *Strongylopus grayii*

Colours and patterns vary considerably. Dark spots usually present. Horizontal pupils. Belly white. **Dark bars across legs.** Toes not as long as in previous species. Call: monotonous wooden tapping or clicking. Alongside any water body in sw and e coastal regions and temperate high rainfall areas at high and low altitudes.
**Similar**
NAMAQUA STREAM FROG  *S. springbokensis*
Confined to Namaqualand where (3) does not occur.

**4    PLAIN STREAM FROG**      *Strongylopus wageri*

**Plain cream to russet**, occasionally with light stippling. Horizontal pupils. Snout slightly paler than back. Belly white. Sometimes has bars across legs. Toes very long. Call: raucous cackle repeated at regular intervals. Wooded streams in Drakensberg and e escarpment.

**5    BERG STREAM FROG**      *Strongylopus hymenopus*

Rough, warty skin. Mottled grey or brown. Horizontal pupils. Head flat and broad. Rounded snout. **No facial mask.** Belly white, dark spots on throat. Bars across legs. Call: rapid chattering interspersed with long pauses. Streams and seepage in high Drakensberg grassland.

**6    COMMON PLATANNA**      *Xenopus laevis*

Slimy skin. Streamlined oval body. Mottled grey. Round pupils. Belly greyish-white, occasionally spotted. Forelimbs diminutive with feeble, tapering fingers. Hindlimbs massive with extensively webbed feet and clawed toes. Call: soft underwater buzzing. Migrates to new breeding grounds in rainy weather. Remains almost permanently submerged in any water body throughout Africa.
**Similar**
CAPE PLATANNA  *X. gilli*
Elongated dark markings on back. Sw Cape only.
TROPICAL PLATANNA  *X. muelleri*
Short tentacle (2 mm) below each eye. Tropical and subtropical lowveld.

1

45 mm

2

45 mm

3

40 mm

4

40 mm

5

60 mm

6

50-100 mm

**1 & 2   GIANT BULLFROG**          *Pyxicephalus adspersus*

Massive, flaccid body. Olive-green with numerous skin ridges. Orange or yellow in armpits and groin. Head broad, heavy. **No facial markings.** Belly yellow. Large digging tubercle on heel. Juvenile (2) bright green with black stippling; usually has vertebral stripe. Call: deep bellow lasting about a second. If molested gives loud open-mouthed bray. Breeds in temporary pans in central highveld.
**Similar**
**AFRICAN BULLFROG**  *P. edulis*
Dark spots on green-brown back extending to face. Wide sub-tropical distribution.

**3   NATAL SAND FROG**          *Tomopterna natalensis*

Stocky body. Mottled grey or russet. Slightly pointed snout. **Two glandular ridges from eye and mouth converge above shoulder.** Horizontal pupils. Belly white. Male has black throat. Call: penetrating yelps preceded by build-up of accelerating croaks. Breeds in streams and vleis in grassland in temperate, high rainfall areas of highveld and e escarpment.

**4   TREMOLO SAND FROG**          *Tomopterna cryptotis*

Stocky body. Mottled brown, grey and reddish, often with one or more pale stripes down back. Pale patch between shoulders. Blunt snout. Whitish glandular ridge from mouth to shoulder. Horizontal pupils. Belly white. Male has black throat. Call: rapid series of short, clear pips, about 12 per second. Breeds in pans and vleis throughout s Africa except in arid w areas and sw Cape.
**Similar**
**KNOCKING SAND FROG  T. krugerensis**
Indistinguishable. Call: percussive wooden knocking, four or five times per second.
**CAPE SAND FROG  T. delalandii**
sw Cape. Meets but does not overlap range of (4) near Grahamstown.

**RUSSET-BACKED SAND FROG   Tomopterna marmoratus**

Stocky body. Marbled russet without conspicuous dark markings. Pale patch between shoulders. Blunt snout. Whitish glandular ridge from mouth to shoulder. Horizontal pupils. Belly white. Male has black throat. Call: piping note repeated at variable rate. Calls from sand banks along rivers in Kruger National Park area, Zimbabwe and s Mozambique.

**6   FOAM NEST FROG**          *Chiromantis xerampelina*

Grey or tan with variable number of dark spots. May turn almost white during daylight. Horizontal pupils. Belly white, dark stippling on throat. Long limbs without much strength. Fingers, toes have large adhesive terminal discs. Call: soft discordant chirping. Eggs laid in foam nests on branches overhanging water. Bushveld from e subtropical lowveld and Limpopo basin northwards.

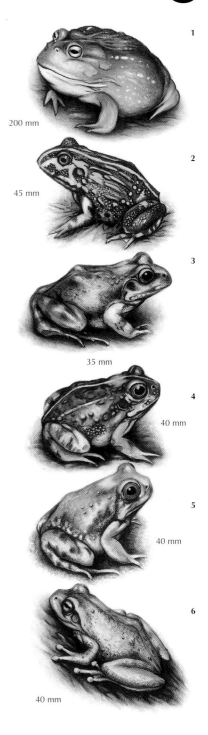

1

200 mm

2

45 mm

3

35 mm

4

40 mm

5

40 mm

6

40 mm

# REPTILES

Reptiles are a class of vertebrates with dry, cornified skin which distinguishes them from the
amphibians and fishes, and ectothermic metabolism (body temperature dependent on the temperature
of the environment) which distinguishes them from birds and mammals.

Of the four orders of reptiles, three are well represented in southern Africa: the shelled reptiles (chelonians),
the scaled reptiles (squamates) and the crocodiles (crocodilians). The fourth order includes the tuataras, which
now exist only on a few New Zealand islands. The reptilian orders occurring in the southern African region
are so different that they require separate descriptions:

- **Chelonians** include tortoises (land dwelling), turtles (sea dwelling) and terrapins (freshwater dwelling). They
  are easily recognisable by their characteristic shell which is a horn-covered bony extension of the rib cage. The
  carapace (upper shell) is domed and the plastron (lower shell) is flat in females and usually concave in males.

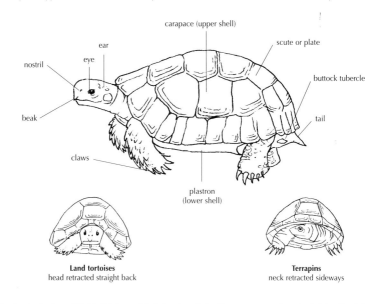

**Land tortoises**
head retracted straight back

**Terrapins**
neck retracted sideways

**Squamates** (scaled reptiles) include the amphisbaenas, snakes and lizards:

**Amphisbaenas** (sometimes called worm lizards, but not to be confused with legless lizards) are burrowing animals that are very rarely encountered. Most are pinkish and about 15-30 cm long. Eyes are hidden and the head is protected in some species by a thick shield resembling a fingernail.

**Snakes** are all legless. They lack eyelids and ears but can detect sound vibrations through the substrate. The lower jaw can be dislocated to enable large prey items to be swallowed whole. The teeth are generally long and in some species they are adapted to inject venom.

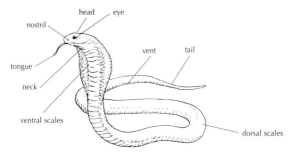

**Lizards** generally have four legs although in a few species these have become vestigial and they appear to be legless. They have visible ear openings and movable eyelids. The upper and lower jaws are fused. Belly scales are small and this distinguishes the legless lizards from most snakes, which have large ventral scales. Many species of lizards have long tails that can be shed and regenerated. No southern African species is venomous.

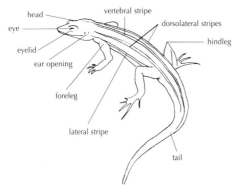

**Crocodilians** are represented by one species, the Nile crocodile.

## Scope of this chapter

Southern Africa has the widest diversity of land tortoises in the world. All 13 species are described in this chapter, as well as all marine turtles that visit southern African shores, including those that do not breed here. All indigenous hard-shelled terrapins are covered in the chapter. Excluded are the soft-shelled terrapins from north and east Africa which have been recorded at the peripheries of the southern African region but are very seldom seen. Also excluded is the American red-eared terrapin which has escaped from captivity. It has a green shell when young, brightly striped head and webbed feet.

The 12 southern African amphisbaenas have not been included as they are very rarely seen and the different species are difficult to identify (see picture above).

Of the 130 southern African species of snakes, 90 are described. These include all those that are most likely to be encountered. In cases where there is a group of similar-looking, inconspicuous species, such as the blind snakes, a few species have been described as representative of the group as a whole.

The same criteria have been used to select the 103 lizards that are included, out of the nearly 250 southern African species. A large number of lizards are difficult to distinguish from others in a closely related group therefore the more common species representing these groups have been described.

The Nile crocodile, the only crocodilian in southern Africa, is described.

## Distribution

Reptiles are distributed throughout southern Africa. Like all forms of wildlife, their numbers and diversity increase towards the warmer and wetter north-east. However, this is less marked in reptiles than in most other animals because, more than almost any other group, reptiles have adapted to desert conditions.

Crocodiles were once widespread but their range has now been reduced to nature reserves and remote areas in the north. The distribution of other reptiles has probably been less affected by humans, although their numbers and conservation status most certainly have. Some tortoises with restricted ranges in the southern Cape have become severely endangered.

## Reproduction and development

The mating season for reptiles is usually spring, and it is at this time that they are most frequently encountered. Fertilisation is internal. Sperm is transferred to the female via a single penis in crocodiles and chelonians, and paired hemipenes in snakes and lizards (although only one hemipenis is used at a time).

The majority of reptiles lay their eggs in warm, moist, secluded sites. Marine turtles come ashore along the north-eastern coastline to nest, returning every summer to the same sites. The eggs are laid in holes dug on the beach above the high water mark and then covered and disguised by the female scuffing the sand in a large area around the nest. In April, the young hatch and run a gauntlet of crabs, sea birds and other predators to reach the security of the surf. They remain at sea until sufficiently mature to breed. Other chelonians also bury their eggs in holes which they dig in carefully selected sites.

Crocodiles, too, bury their eggs in sandy banks. At the time of hatching the female — in response to the vocalising babies — re-excavates the nest and carries the hatchlings to the water. She also cracks open unhatched eggs with her teeth to free the hatchlings. For some time thereafter both male and female guard the young crocodiles in the water. A few species of snakes and lizards also protect their eggs and young while they develop.

The sex of young crocodiles and chelonians is determined in the egg by the incubation temperature. Male crocodiles develop in high temperatures and females in low temperatures; the opposite is true for turtles.

A few species of snakes and lizards give birth to live young.

## Feeding

Land tortoises are vegetarian but will occasionally scavenge carrion for calcium. Turtles and terrapins are mainly carnivorous.

Snakes capture and eat live prey. Small prey items such as slugs are simply swallowed. Larger prey is first subdued, either by constriction or by injection of venom.

Lizards are insectivorous except the two monitor species, which take larger prey including small mammals and nestling birds. They are not venomous and rely on their stealth and agility to hunt and capture prey.

Crocodiles take live prey, mostly fish, under water, as well as animals that come down to drink.

## Snakebite and venom

Of the 130 species of snakes in southern Africa, 34 are venomous and 14 are known to have caused human death. Both venomous and non-venomous snakes will strike in defence and some of the cobras and the rinkhals can spray venom at potential attackers.

Venom can be neurotoxic, causing dizziness, convulsions and respiratory difficulty, or cytotoxic, causing destruction of tissue and internal bleeding. In general, the mambas and cobras possess neurotoxic venom and adders possess cytotoxic venom, but there are exceptions.

In the event of snakebite, apply a firm, crepe pressure bandage to the full length of the affected limb and obtain professional medical attention as quickly as possible. Other first aid treatment should only be undertaken if medical help is more than several hours away. Identification of the snake is useful, but should not be allowed to delay treatment of the victim.

## Dimensions

In the case of tortoises, terrapins and turtles, the measurement given with the illustration refers to the length of the carapace with the head and tail retracted. The dimensions of snakes, lizards and crocodiles refer to the full length from the snout to the tip of the tail.

**1**

30-45 cm

**2**

15-25 cm

**3**

8-12 cm

**4**

13-18 cm

**5**

7-10 cm

**1   MOUNTAIN TORTOISE**                    *Geochelone pardalis*
Shell heavily blotched or streaked, almost dark grey in large adults. Hatchling bright yellow, each scute having 1-2 black spots. **Upper shell has no small scale above neck.** Up to six clutches (each with 6-15 eggs) laid in summer. Widespread except most of highveld, succulent Karoo and Namib desert.

**2   ANGULATE TORTOISE**                    *Chersina angulata*
Shell light straw-yellow with dark edges to scutes. **Single scute beneath throat,** larger in males and used to overturn opponents. In w Cape often has bright red underside. Female lays single, large egg at 4-6 week intervals. S coastal areas, extending inland into moist areas.

**3   GEOMETRIC TORTOISE**                *Psammobates geometricus*
Shell high, domed. Bright yellow and black radiating markings. Shell has only slightly upturned rear margin. **Scutes along bridge higher than they are broad. Lacks buttock tubercles.** Female larger, has smaller tail than male. 2-4 eggs laid in September. Endangered (only 2 000-3 000 remain). Restricted to coastal renosterbosveld in SW.
**Similar**
**KAROO TENT TORTOISE  *P. tentorius***
Scutes on bridge broader than high. Karoo and w Cape.
**KALAHARI TENT TORTOISE  *P. oculiferus***
Buttock tubercles present, shell spiny. Kalahari.

**4   SPEK'S HINGEBACK**                        *Kinixys spekii*
Brown, flattened upper shell has hinge at back. Tail ends in spine. Beak has single cusp. Male has hollow belly. Shelters in rock cracks and hollow logs. Readily eats fungi, snails, millipedes, as well as other plants. 2-4 eggs laid in summer. N South Africa and Zimbabwe.
**Similar**
**BELL'S HINGEBACK  *K. belliana***
Shell domed with radiating pattern. Mozambique plain.
**NATAL HINGEBACK  *K. natalensis***
Weak hinge. Beak has three cusps. KwaZulu-Natal midlands.

**5   PARROT-BEAKED TORTOISE**              *Homopus areolatus*
Green shell with black margins in female, orange in male. **Dorsal scutes have depressed centres. Only four toes on forefeet.** Lacks buttock tubercles. Beak strongly hooked. Breeding male has bright orange nose. Small, shy. 2-3 small eggs laid in summer. Cape coastal regions.
**Similar**
**GREATER PADLOPER  *H. femoralis***
Shell brown. Buttock tubercle present. Karoo and Free State.
**SPECKLED PADLOPER  *H. signatus***
Very small. Speckled shell. Five toes on forefeet. Namaqualand.
**KAROO PADLOPER  *H. boulenger***
Shell uniform brown. Five toes on forefeet.
**NAMA PADLOPER  *H. bergeri***
Shell yellow. Only around Aus, Namibia.

**1 SERRATED HINGED TERRAPIN**     *Pelusios sinuatus*

Neck withdrawn sideways. Black with yellow, angular-edged blotch in centre of belly. **Shell domed, front hinge on underside, serrated rear edge.** Keels along backbone (particularly in juveniles). Often seen basking on floating logs. 7-13 soft-shelled eggs laid in spring. Large rivers and pans in NE.

**Similar**

**PAN TERRAPIN**  *P. subniger*

Shell rounded. Yellow centres to belly scutes. NE.

**BLACK-BELLIED HINGED TERRAPIN**  *P. rhodesianus*

Carapace black. Plastron black. N and NE.

**YELLOW-BELLIED HINGED TERRAPIN**  *P. castanoides*

Carapace yellowish-black. Plastron yellow. NE.

**OKAVANGO HINGED TERRAPIN**  *P. bechuanicus*

Head noticeably large. Carapace black. Plastron black. Okavango and Zambezi.

30-45 cm

**2 MARSH TERRAPIN**     *Pelomedusa subrufa*

Neck withdrawn sideways. **Shell hard, very flat with no hinge on belly. Two soft tentacles on chin.** Leaves drying pans and digs into soil to await rains. Eats almost anything, including small birds coming to drink. 10-30 soft-shelled eggs laid in sandbank after summer rains. Pans, vleis, slow-moving rivers throughout s Africa.

20-30 cm

**3 LEATHERBACK TURTLE**     *Dermochelys coriacea*

Largest sea turtle. Shell pliable, rubbery, with 12 prominent ridges. Long flippers. Young blue-grey. Cannot withdraw head. Specialist feeder on jellyfish. May dive more than 300 m. Female nests at high tide on moonless night from November to January. Lays 6-9 clutches of 100-120 eggs. Marine. Around entire coast, but breeds only in Maputaland.

130-170 cm

**4 LOGGERHEAD TURTLE**     *Caretta caretta*

Head has strong jaws. Elongate shell tapers at rear. 15 scutes, excluding marginals. Scutes smooth (keeled in hatchlings) and non-overlapping. Each limb has two claws. Adults and young brown. Hunts for crabs, molluscs, sea urchins around reefs, rocky estuaries. Nests in summer, laying up to five clutches of 100 eggs at 15-day intervals. Marine. Around E coast, but breeds only in Maputaland.

**Similar**

**OLIVE RIDLEY TURTLE**  *Lepidochelys olivacea*

17 or more scutes, exluding marginals. One claw on each limb.

70-100 cm

**5 GREEN TURTLE**     *Chelonia mydas*

Hard shell smooth with non-overlapping scutes, 12 scutes along edge on each side. Front flipper has single claw. Shell brown with light streaks. Slow-growing; 10-15 years to mature. Enters estuaries to feed on sea grasses. Marine. Non-breeding visitor to E and W coasts.

**Similar**

**HAWKSBILL TURTLE**  *Eretmochelys imbricata*

Shell tear-shaped. Overlapping scutes. Beak hooked. E coast.

98-120 cm

**1**

35-40 cm

**2**

60-80 cm

**3**

18-24 cm

**4**

300-500 cm

**5**

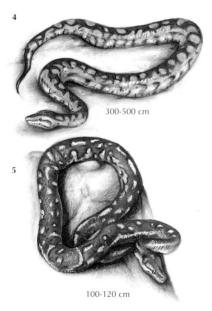

100-120 cm

### 1 BIBRON'S BLIND SNAKE — *Typhlops bibronii*

Primitive snake. Head blunt. Eye reduced to black spot beneath skin. No teeth in lower jaw. Plain brown with lighter belly. Thick body covered in small, smooth, overlapping scales. Very short tail ends in spine. Burrows. Feeds on ant and termite larvae. Highveld and coastal grassland.

### 2 SCHLEGEL'S BLIND SNAKE — *Rhinotyphlops schlegelii*

Large, thick-bodied. Head blunt. Eye reduced to black spot beneath skin. Prominent horizontal edge to snout. Thick body covered in overlapping scales on back and belly. Very short tail ends in spine. Colour varies: blue-grey when first shed, turning to rust-red. May have dark blotches or fine stripes. Burrows. Feeds on ant and termite larvae. N savanna.
**Similar**
DELALANDE'S BLIND SNAKE *R. lalandei*
Slender. Pink-grey with pale belly. E.

### 3 PETER'S THREAD SNAKE — *Leptotyphlops scutifrons*

Minute, very thin grey-black snake. Body covered in small, smooth overlapping scales on back and belly. Eye of blunt head reduced to black spot beneath skin. Longish tail ends in spine. Burrows, feeding on ant and termite larvae. Lays 3-7 small, elongate eggs, joined like string of sausages. N areas except Namib desert.
**Similar**
WESTERN THREAD SNAKE *L. occidentalis*
Very thin. Grey-brown to purple-brown. Rocky desert of Namibia.
BLACK THREAD SNAKE *L. nigricans*
Black; shortish tail. S Cape and highveld.

### 4 AFRICAN ROCK PYTHON — *Python sebae*

Africa's largest snake. Thick, muscular body has very small, smooth scales. Triangular head covered in small scales. Two heat-sensitive pits on upper lip. Body olive with dark blotches. Large, dark spearhead mark on head. Eats mammals, birds. Up to 100 eggs (size of an orange) laid in hollow tree, antbear hole, etc. Female coils around eggs to protect them. Rock outcrops and bush near water in N.

### 5 ANCHIETA'S DWARF PYTHON — *Python anchietae*

Muscular body covered in small, tubercular scales. Triangular head covered in small scales. Five heat-sensitive pits on upper lip. Pale, red-brown with small, scattered, black-edged white spots and bands. Eats small birds, rodents. 5-6 large eggs laid in summer. Rocky areas of n Namibia and Angola.

**1  COMMON BROWN WATER SNAKE**   *Lycodonomorphus rufulus*

Slim with small head. Elliptical pupils. Body plain olive with smooth scales, pale yellow-pink belly. Nocturnal. Catches and constricts small frogs, tadpoles. 6-10 eggs laid in late summer. Moist places from w Cape to Zimbabwe.
**Similar**
**DUSKY-BELLIED WATER SNAKE  *L. laevissimus***
Dark belly band. Spotted upper lip. Rivers of e Cape and KwaZulu-Natal.

**2  BROWN HOUSE SNAKE**         *Lamprophis fuliginosus*

Muscular body with obvious head. Body scales smooth, shiny. Body rust-red with pair of thin yellow stripes on each side of head, pale belly. Terrestrial, nocturnal, constrictor. Eats mice, rats, sometimes lizards. Common around houses, useful in controlling pests. Up to 18 eggs laid in summer. Throughout s Africa.

**3  OLIVE HOUSE SNAKE**         *Lamprophis inornatus*

Muscular body with obvious head. Body scales smooth, shiny. Body plain olive-green with paler belly. Terrestrial, nocturnal, constrictor. Hunts mice, rats, sometimes other snakes. Common around houses, useful in controlling pests. Up to 15 eggs laid in summer. S Cape to ne escarpment.

**4  AURORA HOUSE SNAKE**        *Lamprophis aurora*

Small-headed, gentle snake. Prominent orange dorsal stripe on green body. Vertical pupils. Young speckled yellow. Nocturnal, constrictor. Eats nestling rodents, lizards. 8-12 eggs laid in summer. Cape Town to highveld.
**Similar**
**SPOTTED HOUSE SNAKE  *L. guttatus***
Light brown with dark brown blotches. Karoo and e mountains.

**5  CAPE WOLF SNAKE**           *Lycophidion capense*

Head flattened, small eyes, vertical pupils. Body uniform grey-black (browner in S), usually with white-tipped scales. Nocturnal. Catches and constricts lizards as they sleep in their retreats. 3-8 eggs laid in summer. Widespread in E.
**Similar**
**VARIEGATED WOLF SNAKE  *L. variegatum***
Slender. White mottling on back. N KwaZulu-Natal to Zimbabwe.
**NAMIBIAN WOLF SNAKE  *L. namibensis***
Dark brown back, brown belly stripe. N Namibia.

60-80 cm

60-100 cm

60-100 cm

50-80 cm

30-50 cm

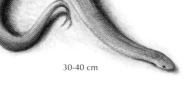

100-150 cm

30-40 cm

100-150 cm

45-60 cm

45-60 cm

**1   CAPE FILE SNAKE**                    *Mehelya capensis*

Thickset, triangular body with very flat head. Body scales conical, strongly keeled, separated by bare, pink skin. Scales along backbone white, large, keeled. Grey-brown with cream belly and flanks. Constricts lizards and other snakes. 5-13 large eggs laid in summer. Rare, docile, never bites. N.

**Similar**

**BLACK FILE SNAKE  *M. nyassae***

Smaller, body black. NE.

**2   COMMON SLUGEATER**                   *Duberria lutrix*

Stout-bodied, scales smooth, small head indistinct from neck. Body brick-red to pale brown with pale sides. Cream belly. Feeds on slugs, snails. 6-18 young born in summer. Rolls into tight spiral when handled. Damp situations from Cape Town to e Zimbabwe.

**Similar**

**VARIEGATED SLUGEATER  *D. variegata***

Larger. Three rows of blackish spots. E coast to Mozambique.

**3   MOLE SNAKE**                         *Pseudaspis cana*

Body thickset with small head. Slightly hooked snout. Small eyes with round pupils. Colour light brown in deserts, black in S, dark brown elsewhere. Young spotted. Powerful constrictor. Hunts rodents and moles underground. Up to 95 young born in late summer. Throughout s Africa.

**4   MANY-SPOTTED SNAKE**    *Amplorhinus multimaculatus*

Head small. Round pupils. Tail longish. Body green to olive-brown with dark blotches, sometimes flecked with white and with pale stripe on each side. Hunts frogs at dusk in reedbeds and waterside vegetation. 4-12 young born in late summer. Back-fanged but harmless. Rare. Restricted to cool e areas.

**5   WESTERN KEELED SNAKE**      *Pythonodipsas carinatus*

Body long, thin. Flattened head covered in small scales, large eyes have vertical pupils. Nostrils swollen and on top of snout. Pastel-coloured with dark-edged blotches that may fuse into zigzag. Feeds at dusk on small lizards, rodents. Lays eggs. Viper-like but harmless. Restricted to rocky Namib.

**1 SUNDEVALL'S SHOVEL-SNOUT** *Prosymna sundevallii*
Cylindrical body has smooth scales. Short tail ends in spine. Snout flattened, shovel-like, slightly upturned. Body dark brown with paired (S and central) or single (N and E) dark spots. Belly white. Shovels in soft soil for reptile eggs to eat. 3-5 eggs laid in summer. Central areas from Cape to Zimbabwe.
**Similar**
**TWO-STRIPED SHOVEL-SNOUT** *P. bivittata*
Prominent dorsal orange stripe. Arid Kalahari savanna.
**SOUTH-WESTERN SHOVEL-SNOUT** *P. frontalis*
Slender. Dark brown collar on neck. Namaqualand and Namibia.

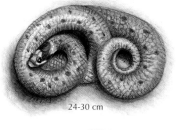

1

24-30 cm

**2 FOREST MARSH SNAKE** *Natriciteres variegata*
Pencil-thin body with long tail. Smooth scales. Back dark olive to chestnut, usually with dark dorsal band bordered by white dots. Faint yellow collar may be present. Under dead logs and rotting vegetation. Eats frogs. Lays up to six eggs in summer. Dune forest and swamp in n KwaZulu-Natal and e Zimbabwe.

2

30-40 cm

**3 STRIPED SWAMP SNAKE** *Limnophis bicolor*
Body cylindrical. Small head. Large eyes have round pupils. Scales smooth, shiny. Body olive-brown with 3-4 black-edged stripes. Belly bright yellow to brick-red. Aquatic. Hunts small frogs and fish. Lays a few large eggs. Shy, never bites. Restricted to Okavango delta and Zambezi valley.

**4 SPOTTED BUSH SNAKE** *Philothamnus semivariegatus*
Slender-bodied with long tail. Belly flat-bottomed with edge on both sides. Body green, merging to bronze on tail, with black blotches on forebody. Excellent, speedy climber. Catches lizards, tree frogs in low bush and rock outcrops. Lays 3-12 eggs in summer. Inflates throat to show blue skin in threatening defence. Bites readily but harmless. N savanna and thickets.

**5 NATAL GREEN SNAKE** *Philothamnus natalensis*
Body slender, bright green. Easily mistaken for young green mamba but has flat belly with edge on both sides. Two rows of scales behind eye. Hunts frogs, sometimes lizards, during day in reedbeds and along river banks. Lays 4-8 elongate eggs in summer. E lowlands northwards into interior.
**Similar**
**GREEN WATER SNAKE** *P. hoplogaster*
Head rounder. Single scale rose behind eye. E Cape to Zimbabwe.

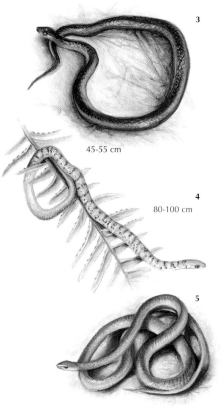

3

45-55 cm

4

80-100 cm

5

70-100 cm

80-120 cm

100-140 cm

90-120 cm

80-100 cm

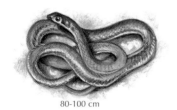

50-80 cm

**1   RHOMBIC SKAAPSTEKER      *Psammophylax rhombeatus***
Boldly patterned. Slim body. Few scale rows (17). Longish tail. Back yellowish-brown with 3-4 rows of dark-edged blotches (sometimes striped in e specimens). Hunts small prey in grassland. Lays up to 30 eggs. Coils around them until they hatch. Not dangerous. Throughout s Africa but rare in W.
**Similar**
**STRIPED SKAAPSTEKER  *P. tritaeniatus***
Smaller. Grey body with bold dark stripes. S and E.

**2   OLIVE GRASS SNAKE        *Psammophis phillipsii***
Robust snake. Obvious head. Long tail, large scales. Body olive-brown, paler towards tail, sometimes with scattered black flecks or thin stripes. Cream belly may have black streaks. Active, diurnal hunter. Eats small vertebrates. Lays up to 30 eggs in summer. Shy. Mild venom. N savanna.
**Similar**
**SHORT-SNOUTED GRASS SNAKE  *P. sibilans***
Slender. Light band on sides and white "stitch" down backbone. Central grasslands and E coast; also n Namibia.

**3   STRIPE-BELLIED SAND SNAKE  *Psammophis subtaeniatus***
Body slender. Head lance-shaped with large eyes. Back has broad black-edged dorsal band. Cream and brown stripes on sides. Bright yellow belly, bordered by black and white stripes. Eats birds, lizards, mice. Lays 4-10 elongate eggs in summer. Open savanna in N.
**Similar**
**WESTERN SAND SNAKE  *P. trigrammus***
Very slender with reddish lateral stripe. Namibia.

**4   KAROO SAND SNAKE         *Psammophis notostictus***
Slender body. Narrow head, large eyes. Long tail. Body may be plain grey-brown, but usually lightly striped on sides and with thin stripe along backbone. Chases down lizards on sandy flats. Shelters at night in rock cracks or holes. Lays 3-4 elongate eggs in summer. Common in Karoo and adjacent desert.
**Similar**
**NAMIB SAND SNAKE  *P. leightoni***
Boldly striped. Top of head spotted or barred. W desert.

**5   CROSS-MARKED GRASS SNAKE     *Psammophis crucifer***
Small, robust body. Relatively short tail. Body silver-grey with black-edged brown stripes along backbone and on sides. Prominent dark-edged light crossbars on head. Rare variant has no pattern. Hunts in fynbos and mountain grassland for lizards, frogs. Lays 5-13 eggs in midsummer. S coast and highveld grassland.

**1 DWARF BEAKED SNAKE** *Dipsina multimaculata*

Small, slender body. Short tail. Head has dark V-shaped mark and prominent hooked snout. Colours match sandy habitat. 3-5 rows of dark, sometimes pale-centred, blotches or crossbands on back. Shy, slow-moving. Ambushes small lizards. Lays 2-4 elongate eggs in summer. Coils and hisses in threat, but harmless. Karoo and rocky desert.

**2 RUFOUS BEAKED SNAKE** *Rhamphiophis oxyrhynchus*

Large, stout-bodied. Prominent hooked snout. Long tail. Distinctive dark brown eye stripe on head. Body plain yellow-orange to red-brown, sometimes with pale-centred scales. Shelters in burrow. Eats small vertebrates, including snakes. Lays 8-17 large eggs in summer. N bushveld.

**3 BARK SNAKE** *Hemirhaggheris nototaenia*

Small, slender. Head distinctly flattened, eyes large with vertical pupils. Back grey with dark dorsal stripe and series of black spots on sides. Secretive, sheltering under loose bark or in hollow trees. Hunts lizards, tree frogs. Shy, never bites. Lays 2-8 elongate eggs in hollow tree. N savanna.
**Similar**
**NAMIBIAN BARK SNAKE** *H. viperinus*
Blotches more vivid, forming zigzag. Central Namibia.

**4 BICOLOURED QUILL-SNOUTED SNAKE** *Xenocalamus bicolor*

Thin, elongate. Quill-shaped head, underslung mouth and short, blunt tail. Minute eyes with round pupils. Coloration may be striped, spotted or all-black. Burrows in deep sand hunting worm lizards. Lays 3-4 very elongate eggs in summer. Scattered populations in n bushveld.
**Similar**
**SLENDER QUILL-SNOUTED SNAKE** *X. mechowii*
Body very long and thin. Two rows of blotches. Caprivi region.

**5 CAPE CENTIPEDE-EATER** *Aparallactus capensis*

Small, slender. Small head, rounded snout, prominent black collar. Body varies from red-brown to grey-buff. Belly cream. Lives underground, particularly in old termitaria. Hunts centipedes. Harmless. Lays 2-4 small eggs in summer. E.
**Similar**
**RETICULATED CENTIPEDE-EATER** *A. lunulatus*
Body dark. Two yellow collars on neck. Zimbabwe and lowveld.

1

30-45 cm

2

120-140 cm

3

25-40 cm

4

45-60 cm

5

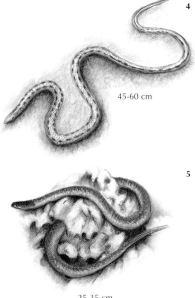

25-35 cm

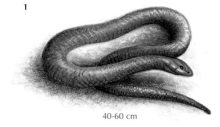

40-60 cm

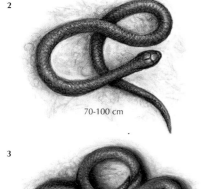

70-100 cm

40-50 cm

30-40 cm

55-90 cm

**1   PURPLE-GLOSSED SNAKE**          *Amblyodipsas polylepis*

Stocky with blunt head. Small eyes. Smooth shiny scales. Scales under tail in two rows. Body and belly black, with purple gloss when freshly shed. Burrows underground. Eats other burrowing reptiles, particularly blind snakes. Breeding habits unknown. Slow, rarely bites. Ne savanna.

**2   NATAL BLACK SNAKE**          *Macrelaps microlepidotus*

Stocky body, all-black. Blunt head. Easily confused with (1) but lacks purple sheen and has single scales under tail. Lays up to 10 eggs in summer. Eats small vertebrates. Bite may lead to unconsciousness. Restricted to E coast.

**3   BIBRON'S BURROWING ASP**          *Atractaspis bibronii*

Thinnish black body (sometimes with white belly). Blunt head. Small eyes. Short tail ends in spine. Shelters in rock piles, old termitaria, etc. Eats other burrowing reptiles. Lays up to seven eggs in summer. Has long fangs and painful venom. Cannot be held safely behind head. N.
**Similar**
**DUERDEN'S BURROWING ASP  *A. duerdeni***
Snout bluntly hooked. E Botswana and central Namibia.

**4   GERARD'S BURROWING SNAKE *Chilorhinnophis gerardi***

Very slender. Blunt head. Short, rounded tail. Body bright yellow with three black stripes. White belly. Head and tail tip black, easily confused. When threatened, holds tail up as mock head which may even appear to strike. Burrows in loose sand. Eats worm lizards, thread snakes. Lays six eggs in summer. N Zimbabwe.

**5   COMMON EGGEATER**          *Dasypeltis scabra*

Slender. Blunt head. Long tail. Rough, keeled scales. Dirty grey body with numerous blotches. Prominent V-shaped mark on neck. Feeds on bird eggs. Harmless but strikes readily and reveals threatening wide black gape. Also hisses by rubbing keeled scales together. Throughout s Africa.
**Similar**
**BROWN EGGEATER  *D. inornatus***
Uniform brown colour, longer tail. E coastal areas.

**1 MARBLED TREE SNAKE** *Dipsadoboa aulica*

Body elongate with long tail. Large head. Big eyes with vertical pupils. Head finely marbled white. Back light brown with many light, dark-edged crossbands in juveniles, decreasing in size and number with age. Feeds on geckos and frogs. Lays up to eight small eggs in summer. E coast and lowveld swamplands.

**2 EASTERN TIGER SNAKE** *Telescopus semiannulatus*

Distinctive thin body. Long tail. Large head. Big eyes with vertical pupils. Dull orange body has 22-50 dark blotches that are larger on forebody. Terrestrial but climbs trees and roofs readily in search of small birds, bats, lizards. Lays 6-20 eggs in summer. Bites readily but venom mild. N and e half of region.
**Similar**
**NAMIB TIGER SNAKE** *T. beetzi*
Sandy-buff colour. 42-59 dark blotches. Karoo and w desert.

**3 RED-LIPPED SNAKE** *Crotaphopeltis hotamboeia*

Body elongate with long tail. Obvious glossy black head. Large eyes. Distinctive bright red-orange lips. Body olive with white flecks. Nocturnal. Hunts in marshy areas for small frogs. Lays up to 12 eggs in early summer. Flattens head to display lips. Harmless. E half of region and SW coast.

**4 BOOMSLANG** *Dispholidus typus*

Head blunt. Very large eyes. Body covered with oblique, strongly keeled scales. Colour varies: juvenile twig-coloured but with bright emerald eyes and white throat. Female drab olive. Male may be mottled in black and gold, or uniform bright green, red or powdery blue. Shy. Diurnal. Hunts chameleons, small birds. Lays up to 25 eggs in summer. Inflates throat in threat, may bite readily. Potent venom may cause death from internal bleeding in 1-3 days. Widespread except dry, treeless w areas.

**5 TWIG SNAKE** *Thelotornis capensis*

Body and tail very thin, elongate. Lance-like head has large eyes with keyhole-shaped pupils. Grey-brown with black and pink flecks and series of diagonal pale blotches. Head uniform green or blue-green (NE), heavily speckled (SE) or with Y-shaped mark (N). Completely arboreal. Eats lizards, frogs, other snakes. Lays 4-18 elongate eggs in summer. Inflates throat in threat. Potent venom may cause death from internal bleeding. N and E.

60-80 cm

60-90 cm

60-75 cm

120-160 cm

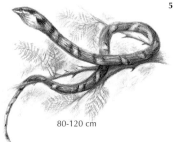

80-120 cm

60-80 cm

35-55 cm

40-70 cm

45-65 cm

50-80 cm

**1   YELLOW-BELLIED SEASNAKE**          *Pelamis platurus*
Soft-skinned body. Bright yellow and black stripes. Lacks large belly scales. Head flat. Tail oar-like with bold yellow spots. Drifts on surface of sea. Catches small fish. 3-5 young born at sea. Venom may cause paralysis, but no deaths reported. Restricted to Indian Ocean. Uncommon along s African coast.

**2   SPOTTED HARLEQUIN SNAKE**      *Homoroselaps lacteus*
Brightly coloured. Small, slender with rounded head and short tail. Two colour phases: patterned in black and yellow with bright red dorsal stripe (w Cape), or black with yellow dot on each scale and yellow dorsal stripe (N). Burrows underground. Eats other snakes, legless lizards. Lays up to six eggs in December. Venom causes pain, but not fatal. Only in South Africa.
**Similar**
**STRIPED HARLEQUIN SNAKE  *H. dorsalis***
Minute. Black with yellow stripe. Highveld and e escarpment.

**3   CORAL SNAKE**                      *Aspidelaps lubricus*
Stocky. Bold black and orange bands (faded bands and dark head in n Namibia). Belly cream with black bands under neck. Head broad with large scale on nose. Hunts lizards, mice. Lays 3-11 eggs in summer. Threatens and puffs with small cobra-like hood. Venom mild but can be serious. Arid W.

**4   SHIELD-NOSE SNAKE**              *Aspidelaps scutatus*
Short, thickset. Large "bulldozer" scale on nose. Scales rough on rear of body. Body tan, speckled with black. Head, neck black with white throat band. In E has faint dorsal blotches. Burrows in loose sand. Hunts mice and frogs at night. Lays up to 12 eggs in summer. Rears like small cobra with very narrow hood. Venom mild but can be serious. N savanna.

**5   SUNDEVALL'S GARTER SNAKE**      *Elapsoidea sundevallii*
Stout body. Slightly pointed snout. Short tail. Scales smooth, glossy. Colour varied: juvenile banded cream, brown and white. Bands persist in adults in S but fade elsewhere to plain slate-grey or black body with pink-buff belly. Slow-moving. Nocturnal. Eats mice, lizards, other snakes. Lays up to 10 small eggs. Venom is mild, causing dizziness, nasal congestion. E areas and n Namibia.
**Similar**
**BOULENGER'S GARTER SNAKE  *E. semiannulata***
Smaller, snout rounded, bands black and white. N savanna.

**1 RINKHALS** *Hemachatus haemachatus*

Large, stout. Wide head. Keeled body scales. Colour varied: juvenile has about 40 black and tan bands. These may persist in some adults (Cape, e areas and Zimbabwe) or fade in others (central highveld). **White throat band present in all.** Nocturnal. Hunts toads, mice in damp grassland. Up to 63 young born in autumn. Shams death if threatened. Can rear and spit venom up to 3 m. Toxic venom is potentially fatal. S and e half of region.

**2 MOZAMBIQUE SPITTING COBRA** *Naja mossambica*

Small. Blunt head. Smooth scales. Body pink-grey to dark olive. Scales black-edged. Belly pinkish, sometimes with black crossbands or blotches on throat. Nocturnal. Eats mice, lizards, frogs. Lays 10-22 eggs in summer. Rears to spread broad hood. Spits and bites readily, causing swelling and skin loss, but fatalities rare. KwaZulu-Natal northwards to Caprivi.

**Similar**

**WESTERN BARRED SPITTING COBRA** *N. nigricollis nigricincta*

Numerous dark bands on grey-pink body. N Namibia.

**BLACK SPITTING COBRA** *N. nigricollis woodi*

Large. All-black. Diurnal. W Cape to s Namibia.

**3 FOREST COBRA** *Naja melanoleuca*

Very large. Slender body. Glossy scales. Head, forebody yellow-brown, heavily speckled black. Tail shiny blue-black. Active at dusk and early evening, usually near water. Eats small vertebrates, including fish. Lays up to 26 large eggs in summer. Rears and spreads narrow hood. Shy but bites readily if cornered. Venom potent neurotoxin leading to death from paralysis if untreated. Forests of n KwaZulu-Natal and e Zimbabwe.

**4 CAPE COBRA** *Naja nivea*

Slender. Broad head. Smooth, dull scales. Juvenile dirty yellow, speckled dark brown, has broad black band on throat. Adult colour varied: usually yellow-brown heavily flecked with dark brown, but may be plain yellow (Kalahari) or dark mahogany (Namaqualand). Black throat band fades with age. Hunts by day. Eats small vertebrates, including snakes. Lays 8-20 large eggs in summer. Rears and spreads broad hood, bites readily but does not spit. Karoo and arid W.

**5 SNOUTED (EGYPTIAN) COBRA** *Naja annulifera*

Thick-bodied. Very broad head. Body scales smooth, dull. Row of small scales between eye and lip. Yellowish-brown, becoming blue-black with age, sometimes with 7-9 broad yellow bands. Belly dull yellow with dark blotches. Juvenile has dark throat band. Nocturnal. Eats small vertebrates. Lays 8-33 large eggs in summer. Rears and spreads broad hood. Bites readily but does not spit. May sham death. Venom potent neurotoxin leading to rapid death from paralysis if untreated. KwaZulu-Natal to Angola.

90-120 cm

90-130 cm

180-210 cm

120-150 cm

150-200 cm

**1**

200-300 cm

**2**

180-220 cm

**3**

40-80 cm

**4**

70-90 cm

**5**

80-120 cm

**1   BLACK MAMBA**               *Dendroaspis polylepis*

Very large, muscular. Scales smooth, dull. Head long, flat-sided (coffin-shaped) with black mouth. Body dirty grey, sometimes olive. Black blotches on pale grey-green belly. Diurnal. Terrestrial but will climb trees. Eats small mammals, birds. Lays 12-18 large eggs in summer. Rears forebody, gapes widely, hisses and spreads very narrow hood in defence. Delivers many quick bites. Venom potent neurotoxin leading to rapid death from paralysis if untreated. N half of region and E coast.

**2   GREEN MAMBA**               *Dendroaspis angusticeps*

Smaller than black mamba, slender. Scales smooth, dull. Head long, flat-sided (coffin-shaped) with white mouth. Body brilliant green with lighter belly. Arboreal, gliding easily through canopy searching for small mammals, birds. Shy, rarely seen. Lays 7-10 eggs in summer. Bites rarely but venom may cause death from paralysis. Restricted to coastal KwaZulu-Natal and e Zimbabwe.

**3   RHOMBIC NIGHT ADDER**            *Causus rhombeatus*

Short, muscular body. Rounded head. Soft, almost smooth scales. Large paired scales on top of head. Body grey-pink. Tail has 20-30 dark, pale-edged, squarish blotches (faded in N). Dark V-shape on head. Nocturnal. Hunts in moist areas for frogs. Lays 15-26 eggs in summer. Mild venom causes swelling and pain. Cape coast to Zimbabwe.
**Similar**
**SNOUTED NIGHT ADDER  C. defilippii**
Snout pointed, upturned. Ne savanna.

**4   PUFF ADDER**                  *Bitis arietans*

Large, thick-bodied. Sluggish. Broad head covered in small scales. Tail very short. Body scales rough. Body yellow-brown to light brown with numerous dark, pale-edged chevrons. Belly pale with scattered blotches. Male brighter than female. Ambushes small mammals. Active at dusk. Up to 30 young born in late summer. May give deep warning hiss. Bites readily. Venom causes swelling and pain, occasionally death. Throughout s Africa.

**5   GABOON ADDER**                *Bitis gabonica*

Very heavy-bodied. Large, triangular head covered in small scales. Pair of horn-like scales on snout. Body has geometric pattern of purple, brown and other pastel colours. Pale head has thin, dark line along crown. Lies camouflaged around bushes. Ambushes small mammals. Up to 43 young born in late summer. Docile, rarely bites. Venom causes massive swelling, can cause limb loss and death. Restricted to NE coast and e Zimbabwe.

**1  BERG ADDER**                    *Bitis atropos*

Small, stout. Very short tail. Elongate head with small scales, no horns. Body scales small, rough. Boldly patterned in grey and blue-black (browner in central areas). Dark arrow-shape on crown. Ambushes frogs, lizards, mice. Up to 15 young born in autumn. Hisses and bites readily. Venom mild, causing drooping eyelids and loss of taste and smell. In mountainous areas from e Zimbabwe to SW.

**Similar**

**DESERT MOUNTAIN ADDER  B. xeropaga**

Buff-grey back. 16-34 dark and light bars. Lower Orange River.

30-45 cm

**2  MANY-HORNED ADDER**              *Bitis cornuta*

Small, stout. Very short tail. Elongate head has small scales, large tuft of 2-4 horns above each eye. Dark marks on crown may form arrowhead-shape. Body scales small, rough. Body boldly blotched in grey-black pattern. 4-10 young born in late summer. Eats small mice, lizards. Bites rare. Venom mild, no deaths reported. Shelters in rocky areas along SW and W coast.

**Similar**

**PLAIN MOUNTAIN ADDER  B. inornata**

Dull brown. No horns. Montane grassland in e Karoo.

30-50 cm

**3  HORNED ADDER**                  *Bitis caudalis*

Small, stout. Very short tail. Elongate head has small scales, single large horn above each eye. Dark V-shape or hourglass-shape on head. Body blotched. Colour varies, matching local ground colour (light grey in Etosha; buff or orange-brown in Kalahari; grey-olive to light brown in Karoo and Northern Province). Belly cream-white, unpatterned. Shuffles into sand at bush base and ambushes small lizards. Up to 27 young born in late summer. Venom mild, no deaths reported. Bites rare. Common in arid W.

25-35 cm

**4  PERINGUEY'S ADDER**            *Bitis peringueyi*

Very small. Very short tail. Elongate head small scales, no horns. Eyes on top of head. Body pale or reddish-brown with faint dark spots. Tail tip may be black. Lives in sand dunes, shuffling into loose sand, leaving only eyes exposed and ambushing small lizards. Up to 10 young born in autumn. Venom very mild, not dangerous. Restricted to Namib desert.

**Similar**

**NAMAQUA DWARF ADDER  B. schneideri**

Very small. Eyes on side of head. Namaqualand and s Namibia.

20-25 cm

**5  SWAMP VIPER**              *Atheris superciliaris*

Medium-sized, robust body. Elongate head. Most head scales small, but large scale above each eye. Body grey-brown with three rows of blackish spots, separated by yellowish bars. Tail yellow-orange below. Hides in rodent burrows, emerging at night to feed on small frogs. Up to eight young born in early summer. Venom causes pain and swelling. Low-lying marshes in Zambezi River floodplain.

40-60 cm

**1**

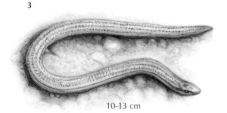

30-45 cm

**2**

16-22 cm

**3**

10-13 cm

**4**

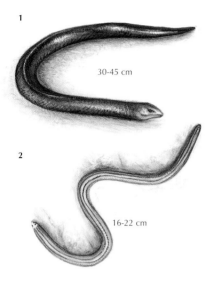

9-10 cm

**5**

8-10 cm

**1   GIANT LEGLESS SKINK**          *Acontias plumbeus*
Very large. Thick body without legs and with short tail. Head broad, elongate. Steel-grey snout. Eyes small with eyelids. Uniform black to dark brown. Burrows in moist leaf litter. Eats worms, insect larvae, burrowing frogs. 2-14 young born in late summer. Lowveld and E coast.
**Similar**
**CAPE LEGLESS SKINK  *A. meleagris***
Golden brown. Speckled in W, striped in E. S Cape.
**STRIPED LEGLESS SKINK  *A. lineatus***
Snout edge spade-like. Fine yellow and black stripes. W Cape to Namibia.

**2   GOLDEN BLIND LEGLESS SKINK**          *Typhlosaurus*
*aurantiacus*
Pencil-thin body. Lacks limbs. Short, blunt tail. Head eyeless with rounded, flattened snout, covered in two strap-like scales. Golden pink in KwaZulu-Natal and Mozambique. Striped or plain black in Mpumalanga and Northern Province. Burrows in sandy soils searching for grubs, termites. 1-3 fully formed young born in late summer.
**Similar**
**STRIPED BLIND LEGLESS SKINK  *T. lineatus***
Slender. Yellow with fine black stripes. Kalahari.
**CUVIER'S BLIND LEGLESS SKINK  *T. caecus***
Very slender. Orange to flesh-coloured. W Cape coastal dunes.

**3   GRONOVI'S DWARF BURROWING SKINK**          *Scelotes*
*gronovii*
Body shiny, silver-grey with vague brown band along backbone. Greyish-white belly often heavily speckled. Almost legless; lacks forelimbs, only single toe on spike-like hindlimbs. Snout flattened. Tail just shorter than body. Burrows. One or two young born in autumn. W Cape coastal dunes.
**Similar**
**ALGOA DWARF BURROWING SKINK  *S. anguina***
Legless. Silvery with dark band along back. Coastal e Cape.

**4   WESTERN DWARF BURROWING SKINK**          *Scelotes*
*capensis*
Slender body covered with smooth, shiny scales. Small limbs each has five toes. Tail long, bright blue. Back olive-brown with coppery sheen; often has lighter stripe on each side. Lives beneath rocks and decaying logs. Restricted to Richtersveld and s Namibia.
**Similar**
**MONTANE DWARF BURROWING SKINK  *S. mirum***
Feet minute. Five toes. Bluish tail speckled. Mpumalanga mountains.

**5   BOUTON'S SKINK**          *Cryptoblepharus boutonii*
Body small, slender. Thin limbs, feet with five toes. Eyes large, snake-like, without eyelids. Scales smooth. Tail tapers to fine point. Back blackish-bronze, pale spots on sides and legs. Hunts small crustaceans and fish among intertidal rocks. Swims readily. One or two eggs laid in sand in summer. Restricted to Black Rocks, Maputaland.

**1  WAHLBERG'S SNAKE-EYED SKINK    *Panaspis wahlbergi***
Slender body covered with smooth scales. Tiny limbs with five toes. Eyes large, snake-like, without eyelids. Tail tapers to fine point. Body grey-bronze, sometimes with six fine dark lines. Breeding male has pinkish-orange belly. Scuttles among grass roots and rotting logs. Feeds on termites, small insects. Lays 2-6 eggs in early summer. E savanna.

**2  SUNDEVALL'S WRITHING SKINK    *Lygosoma sundevallii***
Body fat and shiny, merging into fat, spine-tipped tail. Small, five-toed limbs. Snout flattened. Eyes small with movable eyelids. Bronze body speckled with dark spot on each scale. Burrows under rotting logs and into termite nests. Few eggs laid in summer. Common in n savanna.

**3  WESTERN ROCK SKINK    *Mabuya sulcata***
Graceful, flat, shiny body. Long, thin tail. Female and juvenile olive-brown with six dirty gold stripes. Breeding male jet black with heavily speckled throat, sometimes with dirty bronze on hindbody and tail. 3-5 young born in late summer. Common on rock outcrops in Karoo and Namibia.
**Similar**
**RAINBOW SKINK  *M. quinquitaeniata***
Female and juvenile have blue tail. Male has green body with orange tail. NE.

**4  CAPE SKINK    *Mabuya capensis***
Body very fat with shiny scales. Stubby legs. Long tail. Back light brown with three pale stripes and numerous dark crossbars. Lives in burrows in loose sand beneath rotting logs, etc. Usually 5-18 young born in late summer. Some females lay eggs. Throughout s Africa.
**Similar**
**WESTERN THREE-STRIPED SKINK  *M. occidentalis***
Boldly striped. Earhole with spiny lobes. Karoo and w desert.

**5  STRIPED SKINK    *Mabuya striata***
Thick-bodied. Longish tail. Back dark brown to black with bold white stripes (in E) or numerous small, pale spots (in S and central areas). Breeding male develops yellow-orange throat. 3-9 young born in summer (in S) or throughout year (in N). Widespread except central and w Cape.
**Similar**
**VARIABLE SKINK  *M. varia***
Bright white, dark-edged stripe on side. E savanna.
**VARIEGATED SKINK  *M. variegata***
Back speckled, pale stripe on side. Karoo and Kalahari.

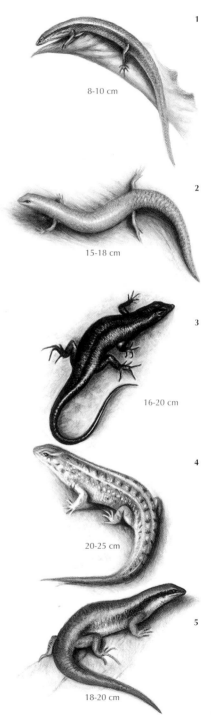

1

8-10 cm

2

15-18 cm

3

16-20 cm

4

20-25 cm

5

18-20 cm

**1**

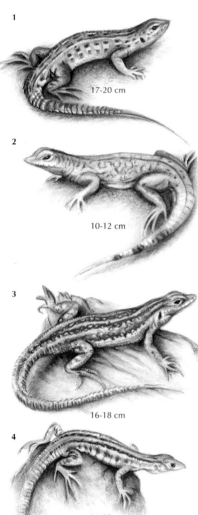

17-20 cm

10-12 cm

**2**

**3**

16-18 cm

**4**

14-17 cm

**5**

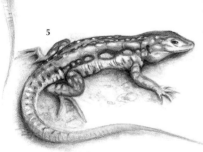

13-17 cm

### 1 COMMON ROUGH-SCALED LIZARD *Ichnotropis squamulosa*

Head small. Body cylindrical, covered in small, strongly keeled scales. Tail just longer than body and tapered. Buff-brown with dark crossbands or blotches and rows of pale spots. Short-lived, laying 8-12 eggs at end of first year and then dying. N and e savanna.
**Similar**
**CAPE ROUGH-SCALED LIZARD *I. capensis***
Black and white stripes on sides. Male has red side stripe and yellow throat. Central areas and N.

### 2 ANCHIETA'S DESERT LIZARD *Meroles anchietae*

Body flattened, with silvery sheen. Black crossbands on tail. Flattened snout with sharp cutting edge. Toes of long hindlimbs have conspicuous fringe. Hunts on slipfaces of sand dunes. Eats insects and plant seeds. Runs quickly and dives into loose sand to hide. Lays one or two large eggs in summer. Central and n Namib dune seas.
**Similar**
**WEDGE-SNOUTED DESERT LIZARD *M. cuneirostris***
Red-orange body with plain tail. S Namib dunes.

### 3 SPOTTED DESERT LIZARD *Meroles suborbitalis*

Body slender. Tail roughly same length as body. Snout rounded. Body scales small, granular. Toes have fringe to aid running on sand. Distinct collar beneath throat. Juvenile boldly striped. Adult matches local soil colour, usually mottled pink-grey to slate, some retaining faint stripes. Hunts small insects on flat, semi-arid gravel plains. Lays 3-7 eggs. Karoo to s Namibia.
**Similar**
**KNOX'S DESERT LIZARD *M. knoxii***
Body has pale spots and faint stripes. W Cape to s Namibia.

### 4 NAMAQUA SAND LIZARD *Pedioplanis namaquensis*

Body slender. Long tail. Granular scales. Distinct collar, faint fold under throat. Juvenile vividly striped, pink-brown tail. Adult cryptically coloured in tans and browns, sometimes with faint stripes, and with orange-brown tail. Very fast, running between bushes on flat, sandy soil. Shelters in burrow dug in loose sand. Lays 3-5 eggs in early summer. Arid W, from Karoo to Angola.
**Similar**
**PLAIN SAND LIZARD *P. inornata***
Plain grey-brown. Lives on rocky flats. N Cape and s Namibia.

### 5 SPOTTED SAND LIZARD *Pedioplanis lineoocellata*

Body slender. Long tail. Distinct collar, faint fold under throat. Black-lined clear "window" in lower eyelid. Juvenile striped. Adult has series of pale blue spots on flanks. Rocky flats, broken ground. Grabs small insects after short dash from shaded cover. Shelters under flat stones. Lays 4-8 eggs in early summer. Throughout s Africa.
**Similar**
**BURCHELL'S SAND LIZARD *P. burchelli***
Tan and brown, lacks spots on flanks. Cape mountain summits.

**1 SOUTHERN ROCK LIZARD** *Australolacerta australis*
Body sleek. Long tail. Granular scales. Well-developed collar. Back dark olive, rows of small pale spots that are bright orange on sides. Forages on rock faces. Locally common but shy. Lays 5-7 eggs in summer. W Cape fold mountains.
**Similar**
**NORTHERN ROCK LIZARD** *A. rupicola*
Reddish-brown back, white stripe on side. Soutpansberg.

**2 COMMON MOUNTAIN LIZARD** *Tropidosaura montana*
Head short. Tail relatively long. Scales spiny, overlapping. Body olive with dark streak along backbone, bordered by pale stripe; pale yellow to bright orange spots on sides. Tail blue-green. Common, but hides in thick cover. Lays 4-5 eggs in summer. S Cape to KwaZulu-Natal.
**Similar**
**CAPE MOUNTAIN LIZARD** *T. gularis*
Bright green, orange spots on sides. Cape fold mountains.

**3 BUSHVELD LIZARD** *Heliobolus lugubris*
Body cylindrical. Well-developed collar. Scales small, keeled. Back grey-tan to red-brown with vague crossbars and three pale stripes. White spots on hindlimbs. Hatchling jet black with three broken yellow-white stripes, sand-coloured tail; mimics distasteful beetles. Lays 4-6 eggs in summer. N savanna.

**4 DELALANDE'S SANDVELD LIZARD** *Nucras lalandii*
Body stout. Head blunt. Tail thick and easily shed, almost twice body length and used as fat store. Back olive-grey with 8-10 rows of white, black-edged spots. Lives in underground burrow, emerging rarely to eat insects and flying termites. Lays 4-9 eggs in summer. E Cape and grassland in NW and N.
**Similar**
**SPOTTED SANDVELD LIZARD** *N. intertexta*
Light brown with white, black-edged spots. Central savanna.

**5 STRIPED SANDVELD LIZARD** *Nucras tessellata*
Elegant with very long tail. Bright black and white bars on sides, merging to bright red on hindlimbs and tail. **Four thin dark stripes along backbone.** Digs up scorpions, large beetles. Shelters under stones. Lays 3-4 eggs in summer. Succulent Karoo and s Namibia.
**Similar**
**KAROO SANDVELD LIZARD** *N. livida*
Six lines along backbone. Tail brown. S and Little Karoo.

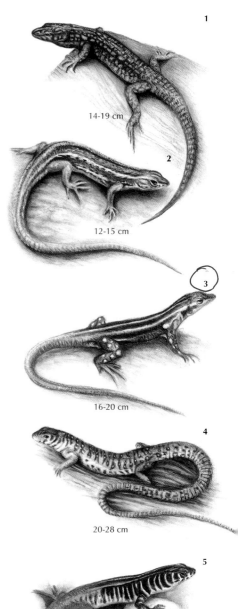

14-19 cm

2

12-15 cm

3

16-20 cm

4

20-28 cm

5

20-25 cm

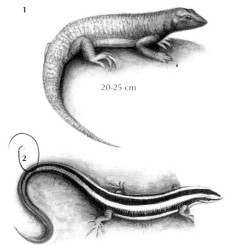

20-25 cm

12-14 cm

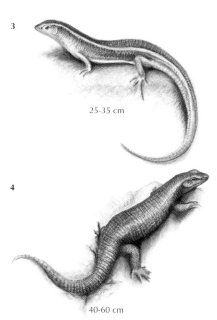

25-35 cm

40-60 cm

18-24 cm

**1   DESERT PLATED LIZARD**   *Angolosaurus skoogi*

Large. Spade-like snout. Tapering, short tail only slightly longer than body. Fold alongside belly. Covered in squarish scales. Adult ivory-coloured with scattered maroon blotches. Juvenile sand-coloured. Chin, throat, lower chest black. Eats windblown insects, dry plant debris. "Swims" into loose sand to sleep and hide. Lays 2-4 large eggs in autumn. N Namib desert dune seas.

**2   DWARF PLATED LIZARD**   *Cordylosaurus subtessellatus*

Small, elegant. Long, bright blue tail. Striped body. Covered in squarish scales. Fold along side. Forages among rocks, hunting small insects. When threatened, wriggles among stones. Readily sheds tail. Lays 2-3 eggs in summer. Succulent Karoo through Namibia to Angola.

**3   YELLOW-THROATED PLATED LIZARD**   *Gerrhosaurus flavigularis*

Large. Body covered in squarish scales. Fold along side. Head small. Tail very long, easily shed. Two bright yellow, dark-edged stripes on sides. Breeding male has bright red throat (sometimes blue). Shelters in burrow at base of bush. Lays 4-6 eggs in summer. E areas from Cape to Zambezi.
**Similar**
**KALAHARI PLATED LIZARD** *G. multilineatus*
Body brown, speckled. Throat, flanks blue. Kalahari.

**4   GIANT PLATED LIZARD**   *Gerrhosaurus validus*

Very large. Body flattened, covered in small, squarish scales. Fold along side. Juvenile black with yellow spots on back and bars on sides, which fade to streaks in adult. Breeding male has pink flush to head. Shy. Lives on koppies. Eats large insects, flowers, soft fruit, leaves. Lays up to five large eggs in summer. N of South Africa into Zimbabwe; also n Namibia.
**Similar**
**ROUGH-SCALED PLATED LIZARD** *G. major*
Body rounded. Light brown. Scales large, rough. Ne bushveld.

**5   COMMON LONG-TAILED SEPS**   *Tetradactylus tetradactylus*

Body thin, short. Long snake-like tail (three times body length). Only four toes on each of very small limbs. Back olive, dark brown stripe on each side, black and white bars on side of neck. Hunts small insects, grasshoppers, in montane grassland or fynbos. Lays 3-5 eggs in summer. S and e Cape.
**Similar**
**SHORT-LEGGED SEPS** *T. seps*
Long tail. Small, fully formed limbs. S Cape to KwaZulu-Natal.

**1 CAPE GIRDLED LIZARD** *Cordylus cordylus*

Body flattened, girdled with rows of spiny scales. Head flat, wide. Tail hard, spiny. Mottled brown, often with pale dorsal stripe. Shelters in rock cracks, using spiny tail to protect head. 1-3 live young born in autumn. Common in s Cape coastal and escarpment mountains.

**Similar**

**TRANSVAAL GIRDLED LIZARD** *C. vittifer*
Orange-red. Elongate scales behind head. Highveld rock outcrops.

**TROPICAL GIRDLED LIZARD** *C. tropidosternum*
Lichen-coloured. Arboreal. Scales rough. N bushveld.

**BLUE-SPOTTED GIRDLED LIZARD** *C. coeruleopunctatus*
Body black with blue spots. Fine scales. S Cape coast.

**2 KAROO GIRDLED LIZARD** *Cordylus polyzonus*

Head flat, wide. Body has numerous narrow girdles. Tail spiny, hard. Colour varies: tan, dark brown or orange. Juveniles and some adults blotched. Black blotch on side of neck. Lives in cracks in shattered boulders, on which it basks. 2-3 young born in autumn. Karoo and arid W.

**3 WARREN'S GIRDLED LIZARD** *Cordylus warreni*

Large. Dark, spiny back spotted and barred yellow. Tail spiny. Small, scattered groups on rocky mountain slopes. Shy; favours deep cracks in shaded boulders. Hunts insects, snails, even small lizards. 2-6 young born in late summer. E escarpment mountains from Zimbabwe to Swaziland.

**4 GIANT GIRDLED LIZARD** *Cordylus giganteus*

Large. Broad head fringed behind with four large spines. Plump body heavily spined. Tail thorny. Terrestrial, living in long burrows in grassland. Basks on termite nest facing into sun. Long-lived, but endangered by habitat destruction and illegal collecting. S highveld.

**5 ARMADILLO GIRDLED LIZARD** *Cordylus cataphractus*

Body thickset, flattened. Head broad, armoured. Girdles strongly keeled, often irregular. Tail very spiny. Back golden. Throat, belly usually blotched. Inhabits large cracks in low rock outcrops. Rolls into ball like hedgehog when threatened. Endangered by illegal collecting. W Karoo and Namaqualand.

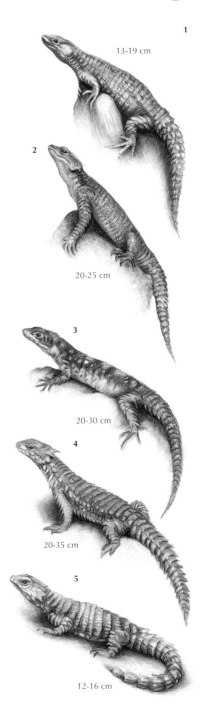

1    13-19 cm

2    20-25 cm

3    20-30 cm

4    20-35 cm

5    12-16 cm

35-40 cm

18-22 cm

25-30 cm

18-21 cm

17-21 cm

## 1  CAPE GRASS LIZARD          *Chamaesaura anguina*

Tan and brown. Body elongate. Limbs minute, spike-like, with only one or two claws. Scales rough. Tail snake-like, 3-4 times body length, easily shed. Hunts grasshoppers, other insects in grassland. Few young born in late summer. S Cape and e escarpment.

**Similar**

**TRANSVAAL GRASS LIZARD** *C. aenea*

Minute feet each with five toes. Boldly striped. E grassland.

## 2  GRACEFUL CRAG LIZARD          *Pseudocordylus capensis*

Body flat. Scales large and squarish on back and belly, but granular on sides. Tail tapering, not spiny. Hindlegs long with slender toes. Back grey-black, with pale yellow streaks on head. Shy; runs quickly over vertical rock faces. Eats insects, particularly bees, wasps. Two or three young born in autumn. Summits of Cape fold mountains.

## 3  CAPE CRAG LIZARD          *Pseudocordylus microlepidotus*

Heavy body. Head broad with strong jaws. Large scales on back and belly, but granular on sides. Breeding male has brightly barred body (orange in E, yellow inland). Juvenile and female drab with yellow and grey-brown bars. Inhabits large rock cracks, dashing out to catch beetles, grasshoppers. 2-6 young born in late summer. Cape coastal and escarpment mountains.

**Similar**

**DRAKENSBERG CRAG LIZARD** *P. melanotus*

Female green-grey, blotched. Male dark with orange sides. E escarpment.

## 4  CAPE FLAT LIZARD          *Platysaurus capensis*

Body very flat, covered in granular scales. Head flat, triangular. Scattered spines on legs. Tail tapered, spiny on sides. Female and juvenile black with three pale stripes. Breeding male has brilliant colours: back, belly bright blue, limbs sometimes yellow, tail coral red. Shelters beneath thin rock flakes. Lays two eggs in summer. Forms dense colonies on granite rocks of lower Orange River.

## 5  COMMON FLAT LIZARD          *Platysaurus intermedius*

Body very flat, covered in granular scales. Head flat, triangular. Scattered spines on sides of neck and legs. Tail tapered, spiny on sides. Breeding male mainly green with orange tail. Head varies from black to green. Female and juvenile black with three pale stripes. Lays two egg clutches during summer. Rock koppies of e escarpment and Zimbabwe.

**Similar**

**EASTERN FLAT LIZARD** *P. orientalis*

Male dark green, tail red. N Drakensberg.

**NATAL FLAT LIZARD** *P. natalensis*

Male has green back and throat, orange tail. N KwaZulu-Natal.

**LEBOMBO FLAT LIZARD** *P. lebomboensis*

Male black, tail and sides brick-red. Lebombo mountains, Swaziland.

**SOUTHERN ROCK AGAMA**      *Agama atra*

Body plump, covered in granules and scattered spines. Head broad with rounded snout, wide mouth, small scales. Tail tapering, cannot be shed. Crest along backbone (larger and extends onto tail in N). Forms small colonies on rock outcrops. Breeding male has bright blue head. Female, juvenile drabber. Lays 7-12 eggs in summer. Cape and adjacent regions.
Similar
**ANCHIETA'S AGAMA**   *A. anchietae*
Smaller. Black-tipped scales on soles. N Cape and Namibia.

**GROUND AGAMA**      *Agama aculeata*

Typical agama body shape. Earhole relatively large. Throat has central network of markings. Regular rows of enlarged spines on back. Body cryptically blotched in browns. Breeding male bluish head. Terrestrial, basking in low bushes, feeding on ants. Shy, solitary. Lays 10-18 eggs in hole in summer. Widespread in savanna and semi-arid areas.

**SPINY AGAMA**      *Agama hispida*

Very similar to ground agama. Earhole smaller and throat dark with irregular pale blotches. Cryptic, except breeding male (vivid, metallic yellow-green). Terrestrial; male displays from boulder. Shy, runs into burrow when disturbed. Lays 10-15 eggs in summer. Karoo and Namaqualand.

**NAMIBIAN ROCK AGAMA**      *Agama planiceps*

Graceful, long-tailed. Hindlegs long, head small. Juvenile and female grey to olive with pale blotches, bright orange shoulder blotch and paired lemon blotches on dark head. Breeding male has metallic dull blue-purple sheen, orange-red head, neck and throat. Tail olive-yellow at base, coral red at tip. Lives in colonies on rock outcrops in n Namibia.

**TREE AGAMA**      *Acanthocerus atricollis*

Very large. Body plump, covered in spiny scales. Large black spot on shoulder. Female, juvenile lichen-coloured. Breeding male develops bright ultramarine head. Clambers on tree trunks, nodding head in display. Will threaten with open mouth showing bright orange lining. Feeds mainly on insects. Lays 4-14 eggs in hole in ground in summer. Common in e bushveld.

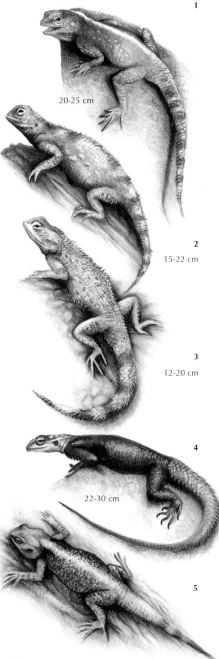

1

20-25 cm

2

15-22 cm

3

12-20 cm

4

22-30 cm

5

20-35 cm

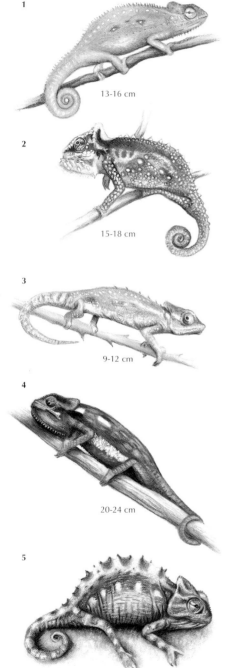

**1**

13-16 cm

**2**

15-18 cm

**3**

9-12 cm

**4**

20-24 cm

**5**

18-22 cm

**1   CAPE DWARF CHAMELEON**   *Bradypodion pumilum*

Head extends behind into scaly casque. Throat has crest of non-overlapping spines. Prehensile tail longer than body. Body lea green, usually with orange-red strip on side. Catches insects wit long, telescopic tongue. 6-10 live young born in bushes. Sw Cape.

**Similar**

**KNYSNA DWARF CHAMELEON   *B. damaranum***

Tail much longer than body. Large, narrow casque. S Cape forests.

**2   NATAL MIDLANDS DWARF CHAMELEON**   *Bradypodion thamnobates*

Head with large, recurved casque. Throat crest of long, overlapping scaly flaps. Crest extends along backbone onto tail. Body mottled, but in display becomes dark blue-green with cream o red-brown lateral patch. Aggressive, threatens other chameleons. Gives birth to up to 30 young in summer. Central KwaZulu-Natal thickets.

**Similar**

**DRAKENSBERG DWARF CHAMELEON   *B. dracomontanum***

Casque large. Throat crest small. Drakensberg kloof forests.

**SOUTHERN DWARF CHAMELEON   *B. ventrale***

Throat crest large, scales overlapping. Tail short. E Cape thickets.

**3   SETARO'S DWARF CHAMELEON**   *Bradypodion setaro*

Very small. Head has narrow, well-developed casque. Throat crest reduced to small spines. Prehensile tail longer than body in male, shorter in female. Body light grey-brown. Throat light gree with white grooves. Up to seven minute young born in summer N KwaZulu-Natal low coastal dune forest.

**Similar**

**SMITH'S DWARF CHAMELEON   *B. taeniabronchum***

Casque small. Throat grooves black. E Cape fynbos.

**4   FLAP-NECKED CHAMELEON**   *Chamaeleo dilepis*

Large chameleon, large skin flaps behind head. Throat crest c small, white scales extends onto belly. Body varies from green t pale yellow or brown, sometimes speckled. In defence gape mouth to reveal orange lining, flattens body and rocks from side to side. Lays up to 57 small eggs in summer that may take nine months to hatch. N savanna and bushveld.

**5   NAMAQUA CHAMELEON**   *Chamaeleo namaquensi*

Bulky, short-tailed, terrestrial. Head large with powerful jaws Casque small. Series of 12-14 large knobs along backbone. Eat large numbers of grasshoppers, beetles, even lizards and snakes Lives in hot deserts and along seashore. Breeds throughout yea laying several clutches of 20 eggs in sand burrow. Arid W.

**1   KAROO FLAT GECKO**          *Afroedura karroica*

Head flat. Large eyes. Depressed body covered in soft, granular skin. Three pairs of pads beneath each toe. Tail segmented. Golden tan, with darker blotches and cream belly. Lays two hard-shelled eggs beneath sun-warmed rock. Communal nest sites may contain hundreds of eggs. Nocturnal, sheltering under rock flakes on large sandstone outcrops in montane grassland of e Cape.
**Similar**
**HAWEQUA FLAT GECKO  A. hawequensis**
Large. Stout body boldly marked. Sw Cape mountains.
**TRANSVAAL FLAT GECKO  A. transvaalica**
Dull brown. Two pairs of pads on each toe. Limpopo valley and e Zimbabwe.

**2   TROPICAL HOUSE GECKO**      *Hemidactylus mabouia*

Head flat. Large eyes. Flattened body covered in soft, granular skin with 10-18 rows of tubercles on back. Toes large, tips flared with paired pads and large claws. Body pale grey with 4-5 wavy, dark crossbars that fade in light. Lays two hard-shelled eggs. Nocturnal, common around house lights in lowveld and warm e coastal areas.
**Similar**
**TASMAN'S HOUSE GECKO  H. tasmani**
Large (15 cm). Bold colour and tubercles. Rock outcrops in central Zimbabwe.

**3   MARBLED LEAF-TOED GECKO** *Phyllodactylus porphyreus*

Body, head flat. Skin smooth, granular. Tail round, unsegmented. Toe tips flared with single pair of pads. Back marbled grey, sometimes with pale dorsal stripe. Nocturnal, sheltering under bark, in rock cracks or houses. Social, up to 20 may share same retreat. S Cape coastal regions.
**Similar**
**STRIPED LEAF-TOED GECKO  P. lineatus**
Tiny. Terrestrial. Grey with dark stripes. W Cape valleys.

**4   CAPE DWARF DAY GECKO**      *Lygodactylus capensis*

Tiny. Rounded body with granular skin. Tiny inner toe; other toes have dilated tips, large claws and paired, oblique pads. Body grey-brown with dark streak from snout to shoulder that may continue as pale lateral stripe. Active by day, feeding on ants, termites. Lays many two-egg clutches. Communal eggs sites common. E.

**5   COMMON BARKING GECKO**      *Ptenopus garrulus*

Small. Body round. Tail short, smooth. Short, rounded head with bulging eyes. Stubby, fringed toes without adhesive pads. Body reddish-brown to greyish-yellow with fine speckles or black crossbars. Breeding male has yellow throat. Digs branched burrows in firm sand at base of a bush. Male calls "ceek, ceek, ceek ..." at entrance at sunset. Arid W.

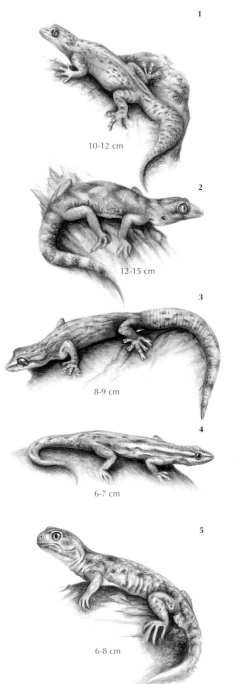

1

10-12 cm

2

12-15 cm

3

8-9 cm

4

6-7 cm

5

6-8 cm

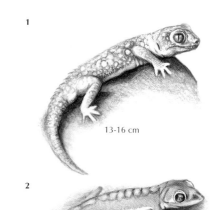

13-16 cm

10-12 cm

14-18 cm

15-19 cm

8-10 cm

### 1 GIANT GROUND GECKO *Chondrodactylus angulifer*

Body stout, cylindrical. Head large, short-snouted, with large eyes. Feet hand-like, short toes lack pads. Tail segmented, with rings of enlarged tubercles. Back pale orange to red-brown, sometimes with pale, dark-edged chevrons. Shelters in burrow, emerging at night to catch insects. When alarmed walks stiff-legged, tail held scorpion-like. Gravel plains, sandy flats of Namib and Karoo.

### 2 WEB-FOOTED GECKO *Palmatogecko rangei*

Body slender, semi-transparent. Flat head, swollen nostrils, large, jewel-like eyes. Thin feet, webbed toes, short, unsegmented tail. Back flesh-pink with dark reticulation, belly white. Spends day in tunnel dug in fine sand, emerging at night to feed on crickets, spiders. Clutches of two large, hard-shelled eggs laid November to March. Wind-blown sands of Namib desert.

### 3 WAHLBERG'S VELVET GECKO *Homopholis wahlbergi*

Body large, soft-skinned. Robust head and limbs. Toes dilated with 8-12 large, unpaired pads and small claws. Back soft grey colour, male with pair of broad, black stripes on back. Belly dirty cream, sometimes flecked. Nocturnal. Arboreal, sheltering under bark or in hollow logs. Lays pairs of large, white eggs in rock cracks or under bark. E savanna.

### 4 BIBRON'S GECKO *Pachydactylus bibronii*

Large. Body stout. Triangular head with powerful jaws. Skin rough with numerous keeled tubercles. Tail segmented with whorls of spiny scales. Back grey with white spots and 4-5 indistinct dark crossbands (more distinct in juvenile). Nocturnal. Lives mainly among rocks but also enters houses. Forms large colonies. Bite painful but not toxic. Widespread.
**Similar**
**SPOTTED GECKO** *P. maculatus*
Small (8-10 cm). Pale grey with black spots. S Cape to Swaziland.
**MARICO GECKO** *P. mariquensis*
Slender, thin-legged. Smooth. Karoo and s Namibia.

### 5 NAMIB DAY GECKO *Rhoptropus afer*

Small, long-legged. Long toes (inner toe minute) with flared tips, each with single pad. Back smooth with granular skin. Dappled grey but lower surfaces of legs, tail and throat bright yellow. Territorial, signalling to each other by lifting tail to reveal bright colour. Diurnal, darting between boulders, eating ants, small beetles. Lays two hard-shelled eggs in rock crack. Rocky Namib plains.
**Similar**
**BARNARD'S DAY GECKO** *R. barnardi*
Reddish without yellow underparts. Semi-desert, n Namibia.

## 1 ROCK MONITOR — *Varanus albigularis*

Nose bulbous. Tail only as long as body. Head, body covered in small bead-like scales. Mottled in tan and black, but dulled with dust and old skin. Roams rocky semi-desert looking for insects, millipedes, anything edible. 20-40 eggs laid in hole in spring. Will bite, but is not poisonous. Tail used as whip. Widespread except w Cape and Namib desert.

## 2 WATER MONITOR — *Varanus niloticus*

Largest African lizard. Head elongate. Flattened tail longer than body. Head, body covered in small bead-like scales. Blotched black and yellow; juvenile brighter than adult. Forages along rivers and pans for crabs, frogs, etc. 20-60 eggs laid in termite nest, hatching 4-6 months later. Widespread except w Cape and most of Namibia.

## 3 KALAHARI ROUND-HEADED WORM LIZARD — *Zygaspis quadrifrons*

Body worm-like with rounded head. Uniform purple-brown above, belly lighter. Burrows in sandy scrub and bushveld, feeding on small insects, larvae. Zimbabwe, Botswana and adjacent Namibia.

**Similar**

**VIOLET ROUND-HEADED WORM LIZARD** *Z. violacea*
Dark purple-brown. S Mozambique.

## 4 CAPE SPADE-SNOUTED WORM LIZARD — *Monopelis capensis*

Body pink, worm-like. Head with "thumb-nail" cutting edge used to dig deep tunnels. 4-6 enlarged, elongate scales on throat. Burrows in deep sand for insect grubs. Seen only during excavations or when floods push it to surface. Up to three young born in late summer. S Kalahari, along Limpopo River to Zimbabwe and s Mozambique.

**Similar**

**ANGOLAN SPADE-SNOUTED WORM LIZARD** *M. anchietae*
Body thick. Purple-brown. N Namibia and Botswana.

## 5 NILE CROCODILE — *Crocodylus niloticus*

Large. Long tail has two raised keels. Hindfeet webbed. Eyes and halved nostrils on top of head. Adult dull olive with cream belly. Hatchling has black markings and straw-yellow belly. 20-80 eggs laid in hole in sandbank. Parents protect nest, hatchlings. Young eat insects, frogs. Adult ambushes mammals, birds, fish. Almost extinct outside reserves. Restricted to N and E.

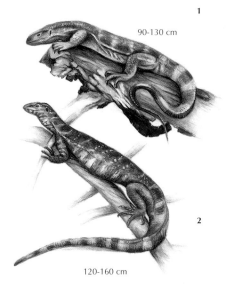

1

90-130 cm

120-160 cm

2

3

16-20 cm

4

25-30 cm

5

250-350 cm

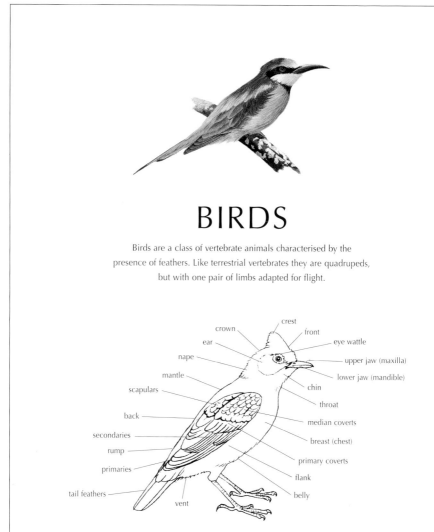

# BIRDS

Birds are a class of vertebrate animals characterised by the
presence of feathers. Like terrestrial vertebrates they are quadrupeds,
but with one pair of limbs adapted for flight.

The bill is characteristic of what the bird eats and thus helps with identification. Similarly the legs and feet are indicators of the habitat and habits of the bird.

Other important features that aid identification are wattles, eye-rings and unfeathered facial skin.

Colour of plumage is a clear factor in identification. Technical reference to types of feathers has been kept to a minimum but certain basic terms have been unavoidable and are shown in the accompanying illustration.

## Scope of this chapter

Over 900 birds are found in southern Africa, of which 620 are covered in this chapter. Birds that are seldom seen because of their habits, or are rare, have been excluded (although some rarities such as the blue swallow are described because of the widespread public concern for their survival).

## Distribution

Most species of birds are closely associated with their preferred habitats (see map on p. 3), which are important when trying to identify particular birds. The main habitat types are:

**Coastal bush**. Typical birds are doves, louries, barbets, bulbuls, robins, shrikes, flycatchers and sunbirds.
**Indigenous forest**. Birdlife is similar to that of coastal bush but may include different species such as bush shrikes, and raptors such as the crowned eagle and African goshawk.
**Bushveld**. Birdlife is very rich, typical birds being drongoes, cuckoos, kingfishers, woodhoopoes, bee-eaters, woodpeckers, hornbills and numerous raptors.
**Grassland**. Francolins, korhaans, cisticolas, larks and pipits are common. In montane grassland cold winters and wind keep vegetation sparse and stunted. Birdlife here includes specialised species such as rockjumpers, rock thrushes and chats. Larger birds are bearded and Cape vultures, black eagles and jackal buzzards.
**Semi-desert and desert**. Terrestrial birds such as larks, sandgrouse and bustards are common, with some species being very localised in their distribution.
**Fynbos**. Some endemic species, including sugarbirds, sunbirds and canaries, are common.
**Wetlands**. Varying in size and vegetation, wetlands are generally prolific in birdlife. Waders, ducks and other waterfowl congregate here and the presence of reedbeds attracts bishops and weavers.
**Artificial habitats**. These are playing an increasing role in the distribution of birds. Mature suburban gardens simulate inland woodland and attract a wide range of species. Man-made dams and ponds are more numerous in some inland areas than natural wetlands, and are rich in waterbirds.

## Migration

About 150 species of birds migrate to this region for the southern African summer months. The majority, e.g. the European swallow and white stork, come from the northern hemisphere where many of them breed. Others, e.g. the flamingoes, come from no further than central Africa. Still others, e.g. the striped swallows, breed here in summer and migrate some distance north into Africa for a few months in winter.

In addition to the long-distance migrants, many species migrate seasonally within the region, generally between high and low altitudes.

Different migrant species appear to use different navigational techniques. Some fly by night and navigate by the stars, others use the sun, and yet others seem able to utilise the earth's magnetic field.

## Status of birds

The following terms are used in the descriptions:

Resident: a bird that stays in the region all year and breeds here
Visitor: a bird that spends one season (usually summer) here but does not breed
Summer/winter resident: a bird that spends only the particular season here but breeds in that time

## Reproduction and development

A great many birds are territorial, and males proclaim and defend their breeding territories by means of song and posturing. These songs are often highly distinctive and provide a useful means of identifying the bird. Males and females also indulge in a variety of courtship rituals such as the presentation of food or nesting material to their mate, aerial display and posturing. Most species construct nests in which to incubate their eggs and rear their young. Some, e.g. the cuckoos and whydahs, lay their eggs in the nests of other species, leaving the unsuspecting host to rear the chick or brood.

## Dimensions

The dimensions given for the birds in this chapter refer to the total length from the tip of the bill to the end of the tail with the bird extended, as when laid out on a table.

63 cm

80-95 cm

51 cm

46-53 cm

16-19 cm

**1   JACKASS PENGUIN**              *Spheniscus demersus*
Black and white facial pattern. White underparts with **encircling black bar.** Call: donkey-like braying. Singly or in groups in coastal waters, or large concentrations on offshore islands. W and S coasts. Resident.

**2   BLACKBROWED ALBATROSS**        *Diomedea melanophris*
**Adult has all-yellow, pink-tipped bill.** Immature has grey bill with dark tip. Huge, narrow-winged pelagic seabird. Glides close to water's surface. Most common albatross in Cape waters. Entire s African coastline. Visitor throughout year but mainly winter.
**Similar**
**YELLOWNOSED ALBATROSS  *D. chlororhynchos***
Yellow confined to upper bill. Common in winter off E coast.
**WANDERING ALBATROSS  *D. exulans***
White face, black markings on tail. Uncommon.
**SHY ALBATROSS  *D. cauta***
Very narrow black borders under wings. Seen mainly in winter.

**3   WHITECHINNED PETREL**          *Procellaria aequinoctialis*
**Pale greenish bill.** White chin variable. Dark, large, long-winged pelagic bird. Stiff-winged flight. Gregarious in large numbers around trawlers. Entire coastline. Visitor.
**Similar**
**NORTHERN GIANT PETREL  *Macronectes halli***
Massive flesh-yellow bill with dark tip.
**SOUTHERN GIANT PETREL  *Macronectes giganteus***
Pale flesh-coloured bill with greenish tip.
**PINTADO PETREL  *Daption capense***
Pied, two white patches on each upperwing.

**4   SOOTY SHEARWATER**             *Puffinus griseus*
Long thin bill, sooty-brown body with conspicuous **pale areas on underwings.** Short rounded tail. Feeds in mixed flocks, sometimes in thousands. Seen close inshore in Cape waters but occurs on entire coastline. Visitor, mainly in winter.
**Similar**
**GREAT SHEARWATER  *P. gravis***
Distinctive black cap, white collar, dark smudges on belly.
**CORY'S SHEARWATER  *Calonectris diomedea***
Yellow bill. No cap. Laboured flight.

**5   WILSON'S STORM PETREL**        *Oceanites oceanicus*
**Broad, rounded wings, uniformly dark underwing pattern.** White rump. Long, spindly legs projecting beyond square tail. Yellow webbed feet, although difficult to detect. Flight action swallow-like. All pelagic waters; usually seen only far out at sea. All-year visitor.
**Similar**
**EUROPEAN STORM PETREL  *Hydrobates pelagicus***
Pointed wings with white stripe below. Legs not projecting beyond tail.

**CAPE GANNET**                  *Morus capensis*

Distinctive black lines on bill and face, plus **long black line** down centre of throat. Large black and white seabird with yellow head and hindneck. Offshore, singly or in straggling groups. Large flocks over fish shoals, with individuals plunge-diving repeatedly. Roosts colonially. Entire s African coastline. Resident.

**GREYHEADED GULL**           *Larus cirrocephalus*

**All-grey hood, pale yellow eyes, red bill and legs.** Immature has white head. Scavenger. Call: loud scream while feeding. Small and large flocks at large inland waters and coast. Widespread except w interior. Resident.
Similar
**HARTLAUB'S GULL   *L. hartlaubii***
White head, dark eyes, deep red bill and legs. W coast.

**KELP GULL**                 *Larus dominicanus*

**Yellow bill with red spot. Dark eyes. Whitish-yellow feet.** Immature mottled dark brown, pale rump; becomes paler with age. Call: harsh "ki-ok". Coastal waters including estuaries and dumps, singly or in small groups. Entire coast. Common resident.

**AFRICAN SKIMMER**        *Rynchops flavirostris*

**Red bill with distinct structure.** Brown and white tern-like body. Feeding action diagnostic: flies low over water with long lower mandible skimming below surface. On large, permanent rivers and lakes. Rests on sandbanks. Okavango, Zambezi and Chobe. Summer resident.

**CASPIAN TERN**           *Hydropogne caspia*

**Massive red bill. Black cap.** Largest tern in s Africa. Deeply forked tail. Agile flight. Call: grating "kraak". Estuaries, lagoons, inland waters. Entire coastline and large inland waters. Resident.
Similar
**SANDWICH TERN   *Sterna sandvicensis***
Long, thin black bill with yellow tip. Summer visitor.
**SWIFT TERN   *Sterna bergii***
Yellow bill. Intermediate size. Resident.
**COMMON TERN   *Sterna hirundo***
Red bill has black tip in breeding plumage. In thousands offshore. Summer visitor.

**WHISKERED TERN**        *Chlidonias hybridus*

**Heavy red bill in breeding plumage**, otherwise black as in other marsh terns. Black cap. Pale grey rump. Call: repeated, hard "zizz". In small numbers at various open freshwater bodies. Widespread. Resident.
Similar
**WHITEWINGED TERN   *C. leucopterus***
Black underwing coverts when breeding. Non-breeding bird has white rump. Summer visitor.

1

84-94 cm

2

42 cm

3

60 cm

4

38 cm

5

52 cm

6

23 cm

**BIRDS**

180 cm

60 cm

♂

♀

90 cm

4

79 cm

41 cm

43 cm

**1   WHITE PELICAN**                    *Pelecanus onocrotalu*
**Bill pink with blue-grey sides and yellowish pouch.** All-white
appearance. During breeding head, neck and body show pale
pink flush. In flocks on coastal islands, estuaries, lagoons, large
inland waters. Often associates with pinkbacked pelican. W, NW
and E. Resident.
**Similar**
**PINKBACKED PELICAN** *P. rufescens*
Pinkish-grey wings. Pale yellow bill with grey pouch.

**2   REED CORMORANT**                *Phalacrocorax africanu*
Yellow bill. Red eyes. Yellow to red facial skin. Male has small
crest. Black with **brown-speckled wings.** Female blotched brown
and off-white below. Singly or in groups on **inland** waters. Wide
spread. Resident.
**Similar**
**BANK CORMORANT** *P. neglectus*
Black with white rump. Crested head. Stocky. W coast.
**CROWNED CORMORANT** *P. coronatus*
All-black. Crested head. Short tail. W coast.
**CAPE CORMORANT** *P. capensis*
Black. No crest. Short tail. Flies over sea in long lines. Almos
entire coast.

**3   WHITEBREASTED CORMORANT**      *Phalacrocorax carbo*
Bright yellow patch at bill base, **white throat and breast,** body
glossy black. Largest cormorant in s Africa. Coastal habitats, large
inland waters. Often perches or nests in dead trees. Roosts and
breeds colonially. Widespread. Resident.

**4   DARTER**                              *Anhinga melanogaste*
**Pointed bill (not hooked),** slender head, long thin neck with characteristic kink, rufous colouring. Call: croak. Inland waters, singly
or in small groups. Swims with body submerged, only head and
neck showing. Perches with outspread wings after swimming.
Widespread. Resident.

**5   GREENBACKED HERON**                *Butorides rufiventri*
Crown black, sides of neck and flanks grey, **upperparts appear**
**grey-green,** feather edges creamy. Call: sharp "kaaek". Wooded
rivers, dams, estuaries, mangrove stands. Singly, during day, hunt-
ing from low perch above water or on shoreline. NE. Resident.
**Similar**
**DWARF BITTERN** *Ixobrychus sturmii*
Slate grey upperparts, heavily streaked underparts. Summer resi-
dent.
**LITTLE BITTERN** *Ixobrychus minutus*
Black cap and upper mandible. Rufous neck and underparts.

**6   SQUACCO HERON**                      *Ardeola ralloide*
Yellowish bill, black culmen, **pale buffy plumage and pale yellow**
**legs.** Lakes, lagoons, streams. Solitary. N and E. Resident or summer visitor.

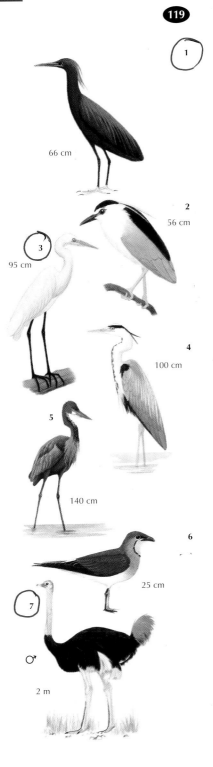

**1   BLACK EGRET**                    *Egretta ardesiaca*

**Overall slaty plumage**, black legs, yellow feet. Lakes, lagoons, floodpans. Singly or in small groups. **Forms canopy with wings when fishing.** N, central and E. Resident.

**2   BLACKCROWNED NIGHT HERON**     *Nycticorax nycticorax*

**Red eyes, black bill, cap and back**, contrasting with grey wings and underparts. River backwaters, lagoons, dams. Singly. Nocturnal, roosts by day in trees or waterside vegetation. Widespread except w and central areas. Nomadic resident.

**3   GREAT WHITE HERON**             *Casmerodius albus*

Orange-yellow bill (black for short period when breeding), yellow eyes, white plumage. Long neck, **long black legs**, black feet. Rivers, dams, estuaries, floodpans. Singly. Stands motionless for long periods in shallows. N, E and S. Resident.

**Similar**

**LITTLE EGRET  *Egretta garzetta***
Long black bill and legs. Yellow feet. Always has head plumes.

**YELLOWBILLED EGRET  *E. intermedia***
Bill yellow. Upper legs yellow. Lower legs and feet dark green.

**CATTLE EGRET  *Bubulcus ibis***
Short yellow bill and legs. Brown feet.

**4   GREY HERON**                    *Ardea cinerea*

Yellow bill. White head and neck. Black eye stripe. Pale yellow legs. **Grey underwings.** Call: loud "kraaunk". Dams, rivers, lagoons. Solitary. Stands motionless in shallows or creeps forward in hunched position. Throughout s Africa. Resident.

**Similar**

**BLACKHEADED HERON  *A. melanocephala***
Black-topped head and hindneck, white throat. Grasslands.

**5   GOLIATH HERON**                 *Ardea goliath*

**Robust. Rufous head and neck.** Grey above, underparts rufous. Call: harsh "kraauk". Rivers, dams, estuaries. Singly or in pairs, standing motionless or walking slowly. Slow, heavy wingbeats. Central and n areas. Resident.

**Similar**

**PURPLE HERON  *A. purpurea***
Slender, thin neck and bill. Solitary, secretive.

**6   REDWINGED PRATINCOLE**          *Glareola pratincola*

Short decurved bill. **Red gape.** Buff throat edged by thin black line. Olive-green above. **Rufous under otherwise black wing.** Large flocks in floodlands, estuaries. Settles briefly with raised wings before rising again. Zambezi, Okavango and E coast. Summer resident.

**Similar**

**BLACKWINGED PRATINCOLE  *G. nordmanni***
Black gape. No rufous under wing. Central interior. Summer visitor.

**7   OSTRICH**                       *Struthio camelus*

Long grey neck. Male black with white wings and chestnut tail. Female drab brown. Call: roar. Wooded grassland, thornveld. Throughout s Africa, often domesticated. True wild birds only in Namibia and Kalahari. Resident.

66 cm

56 cm

95 cm

100 cm

140 cm

25 cm

2 m

♂

**1   SADDLEBILLED STORK**     *Ephippiorhynchus senegalensis*
**Black and red banded bill, yellow saddle at bill base.** Male has brown eyes and yellow wattle. Female has yellow eyes, no wattle. Large rivers, floodplains, dams, marshes. Solitary or in pairs. NE. Resident.

**2   MARABOU STORK**     *Leptoptilos crumeniferus*
Massive bill, **bare head and neck, fleshy pouch on foreneck.** In flight shows black wings, white body and tucked-in nèck. Game reserves, refuse dumps, abattoirs. Small to large flocks. Inactive on sandbanks for much of the time. Soars to great heights. N half of region. Resident.

**3   WHITE STORK**     *Ciconia ciconia*
**Red bill and legs**, black and white body. Grassland, bushveld, vleis, pastures. Singly or in flocks. Often soars, travels at great height. Erratic movements in response to pest infestations, feeding for a few days before moving on. Widespread. Summer visitor.
**Similar**
**WOOLLYNECKED STORK** *C. episcopus*
Woolly white neck. Black face, bill and body. NE. Resident.
**YELLOWBILLED STORK** *Mycteria ibis*
Yellow bill, red face and forehead, pink legs.

**4   ABDIM'S STORK**     *Ciconia abdimii*
Tawny bill, blue face, pale legs with pink ankles and feet. **In flight shows white rump.** Soars at great height, usually in large flocks, associating with white storks. Moves in response to insect outbreaks. Widespread except S and W. Summer visitor.
**Similar**
**BLACK STORK** *C. nigra*
Red bill, long red legs. Singly or in pairs. Resident.
**OPENBILLED STORK** *Anastomus lamelligerus*
Tawny bill with open gap between mandibles. Body appears black.

**5   HAMERKOP**     *Scopus umbretta*
Flattened, heavy black bill, **large backward-directed crest**, dull brown plumage. Call: nasal "wek-wek-wek". Freshwater bodies. Usually singly, feeding in shallows, stalking and stirring its feet to disturb prey. Nest is large dome in waterside tree. Widespread. Resident.

**6   GREATER FLAMINGO**     *Phoenicopterus ruber*
**Pink bill, black tip.** In flight forewings scarlet. Plumage mostly white. Very long red legs and white neck. Call: honk. Shallow lakes, salt pans, estuaries. Small to huge concentrations. Feeds with bill upside down, sifting silt. Widespread. Nomadic resident.
**Similar**
**LESSER FLAMINGO** *Phoeniconaias minor*
Uniform dark red bill; looks black at distance. Plumage appears dark pink.

**7   AFRICAN SPOONBILL**     *Platalea alba*
Long, flattened, **spoon-shaped red and blue bill.** Red legs. White plumage. Call: low "kaark". Dams, seasonal pans, lagoons, rivers. Singly or in groups. Feeds with side-to-side sweeping motion of bill. Widespread except W. Resident.

**1  SACRED IBIS**              *Threskiornis aethiopicus*
Decurved **black bill**, unfeatherd black head, neck and legs, white plumage. Marshy ground, sewage works, dams, croplands. Singly or in flocks. Often fly in V formation. Widespread except some w areas. Resident.

**2  HADEDA IBIS**                *Bostrychia hadedash*
Decurved bill, **red upper mandible. White cheek stripes.** Drab brown plumage with glossy pink shoulder patch. Call: loud "ha-ha-haadada", often in unison. Suburban gardens, grassland, plantations, near water, damp ground. Usually small groups. Roosts in tall tree. N, E and S. Resident.
**Similar**
**BALD IBIS**  *Geronticus calvus*
Dark, glossy blue plumage. Bright red bill, bald head, pink legs. Drakensberg and surrounds.
**GLOSSY IBIS**  *Plegadis falcinellus*
Slender. Bronze-brown. Iridescent green wings and tail.

**3  AFRICAN FINFOOT**          *Podica senegalensis*
**Bright orange bill and legs.** Stout neck. **Speckled plumage on back.** Quiet, densely vegetated rivers. Swims furtively beneath overhanging branches with **body largely submerged**, head and neck stretched forward with each stroke. E coast and NE. Resident.

**4  EGYPTIAN GOOSE**          *Alopochen aegyptiacus*
Pink bill, rufous eye patch, long neck, long pink legs, brown patch on breast. Call: male hisses, female honks; socially very noisy. Most freshwater bodies, also fields, sandbanks, often in pairs. Flies to grazing grounds in evenings. Throughout s Africa. Resident.
**Similar**
**PYGMY GOOSE**  *Nettapus auritus*
Much smaller (33 cm). Short yellow bill, white face, dark green upperparts. NE.

**5  SPURWINGED GOOSE**        *Plectropterus gambensis*
Pink bill and legs. Male has fleshy caruncle on forehead. Glossy black body. Throat, underparts white. Call: "chi-chi-chi" in flight. Large rivers, floodplains, dams. Flocks graze in grassland during day. Widespread except west-central areas. Resident.

**6  WHITEFACED DUCK**          *Dendrocygna viduata*
**White face**, black head and neck, dark plumage. Erect stance. Immature has smudged brown face. Call: three-note whistle. Dams, rivers, estuaries, sewage pans. Pairs or flocks, usually standing ashore. NE. Resident.
**Similar**
**FULVOUS DUCK**  *D. bicolor*
Rufous head, cream flanks, white rump in flight.
**WHITEBACKED DUCK**  *Thalassornis leuconotus*
Pale spot at bill base. Humped brownish back; swims with tail submerged.
**SOUTH AFRICAN SHELDUCK**  *Tadorna cana*
Head of male all-grey. Head of female grey and white. Rufous body. SW.

1

89 cm

2

76 cm

3

63 cm

4

71 cm

5

102 cm

♂

6

48 cm

**1**

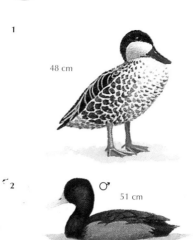

48 cm

**2**

♂  51 cm

**3**

53-58 cm

**4**

♂

64-79 cm

**5**

20 cm

**6**

43 cm

**1   REDBILLED TEAL**                    *Anas erythrorhyncha*

**Red bill, pale cheeks, dark cap.** Spotted body. In flight shows creamy speculum. Dams, floodplains, sewage pans. Large mixed flocks, smaller groups or pairs during rainy season. Throughout s Africa. Resident.
**Similar**
**HOTTENTOT TEAL  *A. hottentota***
Grey-blue bill. Creamy cheeks with dark smudge
**CAPE TEAL  *A. capensis***
Pink upturned bill. Speckled head. Small, pale body.

**2   SOUTHERN POCHARD**              *Netta erythrophthalma*

Pale patch at bill base. Male has red eyes. Female has pale **crescent** from eye to neck. Blue bill and feet, dark rufous plumage. **White wing-bar in flight.** Deep fresh waters in pairs or flocks. Throughout s Africa. Resident.
**Similar**
**MACCOA DUCK  *Oxyura maccoa***
Female and non-breeding male have **horizontal** white facial stripe. Male in breeding plumage has cobalt blue bill, large black head, chestnut-brown body.

**3   YELLOWBILLED DUCK**              *Anas undulata*

**Bright yellow bill with black central patch.** Brown feathers edged white, appearing ashy. Upperwing shows green speculum with white border in flight. Female quacks when taking off. Pairs and flocks on open water. Widespread except NE and arid W. Resident.
**Similar**
**AFRICAN BLACK DUCK  *A. sparsa***
Dark bill. Black with white spots on back. Rivers, streams.
**CAPE SHOVELLER  *A. smithii***
Large dark spatulate bill. Orange legs. Speckled brown body.

**4   KNOBBILLED DUCK**                *Sarkidiornis melanotos*

Head, neck speckled grey. Male has large fleshy caruncle on forehead and bill. Glossy blue upperparts, white underparts. Temporary bushveld pans, marshes, rivers. Pairs or flocks. Often perches in dead tree near water. N and E. Nomadic resident.

**5   DABCHICK**                        *Tachybaptus ruficollis*

**Rufous neck. Creamy spot at base of bill when breeding.** Small dark body. Call: descending whinnying trill. Freshwater bodies. Dives frequently. Skitters across water chasing rivals. Widespread. Resident.
**Similar**
**BLACKNECKED GREBE  *Podiceps nigricollis***
Red eyes. Dark upperparts. Silvery white underparts.
**GREAT CRESTED GREBE  *Podiceps cristatus***
Ruby-red eyes. Dark double crest. White cheeks. Dark ruff.

**6   REDKNOBBED COOT**                *Fulica cristata*

Red eyes. **White bill and frontal shield with double red knobs on forehead. All-black plumage.** Call: harsh "crornk". Freshwater bodies with reedbeds. Singly or in numbers along reed edges or ashore. Noisily pursues rivals across water. Widespread except NE. Resident.

**1   PURPLE GALLINULE**          *Porphyrio porphyrio*

**Massive red bill and red frontal shield. Purple and turquoise plumage. Pink legs.** Call: various shrieks, groans, wails. Marshes, reedbeds, sewage pans. Singly or in pairs walking on mud flats and vegetation or clambering through tangled reeds. Widespread except west-central areas. Resident.
**Similar**
**LESSER GALLINULE  *P. alleni***
Red bill. Blue shield. Green above. Dark blue head and body. Summer resident.

**2   MOORHEN**          *Gallinula chloropus*

Red bill with yellow tip. Red frontal shield. Body sooty black with white flank feathers. **Legs yellow-green.** Call: sharp "kr-rrrk". Freshwater bodies with fringing reedbeds and grass. Singly or in pairs in open water or feeding ashore in marshlands. Widespread. Resident.
**Similar**
**LESSER MOORHEN  *G. angulata***
Mainly yellow bill. Greenish legs. Small, blackish waterbird. Summer resident.

**3   BLACK CRAKE**          *Amaurornis flavirostris*

**Bright yellow bill.** Red eyes and legs. **Black plumage.** Call: harsh "rr-rr-rr", ending in croak. Dams, quiet rivers, floodplains with reedbeds. Singly or in loose groups at water's edge or walking on floating vegetation. Shy. Widespread except w and central areas. Resident.
**Similar**
**AFRICAN CRAKE  *Crex egregia***
Plain grey head and neck. Mottled upperparts. Barred below. Summer resident.

**4   AFRICAN RAIL**          *Rallus caerulescens*

**Long, decurved red bill.** Red legs. Dark grey head and breast. Brown upperparts. White-barred flanks and tail. Call: shrill whistle "cree-crak-crak-crak". Reedbeds, dense marshy vegetation. Shy, skulking, fast-moving. Flicks tail continuously. Emerges at reed clearings, often in early morning. Central, ne areas and along S coast. Resident.

**5   REDCHESTED FLUFFTAIL**          *Sarothrura rufa*

Male has **rufous head and breast.** Dark streaked body and tail. Female has dark streaked plumage. Pale throat. Call: repeated low hoot mainly at night and on dull days. Marshes, vleis, damp valleys. Solitary, always well concealed in vegetation. S and E. Resident.
**Similar**
**BUFFSPOTTED FLUFFTAIL  *S. elegans***
Male has rufous head and neck. Spotted. Female more uniform.

**6   AFRICAN JACANA**          *Actophilornis africanus*

**Blue frontal shield, yellow upper breast, rufous body.** Call: loud "krrrk". Pans, river backwaters with water lilies. Singly or in loose groups walking on floating vegetation. Often chase one another while calling noisily. N and E. Resident.
**Similar**
**LESSER JACANA  *Microparra capensis***
Rufous crown and eye-stripe, white belly, pale body. Small.

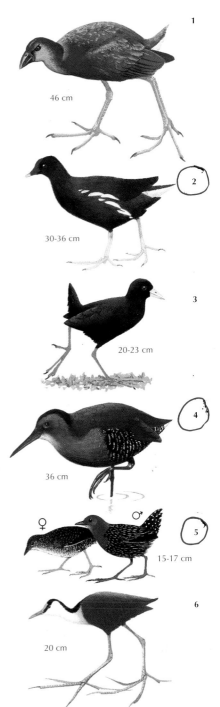

1

46 cm

2

30-36 cm

3

20-23 cm

4

36 cm

♀   ♂   5

15-17 cm

6

20 cm

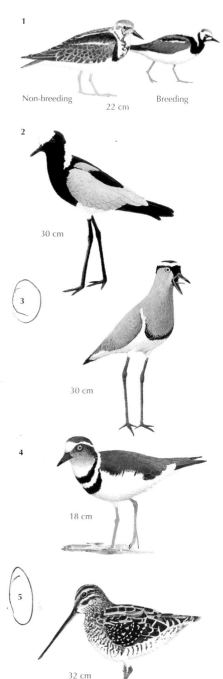

Non-breeding
22 cm
Breeding

30 cm

3

30 cm

4

18 cm

5

32 cm

**1  TURNSTONE**          *Arenaria interpres*
Short black bill. Striking patterns on breast. Blackish upperparts (rufous when breeding). Orange legs. Distinct white bar on wings and back in flight. Call: hard "tuc-a-tuc". Small flocks. Mud flats, rocky shores. Flicks stones and debris with its bill. Entire coastline. Summer visitor.

**2  BLACKSMITH PLOVER**          *Vanellus armatus*
Black bill and legs. Pied plumage with **grey wings and mantle.** Call: metallic "tink-tink-tink". Calls repeatedly when disturbed. Margins of inland water bodies, moist grassland. Pairs, individuals or non-breeding flocks. Throughout s Africa. Resident.

**3  CROWNED PLOVER**          *Vanellus coronatus*
Bill base red, tip black. Eyes pale yellow. **Black cap, white crown, brown upperparts, long red legs.** Call: noisy "kreep-kreep-kreeip" repeated day and night. Dry open ground, short grassy fields, parks, fallow land. Pairs or small groups. Often circles high up, calling repeatedly. Widespread. Resident.
**Similar**
**WATTLED PLOVER  *V. senegallus***
Bright yellow bill, wattles and legs. Streaked neck. NE.
**WHITECROWNED PLOVER  *V. albiceps***
Long yellow wattles. White band extends from bill over crown. Along large ne rivers.
**LESSER BLACKWINGED PLOVER  *V. lugubris***
White forecrown, forward of eye. Eye-ring pale yellow. Mainly Mozambique.
**BLACKWINGED PLOVER  *V. melanopterus***
Red eye-ring. White forecrown extending above eye. Red legs. E coast.

**4  THREEBANDED PLOVER**          *Charadrius tricollaris*
**Red eye-ring.** Red bill with black tip. Two black breast bands. Call: high-pitched "wick-wick". Singly or in pairs walking on sandy shores or in shallows. Throughout s Africa. Resident.
**Similar**
**CASPIAN PLOVER  *C. asiaticus***
Pale eyebrow stripe. Breeding male has chestnut breast band with black border. Summer visitor.
**CHESTNUTBANDED PLOVER  *C. pallidus***
Thin chestnut breast band, extending to crown in male.
**RINGED PLOVER  *C. hiaticula***
Yellow bill base, black tip. Black breast band. White collar. Summer visitor.
**KITTLITZ'S PLOVER  *C. pecuarius***
Black forehead stripe, extending through eye and around hindneck. Buff breast.
**WHITEFRONTED PLOVER  *C. marginatus***
Dark line from bill through eye. Slender bill. White collar.

**5  AFRICAN SNIPE**          *Gallinago nigripennis*
Long straight bill, striped head, barred tail and flanks, white belly. Call: drumming sound created by vibrating fanned tail feathers in steep downward flight. Wetlands, marshes, sewage pans, singly or in pairs. Widespread except W. Resident.
**Similar**
**GREAT SNIPE  *G. media***
Very similar. Extreme N and NE. Summer visitor.
**PAINTED SNIPE  *Rostratula benghalensis***
White eye patch. Female has striking red-brown neck and breast.

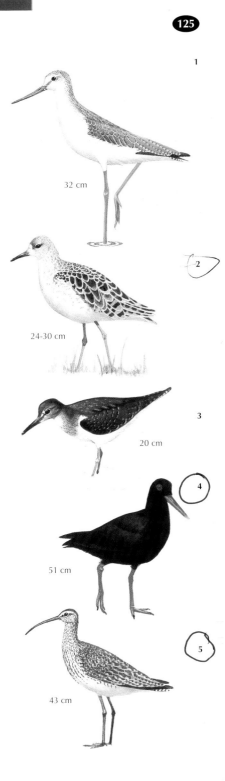

**1   GREENSHANK**                    *Tringa nebularia*

Robust, slightly upturned bill. **Green-grey legs.** White underparts. **White back in flight.** Call: triple "tew-tew-tew". Coastal and inland waters. Solitary. Throughout s Africa. Summer visitor.

**Similar**

**MARSH SANDPIPER  T. stagnatilis**

Straight slender bill. Yellowish legs.

**2   RUFF**                    *Philomachus pugnax*

Short, straight bill with bulbous tip. **Boldly scaled upperparts.** Legs orange. In flight **white oval patches on sides of tail.** Coastal and inland waters. Singly or in flocks, standing in shallows. Takes flight in dense flocks. Throughout s Africa. Summer visitor.

**Similar**

**LITTLE STINT  Calidris minuta**

Much smaller (14 cm). Slender bill. Heavily blotched upperparts.

**3   COMMON SANDPIPER**              *Tringa hypoleucos*

Medium to short, robust bill. **White area above shoulder.** Brown upperparts, barred tail. Call: shrill "weet-a-weet". Singly on shoreline of variety of wetlands. Often bobs hindquarters. Flies low with stiffly bowed wings, shallow wingbeats between short glides. Throughout s Africa. Summer visitor.

**Similar**

**WOOD SANDPIPER  T. glareola**

Straight bill. Broad eyebrow. Dark, well-spotted upperparts.

**CURLEW SANDPIPER  Calidris ferruginea**

Decurved bill. Broad white rump in flight. Plain grey.

**SANDERLING  Calidris alba**

Short thick bill. Dark shoulder patch. Pale shorebird.

**KNOT  Calidris canutus**

Larger (25 cm). Short bill. Short-legged, dumpy. In flocks along entire coast.

**TEREK SANDPIPER  Xenus cinereus**

Long upcurved bill. Short orange-yellow legs. Along coast.

**GREY PLOVER  Pluvialis squatarola**

Larger (29 cm). Stout bill. Tucked-in neck. Grey body. Black armpits in flight.

**4   AFRICAN BLACK OYSTERCATCHER** *Haematopus moquini*

Bright red bill, eyes and legs. **Black plumage.** Call: "klee-kleep". Rocky coastlines, estuaries, lagoons. In pairs or small flocks. Forages for food along shoreline. Threatened. S and w coastline. Endemic resident.

**5   WHIMBREL**                    *Numenius phaeopus*

Decurved bill. **Dark cap, pale eyebrow, central stripe on head.** In flight extensive white rump and back. Call: twittering "peep-pee-pee-ee". Estuaries, coastal lagoons, mud flats. Singly or in small groups standing or probing for food. Entire coastline. Summer visitor.

**Similar**

**CURLEW  N. arquata**

Much larger (59 cm). Longer decurved bill. Paler plumage, lacking head stripes.

**BARTAILED GODWIT  Limosa lapponica**

Smaller (39 cm). Long, slightly upcurved bill with red base.

32 cm

24-30 cm

20 cm

51 cm

43 cm

1

43 cm

2

44 cm

3

20 cm

4

53 cm

5

53 cm

### 1   AVOCET                    *Recurvirostra avosetta*

**Thin, upturned bill.** Black cap and hindneck. Black and white plumage. **Long grey legs.** Call: liquid "kloot". Lakes, pans, lagoons, estuaries. Small to large flocks. Sweeps bill from side to side in shallows. Widespread. Nomadic resident.
Similar
**BLACKWINGED STILT** *Himantopus himantopus*
Slender, straight black bill. Long red legs.

### 2   SPOTTED DIKKOP                  *Burhinus capensis*

**Large yellow eyes. Spotted below.** Yellow legs. Call: shrill "chwee-chwee" while flying about restlessly at night. Short grass, open rocky areas. Singly or in pairs. Mainly nocturnal. When disturbed runs with lowered head. Throughout s Africa. Resident.
Similar
**WATER DIKKOP** *B. vermiculatus*
Grey panel with black edges on folded wing. River edges.

### 3   TEMMINCK'S COURSER             *Cursorius temminckii*

Sharp, decurved bill. **Rufous cap.** Black and white stripes behind eye. Grey-brown above, rufous below. White legs. Call: sharp "err-err-err". Short or burnt grassland. Pairs or groups. Stands upright, bobs head and tail, runs swiftly, then resumes feeding. Widespread except SW. Nomadic resident.
Similar
**BURCHELL'S COURSER** *C. rufus*
Back of head grey. White bar on secondaries in flight.
**BRONZEWINGED COURSER** *Rhinoptilus chalcopterus*
Distinctive black and white mask. Red eye-ring, red legs.
**DOUBLEBANDED COURSER** *Smutsornis africanus*
Two thin black bands encircling upper breast. Pale body.
**THREEBANDED COURSER** *Rhinoptilus cinctus*
Three bands on neck and breast. Yellow bill base and eye-ring.

### 4   REDCRESTED KORHAAN             *Eupodotis ruficrista*

Long neck. **Upperparts have creamy-white V markings.** Black below. Female has white breast band. Red crest rarely seen. Call: series of clicks followed by shrill whistles. Singly or in pairs in grassland, bushveld. Displaying male flies up and suddenly tumbles out of the sky. N. Resident.

### 5   BLACK KORHAAN *Eupodotis afra*

Pink bill. Barred above. Male has black neck, white ear patches. S, W and central areas. Endemic residents.
Similar
**WHITEQUILLED KORHAAN** *E. afroides*
Identical except for white on wing tips in flight. Arid central areas.
**BLACKBELLIED KORHAAN** *E. melanogaster*
Male has black extending in a line up neck to chin. Female is white below. NE.
**WHITEBELLIED KORHAAN** *E. cafra*
Front of neck blue-grey. White belly. Male has dark cap and throat.
**BLUE KORHAAN** *E. caerulescens*
Blue-grey neck and underparts. Blue in wings in flight.
**KAROO KORHAAN** *E. vigorsii*
Black throat patch. Grey-brown head and neck. Arid SW.
**RÜPPELL'S KORHAAN** *E. rueppellii*
Similar to Karoo korhaan. Nw Namibia.

**1   KORI BUSTARD** *Ardeotis kori*
Yellow eyes and lower bill. **Dark crest, grey neck.** Call: booming "wum-wum-wummm". Grassland, dry woodland. Singly or in pairs walking slowly or in slow flight. Elaborate courtship display. Largely restricted to game reserves. Resident.
**Similar**
**LUDWIG'S BUSTARD** *Neotis ludwigii*
Smaller (90 cm). Brown cap. Dark brown neck and breast. Little white on wings.
**STANLEY'S BUSTARD** *Neotis denhami*
Black cap. Conspicuous white markings in wing.

**2   SECRETARYBIRD** *Sagittarius serpentarius*
**Orange face. Loose black feathers behind head.** Tail feathers project beyond legs in flight. Grassland, savanna. Walks or runs with wings outstretched. Soars to great heights. Roosts on top of trees. Throughout s Africa. Resident.

**3   NATAL FRANCOLIN** *Francolinus natalensis*
Red bill, yellow base. Brown upperparts, **black and white barred underparts.** Red legs. Call: harsh "kwali, kwali, kwali". Utters raucous cackling in alarm. Small parties in wooded, rocky habitat. NE. Resident.
**Similar**
**REDBILLED FRANCOLIN** *F. adspersus*
All-red bill. Yellow eye-ring. Finely barred underparts. NW.
**CAPE FRANCOLIN** *F. capensis*
Dark cap. Pale cheeks. Dark brown underparts streaked white. S coastal areas.

**4   SWAINSON'S FRANCOLIN** *Francolinus swainsonii*
**Red face and neck. Black bill and legs.** Plumage uniform brown. Call: harsh "krrraaak-krrraaak-krrraaak" fading at the end. Male calls from low branch or anthill. Singly or in groups in woodland, bushveld. North-central areas. Resident.
**Similar**
**REDNECKED FRANCOLIN** *F. afer*
Face, bill, throat and legs all red. Black and white below. Also occurs far S.

**5   CRESTED FRANCOLIN** *Francolinus sephaena*
**Dark cap with broad white eyebrow.** Dark blotched upper breast. Rufous above, pale below. **Tail often raised.** Call: shrill "kwerri-kwetchi" repeated. Bushveld, riverine thickets. In pairs or small groups. N and NE. Resident.
**Similar**
**ORANGE RIVER FRANCOLIN** *F. levaillantoides*
Red spotting on underparts extending up to white throat.
**REDWING FRANCOLIN** *F. levaillantii*
Rufous from eye to lower hindneck. Black speckling on breast. SE.
**GREYWING FRANCOLIN** *F. africanus*
Throat freckled grey. Underparts finely barred. Greyish body. S.
**SHELLEY'S FRANCOLIN** *F. shelleyi*
Clear white throat, black surround. Black-barred belly.
**COQUI FRANCOLIN** *F. coqui*
Male has tawny head. Female has white throat with black border.
**HARTLAUB'S FRANCOLIN** *F. hartlaubii*
Large bill. Streaked underparts. North-central Namibia.

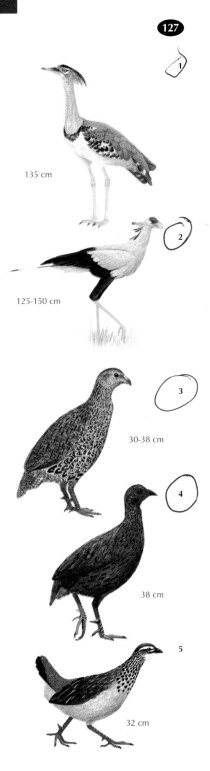

135 cm

125-150 cm

30-38 cm

38 cm

32 cm

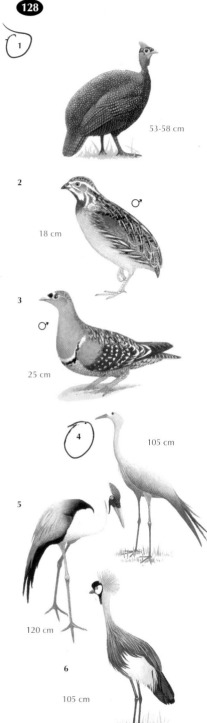

53-58 cm

18 cm

25 cm

105 cm

120 cm

105 cm

**1  HELMETED GUINEAFOWL**          *Numida meleagris*
**Blue neck, red cap, bare casque on crown.** Grey and white flecked body. Call: "ker-bek-ker-bek-ker-bek" repeated. Grassland, bushveld, farmlands. Forms large flocks when not breeding. Roosts in trees. Widespread except extreme W. Resident.
**Similar**
**CRESTED GUINEAFOWL  *Guttera pucherani***
Black head plumes. Red eyes. Black plumage with white spots. Ne forests.

**2  COMMON QUAIL**          *Coturnix coturnix*
Pale underparts. Pale facial markings. Call: piercing "whit-wit-tit", repeated day or night at intervals. Bushveld, grassland, fields. Usually in pairs. Widespread except NE, north-central and some w areas. Resident.
**Similar**
**HARLEQUIN QUAIL  *C. delegorguei***
Dark throat markings, especially in male. Chestnut underparts.
**KURRICHANE BUTTONQUAIL  *Turnix sylvatica***
Pale eyes. Black spots on sides of neck and breast. Pale face.
**BLACKRUMPED BUTTONQUAIL  *Turnix hottentotta***
Brown eyes. Chestnut breast and face. Dark rump in flight.

**3  DOUBLEBANDED SANDGROUSE**          *Pterocles bicinctus*
Yellow eye-ring. **Male has black and white bands on forehead and across breast.** Female is finely barred. Call: soft, quick "weep-wee-choo-chippi". Flocks come to drink after sunset. N half of region. Resident.
**Similar**
**NAMAQUA SANDGROUSE  *P. namaqua***
No forehead bands. Brown and white breast band. Long tail.
**BURCHELL'S SANDGROUSE  *P. burchelli***
Uniform ochre colouring with distinct white spots all over.
**YELLOWTHROATED SANDGROUSE  *P. gutturalis***
Pale yellow throat. Male's throat bordered by black band.

**4  BLUE CRANE**          *Anthropoides paradiseus*
**Bulbous head.** Slender neck and trailing wing plumes. **Blue-grey plumage.** Call: far-carrying, nasal "kraaaarrk". Hilly grassland, farmland, dams, vleis. Pairs or small groups. Non-breeding birds nomadic and gather in large flocks, preferring higher altitudes. Endangered. SE and NW. Endemic resident.

**5  WATTLED CRANE**          *Bugeranus carunculatus*
White head and neck, grey crown. Red upper bill and face. **Large white wattles on either side of face.** Dark upperparts and tail. Call: loud, drawn-out, bell-like "horuk". Pairs or small groups in vleis, marshes and high grassland in scattered localities. Endangered resident.

**6  CROWNED CRANE**          *Balearica regulorum*
**Golden crown. White upperwings in flight.** Call: two-syllabled trumpeting "may hem". Grassland, vleis, farmlands, dams. Usually in flocks. Roost in estuarine reedbeds or trees. N and along SE coast into interior. Nomadic when not breeding. Resident.

**1   CAPE VULTURE**                     *Gyps coprotheres*

**Honey-coloured eyes.** Pale creamy plumage, back is almost white. **Two bare patches of blue skin at base of neck.** Immature is rufous with pink neck. Breeds in large colonies on cliffs. Ranges far, singly or in small groups. Perches on pylons. Widespread in interior. Threatened. Endemic resident.

**Similar**
**WHITEBACKED VULTURE** *G. africanus*
Almost identical but eyes dark. White lower back visible from above.

**2   BEARDED VULTURE**                  *Gypaetus barbatus*

**Black mask across face, ending in "beard".** Loosely feathered head and legs. Rufous underparts. **Wedge-shaped tail in flight.** Remote high mountains. Soars by day. Nests on cliff ledges. Solitary. Restricted to Drakensberg in Lesotho and surroundings. Resident.

**3   LAPPETFACED VULTURE**              *Torgos tracheliotus*

**Red skin on head and neck.** Large bill. Dark body. Streaked underparts, white "trousers". Bushveld, thornveld, desert. Nests on tree tops. Usually solitary. Confined largely to major reserves. N half of region. Resident.

**Similar**
**HOODED VULTURE** *Necrosyrtes monachus*
Thin-billed. Pink face and neck. White ruff and white "trousers".
**WHITEHEADED VULTURE** *Trigonoceps occipitalis*
Red and blue bill. Pink face and legs. White head and neck.

**4   AFRICAN FISH EAGLE**               *Haliaeetus vocifer*

**White head and breast.** Dark rufous upperparts, chestnut belly. Call: far-reaching, ringing "kiow-kiw-kiw" uttered while perched or in the air. Large rivers, lakes, dams, estuaries, lagoons. Usually in pairs, conspicuously perched. Flies low over water surface. Very vocal. Widespread except arid w and central areas. Resident.

**Similar**
**PALMNUT VULTURE** *Gypohierax angolensis*
White head, neck and body. Black lower wing feathers and tail. E and nw borders of region.
**OSPREY** *Pandion haliaetus*
Crested. White underparts, dark upperparts. Near water. See main description on p. 132.

**5   YELLOWBILLED KITE**                *Milvus migrans parasitus*

**Yellow bill.** Brown head and body. **Deeply forked tail constantly manoeuvred as rudder.** Call: "kleeuw" in flight. Wide range of habitats. Singly, in pairs or large flocks at food source. Associates with similar black kite. Widespread. Summer resident.

**Similar**
**BLACK KITE** *M. migrans migrans*
Black bill, pale grey head. Tail less forked.

**6   BATELEUR**                         *Terathopius ecaudatus*

**Scarlet face and legs. Tawny back. Long tapered wings, very short tail.** Call: bark-like "kaw-aaaw". Bushveld, savanna. Singly or in pairs. Glides with sideways rocking motion as though balancing; very little wing flapping. Mostly in game reserves. N and E. Resident.

1

105-115 cm

2

110 cm

3

98-105 cm

4

5

63-73 cm

55 cm

6

♀

55-70 cm

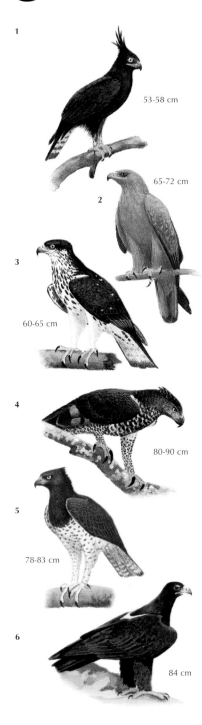

**1   LONGCRESTED EAGLE**                    *Lophaetus occipitalis*
Pale eyes. **Long crest.** Dark plumage. Tail barred in flight. White
wing bases. Call: shrill "wee-ar". Wooded hills and valleys, plantations. Perches conspicuously. Soars early morning. N and e
forests. Resident.

**2   TAWNY EAGLE**                                   *Aquila rapax*
Yellow cere and gape. **Gape extends to below centre of eye.** Vari-
able mottling on wing from pale buff to dark brown. In flight **lit-
tle white on wings, none on upper tail coverts.** Bushveld,
thornveld. Singly or in pairs. Confined mostly to major reserves.
Widespread except S. Resident.
**Similar**
**STEPPE EAGLE  *A. nipalensis***
Yellow gape extends beyond centre of eye. Adult dark brown.
Summer visitor.
**WAHLBERG'S EAGLE  *A. wahlbergi***
In flight narrow, parallel wings and longish, square tail. Summer
resident.
**LESSER SPOTTED EAGLE  *A. pomarina***
White spots on brown folded wings. Narrow "stovepipe" legs.
Summer visitor.
**BROWN SNAKE EAGLE  *Circaetus cinereus***
White, unfeathered legs. Upright stance.
**BOOTED EAGLE  *Hieraaetus pennatus***
White shoulder patch. Short broad tail, broad wings. Mainly SW.

**3   AFRICAN HAWK EAGLE**               *Hieraaetus spilogaster*
**Dark cap. Spotted breast.** White, unspotted thighs. In flight
underwing whitish, upperwing dark brown with white patches.
Broad terminal tail band. Call: whistle, "klu-klu-klee". Woodland,
savanna. Soars singly or in pairs in morning. Perches in leafy tree.
N. Resident.
**Similar**
**AYRES' EAGLE  *H. ayresii***
Underwing dark, barred. White shoulder patch on folded wing.

**4   CROWNED EAGLE**                  *Stephanoaetus coronatus*
Crested head. Dark above, heavily blotched underparts. **Underwing coverts rufous.** Short rounded wings. Long barred tail. Call:
"kewee-kewee-kewee" during aerial display. Female's call lower-
pitched. Evergreen forest and along large rivers. E. Resident.

**5   MARTIAL EAGLE**                        *Polemaetus bellicosus*
**Dark brown head, throat, upper breast. Shows dark underwings
in flight. Spotted underparts.** Call: loud "kloo-ee, kloo-ee". Vari-
ety of habitats, usually bushveld, savanna. Solitary. Hunts from
perch or in flight. Widespread but scarce outside major reserves.
Resident.
**Similar**
**BLACKBREASTED SNAKE EAGLE  *Circaetus pectoralis***
Shows whitish underwings in flight. Unspotted underparts, bare
legs.

**6   BLACK EAGLE**                             *Aquila verreauxii*
**Black with white V on back, white panels under wings.** In flight
wings are narrow at base, broadening towards middle. Mountainous regions, rocky hills, cliffs. Usually in pairs. Perches on rocks
or flies quite low. Widespread except most of Botswana and
Mozambique. Resident.

**1   STEPPE BUZZARD**                    *Buteo buteo vulpinus*

Dark eyes. Plumage varies from pale to dark brown. **Pale zone across breast** dividing streaked upper breast from banded underparts. Call: "kreeee" in flight. Grassland, open bushveld. Singly or in small groups, sitting on roadside poles or slowly circling overhead. Forms flocks when migrating. Widespread except in desert. Summer visitor.

**Similar**

**FOREST BUZZARD   B. trizonatus**

Underparts have vertical blotches with clear patches. S and e forests. Endemic resident.

**2   JACKAL BUZZARD**                    *Buteo rufofuscus*

Dark head and upperparts. **Chestnut breast and tail.** Rounded wings. Call: high-pitched "kwea-ka-ka-ka". Montane areas and adjacent grassland, singly or in pairs. Perches on roadside poles. Central areas, S and W. Endemic resident.

**Similar**

**AUGUR BUZZARD   Buteo augur**

White underparts and underwings. Zimbabwe and nw Namibia.

**3   BLACKSHOULDERED KITE**             *Elanus caeruleus*

Red eyes. Grey upperparts. White underparts and **black shoulder patch.** In flight pale plumage contrasts with black wing tips. Call: soft "weeep-weeep". Grassland, open woodland. Usually singly. Perches conspicuously on roadside poles, cables, bare trees. Frequently hovers. Throughout s Africa. Resident.

**Similar**

**LIZARD BUZZARD   Kaupifalco monogrammicus**

Vertical black streak down throat. Two broad white tail bands. NE.

**PALLID HARRIER   Circus macrourus**

Yellow eyes. Tall. Pale grey upperparts, white underparts. Summer visitor.

**4   GABAR GOSHAWK**                     *Micronisus gabar*

Red eyes. Red cere and legs. Grey throat and breast. **Broad white rump** in flight. Melanistic form lacks white rump. Call: high-pitched whistle "pi-pi-pi ...". Thornveld, mixed bushveld; favours semi-arid regions. Singly. Hunts from a concealed perch or in low flight across open savanna. Central areas and N. Resident.

**Similar**

**LITTLE SPARROWHAWK   Accipiter minullus**

Yellow eyes. Slender yellow legs. Two white spots on uppertail.

**LITTLE BANDED GOSHAWK   Accipiter badius**

Red eyes. Yellow legs. Lacks white rump and tail spots.

**OVAMBO SPARROWHAWK   Accipiter ovampensis**

Brown eyes. Grey barring on underparts up to throat. Cere and legs usually yellow, sometimes red. Black and grey barred tail.

**5   GYMNOGENE**                         *Polyboroides typus*

**Bare yellow face, small head.** Wings grey with black edging, broad and floppy. Black tail with **single white central band.** Long yellow legs. Call: whistled "peee-oooo". Woodland, bushveld. Clambers about trees using legs to extract prey from cavities. Widespread except arid W. Resident.

1

45-50 cm

2

44-53 cm

3

30 cm

4

30-34 cm

5

60-66 cm

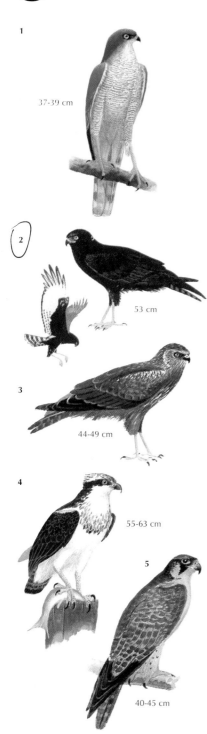

37-39 cm

53 cm

44-49 cm

55-63 cm

40-45 cm

**1   AFRICAN GOSHAWK**                    *Accipiter tachiro*
Yellow eyes. Adult finely barred red-brown on front. Immature
has bold dark blotches on underparts and grey cere. Male has
grey upperparts and two white spots in tail. Female is much larger with brown upperparts and no tail spots. Call: "krit" by male
during territorial display. Flies high with fast wing beats alternat-
ed with gliding. Riverine forests, montane woodland and other
well wooded regions. Active early mornings and evenings. Main-
ly NE to S. Resident.
**Similar**
**REDBREASTED SPARROWHAWK** *A. rufiventris*
Dark head and upperparts. Uniform rufous underparts.
**CUCKOO HAWK** *Aviceda cuculoides*
Crest. Grey throat, rufous-barred belly. Buoyant flight.
**PALE CHANTING GOSHAWK** *Melierax canorus*
Pale grey. Pink cere and legs. Upright stance. W half of region.
**DARK CHANTING GOSHAWK** *Melierax metabates*
Darker grey than pale chanting goshawk. Upright stance. N and
NE.

**2   BLACK HARRIER**                          *Circus maurus*
Yellow eyes. Black plumage. In flight long white flight feathers,
white rump and long banded tail. Call: "pee-pee-pee" during dis-
play. Grassland, scrub, arid and mountainous regions. Singly or in
pairs. S half of region. Endemic resident.
**Similar**
**BLACK SPARROWHAWK** *Accipiter melanoleucus*
Red eyes. White or blotched underparts. E and NE.
**BAT HAWK** *Macheiramphus alcinus*
Pointed wings. White legs. Crepuscular. NE.

**3   AFRICAN MARSH HARRIER**              *Circus ranivorus*
Yellow eyes. Dark upperparts, rich rufous brown below. Barred
flight feathers and tail. Long yellow legs. Immature has **pale
breast band.** Marshland, reedbeds, adjoining fields. Singly, **flying
low, head bent down,** resting on ground or post. Widespread
except arid W. Resident.

**4   OSPREY**                              *Pandion haliaetus*
Crested head. Black mask through eye. White underparts. Sometimes has streaky breast band. Singly on perches at water. Hunts
fish in estuaries, large inland waters. N, E and S. Visitor, mainly in
summer.

**5   LANNER FALCON**                        *Falco biarmicus*
**Rufous crown.** Slate-grey above, pinkish-brown below. Immature
more heavily blotched than immature peregrine falcon. Yellow
feet. Call: harsh "kak-kak-kak". Often along cliffs, sometimes
around tall urban buildings. Flight characterised by wing flapping
followed by circling glides. Throughout s Africa. Resident.
**Similar**
**PEREGRINE FALCON** *F. peregrinus*
Dark crown. Underparts barred black and white.
**REDNECKED FALCON** *F. chicquera*
Chestnut crown and nape. Arid areas with acacia or palm trees.
**HOBBY FALCON** *F. subbuteo*
Heavily streaked underparts, rufous thighs and vent.

**1   GREATER KESTREL**          *Falco rupicoloides*

**Whitish eyes.** All-rufous plumage with blackish streaks and spots.
White underwings in flight. Call: "kee-kee-krik" during display.
Dry grassland, arid thornveld. Singly or in pairs, usually perched
on poles or thorn trees. Sometimes hovers. Central areas and W.
Resident.
**Similar**
**ROCK KESTREL**  *F. tinnunculus*
Blue-grey head (sometimes brown in females). Rocky hilly terrain.
**LESSER KESTREL**  *F. naumanni*
Pale underparts. In flocks in open grassland.
**AFRICAN HOBBY FALCON**  *F. cuvierii*
Dark upperparts. Unstreaked rufous underparts. North-central
areas. Summer resident.

**2   DICKINSON'S KESTREL**          *Falco dickinsoni*

Yellow around eyes, yellow cere. Pale grey head and neck. Grey
body, pale rump. Yellow feet. Call: shrill "keee-keee-keee".
Bushveld, often in baobabs or palms. Singly or in pairs. Hunts
from tree. N and NE. Resident.
**Similar**
**EASTERN REDFOOTED KESTREL**  *F. amurensis*
No rufous. Red feet. Male slate-grey, female barred below. Sum-
mer visitor.
**WESTERN REDFOOTED KESTREL**  *F. vespertinus*
Red feet. Male grey with rufous vent. Female pinkish below. Sum-
mer visitor.
**SOOTY FALCON**  *F. concolor*
Blackish face. Yellow legs. E coastal bush. Summer visitor.

**3   PYGMY FALCON**          *Polihierax semitorquatus*

Red eyes. Grey upperparts, white underparts. Female has chestnut
back. Wings speckled in flight. Red legs. Pairs usually perch in
trees close to nests of sociable weavers or redbilled buffalo
weavers with which they live in close association. Arid west-central areas. Resident.

**4   NARINA TROGON**          *Apaloderma narina*

**Emerald green head, upper breast (male) and back. Crimson
underparts.** Female has upper breast rufous to grey. Call: drawn-
out, low, repeated "hoot-hoot". Usually in pairs in forest, coastal
bush. Secretive. Flight is rapid. Extreme N and E. Resident.

**5   GREY LOURIE**          *Corythaixoides concolor*

Entirely grey plumage with distinct head crest. Call: harsh "kweh-
h-h". Alternative name is go-away bird. Bushveld, dry woodland,
gardens. Pairs or small parties, noisy and conspicuous, clambering about in trees or flying low with floppy wing beats. N. Resident.

**6   PURPLECRESTED LOURIE**          *Tauraco porphyreolophus*

Red eye-ring. **Purple crest.** Bluish wings and tail, ochre-washed
breast. Red in wings is conspicuous in flight. Call: loud "kok-kok-
kok-kok ..." rising in volume and accentuated towards end.
Coastal and riverine forests, woodland. Usually in pairs, furtively
clambering through dense foliage. NE. Resident.
**Similar**
**KNYSNA LOURIE**  *T. corythaix*
White eye-ring and tips to crest. Green head and body.

1

36 cm

2

28-30 cm

3
♀

19,5 cm

♂

4

29-34 cm

5

47-50 cm

6

47 cm

**1 CAPE TURTLE DOVE** *Streptopelia capicola*

Pale grey head. Black eyes. Black half-collar. Pallid grey underparts, darker upperparts. **White-tipped tail** visible in flight. Call: "kuk-cooo-kuk" repeated. Most habitats. Throughout s Africa. Resident.

**Similar**

**MOURNING DOVE** *S. decipiens*

Grey head. Yellow eyes with red eye-rings. Call: "kur-r-r-r". Along Zambezi and Limpopo.

**REDEYED DOVE** *S. semitorquata*

Grey crown. Red eyes with purple eye-rings. Breast deep pink.

**2 LAUGHING DOVE** *Streptopelia senegalensis*

Pinkish head and neck. Cinnamon breast with black spots, **cinnamon back.** In flight white outer tail feathers conspicuous. Call: soft "coo-coo-cook-coo-coo". Wide variety of habitats. Throughout s Africa. Resident.

**3 NAMAQUA DOVE** *Oena capensis*

Yellow bill. Male has black face and throat. Small, with **long tail** and chestnut flight feathers. Call: hooting "twoo-hoo". Dry grassland, thornveld, fallow fields. Singly or in pairs. Swift flight. Widespread. Nomadic resident.

**4 EMERALDSPOTTED DOVE** *Turtur chalcospilos*

Dark bill. Pale grey forehead. Grey-brown upperparts. Buffy underparts, **green wing-spots.** Call: low, descending cooing "du-du ... du-du ... du ... du-du-du-du-du-du". Woodland, bushveld, riverine and coastal bush. Often seen on ground, flying quickly when disturbed. N and E. Resident.

**Similar**

**TAMBOURINE DOVE** *T. tympanistria*

White face and underparts. Brown upperparts. E forests.

**CINNAMON DOVE** *Aplopelia larvata*

Whitish face, cinnamon body. Call: soft drawn-out hoot. E forests.

**5 GREEN PIGEON** *Treron calva*

White eyes. Red bill base. **Bright green and yellow plumage.** Red feet. Call: liquid bubbling notes, descending in pitch. Riverine forest, wooded bushveld; associated with wild figs. Flocks remain well concealed while climbing around trees, often hanging upside down on branches in search of fruit. Flies off rapidly if disturbed. N and E. Resident.

**6 ROCK PIGEON** *Columba guinea*

Bill black. **Bare red eye patch. Rufous, white-spotted upperparts.** Legs red. Call: deep cooing "doo-doo-doo", rising then falling. Mountains, cliffs, cities. Often in flocks, travelling long distances for water or to feed in grain fields. Widespread except north-central areas and NE. Common resident.

**Similar**

**FERAL PIGEON** *C. livia*

Plumage variable, largely grey, blue, black and white.

**RAMERON PIGEON** *C. arquatrix*

Yellow bill, eye-ring and feet. White-speckled plumage.

**1  MEYER'S PARROT**                    *Poicephalus meyeri*

Yellow bar on crown. Brown head, breast and upperparts. Green belly. In flight **blue-green rump and yellow underwing coverts conspicuous.** Call: high-pitched screeching. Small flocks. Woodland. N. Resident.

**Similar**

**BROWNHEADED PARROT  *P. cryptoxanthus***
Brown head. Green body. Bright yellow underwings. NE.

**RÜPPELL'S PARROT  *P. rueppellii***
Grey head. Female has blue rump and belly. North-central Namibia.

**CAPE PARROT  *P. robustus***
Orange forehead, shoulders, leg feathers. Grey or brown neck.

**ROSYFACED LOVEBIRD  *Agapornis roseicollis***
Pink face and throat, bright blue back and rump. NW.

**2  DIEDERIK CUCKOO**                *Chrysococcyx caprius*

Black bill. **Red eyes.** White marks **before and behind eye. Multiple white marks on wings.** Female more coppery on upperparts. Immature has red bill. Call: clear "dee-dee-dee-deederik". Various habitats including suburbia. Widespread. Summer resident.

**Similar**

**KLAAS'S CUCKOO  *C. klaas***
Dark eyes with white mark only behind. Green bill, no white in wing.

**EMERALD CUCKOO  *C. cupreus***
Male has yellow belly, green back. Female has bronze barring. E forests.

**3  JACOBIN CUCKOO**                    *Clamator jacobinus*

Black crest. Dark form: black except for white wing-bar. Pale form: clear white underparts. Call: shrill, far-carrying "kleeuw-kewp-kewp-kleeuw ...". Noisy. Woodland. S and E coast (dark form); n interior (pale form). Summer resident or visitor.

**Similar**

**STRIPED CUCKOO  *C. levaillantii***
Larger (40 cm). Heavy black streaking on throat and breast.

**THICKBILLED CUCKOO  *Pachycoccyx audeberti***
Heavy bill. Grey-brown upperparts. White underparts. NE.

**BLACK CUCKOO  *Cuculus clamosus***
All-black. Lacks crest and white wing-bars.

**4  GREAT SPOTTED CUCKOO**            *Clamator glandarius*

**Long grey crest.** White-spotted upperparts. Creamy-white underparts. Long wedge-shaped tail. Call: loud, rapid "keeow-keeow-keeow ...". Woodland, thornveld. N half of region. Summer visitor or resident.

**5  REDCHESTED CUCKOO**              *Cuculus solitarius*

Yellow eye-ring. Grey head and upperparts. **Broad russet upper breast.** Widely spaced barring on underparts. Juvenile lacks russet breast. Call: male calls "Piet-my-vrou", loud and far-carrying. Woodland, plantations, suburbia. Flight hawk-like. Widespread except arid w areas. Summer resident.

**Similar**

**AFRICAN CUCKOO  *C. gularis***
Conspicuous yellow gape. Barred undertail. Call: "hoop-hoop".

1

22-23 cm

2

♂

18,5 cm

3

33-34 cm

4

38-40 cm

5

28 cm

1

38-44 cm

2

36 cm

3

30-36 cm

4

30-33 cm

5

15-18 cm

**1   BURCHELL'S COUCAL**               *Centropus burchellii*
Red eyes. Black head and neck. Chestnut back. Creamy white
underparts. **Fine rufous barring on rump and base of black tail.**
Call: deep bubbling "doo-doo-doo ..." up to 20 times, descending
then ascending. Riverine bush, reedbeds, tall rank grassland, sub-
urbia. Secretive within lower stratum but may perch conspicu-
ously. E coast and highveld interior. Resident.
**Similar**
**WHITEBROWED COUCAL  *C. superciliosus***
White eyebrow, white streaks on crown and mantle. Along n bor-
der of region.
**SENEGAL COUCAL  *C. senegalensis***
Dark rump. Unbarred tail. Zimbabwe, n Botswana, ne Namibia.
**BLACK COUCAL  *C. bengalensis***
Smaller (37 cm). Black head and underparts. Chestnut wings and
back. NE.
**GREEN COUCAL  *Ceuthmochares aereus***
Smaller (33 cm). Yellow bill. Dull green upperparts, long green
tail. E forests.

**2   MARSH OWL**                          *Asio capensis*
Large dark brown eyes. Rounded buffy facial disc with black rim.
Short "ear" tufts. Uniform brown body. Russet wings in flight.
Call: harsh "kraak-kraak" in flight. Marshy grassland, vleis. Singly
or in pairs, sometimes in loose groups. Most active early morning
and late afternoon. Hunts by quartering ground in flight. Often
perches on roadside poles. When flushed, circles low before
resettling. Widespread except arid W. Resident.

**3   WOOD OWL**                      *Strix woodfordii*
Large dark brown eyes. Finely barred white facial disc. No "ear"
tufts. Russet-brown back, white spots on wings, heavily barred
underparts. Call: rapid "HU-hu, HU-hu-hu, hu-hu" (male), high-
er-pitched "Hoo" (female). Evergreen and riverine forest, mature
woodland, exotic plantations. Usually in pairs. Strictly nocturnal.
Roosts in tree during day. Along S and E coast and in NE.
Localised resident.

**4   BARN OWL**                            *Tyto alba*
Small dark eyes, heart-shaped white facial disc. Pale upperparts
and whitish underparts, slim build. Call: eerie screech. Large vari-
ety of habitats such as caves, large hollow trees, old buildings.
Often in suburbia. Singly or in pairs. Throughout s Africa. Resi-
dent.
**Similar**
**GRASS OWL  *T. capensis***
Darker upperparts, pale underparts. Moist grassland in E.

**5   SCOPS OWL**                     *Otus senegalensis*
Grey face. Yellow eyes. "Ear" tufts. Small owl with grey plumage
resembling tree-bark. Call: soft "prrrp", repeated at intervals.
Perches close to tree trunk during the day, using excellent cryptic
colouring to create illusion of being part of the tree. Acacia and
broadleafed woodland, bushveld. Singly or in pairs. N half of
region. Resident.
**Similar**
**WHITEFACED OWL  *O. leucotis***
Orange eyes, distinct broad black outline to white facial disc,
"ear" tufts.

**1 PEARLSPOTTED OWL** *Glaucidium perlatum*

Rounded head, no "ear" tufts. Pair of black spots on nape resemble eyes. Upperparts brown with white spots, underparts white with brown streaks and white spots. Smallest owl in s Africa. Call: rising whistle "tee-tee-tee-tee-tee-tee", then descending "teeew, teeew, tew, tew, tew, tew ...". Woodland, bushveld, riverine forest. Sometimes active during day. Mobbed by other birds. N half of region. Resident.

**Similar**

**BARRED OWL** *G. capense*

Upperparts and tail barred. Underparts have brown spots in rows. Row of large white spots from shoulder along edge of wing.

15-18 cm

**2 GIANT EAGLE OWL** *Bubo lacteus*

**Pink eyelids**, dark brown eyes. Pale grey plumage. "Ear" tufts not always raised. Largest owl in s Africa. Call: series of low grunts "ungh-ugh-ugh, ugh-ugh", female utters drawn-out whistle. Singly in large trees, deep within canopy. Thornveld, riverine forest, woodland. Central areas and N. Resident.

**3 SPOTTED EAGLE OWL** *Bubo africanus*

Pale yellow eyes. Grey-brown plumage, lightly blotched breast, fine barring on belly and flanks. Call: "hu-hoo" (male), "hu-hu-hoo" (female). Wide variety of habitats from bushveld to suburbia. Usually in pairs, commonly seen or heard in gardens. Throughout s Africa. Resident.

**Similar**

**CAPE EAGLE OWL** *B. capensis*

Orange eyes. Bold blotching and barring on underparts.

60-65 cm

**4 RUFOUSCHEEKED NIGHTJAR** *Caprimulgus rufigena*

Large eyes. Short bill with wide gape. Mottled grey and russet with buff collar. Call: "chwop, chwop, kewook-kewook" or a sustained purring. Insectivorous. Nocturnal. Rests by day on ground under tree. Woodland, thornveld, Kalahari sandveld. Widespread except E coast. Summer resident.

**Similar**

**FIERYNECKED NIGHTJAR** *C. pectoralis*

Rufous around neck. Call: slow, slow, quick, quick, quick, quick (likened to the phrase "Good Lord, deliver us"), descending in pitch. Resident.

**EUROPEAN NIGHTJAR** *C. europaeus*

Dark. Roosts lengthwise on horizontal branch. Summer visitor.

**MOZAMBIQUE NIGHTJAR** *C. fossii*

Call: engine-like gurgling. Roosts on sandy ground. NE. Resident.

**FRECKLED NIGHTJAR** *C. tristigma*

Granite-like freckles overall. Call: "cow-cow". Roosts on rocks. Resident.

**PENNANTWINGED NIGHTJAR** *Macrodipteryx vexillaria*

Male has long wing pennants. Call: high squeak. NE. Summer resident.

43-50 cm

23-24 cm

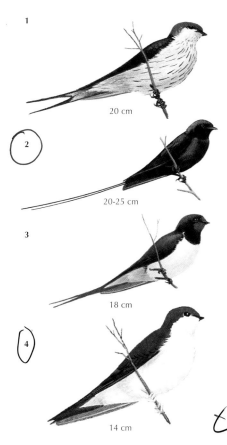

20 cm

20-25 cm

18 cm

14 cm

**Swallows and martins**
Broader, rounded wings, bent at shoulder.
Glide frequently between bouts of flapping.
Swallows can perch.

**1  GREATER STRIPED SWALLOW**          *Hirundo cucullata*
Rufous crown. White ear coverts. **Pale streaked underparts.**
Rufous rump. Call: soft "chissik" in flight. Glides over open, rocky
or urban terrain near water. Perches on trees and wires. Wide-
spread except NE. Summer resident.
**Similar**
**LESSER STRIPED SWALLOW  *H. abyssinica***
Rufous ear coverts. Heavily streaked underparts.
**REDBREASTED SWALLOW  *H. semirufa***
Blue cap and ear coverts. Entirely rufous underparts.

**2  BLUE SWALLOW**          *Hirundo atrocaerulea*
**Entirely glossy blue-black.** Very long tail shafts. Call: wheezy chit-
tering. Singly or in small parties. Nests in holes underground.
Rare. Restricted to localised areas of e montane grassland, threat-
ened by forest plantations. Endangered summer resident.
**Similar**
**BLACK SAW-WING SWALLOW  *Psalidoprocne holomelas***
Entirely black. Tail shafts shorter. S and E coast and mistbelt hills.
Resident.

**3  EUROPEAN SWALLOW**          *Hirundo rustica*
**Dark red forehead and throat.** Black breast band. Long tail shafts.
Call: soft twittering made by flocks. Mixes with other swallows
and swifts. Flocks perch on wires and on roads. Numerous.
Throughout s Africa. Summer visitor.
**Similar**
**WHITETHROATED SWALLOW  *H. albigularis***
Red forehead. Clear white underparts with black breast band.
Summer resident.
**WIRETAILED SWALLOW  *H. smithii***
Dark orange cap. White underparts with partial breast band. NE.
Resident.
**PEARLBREASTED SWALLOW  *H. dimidiata***
Blue upperparts. White underparts. No tail streamers. Resident.
**GREYRUMPED SWALLOW  *Pseudhirundo griseopyga***
Grey-brown cap, pale grey rump. White underparts. NE. Resi-
dent.

**4  HOUSE MARTIN**          *Delichon urbica*
**Blue cap and back. White rump.** Short, slightly forked tail. White
underparts. Short, broad-based wings. Call: single "chirrup".
Often associates with European swallow. Widespread except SW.
Summer visitor.
**Similar**
**(EUROPEAN) SAND MARTIN  *Riparia riperia***
Brown except for white throat and belly.
**BROWNTHROATED MARTIN  *Riparia paludicola***
Entirely brown except for white belly. Resident.
**BANDED MARTIN  *Riparia cincta***
Larger (17 cm). White eyebrow. Brown upperparts. White under-
parts, broad brown breast band.
**ROCK MARTIN  *Hirundo fuligula***
Dark brown upperparts, light brown underparts. White "win-
dows" in fanned tail. Broad wings. Resident.

**1 PALM SWIFT** *Cypsiurus parvus*

**Entirely grey-brown.** Slender, long-tailed. In small flocks near palm trees where they roost and nest. Flight rapid. Sometimes associates with other swifts. N. Resident.
**Similar**
**BLACK SWIFT** *Apus barbatus*
Shorter tail. Dark with slightly paler wings. S and NE.
**EURASIAN (EUROPEAN) SWIFT** *Apus apus*
Uniformly dark, including wings. Mainly N of Orange River. Summer visitor.
**BRADFIELD'S SWIFT** *Apus bradfieldi*
Greyish underparts and underwings, otherwise black. Namibia and arid west-central interior.

**2 LITTLE SWIFT** *Apus affinis*

**White throat.** Dark brown or black plumage. **White rump patch wraps around sides.** Square tail. Stiff, rounded wings. Call: soft twittering. Mixes with other swifts. Breeds under eaves and bridges. Widespread except most of Botswana. Resident.
**Similar**
**HORUS SWIFT** *A. horus*
White rump patch extends onto sides. Forked tail.
**WHITERUMPED SWIFT** *A. caffer*
Narrow white crescent on rump. Deeply forked tail. Summer resident.
**ALPINE SWIFT** *A. melba*
Larger (22 cm). White belly and throat. Flies fast. Seen at cliffs.
**BÖHM'S SPINETAIL** *Neafrapus boehmi*
Smaller (9 cm). White rump and underparts. Virtually tailless. Mozambique and Zambezi valley.

**3 REDFACED MOUSEBIRD** *Urocolius indicus*

**Red facial mask.** Buffish head and breast. Pale grey rump. Red feet. Call: descending whistle "shree-ree-ree". Thornveld, woodland, suburbia. Flight fast and direct, in small compact groups, often calling on the wing. Widespread. Resident.
**Similar**
**SPECKLED MOUSEBIRD** *Colius striatus*
Black and white bill. Dull brown plumage. Floppy flight in straggling groups. S and E.
**WHITEBACKED MOUSEBIRD** *Colius colius*
Whitish bill. Grey upperparts, white back. Buff underparts. S and W.

1

17 cm

2

14 cm

3

32-34 cm

**Swifts**
Slender, straight swept-back wings.
Fly rapidly with only brief gliding spells.
Swifts do not perch.

17 cm

33-38 cm

25-29 cm

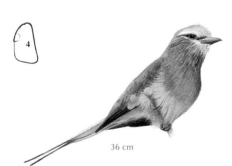

36 cm

**1   LITTLE BEE-EATER**                        *Merops pusillus*

Yellow throat, black collar. Green back. Orange-yellow belly and underwing. **Squarish tail.** Small. Call: quiet "chip-chip". Often in pairs on low perch near water. Savanna, thornveld. N and E. Resident.

**Similar**

**SWALLOWTAILED BEE-EATER** *M. hirundineus*
Bright blue collar. Bluish underparts. Forked tail.

**BLUECHEEKED BEE-EATER** *M. persicus*
Larger (30 cm). Brown and yellow throat. Turquoise belly.

**2   CARMINE BEE-EATER**                    *Merops nubicoides*

Crown deep blue. **Carmine plumage** with pale blue rump and vent. Call: deep "terk-terk". Flocks hawk insects from perches or the ground, twittering in flight. Riverine woodland, marshes, bushveld. Breeds colonially in holes in river bank. NE. Summer visitor and resident.

**3   EUROPEAN BEE-EATER**                    *Merops apiaster*

Turquoise-blue forehead. Yellow throat. **Golden-brown head and back.** Blue underparts. Call: distinctive "quilp". Open woodland, thornveld, fynbos, even urban parks. Loose flocks hawk insects from trees and telephone wires or while flying at great height. Widespread. Summer visitor.

**Similar**

**WHITEFRONTED BEE-EATER** *M. bullockoides*
White forehead. White and red throat. Lacks long tail feathers.

**4   LILACBREASTED ROLLER**                *Coracias caudata*

White face. **Lilac throat and breast.** Blue belly, vent and undertail. Brown upperparts. Tail shafts straight, often absent. Shows electric blue wings in flight. Call: harsh rattling. Perches conspicuously in open woodland, thornveld. Display flight involves spectacular aerial tumbling. N half of region. Resident.

**Similar**

**EUROPEAN ROLLER** *C. garrulus*
Blue head, breast and underparts. No tail shafts. Summer visitor.

**RACKET-TAILED ROLLER** *C. spatulata*
Blue throat and breast. Spatulate tail shafts. NE.

**PURPLE ROLLER** *C. naevia*
Red-brown underparts streaked with white. Green upperparts.

**BROADBILLED ROLLER** *Eurystomus glaucurus*
Large yellow bill. Purplish underparts. Cinnamon upperparts. NE. Summer resident.

**1 GIANT KINGFISHER** *Ceryle maxima*

Large, heavy bill. **Black upperparts with white spots. Male has rufous breast; female has rufous belly.** Call: harsh "kek-kek-kek-kek". Wooded waters; eats fish. Perches on overhanging branch, occasionally hovers. Widespread except arid W. Resident.

**2 PIED KINGFISHER** *Ceryle rudis*

**Entirely black and white.** Male has double breast band; female has partial breast band. Call: high-pitched twittering, often by more than one bird. Pairs or small groups at open water bodies. Hovers and dives for fish. Widespread except some central areas and NW. Resident.

**3 WOODLAND KINGFISHER** *Halcyon senegalensis*

Red and black bill (immature has all-red bill). Black stripe from bill through eye to ear coverts. Pale head. Call: loud, descending "trrp-trrrrrrrr". Woodland, savanna. Pairs hunt insects from perch. N and NE. Summer visitor.

Similar

**MANGROVE KINGFISHER** *H. senegaloides*

All-red bill. No stripe behind eye. In mangroves and estuaries on E coast. Resident.

**GREYHOODED KINGFISHER** *H. leucocephala*

All-red bill. No stripe behind eye. Chestnut belly.

**4 BROWNHOODED KINGFISHER** *Halcyon albiventris*

Red bill. Streaked brown head. Buff breast patches, streaked flanks. **Deep blue back and rump in flight.** Male has black wings; female has brown wings. Call: loud "kee-kee-kee". Bushveld, riverine and coastal woodland. Hunts insects from low perch. S coast to NE. Resident.

Similar

**STRIPED KINGFISHER** *H. chelicuti*

Smaller (18 cm). Black and red bill. Dark, streaked head. White collar.

**5 MALACHITE KINGFISHER** *Alcedo cristata*

Red bill (immature has black bill). **Turquoise crown down to eye. Rufous ear coverts** and underparts. Turquoise upperparts. Call: shrill "peep-peep". Open-water bodies with fringing vegetation. Perches on low reeds or branches in search of fish. E half of region and W along Orange and Zambezi rivers. Resident.

Similar

**PYGMY KINGFISHER** *Ispidina picta*

Mauve patch on ear coverts. Turquoise crown ends above eye. Away from water.

**HALFCOLLARED KINGFISHER** *Alcedo semitorquata*

Larger (20 cm). Black bill. Blue upperparts and ear coverts. Rufous belly.

1

43-46 cm

♂

2

♂

28-29 cm

3

23-24 cm

4

23-24 cm

5

14 cm

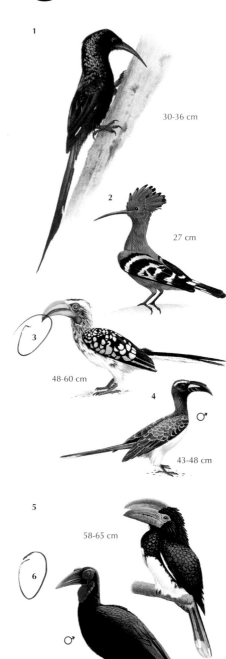

1

30-36 cm

2

27 cm

3

48-60 cm

4

43-48 cm

♂

5

58-65 cm

6

♂

90 cm

**1   REDBILLED WOODHOOPOE**     *Phoeniculus purpureus*
Decurved red bill (immature has black bill). Dark glossy blue
plumage. White wing-bars. Long tail. Red legs. Call: loud cackles
uttered by flock. Woodland, thornveld, suburbia. Flies from tree
to tree in small straggling groups. E and N. Resident.
**Similar**
**SCIMITARBILLED WOODHOOPOE** *Rhinopomastus*
*cyanomelas*
Smaller (26 cm). Strongly decurved black bill. Black legs.

**2   HOOPOE**     *Upupa epops*
Long, slightly decurved bill. Erects crest when alarmed. **Cinnamon plumage. Black and white striped wings.** Call: continuous
"hoop-hoop-hoop". Bushveld, suburbia. Walks about probing for
food. Throughout s Africa. Resident.

**3   SOUTHERN YELLOWBILLED HORNBILL**     *Tockus*
*leucomelas*
**Large yellow bill.** Red bare skin around eyes. Black and white
plumage. Long tail. Call: "wurk-wurk-wukwukuk, wukwukuk,
wurk, wurk ...", building up then receding. During display calling
pairs bow their heads and fan their wings. Dry woodland, mixed
bushveld. Pairs or small groups feed on the ground. N. Resident.
**Similar**
**REDBILLED HORNBILL** *T. erythrorhynchus*
Smallest hornbill (46 cm). All-red bill. Broad white eyebrow.
**CROWNED HORNBILL** *T. alboterminatus*
Red bill with casque. Plain dark brown upperparts. Forests in N
and E.

**4   GREY HORNBILL**     *Tockus nasutus*
Male has small, greyish bill with casque. Female has smaller
casque, upper mandible cream, red tip. Dark head and breast.
Upperparts grey, speckled. Call: plaintive notes ascending then
descending "phee, phephee, phee, pheeoo, pheeoo ...". Pairs or
small flocks in mixed bushveld. Central areas and N. Resident.
**Similar**
**MONTEIRO'S HORNBILL** *T. monteiri*
Red bill. Much white on wings and tail. Nw Namibia.
**BRADFIELD'S HORNBILL** *T. bradfieldi*
Orange bill. Brown wings and tail. Ne Namibia, n Botswana into
w Zimbabwe.

**5   TRUMPETER HORNBILL**     *Bycanistes bucinator*
Large casque on bill. Pink bare skin around eyes. Black throat,
breast and upperparts. White belly. Call: loud, nasal "whaa-aa-
aaa-aaaa". Sometimes several birds call together. Riverine and
lowland forest. Small groups feed in large fruit trees. Extreme E.
Resident.

**6   GROUND HORNBILL**     *Bucorvus leadbeateri*
Large: turkey-sized. Black, decurved bill. **Red face and throat
pouch.** Female has blue central patch on pouch. Plumage and feet
all-black. Call: deep, booming "oomph, oomph-oomph", usually
at dawn. Woodland, savanna, bushveld. Largely terrestrial in
small family flocks. Walks slowly in search of food. May take
flight if disturbed, then broad white wing patches visible. N and
E. Resident.

**BLACKCOLLARED BARBET**       *Lybius torquatus*

Heavy black bill. Bright red forehead, face and throat, bordered
by black collar. Yellowish belly. Call: unmistakable duet, starting
with a harsh "kerrr-kerr" then "tooo-puddely, tooo-puddely-tooo-
puddely ..." accompanied by bobbing and wing-quavering.
Woodland, savanna, suburbia. Pairs or small groups. N and E.
Resident.

**CRESTED BARBET**       *Trachyphonus vaillantii*

Yellow face with red scaling. **Black crest, broad black collar.**
Black and white scalloped upperparts. Call: trilling "trrrrr ..." by
male, female responds "puta-puta-puta-puta". Woodland, savanna, riverine forest, suburbia. Singly or in pairs. Fruit-eating. NE to
central areas. Resident.

**YELLOWFRONTED TINKER BARBET**       *Pogoniulus*
*chrysoconus*

Yellow or orange forehead (never red). Underparts pale yellow.
Call: monotonous, low-pitched "tink, tink, tink" continued for
long periods. Woodland, riverine bush, savanna. Attracted to *Vis-
cum* and *Loranthus* mistletoe-type parasites. N. Resident.
Similar
**REDFRONTED TINKER BARBET** *P. pusillus*
Bright red forehead. Darker appearance. Along section of E coast.
**PIED BARBET** *Tricholaema leucomelas*
Larger (17 cm). Black throat. White underparts. Broad black eye-
stripe. Widespread except NE.

**GROUND WOODPECKER**       *Geocolaptes olivaceus*

Olive head. **Red breast, belly and rump.** Male has moustachial
stripe. Call: loud, harsh "kee-urr, kee-urr". Hilly, boulder-strewn
grassland, gullies, mountains. **Entirely terrestrial.** Often perches
on boulders. Singly or in groups. S and into e interior. Endemic
resident.

**CARDINAL WOODPECKER**       *Dendropicos fuscescens*

Smallest woodpecker. Black moustachial stripe. **Male has brown
forehead, red crown. Female has black crown and nape.** Streaked
breast. Plumage appears dull black and white. Call: high-pitched
"kekekekek". Broadleafed woodland, thornveld, riverine bush.
Pairs often seen in mixed bird parties, gleaning food from trees.
Easily overlooked unless calling. Widespread. Resident.
Similar
**GOLDENTAILED WOODPECKER** *Campethera abingoni*
Streaked underparts. Male has red moustachial stripe and crown.
Female has red nape.
**BENNETT'S WOODPECKER** *Campethera bennettii*
Spotted underparts. Male has red moustachial stripe and crown.
Female has brown facial and throat patch.
**BEARDED WOODPECKER** *Thripias namaquus*
Larger (24 cm). Banded underparts. Both sexes have black mous-
tachial stripe and ear patch.

**REDTHROATED WRYNECK**       *Jynx ruficollis*

Rust-brown throat and upper breast. Brown-streaked and mottled
plumage. **Black broken line from crown to mantle.** Call: high-
pitched "kek-kek-kek-kek", uttered frequently. Open woodland,
grassland, suburbia. Singly or in pairs. Creeps around trees like a
woodpecker. Easily overlooked. Along SE coast and into central
interior. Localised resident.

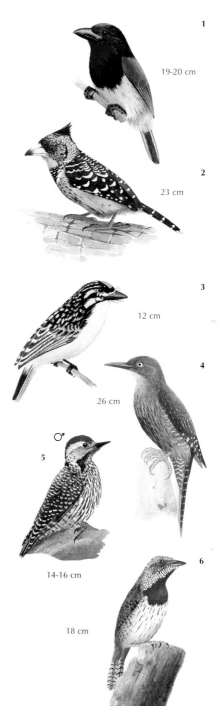

1

19-20 cm

2

23 cm

3

12 cm

4

26 cm

♂

5

14-16 cm

6

18 cm

19-20 cm

18-19 cm

Clapper lark

Flappet lark

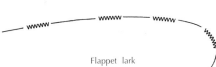

12-13 cm

**1   GREATER HONEYGUIDE**      *Indicator indicato.*
Male has **pinkish bill, dark crown and throat, white ear coverts**
Female has dark bill, speckled moustachial stripe. Yellow shoul
der patch not always present. White outer tail feathers. Immature
has yellow underparts. Call: "vic-torr, vic-torr ..." for long periods
Guides people to bees' nests, using harsh chattering sound
Woodland, bushveld, suburbia. E half of region. Resident.
**Similar**
**LESSER HONEYGUIDE** *I. minor*
Thick bill with pale patch at base. White outer tail feathers.
**SCALYTHROATED HONEYGUIDE** *I. variegatus*
Streaky head. Throat feathers scale-like. E coastal forests.

**2   RUFOUSNAPED LARK**      *Mirafra african.*
Rufous head, nape and wing-feather edges. Brownish-gre
plumage. Speckled upperparts. Pale underparts, usually wit
some streaking on breast. Terrestrial. Best recognised by cal
mournful, often repeated "tseep-tseeooo". Flaps wing feather
and raises crest while calling. Open grassland, fallow land, thorn
veld. Solitary. Often perches on posts, bushes or anthills. Wide
spread except SW. Resident.
**Similar**
**SABOTA LARK** *M. sabota*
White eyebrow distinctive. Short, dark bill, lower half pale.
**MONOTONOUS LARK** *M. passerina*
No distinct eyebrow. Call: "corr-weeooo" by male in summer.
**FAWNCOLOURED LARK** *M. africanoides*
Slightly streaked breast on white underparts.
**FLAPPET LARK** *M. rufocinnamomea*
In display male flies high with intermittent wing flaps. NE.
**CLAPPER LARK** *M. apiata*
In display male flies upwards, hovers and clap wings, then drop
with long whistle.
**LONGBILLED LARK** *M. curvirostris*
Long decurved bill. In display male flies high then drops wi
loud "cheeeeeeeooo".
**REDCAPPED LARK** *Calandrella cinerea*
Rufous cap. Clear white underparts. Rufous on side of breast.
**SPIKEHEELED LARK** *Chersomanes albofasciata*
Upright stance. Long bill. White throat. Short white-tipped tail.

**3   CHESTNUTBACKED FINCHLARK**      *Eremopterix leucot*
Male has black crown, white ear coverts, chestnut back and wi
coverts, black underparts. Female is mottled brown with bla
lower belly. Call: sharp "chip-chwep" uttered in flight. Cultivat
lands, open grassland, thornveld. Flocks fly low and erratical
suddenly settling on the ground. Central arid savanna, N and
Resident.
**Similar**
**GREYBACKED FINCHLARK** *E. verticalis*
Grey upperparts. W half of region.
**BLACKEARED FINCHLARK** *E. australis*
Male has no white plumage. Female no black on belly. South-ce
tral areas.

### GRASSVELD PIPIT     *Anthus cinnamomeus*
**Yellow base to lower mandible. Bold facial markings and breast streaks. White outer tail feathers.** Call: "chree-chree-chree" in flight with undulating dip. Usually solitary in open, often burned, grassland. If disturbed flies off, resettling close by. Throughout s Africa. Resident.
**Similar**
**BUFFY PIPIT** *A. vaalensis*
Pink base to bill. Rich, buff-coloured flanks.
**LONGBILLED PIPIT** *A. similis*
Buff outer tail feathers. Dull moustachial stripe.
**ROCK PIPIT** *A. crenatus*
Drab plumage. Pale eye-stripe. Calls with erect stance. S.
**PLAINBACKED PIPIT** *A. leucophrys*
Buff outer tail feathers. Uniform plumage on back.
**BUSHVELD PIPIT** *A. caffer*
Off-white throat with faint streaking. Flies erratically before resetting. NE.
**TREE PIPIT** *A. trivialis*
Short bill. White throat and breast with tear-shaped markings. Mainly Zimbabwe.
**STRIPED PIPIT** *A. lineiventris*
Yellow-edged wing feathers. Boldly streaked breast and belly. E.

### ORANGETHROATED LONGCLAW     *Macronyx capensis*
**Orange throat encircled with black.** Deep yellow underparts. Buff edges to wing feathers. Call: nasal mewing "mee-yi", also high-pitched whistle. Singly or in pairs in grassland. Usually on the ground, but readily flies to low perches. S and E coast into east-central interior, also ne interior. Resident.
**Similar**
**PINKTHROATED LONGCLAW** *M. ameliae*
Pink throat and breast, black collar. White outer tail feathers.
**YELLOWTHROATED LONGCLAW** *M. croceus*
Yellow throat and belly, black collar. Brown upperparts. Moist grassland.

### CAPE WAGTAIL     *Motacilla capensis*
**Brown-grey upperparts. Thin black breast band.** Buffy belly and flanks. Call: loud, clear "tseep". At waterside or suburban gardens. Singly or in pairs running along the ground, occasionally wagging its tail. Tame and confiding. Widespread except NE. Resident.

### AFRICAN PIED WAGTAIL     *Motacilla aguimp*
**Black upperparts, white wing coverts. White underparts with black breast band.** Singly, in pairs or small groups near any water. N and E, plus W along Orange and Zambezi rivers. Resident.
**Similar**
**LONGTAILED WAGTAIL** *M. clara*
Grey and white. Very long tail. Fast-running streams. Pairs.

### YELLOW WAGTAIL     *Motacilla flava*
Yellow underparts. Grey upperparts. Grey or black head. N and along E and S coast. Summer visitor.

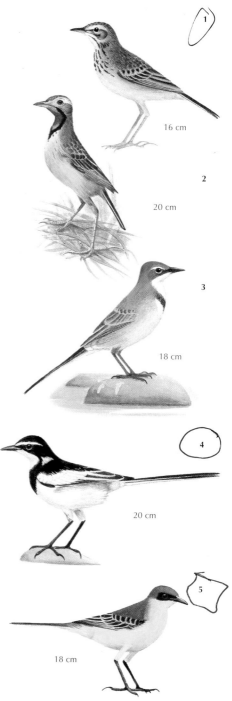

1    16 cm

2    20 cm

3    18 cm

4    20 cm

5    18 cm

25 cm

19-22 cm

♂

22 cm

♀

46-52 cm

25 cm

**1  FORKTAILED DRONGO**          *Dicrurus adsimili*

Red eyes. All-black plumage. **Deeply forked tail with outer feath ers curved outwards.** Call: variety of twanging and shrill notes also mimics other birds. Vocal and aggressive. Singly or in pairs Savanna, bushveld. Widespread except SW coast and Karoo. Res ident.
**Similar**
**SQUARETAILED DRONGO**  *D. ludwigii*
Red eyes. Small, rounded head. Tail only slightly forked. Extreme I

**2  BLACK FLYCATCHER**          *Melaenornis pammelain*

Brown eyes. Tail slightly indented at tip. Outer tail feathe straight. Mostly quiet. NE. Resident.

**3  BLACK CUCKOOSHRIKE**          *Campephaga flav*

Male has **orange-yellow gape**, black plumage; may have yellow shoulder. Female is brownish with barred underparts, brown an yellow wing coverts, bright yellow outer tail feathers. Call: hig pitched trill "trrrrr ...". Woodland, thornveld, bushveld, coast bush. Pairs move through trees unobtrusively, often in bird partie N and along E coast. Resident or summer visitor.
**Similar**
**WHITEBREASTED CUCKOOSHRIKE**  *Coracina pectoralis*
Pale grey upperparts. White underparts.
**GREY CUCKOOSHRIKE**  *Coracina caesia*
All-grey plumage. S coast and E.

**4  PIED CROW**          *Corvus alb*

All-black plumage except white breast and collar. Call: lou harsh cawing. Wide range of habitats, usually in association wi human settlement. Scavenges scraps from refuse dumps, hig ways, fields. Often circles in loose flocks. Widespread except ce tral arid savanna. Resident.
**Similar**
**WHITENECKED RAVEN**  *C. albicollis*
Black with white nape only. Large head. Massive black bill.
**HOUSE CROW**  *C. splendens*
Black with grey nape, mantle and breast. Durban vicinity.
**BLACK CROW**  *C. capensis*
Entirely glossy black.

**5  BLACKHEADED ORIOLE**          *Oriolus larvat*

Red eyes and bill. **Black head.** Yellow-green upperparts. Yello underparts. Call: loud, liquid whistle "pheeoo"; harsh "chee alarm call. Broadleafed and riverine woodland, exotic plan tions, mixed bushveld. Vocal and conspicuous. Singly or in pa in canopy. N, NE and E. Resident.
**Similar**
**EUROPEAN GOLDEN ORIOLE**  *O. oriolus*
Yellow with black wings. Black stripe in front of eye. Summer v itor.
**AFRICAN GOLDEN ORIOLE**  *O. auratus*
All-yellow except for black wing edges and black stripe throu and behind eye. Summer resident.

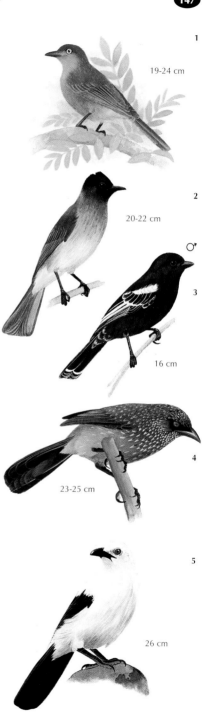

### SOMBRE BULBUL — *Andropadus importunus*

**White eyes.** Dull olive-green plumage. Call: piercing "Willie!" followed in breeding season by babbling trill. Forests, coastal bush. Singly. Highly vocal but camouflaged within canopy. E areas from N to S. Resident.

**Similar**

**YELLOWSPOTTED NICATOR** *Nicator gularis*
Heavy bill. Bright yellow spots on wings. NE.

**YELLOWBELLIED BULBUL** *Chlorocichla flaviventris*
Reddish eyes. White eyelids. Bright yellow underparts. N and E.

19-24 cm

### BLACKEYED BULBUL — *Pycnonotus barbatus*

Dark crested head. Yellow vent. Call: "chit, chit, chit ..." in alarm, and several cheerful liquid calls. Bushveld and woodland, including suburbia, but not evergreen forests. Gregarious. N and E. Common resident.

**Similar**

**REDEYED BULBUL** *P. nigricans*
Red eye wattle. Arid W.

**CAPE BULBUL** *P. capensis*
White eye wattle. Brownish head. Endemic to extreme S and SW.

**TERRESTRIAL BULBUL** *Phyllastrephus terrestris*
Yellowish gape. White throat. Drab brown plumage.

**YELLOWSTREAKED BULBUL** *Phyllastrephus flavostriatus*
Long bill. Dark eyes. Often flicks open one wing. E.

20-22 cm

### SOUTHERN BLACK TIT — *Parus niger*

Short stout bill. Black and white plumage. Greyish underparts in female. Call: harsh, rasping "twiddy-zeet-zeet-zeet" or "zeu-zeu-zu-twit". Wooded habitat. Pairs or groups. N and E. Common resident.

**Similar**

**CARP'S BLACK TIT** *P. carpi*
Small bill. More white in wing. Nw Namibia.

**SOUTHERN GREY TIT** *P. afer*
Grey-brown mantle and back. Buffy belly. Short tail. S and NW.

**ASHY TIT** *P. cinerascens*
Blue-grey mantle, back, flanks and belly. Central interior and NW.

16 cm

### ARROWMARKED BABBLER — *Turdoides jardineii*

Orange eyes. White, arrow-like streaks on underparts. Brown rump. Call: excitable, babbling "scurr-scurr-scurr ...". Woodland, mixed bushveld. Parties move through trees calling frequently. ... Resident.

### PIED BABBLER — *Turdoides bicolor*

All-white except black wings and tail. Dry thornveld, woodland. W. Resident.

**Similar**

**BARECHEEKED BABBLER** *T. gymnogenys*
Black skin below eye. Sides of neck tawny. Nw Namibia.

**WHITERUMPED BABBLER** *T. hartlaubii*
Orange eyes. White rump and vent. White scallops on head and body. Okavango-Zambezi area.

23-25 cm

26 cm

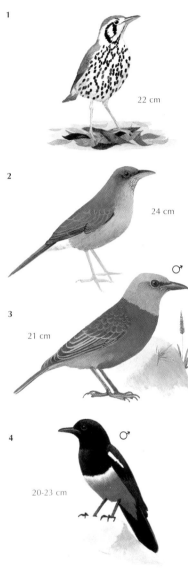

**1    GROUNDSCRAPER THRUSH**          *Turdus litsitsirup*

Black facial markings. Heavily spotted underparts. In flight wing show orange. Call: loud, clear "litsitsirupa". Dry bushveld, wood land, gardens. Singly, often on bare ground. Calls from trees. half of region. Resident.
**Similar**
**SPOTTED THRUSH**  *Zoothera guttata*
Looks like previous species but has white wing spots. Some coast forests.
**DUSKY LARK**  *Pinarocorys nigricans*
Darker facial markings and back. Summer visitor.

**2    OLIVE THRUSH**                          *Turdus olivaceu*

Yellow bill. Speckled throat. Olive-orange underparts. Call: th "wheet" or "wheet-troo-wheet-wheetrroo ...". Woodland, subu bia. Singly or in pairs. Male displays with drooped wings and ta dragging. S half of region. Resident.
**Similar**
**KURRICHANE THRUSH**  *T. libonyana*
Orange bill and eye-ring. Black and white throat markings. NE.

**3    CAPE ROCK THRUSH**                  *Monticola rupestr*

Male has blue-grey head and neck. Female has brown streake head. Rich orange underparts. Call: soft "checheroo" followed loud, repeated whistling "cheewoo-chirri-cheewootiriri". Pa frequent rocky terrain and bush-covered slopes. S. Endemic re dent.
**Similar**
**SHORT-TOED ROCK THRUSH**  *M. brevipes*
Male has whitish-blue crown. Arid W.
**SENTINEL ROCK THRUSH**  *M. explorator*
Male's blue-grey head extends onto mantle and breast.

**4    MOCKING CHAT**            *Thamnolaea cinnamomeivent*

**Black upper body. Chestnut belly, vent and rump.** Male has wh shoulder stripe. Call: melodious sounds, largely imitating oth birds. Pairs in rocky habitats. Frequently raises rear of body. Resident.
**Similar**
**CAPE ROCKJUMPER**  *Chaetops frenatus*
Male has black and white head, rufous underparts. Extreme S.
**ORANGEBREASTED ROCKJUMPER**  *Chaetops aurantius*
Male has orange-yellow underparts. S Drakensberg.

**5    MOUNTAIN CHAT**                    *Oenanthe montico*

Male is pale grey or black with grey cap. Female is blacki brown. White rump, shoulder and outer tail feathers. Call: cl warbling notes, early and late in day. Grassy slopes with rocks anthills. Flies short distance before perching on rock. Widespre except E and NE. Resident.
**Similar**
**ARNOT'S CHAT**  *Thamnolaea arnoti*
Male has white cap, black rump and tail. Female has white thro N.

### CAPPED WHEATEAR — *Oenanthe pileata*

lack cap. White forehead and eyebrow. Broad black breast col-
r. Buff flanks. Short tail. Long legs. Call: melodious whistles.
pen or burnt ground. Nests in burrow. Widespread except
xtreme E. Summer resident, depending on food supply.
imilar
**UFFSTREAKED CHAT  O. bifasciata**
ale has black face, breast and wings, buffy belly.

### STONECHAT — *Saxicola torquata*

ale has black head and back, white on neck, wings and rump,
estnut breast. Female is dull with white wing patches. Call:
ating "tsak, tsak". Grassy hillsides. In pairs. Usually perches
ominently. E half of region. Resident.

### FAMILIAR CHAT — *Cercomela familiaris*

rab grey-brown. Rump and outer tail feathers dark rufous. Call:
huck, chuck" in alarm. Rocky hillsides, farms. Tame and con-
ling. Usually perches prominently. Often flicks wings. Wide-
read except Mozambique and n Botswana. Resident.
imilar
**CKLEWINGED CHAT  C. sinuata**
le underparts contrast with darker upperparts.
**AROO CHAT  C. schlegelii**
le grey plumage. Grey rump. White outer tail feathers.
**NTEATING CHAT  Myrmecocichla formicivora**
ark brown. Conspicuous white underwings. Upright stance.

### CAPE ROBIN — *Cossypha caffra*

hite eyebrow stripe. Orange upper breast, tail and back. Pale
y underparts. Call: melodious variation of four notes. Forest
ges, bushveld, scrub, gardens. Usually near ground, close to
ver. S half of region. Resident.
milar
**EUGLIN'S ROBIN  C. heuglini**
ld white eyebrow stripe. Deep orange underparts. NE.
**HITETHROATED ROBIN  C. humeralis**
hite throat, breast and wing-bar.
**HORISTER ROBIN  C. dichroa**
eyebrow. Orange-yellow underparts, including throat. E
ests.
**ARRED ROBIN  C. stellata**
eyebrow. Grey head and throat. White spot on forehead. Yel-
 underparts. E forests.
**ATAL ROBIN  C. natalensis**
eyebrow. Entirely orange except grey cap and back. Forests in
nd NE.

### WHITEBROWED ROBIN — *Erythropygia leucophrys*

ite eyebrow. White wing-bars and tail tip. Brownish plumage.
eaked breast. Call: repetitive, whistling tune. Bushveld, wood-
d thickets. Secretive but may call from exposed perch. N and
ng SE coast. Resident.
milar
**LAHARI ROBIN  E. paena**
ite eyebrow. Sandy brown. Plain breast. Tail has broad black
d.

18 cm

O'  14 cm

15 cm

18 cm

15 cm

1

12 cm

2

12-13 cm

3

9-10 cm

4

10-12 cm

5

15 cm

**1 WILLOW WARBLER** *Phylloscopus trochilu*
**Creamy-white eyebrow.** Pale yellow throat and breast. Oliv
upperparts. **Scalloped tail tip.** (Sometimes entirely brown upper
parts and white underparts.) Call: soft "foo-eet". Woodland
thornveld. Singly, often in bird parties. Active leaf-gleaner. Wide
spread except extreme W. Summer visitor.
**Similar**
**ICTERINE WARBLER** *Hippolais icterina*
Lower mandible orange. More yellow on wings.
**YELLOW WARBLER** *Chloropeta natalensis*
All-yellow underparts. E thickets and reeds. Resident.
**YELLOWTHROATED WARBLER** *Phylloscopus ruficapillus*
Yellow throat and breast. Whitish belly. S and e forests. Residen

**2 BARTHROATED APALIS** *Apalis thoracic*
**Pale eyes.** Dark upperparts. Pale underparts. **Black throat bar**
(sometimes lacking in female). **White outer tail feathers.** Call: di
tinctive "tilly-tilly-tilly". Woodland, forest. Pairs, often in bird pa
ties. S and E. Resident.
**Similar**
**YELLOWBREASTED APALIS** *A. flavida*
Grey head. White throat. Yellow breast. White belly. N and E.
**BURNTNECKED EREMOMELA** *Eremomela usticollis*
Brown around eyes. Brown throat-bar (sometimes absent). Yello
underparts. N.
**RUFOUSEARED WARBLER** *Malcorus pectoralis*
Black bar on white underparts. Rufous face. Arid W.

**3 YELLOWBELLIED EREMOMELA** *Eremomela icteropygia*
Greyish-white throat and breast. Yellow belly and flanks. Uppe
parts grey. Call: high-pitched "chirri-chee-chee-choo". Pairs fee
in low scrub, open woodland. Often in bird parties. Widespre
except S and E. Resident.
**Similar**
**GREENCAPPED EREMOMELA** *E. scotops*
Green crown. Yellow throat and breast. Pale yellow belly. NE.

**4 LONGBILLED CROMBEC** *Sylvietta rufesce*
Long bill. Brown-grey upperparts. Buff underparts. Taille
appearance. Call: "tree-treer, tree-treer ...". Bushveld, arid fynbo
Usually in pairs in mixed bird parties, gleaning insects from twig
Widespread. Resident.
**Similar**
**REDFACED CROMBEC** *S. whytii*
Shorter bill. Rufous face. NE.

**5 TITBABBLER** *Parisoma subcaerule*
Pale yellow eyes. Dark grey upperparts. Extensive streaking
throat. **Chestnut vent.** Call: clear, ringing notes "cheriktiktik"
"chu-ti chuu-ti chuu-chuu". Mixed bushveld, woodland. Fora
in dense thickets but shows itself freely. Widespread except
Resident.
**Similar**
**LAYARD'S TITBABBLER** *P. layardi*
White vent. Karoo extending N into Namibia.

**1   CAPE PENDULINE TIT**          *Anthoscopus minutus*

**Mottled black forehead.** Yellow underparts. Tiny body. Short tail.
Call: soft "swee-swee-swee". Thornveld, arid scrub, fynbos. Small
groups feed in trees, calling and flitting from one tree to next. W
half of region. Resident.
**Similar**
**GREY PENDULINE TIT** *A. caroli*
Buff face and forehead. Grey throat and breast. Buff belly. NE.

**2   AFRICAN MARSH WARBLER**    *Acrocephalus baeticatus*

No distinctive eyebrow. Brown upperparts. Whitish underparts.
Sharp face. Call: slow, uninterrupted "chuck-chuck-wee-chirruc-
churr-weee-weee-chirruc". Singly or in pairs, moving through
reeds and tall grass. Throughout s Africa. Summer resident.
**Similar**
**EUROPEAN MARSH WARBLER** *A. palustris*
Underparts buffy. Bush, riverine thickets, hillside briers.
**CAPE REED WARBLER** *A. gracilirostris*
White eyebrow. Pale face and chest. Always near water. Bold.
Resident.
**AFRICAN SEDGE WARBLER** *Bradypterus baboecala*
Eye-stripe. Faint markings on breast. Broad rounded tail. E half of
region. Resident.
**GREAT REED WARBLER** *Acrocephalus aruninaceus*
Robust. Heavy movements. Call: slow, harsh warble.
**BROADTAILED WARBLER** *Schoenicola brevirostris*
Broad black tail. Sits vertically on reeds. Resident.
**GARDEN WARBLER** *Sylvia borin*
Rounded head. Plain brown plumage.

**3   GREENBACKED BLEATING WARBLER**    *Camaroptera*
*brachyura*

Upperparts dark olive-green. Alarm call: plaintive "bleeb"; terri-
torial call: "chirrup, chirrup, chirrup". Secretive in low dense
growth. Cocks its tail. E evergreen forests. Resident.
**Similar**
**GREYBACKED BLEATING WARBLER** *C. brevicaudata*
Grey or dusty-brown upperparts. Dry savanna in N.
**KAROO EREMOMELA** *Eremomela gregalis*
Pale yellow eyes. Yellow vent. Karoo into Namibia.

**4   BARRED WARBLER**          *Calamonastes fasciolatus*

Brown cap and back. Brown bars on buff underparts. Call: three
to five mournful "brreeet-brreeet-brreeet" sounds, continued for
long periods. Pairs feed low in thickets. North-central areas. Res-
ident.
**Similar**
**STIERLING'S BARRED WARBLER** *C. stierlingi*
White underparts, boldly barred. NE.
**CINNAMONBREASTED WARBLER** *Euryptila subcinnamomea*
Cinnamon forehead and breast. Black tail. Karoo into Namibia.

**5   GRASSBIRD**               *Sphenoeacus afer*

Rufous cap. Black facial stripes. **Long straggly tail.** Heavily
streaked underparts, boldly marked upperparts. Call: jangled
musical song. Rank grassland, fynbos. S and E. Resident.

1

9-10 cm

2

13 cm

3

12 cm

4

13-15 cm

5

19-23 cm

10-12 cm

10-11 cm

♂    ♀

23 cm

♂

17-18 cm

### 1   FANTAILED CISTICOLA                *Cisticola juncidis*

Dark streaks on crown and upperparts, paler below. Tail boldly marked, black above and below, with broad white tip. Call: "tink, tink, tink ..." by male in summer, flying at a height of 30-40 m, each note accompanied by dip in flight. Grassveld areas. Widespread except arid W. Resident.

**Similar** (all nearly identical in appearance)

**DESERT CISTICOLA  *C. aridula***
Male flies low, calling "zink, zink, zink ..." and snapping wings.

**CLOUD CISTICOLA  *C. textrix***
Male flies high out of sight, calling "see-see-seesee-chick-chick". S and E.

**AYRES' CISTICOLA  *C. ayresii***
Calls like cloud cisticola but with rapid diving and wing snapping. E.

### 2   NEDDICKY                          *Cisticola fulvicapilla*

Rufous cap. Plain brown back, blue-grey underparts (S and E) or buffy underparts (N). Call: continuous "chirri-chirri-chirri ...". Alarm call is a rapid ticking. Pairs or parties in montane or wooded grassland in e half of region. Resident.

**Similar**

**GREYBACKED CISTICOLA  *C. subruficapilla***
Grey back with black streaks. Scrub in S and W.

**BLACKBACKED CISTICOLA  *C. galactotes***
Boldly streaked back. Reedbeds on E coast and in Okavango.

**LEVAILLANT'S CISTICOLA  *C. tinniens***
Streaked back. Waterside reeds in temperate S and E.

**RATTLING CISTICOLA  *C. chiniana***
Shows black gape when singing. Thornveld in N.

**TINKLING CISTICOLA  *C. rufilata***
Reddish crown and ear patch. Dry scrub in north-central areas.

**WAILING CISTICOLA  *C. lais***
Crown well marked. Belly buff. Hillsides in S and E.

**LAZY CISTICOLA  *C. aberrans***
Like neddicky but often cocks tail. Hillsides in E.

**REDFACED CISTICOLA  *C. erythrops***
Uniform plumage. Waterside vegetation in NE.

**CROAKING CISTICOLA  *C. natalensis***
Thick bill. Grey crown. Heavy-bodied. Grassland in NE.

### 3   PARADISE FLYCATCHER                *Terpsiphone viridis*

**Eye-ring and bill blue.** Dark head and throat. Chestnut back and tail. Call: lively "twee-tiddly-twer-twer"; alarm a sharp "zwee-zwer". Riverine bush, forest edges, gardens. Widespread except some areas in W. Summer resident (all year at coast).

### 4   BLUEMANTLED FLYCATCHER  *Trochocercus cyanomelas*

Black head, slightly crested. Dark grey upperparts. White underparts. White wing-bar. Call: high-pitched "kwew-ew-ew-ew"; alarm call same as paradise flycatcher. Pairs active in mid- and upper strata of coastal forest. S and E. Resident.

**Similar**

**WATTLE-EYED FLYCATCHER  *Platysteira peltata***
Red eye wattles. No wing-bar. E.

**1   TAWNYFLANKED PRINIA**                    *Prinia subflava*
Clear white underparts. Buff flanks. Rufous wing-edges. Long tail, often cocked. Call: rapidly repeated "trink-trink-trink", or plaintive "sbeee-sbeee". Rank grass, gardens. Pairs or small parties. N and E. Resident.
**Similar**
**BLACKCHESTED PRINIA  *P. flavicans***
Black breast band in breeding season or yellow underparts.
**KAROO PRINIA  *P. maculosa*** and **DRAKENSBERG PRINIA  *P. hypoxantha***
Heavily streaked cream or pale yellow breast.
**NAMAQUA WARBLER  *Phragmacia substriata***
Faint streaks on breast. Rufous upperparts, flanks and vent. S.

**2   DUSKY FLYCATCHER**                     *Muscicapa adusta*
Slight streaking on crown. Olive-brown upperparts. Underparts dull white with faint streaks. Call: sibilant "tzeeet". Forest edges. Singly or in pairs, perched quietly hawking prey. Along S and E coast and escarpment. Resident.
**Similar**
**SPOTTED FLYCATCHER  *M. striata***
Streaked crown. Larger and slimmer than dusky flycatcher. Widespread. Summer visitor.
**MARICO FLYCATCHER  *Melaenornis mariquensis***
Larger (18 cm). Brown upperparts contrast with white underparts. N.
**CHAT FLYCATCHER  *Melaenornis infuscatus***
Larger (20 cm). All-brown. Pale wing-edges. W half of region.
**BLUEGREY FLYCATCHER  *Muscicapa caerulescens***
Upperparts blue-grey, underparts lighter grey. NE.
**FANTAILED FLYCATCHER  *Myioparus plumbeus***
Pale grey. Fans tail with white outer feathers. NE.

**3   FAIRY FLYCATCHER**                      *Stenostira scita*
White eyebrow. Grey and black. Conspicuous white wing-bar and outer tail feathers. Call: sibilant trill "kisskisskisskiss". Flits about in bushes. Frequently bobs tail. Central areas: near rivers to the S in summer, moving northwards to woodland in winter. Resident and winter visitor.

**4   CHINSPOT BATIS**                         *Batis molitor*
Yellow eyes. Black face mask. Grey above. White wing-bar. Male has black breast band. Female has rufous breast band and chinspot. Call: two or three descending notes "teuu-tuuu-tuuu". Woodland, savanna. Pairs or groups in well defined territory. E and N. Resident.
**Similar**
**CAPE BATIS  *B. capensis***
Rufous on flanks of both sexes. S and e forests.
**PRIRIT BATIS  *B. pririt***
Female has buff throat and breast. W half of region.
**MOZAMBIQUE BATIS  *B. soror***
Markings less distinct than in chinspot batis. Mozambique.

10-15 cm

12-13 cm

12 cm

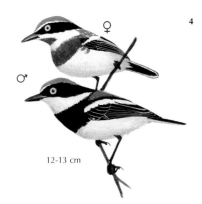

12-13 cm

40-50 cm

2

♂

23 cm

3

23-25 cm

4

18 cm

♂

5

23 cm

6

23 cm

**1   LONGTAILED SHRIKE**               *Corvinella melanoleuca*
Black with white wing-bar and wing tips. **Long black tail.** Call: whistled "prooit-preooo", first note descending, latter ascending. Acacia thornveld. Small groups, perching conspicuously. Takes prey from ground. North-central savanna. Resident.

**2   FISCAL SHRIKE**                           *Lanius collaris*
Black upperparts. White bar across shoulders. White underparts. W races have white eyebrow. Female has rufous flanks. Call: harsh "gercha, gercha". Variety of habitats except forest. Perches prominently, flying down to catch prey. Territorial. Impales prey on thorns. Widespread except NE. Resident.
**Similar**
**FISCAL FLYCATCHER  Sigelus silens**
White bar on wings, not shoulders. White windows in tail.

**3   WHITECROWNED SHRIKE**        *Eurocephalus anguitimens*
**White crown and forehead.** Dark eyes. Black mask. Throat and breast white. Belly buff. Call: shrill "kwee-kwee-kwee". Thornveld, mixed woodland. Usually in small groups, maintaining contact by loud calling. Hunts from prominent perch. North-central areas. Endemic resident.
**Similar**
**WHITE HELMETSHRIKE  Prionops plumatus**
Yellow eye-ring. Grey crown. Black and white wings. In groups.
**LESSER GREY SHRIKE  Lanius minor**
Grey crown and back. Black forehead and mask. Solitary. Summer visitor.
**REDBACKED SHRIKE  Lanius collurio**
Male has grey crown. Chestnut back. Black face mask. Solitary. Summer visitor.

**4   PUFFBACK**                               *Dryoscopus cubla*
Red eyes. Pied plumage. Distinctive wing-bar. Male puffs up white rump in display. Female has white forehead and eyebrow. Call: sharp "chick-weeu, chick-weeu". Woodland, forest. Pairs, often in mixed bird parties. Forages in canopy. Noisy, purring flight. N and E. Resident.
**Similar**
**BRUBRU  Nilaus afer**
Dark eyes. Rich rufous flanks. Thick bill.
**WHITETAILED SHRIKE  Lanioturdus torquatus**
Grey back and lower breast. Short white tail. Long legs. Nw Namibia.

**5   SOUTHERN BOUBOU**                 *Laniarius ferrugineus*
Black upperparts. White bar across shoulders and wings. Rufous belly and vent. Call: duet, "ko-ko" replied to with "kweet" and wide variety of other sounds. Thickets, forest edges. Pairs move secretively near ground in tangled undergrowth. S and E. Resident.
**Similar**
**SWAMP BOUBOU  L. bicolor**
All-white underparts. Zambezi, Chobe and Okavango rivers.
**TROPICAL BOUBOU  L. aethiopicus**
Underparts lightly washed pink. NE.

**6   CRIMSON BOUBOU**              *Laniarius atrococcineus*
Like other boubous but with striking scarlet underparts. Arid NW and central areas. Resident.

**1   BLACKCROWNED TCHAGRA**          *Tchagra senegala*

Black crown. Broad white eyebrow. Pale back. Chestnut wings. Shows white outer tail feathers in flight. Call: "CHEER-tcharee, trichi, cheeroo, cheeroo". Singly in lower strata of woodland, thornveld. N and E. Resident.
**Similar**
**THREESTREAKED TCHAGRA   *T. australis***
Pale grey-brown crown. Frequently on ground.
**SOUTHERN TCHAGRA   *T. tchagra***
Reddish-brown crown. Olive-brown back. S and E coast.

**2   ORANGEBREASTED BUSH SHRIKE**          *Telophorus sulfureopectus*

Blue-grey crown. Yellow forehead and eyebrow. Yellow underparts. Orange breast. Call: "po-po-po-poooo" or "pipit-eeez". Usually in pairs. Riverine thornveld, often in lower and mid-strata. Not secretive. N and E. Resident.
**Similar**
**OLIVE BUSH SHRIKE   *T. olivaceus***
Russet breast with blue-grey crown and white eyebrow, or yellowish breast with green crown and no white eyebrow. S and e forests.
**BLACKFRONTED BUSH SHRIKE   *T. nigrifrons***
No yellow eyebrow. Orange underparts. Mountains in NE.
**GORGEOUS BUSH SHRIKE   *T. quadricolour***
Scarlet throat. E forests and coastal bush.

**3   BOKMAKIERIE**          *Telophorus zeylonus*

Grey and green upperparts. Bright yellow underparts with broad black breast band. Call: duet, "bok-bok-chit" and variations. Pairs in bush, grassland, rocky hillsides. Widespread except N and E. Resident.

**4   GREYHEADED BUSH SHRIKE**          *Malaconotus blanchoti*

**Heavy, hooked bill.** White patch in front of yellow eye. Yellow-orange underparts. Call: haunting, drawn-out whistle "hooooooooop". Riverine woodland, bushveld. Singly or in pairs, feeding in mid- and lower strata. Not secretive but prefers cover. E coast and NE. Resident.

**5   REDBILLED HELMETSHRIKE**          *Prionops retzii*

Red bill, eye-ring and legs. Black plumage with white vent and tail tips. Call: harsh "cherow", often in chorus. Parties in mid- and lower strata of woodland and mature riverine forest. NE. Resident.

**6   INDIAN MYNA**          *Acridotheres tristis*

Yellow bill and skin around eye. Glossy black and brown plumage. White wing patches conspicuous in flight. Yellow legs. Call: varied, discordant chattering. Urban habitats. Roosts in large flocks or in pairs. Struts and forages on lawns. Aggressive when nesting. Introduced. E coast into interior. Resident.

1

21-23 cm

2

19 cm

3

23 cm

4

25-27 cm

5

22 cm

6

25 cm

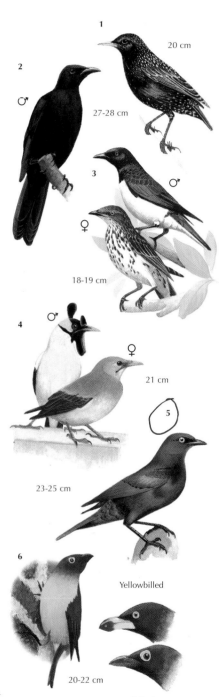

1

20 cm

2

♂

27-28 cm

3

♂

♀

18-19 cm

4

♂

♀

21 cm

5

23-25 cm

6

Yellowbilled

20-22 cm

Redbilled

**1 EUROPEAN STARLING** *Sturnus vulgaris*

Bill yellow when breeding. Blackish plumage with purple-green sheen and pale speckling. Call: harsh "cherr". Flocks in suburbia, playing fields, farmland. Walks rapidly with jerking action. Probes ground for food. Introduced. S. Resident.

**2 REDWINGED STARLING** *Onychognathus morio*

Dark eyes. Blue-black plumage. Female has grey head. Bright red-brown flight feathers. Call: loud whistle "spreeooo". Roosts on cliffs but flocks disperse widely. Perches conspicuously. S, E and NE. Resident.
**Similar**
**PALEWINGED STARLING** *O. nabouroup*
Orange eyes. Whitish flight feathers. W.
**PIED STARLING** *Spreo bicolor*
Pale yellow eyes. Orange gape. Brown plumage. White vent. S and central areas.

**3 PLUMCOLOURED STARLING** *Cinnyricinclus leucogaster*

Male has glossy violet upperparts, head and throat; white underparts. Female has yellow gape; mottled brown above, brown streaks on white below. Call: short slurred whistles. Woodland, riverine forest. In pairs or flocks. N and E. Summer resident.

**4 WATTLED STARLING** *Creatophora cinerea*

Pale grey. Breeding male has yellow and black skin and wattles on head. Non-breeding male and female drab. Black wings. White rump visible in flight. Call: rasping squeak. Gregarious flocks in grassland. Nests colonially in bushes. Throughout s Africa. Nomadic resident.

**5 CAPE GLOSSY STARLING** *Lamprotornis nitens*

Yellow eyes. **Uniform blue-green ear patch.** Head and underparts uniform blue-green. Call: harsh "trrr-tree-cherr". Upright stance. Pairs or flocks in thornveld, woodland, suburbia. Bold. Omnivorous. Widespread except extreme S. Resident.
**Similar**
**BLACKBELLIED GLOSSY STARLING** *L. corruscus*
Glossy blue-black. Black belly and flanks. E coast forests.
**GREATER BLUE-EARED GLOSSY STARLING** *L. chalybaeus*
Black ear patch. Royal blue belly and flanks. NE.
**LONGTAILED GLOSSY STARLING** *L. mevesii*
Dark eyes. Long pointed tail. Limpopo-Cunene-Zambezi area.
**BURCHELL'S GLOSSY STARLING** *L. australis*
Dark eyes. Black ear patch. Long square tail. North-central areas.

**6 REDBILLED OXPECKER** *Buphagus erythrorhynchus*

**All-red bill.** Large yellow eye wattle. Dark rump. Call: rasping "churrrr" in flight. Savanna, especially game reserves. Family groups associate with game, feeding on ticks. Roosts communally. N and E. Resident.
**Similar**
**YELLOWBILLED OXPECKER** *B. africanus*
Yellow bill with red tip. Pale rump.

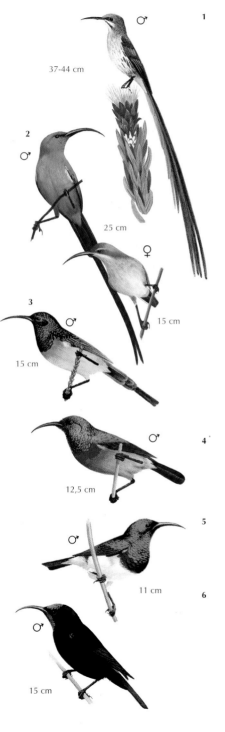

**1   CAPE SUGARBIRD**              *Promerops cafer*

Distinct moustachial stripe. Pale rufous breast. Male has very long, wispy tail, female's tail shorter. Call: jangled, metallic notes. Visits proteas on coastal mountains and flats. Male calls from prominent perch and displays over territory. Extreme S. Endemic resident.
**Similar**
**GURNEY'S SUGARBIRD**  *P. gurneyi*
Bold rufous breast and cap. E escarpment.

**2   MALACHITE SUNBIRD**          *Nectarinia famosa*

Male has long tail. Breeding male is iridescent green with yellow pectoral tufts. Female has short tail, brown back, pale yellow underparts. Call: loud "sseep". Slopes with proteas and aloes, scrub. Temperate S and interior. Resident.

**3   ORANGEBREASTED SUNBIRD**     *Nectarinia violacea*

Male has **metallic green head, purple breast band, orange underparts**, long central tail feathers. Female is olive-green. Call: metallic "shink-shink". Open fynbos. Male perches conspicuously. Extreme S. Endemic resident.

**4   LESSER DOUBLECOLLARED SUNBIRD**     *Nectarinia chalybea*

Male has **metallic green head, blue and red breast band**, grey belly, blue rump. Female is dull grey. Call: abrupt "zwik-zwik". Forest, coastal scrub, fynbos, gardens. May become quite confiding. SW and E. Resident.
**Similar**
**GREATER DOUBLECOLLARED SUNBIRD**  *N. afra*
Wider breast band; red extends to belly. Longer bill.
**MIOMBO DOUBLECOLLARED SUNBIRD**  *N. manoensis*
Almost identical to lesser doublecollared sunbird. Zimbabwe.
**MARICO SUNBIRD**  *N. mariquensis*
Purple breast band. Black belly. Sharply decurved bill. N and W.
**PURPLEBANDED SUNBIRD**  *N. bifasciata*
Purple breast band. Black belly. Short, only slightly decurved bill. NE.

**5   WHITEBELLIED SUNBIRD**       *Nectarinia talatala*

Male has **blue-green head, neck and breast**, white underparts. Female has olive-brown upperparts, off-white underparts. Call: loud "chu-ee, chu-ee, chuee-trrrrr". Dry open bushveld, suburbia. Male calls from conspicuous perch. N and E. Resident.
**Similar**
**COLLARED SUNBIRD** *Anthreptes collaris*
Rich yellow underparts. Short bill. E and NE.

**6   BLACK SUNBIRD**              *Nectarinia amethystina*

Male is black with green iridescence on head, metallic purple on throat. Female is brown above, cream below, with yellow moustachial streak. Call: fast "tshiek", often in flight. Woodland, forest edges, bush, suburbia. Conspicuous. S, E and N. Resident.
**Similar**
**SCARLETCHESTED SUNBIRD**  *N. senegalensis*
Male is black with large scarlet breast patch.

1

2

3

24 cm

4

18 cm

5

14 cm

6

13 cm

11-13 cm

15 cm

**1　CAPE WHITE-EYE**　　　　　　　*Zosterops pallidus*

**White eye-ring.** Olive-green upperparts. Underparts greyish (SW) or greenish-yellow (NE) or pale with cinnamon flanks (arid W). Call: soft "twee". Thick bush, gardens. Parties move through bush gleaning food. Throughout South Africa and most of Namibia. Resident.
**Similar**
**YELLOW WHITE-EYE** *Z. senegalensis*
Bright yellow underparts. N and E of South African border.

**2　CAPE SPARROW**　　　　　　　*Passer melanurus*

Male has **black crown and face joining wide black breast-bar.** Female has grey head. Black bill. Chestnut back. Call: musical "chirrup". Dry grassland, scrub, associated with human habitation. Flocks in non-breeding season, otherwise in pairs. Tame and confiding. Widespread except NE. Resident.
**Similar**
**HOUSE SPARROW** *P. domesticus*
Male has grey cap, black bib; female pale bill and plumage. Around human habitation.
**GREAT SPARROW** *P. motitensis*
Oval black breast patch. Chestnut sides of head.
**SOUTHERN GREYHEADED SPARROW** *P. diffusus*
Entirely grey head. Dark bill. Single white wing-bar.
**YELLOWTHROATED SPARROW** *Petronia superciliaris*
Broad white eyebrow. Yellow throat-spot not always clear.

**3　REDBILLED BUFFALO WEAVER**　　*Bubalornis niger*

Male has **large red bill, black plumage, white wing patches.** Female is browner. Call: mellow trill. Dry open bushveld. Noisy flocks forage under trees. Large untidy nests in large trees. N. Resident.

**4　WHITEBROWED SPARROW-WEAVER** *Plocepasser mahali*

**Broad white eyebrow.** White underparts. **White rump.** Short tail. Plump. Call: harsh "chik-chik". Dry thornveld. Pairs or loose flocks. Untidy straw nests in trees or on poles. Central areas and W. Resident.

**5　SOCIABLE WEAVER**　　　　　　*Philetairus socius*

**Pale bill. Black face and chin.** Brown cap. Scaly back, black-barred flanks. Call: excitable twittering at nest. Open dry acacia thornveld. Flocks feed on ground near massive communal nests. W semi-desert. Endemic resident.
**Similar**
**SCALYFEATHERED FINCH** *Sporopipes squamifrons*
Pink bill. Scaly forehead. Black moustachial stripe. White-edged wing feathers. More widespread.

**6　REDBILLED QUELEA**　　　　　　*Quelea quelea*

Breeding male has red bill, black mask surrounded by pink, yellow or buff wash, red legs. Breeding female has yellow bill. Non-breeding birds have red bill and plain plumage. Call: chittering when flying and nesting. Flocks may number tens of thousands where food is abundant. Flies in tight formation. Colonies are heavily preyed upon by raptors. Nomadic when not breeding. Widespread except S and extreme W. Resident.

**1 MASKED WEAVER** *Ploceus velatus*

Breeding male has red eyes, black forehead and mask extending to a point on throat and surrounded by chestnut wash; plain olive-green back. Female and non-breeding male lack mask; olive above, pale yellow below, whitish chin. Call: prolonged sizzling when breeding. Open savanna, thornveld, suburbia. Nests in colonies in trees, often over water. Nomadic when not breeding. Widespread except extreme SE. Resident.

**Similar**

**LESSER MASKED WEAVER** *P. intermedius*
Yellow eyes. Mask extends onto crown. N.

**SPOTTEDBACKED WEAVER** *P. cucullatus*
Back spotted black and yellow. No black above bill (South African race) or head entirely black (n race). N and E.

**2 CAPE WEAVER** *Ploceus capensis*

Heavy bill. Breeding male has pale eyes, orange wash over face, black line from bill to eye not extending behind eye. Female and non-breeding male paler. Call: rapidly repeated swizzling, harsher than masked weaver. Singly, in pairs or small flocks among trees, usually near water. Nests in small colonies. SW, S and E. Resident.

**Similar**

**YELLOW WEAVER** *P. subaureus*
Red eyes. E coast.

**SPECTACLED WEAVER** *P. ocularis*
Pale eyes. Black line through and behind eye. Male has black bib. E and N.

**BROWNTHROATED WEAVER** *P. xanthopterus*
Brown eyes. Male has brown bib, black bill. Female has pale bill. E and N.

**GOLDEN WEAVER** *P. xanthops*
Yellow eyes. Yellow with no distinct markings. Heavy black bill. E and N.

**3 FOREST WEAVER** *Ploceus bicolor*

Black or brown upperparts. Bright yellow underparts. Call: high-pitched series of varied notes "fo-fo-fo-fwee ...". Riverine, coastal, evergreen forests. In pairs. Quietly clambers about foliage, probing beneath bark for insects. Calls throughout year. Restricted to e forests and coast. Localised resident.

**4 THICKBILLED WEAVER** *Amblyospiza albifrons*

**Massive bill. Dark plumage.** Male has white forecrown and wing patch. Female has streaked underparts. Call: monotonous twittering. Reedbeds, forest fringes. Pairs and small parties. Roosts communally in reedbeds. E areas and n Botswana. Resident.

**5 REDHEADED WEAVER** *Anaplectes rubriceps*

Breeding male has **bright red head, breast and mantle.** Female and non-breeding male have lemon-yellow head. Orange-red bill. White underparts. Call: chattering at nest. Bushveld. N. Resident.

**6 RED BISHOP** *Euplectes orix*

Breeding male has **striking red and black plumage.** Female and non-breeding male are dull, streaked brown. Call: male hisses and wheezes while puffing plumage. Large flocks congregate in reedbeds. Widespread except dry central areas. Resident.

See illustrations of weaver nests on p.163

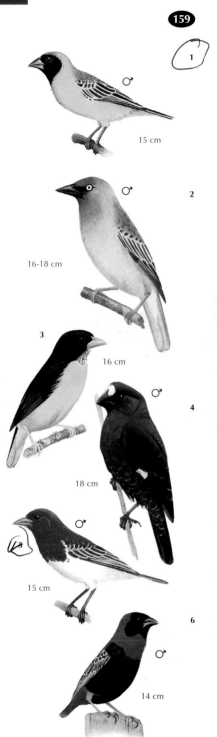

15 cm

16-18 cm

16 cm

18 cm

15 cm

14 cm

19-60 cm

Non-breeding

15-19 cm

12-13 cm

11 cm

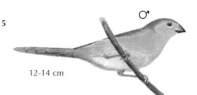

12-14 cm

**1 LONGTAILED WIDOW** *Euplectes progne*

Breeding male has pale bill, red shoulder patch bordered by whitish stripe and full, long black tail. Female and non-breeding male are mottled brown; male retains red wing pattern. Call: swizzling song. Grassland, especially in moist areas. Breeding male flies just above grass with slow, deliberate wing beats. Non-breeding birds form flocks. Temperate east-central areas. Resident.

**Similar**

**REDCOLLARED WIDOW** *E. ardens*

Breeding male has red throat, all-black wings, long wispy tail.

**REDSHOULDERED WIDOW** *E. axillaris*

Breeding male has red shoulders, short tail.

**2 WHITEWINGED WIDOW** *Euplectes albonotatus*

Breeding male has yellow shoulder, white wings, rest of plumage black, broad tail. Female and non-breeding male mottled grey-brown. Call: twittering while fanning tail. Marshes and damp areas in otherwise dry bushveld. E and NE. Resident.

**Similar**

**YELLOWRUMPED WIDOW** *E. capensis*

Breeding male has yellow rump and shoulder. Puffs rump in display. S, E and NE.

**GOLDEN BISHOP** *E. afer*

Breeding male has yellow head and back. Puffs plumage in display.

**3 MELBA FINCH** *Pytilia melba*

Male has red bill, crimson face and throat, black and white barred underparts, green wings. Female has grey head and barred grey breast. Call: single low "wick". Thorn thickets, dry stream beds, often near water. Mixes with other small birds. Feeds on open ground. N half of region. Resident.

**Similar**

**QUAIL FINCH** *Ortygospiza atricollis*

White throat, white lines around eye. Barred breast and flanks. Grey above.

**ORANGEBREASTED WAXBILL** *Sporaeginthus subflavus*

Orange bill. Barred yellow flanks. Orange rump.

**4 JAMESON'S FIREFINCH** *Lagonosticta rhodopareia*

Blackish bill. Upperparts reddish-pink. Underparts rose-pink (male) or orange-pink (female). Call: tinkling trill, followed by "zik-zik-zik". Thornveld, thickets, rank grass. Pairs feed on ground, retreating to cover when disturbed. In parties when not breeding. N and NE. Resident.

**Similar**

**BLUEBILLED FIREFINCH** *L. rubricata*

Black bill. Grey crown and nape. Male has black belly. E.

**REDBILLED FIREFINCH** *L. senegala*

Reddish bill. Yellow eye-ring. Female grey.

**5 BLUE WAXBILL** *Uraeginthus angolensis*

**Blue face, breast and tail.** Female paler than male. Call: high-pitched "weet-weet". Dry thornveld, mixed woodland. Confiding. Pairs or small groups feed largely on ground, flying up when disturbed. Often with other small birds. N and NE. Resident.

**1 VIOLETEARED WAXBILL** *Uraeginthus granatinus*
Red bill. **Blue forehead. Violet cheeks. Dark blue rump.** Long
black tail. Male has dark brown upper- and underparts, black bib.
Female has pale throat and underparts, grey upperparts. Call: soft,
often repeated "tiu-woowee". Dry bushveld. Pairs or small par-
ties, often with melba finches or blue waxbills (previous page). N.
Resident.
**Similar**
**BLACKCHEEKED WAXBILL** *Estrilda erythronotos*
Black facial mask. Dark red belly and rump. Greyish body.
**SWEE WAXBILL** *Estrilda melanotis*
Red rump. Yellow belly. Red lower mandible. Male has black
face. S and E.

**2 COMMON WAXBILL** *Estrilda astrild*
Red bill. **Red eye-stripe. Reddish wash on belly.** Body lightly
barred. Call: loud "ping-ping". Rank vegetation, vleis, reedbeds.
Pairs or flocks constantly on the move, flying off in ones and twos
when disturbed. Feeds from seed heads and on ground. Widespread except very dry areas. Resident.

**3 REDHEADED FINCH** *Amadina erythrocephala*
Male has **red head**, underparts pale with scaled appearance.
Female is lightly barred below. Upperparts brown. Call: "chuck-
chuck". Dry thornveld, grassland. Small flocks feed on ground,
often with other small birds. Central areas and NW. Nomadic res-
ident.
**Similar**
**CUTTHROAT FINCH** *A. fasciata*
Male has red band across throat. Head has scaly appearance.
North-central areas.

**4 BRONZE MANNIKIN** *Spermestes cucullatus*
Black and grey bill. Black head, throat and upper breast. Brown
mantle and back. White underparts with barred flanks. Call: soft
"chuk-chuck-chucka". Grassland, open woodland. Flocks feed on
ground or hanging from grass stems. Often huddle together on
perch. E. Resident.
**Similar**
**REDBACKED MANNIKIN** *S. bicolor*
All-grey bill. Chestnut back. More extensive black on head.

**5 PINTAILED WHYDAH** *Vidua macroura*
Breeding male has red bill, black head and upperparts, white collar and underparts, long straight tail. Female is brown with
streaked head. Call: "tseet-tseet" in display. Wide variety of habitats. Groups comprise male plus several females and immatures.
Breeding male aggressive and dominant at food source. Widespread except NW. Resident.
**Similar**
**SHAFTTAILED WHYDAH** *V. regia*
Breeding male has buff underparts, thin tailshafts with bulbous
ends. NW and central areas.

**6 PARADISE WHYDAH** *Vidua paradisaea*
Breeding male has black bill, head and upperparts, buff collar,
maroon breast band and long, broad tail feathers tapering to
point. Female and non-breeding male buff with broad black eye-
stripe. Call: chirping notes. Acacia thornveld, savanna. Male
perches conspicuously or performs display flight. N. Resident.

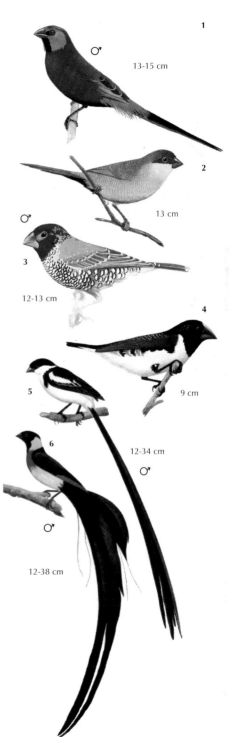

1

13-15 cm

2

13 cm

3

12-13 cm

4

9 cm

5

6

12-34 cm

12-38 cm

11 cm

12 cm

11-12 cm

16 cm

16 cm

**1   STEELBLUE WIDOWFINCH**          *Vidua chalybeata*

**Red bill and legs.** Breeding male has jet black plumage. Female and non-breeding male are brown. Call: mimics redbilled fire-finch (host species). Male calls from prominent perch throughout breeding season. NE. Resident.
**Similar**
**BLACK WIDOWFINCH   V. funerea**
Breeding male has white bill, red legs.
**PURPLE WIDOWFINCH   V. purpurascens**
Breeding male has pale pinkish-white bill and legs.

**2   YELLOWEYED CANARY**          *Serinus mozambicus*

**Bold facial markings.** Greyish crown and nape. Yellow rump. White tail tip. Call: trills and warbles. Woodland. Flocks mix with other canaries and waxbills. Feeds mostly on ground. N and E. Resident.
**Similar**
**FOREST CANARY   S. scotops**
Heavily streaked olive-green and yellow. E forests.
**YELLOW CANARY   S. flaviventris**
Mostly yellow. Darker in south. W half of region.
**CAPE CANARY   S. canicollis**
Grey nape and ear coverts. Yellow face lacks markings. S and E.
**BULLY CANARY   S. suphuratus**
Heavy bill. Olive-green. Paler in north. S and E.

**3   BLACKTHROATED CANARY**          *Serinus atrogularis*

Black throat. Streaked grey upperparts. Yellow rump. White tail tip. Otherwise drab. Call: rambling canary-like warbles. Wood-land, dry river beds. Small nomadic flocks. Drinks regularly. Widespread in interior. Resident.
**Similar**
**WHITETHROATED CANARY   S. albogularis**
Large bill. White throat patch. Dry W.
**STREAKYHEADED CANARY   S. gularis**
Bold white eyebrow. Streaked crown. S and E.
**BLACKHEADED CANARY   S. alario**
Male has black head and bib, chestnut back, white below. Female brown. Arid W.
**PROTEA CANARY   S. leucopterus**
Pale bill. Drab. Two whitish wing-bars. Extreme SW.

**4   CAPE BUNTING**          *Emberiza capensis*

Two white stripes on black face. Whitish throat. Rufous wings. Call: nasal "cheriowee", also "tip-cheeu-tip-cheeu". Rocky terrain in N; sandy, coastal scrub in S. Singly or in pairs. Widespread except N and E. Resident.
**Similar**
**ROCK BUNTING   E. tahapisi**
Three white stripes on black face. Black throat. Rufous underparts. Nw and east-central areas.
**LARKLIKE BUNTING   E. impetuani**
Pale cinnamon. Face markings indistinct. Rufous wing edges.

**5   GOLDENBREASTED BUNTING**          *Emberiza flaviventris*

Two white stripes on black face. Yellow throat and underparts. N and E. Resident.

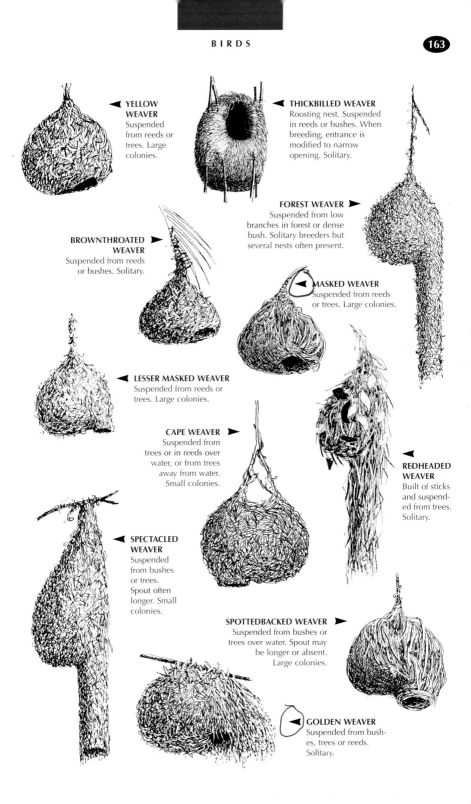

**YELLOW WEAVER**
Suspended from reeds or trees. Large colonies.

**THICKBILLED WEAVER**
Roosting nest. Suspended in reeds or bushes. When breeding, entrance is modified to narrow opening. Solitary.

**FOREST WEAVER**
Suspended from low branches in forest or dense bush. Solitary breeders but several nests often present.

**BROWNTHROATED WEAVER**
Suspended from reeds or bushes. Solitary.

**MASKED WEAVER**
Suspended from reeds or trees. Large colonies.

**LESSER MASKED WEAVER**
Suspended from reeds or trees. Large colonies.

**CAPE WEAVER**
Suspended from trees or in reeds over water, or from trees away from water. Small colonies.

**REDHEADED WEAVER**
Built of sticks and suspended from trees. Solitary.

**SPECTACLED WEAVER**
Suspended from bushes or trees. Spout often longer. Small colonies.

**SPOTTEDBACKED WEAVER**
Suspended from bushes or trees over water. Spout may be longer or absent. Large colonies.

**GOLDEN WEAVER**
Suspended from bushes, trees or reeds. Solitary.

# MAMMALS

Mammals are the class of vertebrates that evolved most recently.
They are endothermic (body temperature is kept constant by their metabolism), and,
except for marine species, they have four limbs and are partly or wholly covered by hair.
The young are born live and are suckled by milk-producing females.

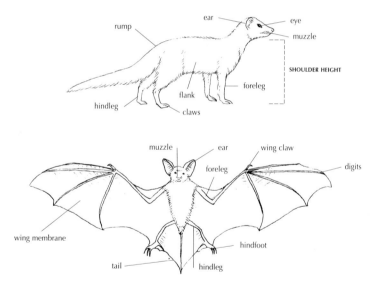

Mammals are unique in their extraordinary range of size, shape and habits; the smallest shrew is less than one millionth the mass of a bull elephant. They generally have keen senses and sophisticated means of communication, which are adapted to the particular way of life of each species.

With a few exceptions, the body form and size of mammals differ clearly from species to species, and most of the common and conspicuous mammals can be easily identified.

Colour is not always a reliable guide to a mammal's identity. In contrast to many birds, mammals' colours are uniform and subdued. Colour also varies within species; individuals from the drier west tend to be greyer than those from the wetter east. The colour of the background can also influence a mammal's appearance, and mammals that wallow or dust-bathe are often coloured by the soil that sticks to their skins.

The shape of antelopes' horns is different for every species and can be used for identification in fully developed adults. When they occur, the horns of females are the same shape as those of males, but they are generally thinner and shorter.

In most species males are larger. Where sexes are distinctly different, both are illustrated in this chapter.

Eyes are set facing forwards for binocular vision in predators and climbing primates, which depend on three-dimensional perception. Herbivores have eyes on the sides of their heads to give a wide field of view in which to see approaching danger. Most mammals have very sensitive ears and can detect sounds that are inaudible to humans. Bats, in particular, have a sense of hearing developed into a precise navigational and hunting tool.

For most mammals the sense of smell is paramount. Many species have a sensory organ, the Jacobsen's organ, situated between the mouth and nasal passages, which enhances their sensitivity to odours and taste.

## Scope of this chapter

About 300 species of mammals occur in southern Africa and this chapter covers 170 of them. In the case of bats, the seven families are described, rather than the 74 species, which are difficult to identify and seldom seen at close quarters. Other species not described are the rare or inconspicuous ones, especially in groups such as shrews and small rodents, which are very unlikely to be encountered.

## Distribution

The distribution of large mammals has been greatly altered by human activity. In most cases the ranges have been reduced, but the translocation of game to re-stock nature reserves has expanded the distribution of some species. The distribution of lesser species has also been disturbed by the destruction of habitat.

## Reproduction and development

The most common mating system among mammals is for a male to mate with many females, and then leave them to bring up the young. Males may search for, court and couple with individual females as they come into oestrus, as in white rhinos; they may actively collect a harem of females before they come into oestrus, as many antelope do, or they may monopolise access to a group of females in a particular territory. Usually the male initiates courtship but in the case of porcupines and lions it is the female who does so.

Only about 5% of mammals are monogamous: aardwolves, elephant shrews, black-backed jackals and some small antelope are examples. Group living does not preclude monogamy; in wild dogs, suricates, dwarf mongooses and porcupines only one pair in the group breeds.

Ungulates are continuously exposed to predation and many give birth to young that are mobile within minutes. In most mammals, however, the young are defenceless at birth and are nurtured for a long period before they become independent. Learning essential behaviour and competencies is important during this time.

## Behaviour

Most mammals are crepuscular because this avoids both the daytime heat and the dangers of moving around in the dark. Animals such as giraffes and elephants, which have to spend long periods feeding, are active around the clock. Shrews lose body heat so quickly from their tiny bodies that they have to feed every few hours, and are active in short bursts throughout the day and night.

Most mammals are solitary but some, e.g. monkeys, baboons, hyaenas and dwarf mongooses, live in closely bonded family groups, with very intricate patterns of social interaction. Herbivores and small carnivores that live in groups do so as a protection against predators. Social large carnivores live in groups so as to be better able to catch their prey and defend their kills and territories from other groups.

The most important means of communication is odour. Faeces, urine or the secretions of special glands can signal social status, sex, reproductive condition, diet and individual identity. Visual communication works only when animals can see each other, so antelope that live in open grassland or savanna, e.g. springbok, gemsbok and sable, have striking coat patterns, e.g. zebras' stripes help herds to keep together when they flee from predators. Sound – a lion's roar, a spotted hyaena's whoop or a black-backed jackal's call – is used to advertise occupation of an area and call group members together.

## Dimensions

For small mammals, dimensions given are the body length from the tip of the snout to the base of the tail, plus the length of the tail. For large mammals the shoulder height in a standing position is given.

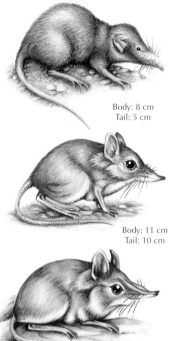

Body: 8 cm
Tail: 5 cm

Body: 11 cm
Tail: 10 cm

Body: 12 cm
Tail: 14 cm

22 cm

80 cm

13 cm

**1   SWAMP MUSK SHREW**               *Crocidura mariquensis*

**Snout long, mobile.** Eyes small. Ears small, rounded. Legs short with pale feet. Blackish-brown overall. Musk glands on flanks. Mainly insectivorous. N and E.
**Similar**
**GREATER MUSK SHREW** *C. flavescens*
Larger (10 cm plus 6 cm tail). S and e coastal areas.
**FOREST SHREW** *Myosorex varius*
Tail has dark line on top. S and E.
**LESSER RED MUSK SHREW** *Crocidura hirta*
Cinnamon or reddish-brown above. Silvery white below.

**2   SHORT-SNOUTED ELEPHANT SHREW**       *Elephantulus brachyrhynchus*

**Snout long, mobile. Large eyes surrounded by white fur.** Large rounded ears. Long hind legs. Tail about same length as body. Fur buffy brown. White underparts. Diurnal. Singly or in pairs. Signals alarm by drumming hind feet. One or two fully-furred young born in summer. NE.
**Similar**
**3   ROCK ELEPHANT SHREW** *E. myurus*
Grey. Black undersides to feet. Central highveld areas.
**FOUR-TOED ELEPHANT SHREW** *Petrodromus tetradactylus*
Larger (19 cm plus 16 cm tail). Ne coastal plains.
**ROUND-EARED ELEPHANT SHREW** *Macroscelides proboscideus*
No white surrounding eye. SW.

**4   SOUTH AFRICAN HEDGEHOG**           *Atelerix frontalis*

**Covered by short sharp prickles.** White on forehead and behind eyes. Legs short. Solitary. Nocturnal. Snuffles through vegetation after insects. Hibernates in winter. Up to nine young born in summer. Central areas.

**5   PORCUPINE**                     *Hystrix africaeaustralis*

Long hair on head and shoulders. **Back covered with black and white quills.** Tail has open-ended quills. Nocturnal. Groups share burrows but forage alone or in pairs. Eats plants, gnaws on old bones. Up to three young born in summer. Widespread except along NW coast.

**6   HOTTENTOT GOLDEN MOLE**   *Amblysomus hottentotus*

Eyes covered by whitish skin. No visible ears. Snout has hard pad for burrowing. Red-brown with bronze-green sheen. Forefeet have large claws. Hindfeet webbed. No tail. Feeds on insects, earth worms. Solitary. Burrows just below surface raising ridges of soil. E and S.
**Similar**
**GIANT GOLDEN MOLE** *Chrysospalax trevelyani*
Larger (23 cm). Long, coarse fur. SE coast.
**CAPE GOLDEN MOLE** *Chrysochlorus asiatica*
Dark brown. Confined to sandy soils in extreme SW.
**YELLOW GOLDEN MOLE** *Calcochloris obtusirostris*
Golden brown. Pale face. Sandy soils in NE.

## 1  EGYPTIAN FRUIT BAT  *Rousettus aegyptiacus*

Head has dog-like muzzle. Simple ears. Large eyes. Two claws on each wing. Wing membrane not extending between hindlimbs. Dark brown above, pale below. Roosts in large colonies in caves, emerging to feed on wild fruits at dusk. Only fruit bat to use echolocation. A single young is born each year. NE and along E and S coast to Cape Town.

**Similar**

**PETERS' EPAULETTED FRUIT BAT**  *Epomophorus crypturus*
Light brown above and below. Roosts in trees.

**STRAW-COLOURED FRUIT BAT**  *Eidolon helvum*
Larger (wingspan 70 cm). Yellowish. Migrates into s Africa in summer.

## 2  SLIT-FACED BATS  Family Nycteridae

Face has paired nose-leaves divided by central slit. Ears elongated. Eyes small. Single claw on each wing. Tail terminates in Y-joint and is totally encased in wing membrane between hindlimbs. Long reddish-brown fur, paler on underside. Insectivorous. Catches prey on the wing and consumes it on feeding perch. Navigates by listening to echo from ultrasonic emissions from nostrils. Roosts in colonies in caves. Six species.

## 3  VESPER BATS  Family Vespertilionidae

Tail totally enclosed within membrane, extends beyond hindlimbs. Simple muzzle lacks nose-leaves. 29 species.

## TOMB BATS and SHEATH-TAILED BATS  Family Emballonuridae

Half of tail length emerges under membrane between hindlimbs. Muzzle lacks nose-leaves. Three species.

## FREE-TAILED BATS  Family Molossidae

More than half the tail protrudes beyond membrane between hindlimbs. Face mastiff-like. 14 species.

## HORSESHOE BATS  Family Rhinolophidae

Horseshoe-shaped nose-leaf with elaborate upward-pointing triangular process behind horseshoe. Tail shorter than hindlimbs, totally enclosed within membrane. 10 species.

## LEAF-NOSED BATS and TRIDENT BATS  Family Hipposideridae

Nose-leaf lacks upward-pointing triangular process behind horseshoe. Tail shorter than hindlimbs, totally enclosed within membrane. Four species.

10-15 cm
Wingspan: 25-35 cm

15 cm
Wingspan: 45 cm

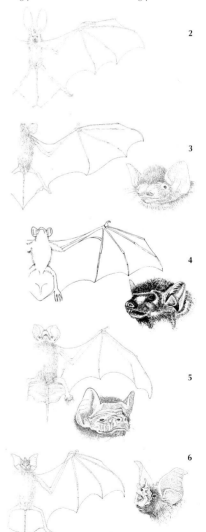

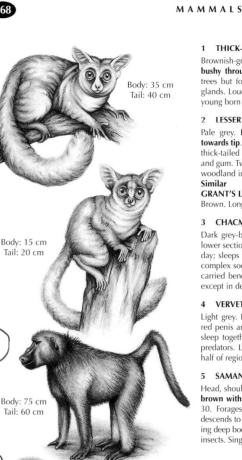

Body: 35 cm
Tail: 40 cm

Body: 15 cm
Tail: 20 cm

Body: 75 cm
Tail: 60 cm

Body: 50 cm
Tail: 60 cm

Body: 60 cm
Tail: 80 cm

**1 THICK-TAILED BUSHBABY** *Otolemur crassicaudatus*
Brownish-grey, paler below. **Small head**, large eyes and ears. **Tail bushy throughout length**. Nocturnal. Roosts in small groups in trees but forages alone. Territory marked with urine and chest glands. Loud baby-like wail. Eats fruit, gum, insects. One or two young born in summer. Moist areas in E and NE.

**2 LESSER BUSHBABY** *Galago moholi*
Pale grey. **Large head**. Huge eyes and ears. Tail **bushy only towards tip**. Tip often darker. Agile climber and leaper. Habits like thick-tailed bushbaby. Wide range of chattering calls. Eats insects and gum. Two litters per year in early and late summer. Forest and woodland in N and NE.
**Similar**
**GRANT'S LESSER BUSHBABY** *Galagoides granti*
Brown. Longer muzzle. Ne Mozambique.

**3 CHACMA BABOON** *Papio cynocephalus*
Dark grey-brown. Large canines. Base of tail carried erect with lower section drooping. Loud, two-syllable alarm call. Forages by day; sleeps in trees or on rock ledges. Troops of up to 100 with complex social structure. Omnivorous and may hunt prey. Young carried beneath mother initially; later on her back. Widespread except in desert.

**4 VERVET MONKEY** *Cercopithecus aethiops*
Light grey. **Black face outlined in white.** Dominant males have red penis and blue scrotum. Troops of up to 20. Forage by day; sleep together in trees. Gives different alarm calls for different predators. Largely vegetarian. Single young born at any time. E half of region and along Orange and Cunene river systems.

**5 SAMANGO MONKEY** *Cercopithecus mitis*
Head, shoulders and limbs black. Back dark reddish-brown. **Face brown with long whitish beard and cheek hair.** Troops of up to 30. Forages by day in trees; sleeps in dense foliage. Seldom descends to ground. Wide range of vocal communications including deep boom and loud "nyah" alarm call. Eats fruit, leaves, bark, insects. Single young born in summer. Confined to forests in E.

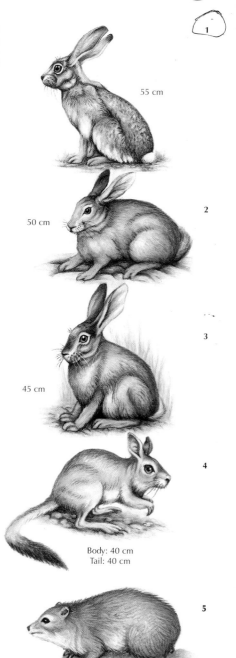

**1 CAPE HARE**          *Lepus capensis*

Greyish-brown above. Yellowish on chest. White abdomen. Eyes large, ears very long. Tail dark above, white below. Solitary. Nocturnal. Lies in shallow depression by day. Eats grass. Up to three **furred and active young.** Open grassland in dry W.
**Similar**
**SCRUB HARE**   *L. saxatilis*
White chest. Bush and thick grass throughout s Africa.

**2 NATAL RED ROCK RABBIT**     *Pronolagus natalensis*

Russet-brown and grey above; rufous rump and underparts. Ears not as long as in hares. **Pale stripe** behind jaw. Tail reddish-brown, **not white beneath.** Nocturnal. Hides among rocks by day. Eats grass. Up to three **naked** young born in fur-lined nest. Confined to rocky areas in SE.
**Similar**
**SMITH'S RED ROCK RABBIT**   *P. rupestris*
Only in Karoo, S and SW.
**JAMESON'S RED ROCK RABBIT**   *P. randensis*
In two areas: central highveld from Vaal River to Zimbabwe, and Namibia.

**3 RIVERINE RABBIT**       *Bunolagus monticularis*

Head grey. Flanks brown. Chest yellowish. Belly white. **White around eye. Dark stripe along lower jaw.** Solitary. Nocturnal. Hides in depression by day. Grazes in summer, browses in winter. One or two young born in burrow in summer. Rare. Confined to river courses in Karoo.
**Similar**
**EUROPEAN RABBIT**   *Oryctolagus cuniculus*
Introduced; confined to several islands off Cape coast.

**4 SPRINGHARE**          *Pedetes capensis*

Fur long, reddish-brown. Ears large but smaller than in rabbits and hares. Tail has **bushy black tip.** Solitary. Nocturnal. Spends day in burrow in sand. Eats grass, roots, seeds. Single young born at any time. In areas with sandy soils throughout s Africa except Cape.

**5 ROCK DASSIE**         *Procavia capensis*

Blunt muzzle. Compact build. Short legs. Toes blunt with rubbery pads. No visible tail. Brown with dark area in middle of back. Diurnal. Colonial. Agile climber in rocky areas, retreating into crevices. Grazes and browses. Up to three young born at end of rainy season. Widespread except n Botswana and Namibia.
**Similar**
**YELLOW-SPOTTED ROCK DASSIE**   *Heterohyrax brucei*
Yellow spot on back. White above eyes. NE.
**TREE DASSIE**   *Dendrohyrax arboreus*
White spot on back. Arboreal. Solitary. Certain e forests.

55 cm

50 cm

45 cm

Body: 40 cm
Tail: 40 cm

45-60 cm

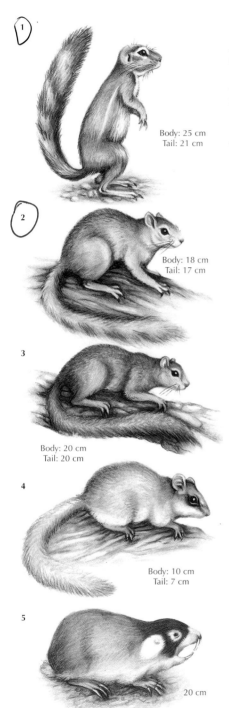

Body: 25 cm
Tail: 21 cm

Body: 18 cm
Tail: 17 cm

Body: 20 cm
Tail: 20 cm

Body: 10 cm
Tail: 7 cm

20 cm

**1   GROUND SQUIRREL**                    *Xerus inauris*
**Blunt muzzle**. Cinnamon above; white underparts. White stripe
on flanks. Long claws for digging. **Tail bushy, striped longitudi-
nally** and often held as sunshade. Colonies live in burrows, forag-
ing by day. **Not arboreal.** Eats plant matter, sometimes insects.
Litters of up to three born at any time. Dry inland areas in W.
**Similar**
**SURICATE see p. 177**

**2   TREE SQUIRREL**                       *Paraxerus cepapi*
Pale grey in W, buff in E. **Underparts only slightly paler than
above. Tail not very bushy.** Diurnal. Arboreal. Lives in small fam-
ily groups but forages alone, sometimes on ground. May move
into roofs of houses. Eats wide range of vegetable matter, insects,
caches excess food. Litters of up to three born mostly in summer.
N and NE.
**Similar**
**GREY SQUIRREL  *Sciurus carolinensis***
Introduced. Grey. Associated with exotic trees in extreme SW.
**STRIPED TREE SQUIRREL  *Funisciurus congicus***
Very small (14 cm plus 16 cm tail). Buff. White stripe on flanks.
N Namibia.
**SUN SQUIRREL  *Heliosciurus mutabilis***
Brown or black. Banded tail. Mozambique and e Zimbabwe.

**3   RED SQUIRREL**                       *Paraxerus palliatus*
Grizzled back and sides. **Underparts and tail bright red or ginger.**
Diurnal. Arboreal. Solitary. Mobs predators, uttering clicks and
trills. Eats plant matter, some insects. One or two young per litter
born in summer. Confined to forests in e Mozambique and along
NE coast of South Africa.

**4   WOODLAND DORMOUSE**               *Graphiurus murinus*
Grey with dark mask around eyes. White below jaw. Underparts
pale grey. Nocturnal. Arboreal. Often shelters in roofs. Eats
insects, seeds. Litters of up to three in summer. Widespread
except arid W.
**Similar**
**SPECTACLED DORMOUSE  *G. ocularis***
Larger (14 cm plus 11 cm tail). White cheeks and chin. Black
face.

**5   CAPE MOLE RAT**                      *Georychus capensis*
**Black and white face.** Massive, protruding incisor teeth. Tiny eyes
and ears. Cylindrical, buff-coloured body. Short legs. Short bristly
tail. Subterranean, occasionally dispersing on soil surface. Pushes
up molehills. Eats plants underground. Litters of up to four. S Cape
coast, Drakensberg foothills.
**Similar**
**COMMON MOLE RAT  *Cryptomys hottentotus***
Plain grey head and body. Widespread.
**CAPE DUNE MOLE RAT  *Bathyergus suillus***
Larger (up to 30 cm). Mottled grey-brown. Sw Cape only.
**NAMAQUA DUNE MOLE RAT  *Bathyergus janetta***
White side stripes. Extreme nw Cape.

**1 GREATER CANE RAT**     *Thryonomys swinderianus*

Nose blunt. Eyes small. Ears almost hidden by hair. Dark brown, coarse hair. Underparts pale grey. Robust limbs. Tail short, hairy. Nocturnal. In dense reeds near water. Eats grass, reeds, cane crops. N and E.

Similar

**DASSIE RAT**   *Petromys typicus*
Much smaller (under 32 cm including 14 cm tail). Namibia and n Cape.
**LESSER CANE RAT**   *T. gregorianus*
Smaller (under 55 cm including tail). South-central Zimbabwe.

**2 GIANT RAT**     *Cricetomys gambianus*

Size distinctive. Grey-brown with paler underparts. Eyes set in dark facial area. **Terminal third of tail white.** Nocturnal. Mainly terrestrial but climbs trees after fruit. NE.

**3 HOUSE RAT**     *Rattus rattus*

Introduced. Hair coarse. Brownish-grey. Underparts pale, sometimes white. Feet large and strong. **Tail scaly, at least body length.** Nocturnal. Omnivorous. Up to 10 young born at any time. Associated with human habitation.

Similar

**WATER RAT**   *Dasymys incomtus*
Dark, woolly hair. Tail shorter than body.
**RED VELD RAT**   *Aethomys chrysophilus*
Reddish-fawn. Flanks lighter. Underside pale grey.

**ANGONI VLEI RAT**     *Otomys angoniensis*

Large ears. Quite long, soft hair. Dark grey tinged with buff above, pale grey below. **Tail about one third body length**, black above. Diurnal. Builds grass nest above water level in swampy areas. Central areas and NE.

Similar

**VLEI RAT**   *O. irroratus*
Tail about half body length. Central areas and S.
**ICE RAT**   *O. sloggetti*
Reddish-brown. High altitudes in Drakensberg and Lesotho.
**BRANTS' WHISTLING RAT**   *Parotomys brantsii*
Tail about two-thirds body length. Kalahari and Namaqualand.
**WOOSNAM'S DESERT RAT**   *Zelotomys woosnami*
Pale grey. White below. Long tail. Kalahari desert.

**STRIPED MOUSE**     *Rhabdomys pumilio*

Reddish-brown to grey-yellow. **Four stripes along back.** White underparts. Tail darker on top. Diurnal. Keeps under cover of vegation, moving rapidly across open spaces. Omnivorous. Nine young born in summer. Widespread except N.

Similar

**SINGLE-STRIPED MOUSE**   *Lemniscomys rosalia*
One dark stripe along back. N.
**LARGE-EARED MOUSE**   *Malacothrix typica*
Large ears. Dark streaks on back and hips. W.

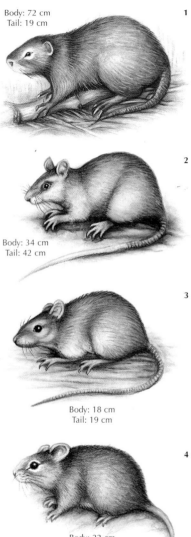

Body: 72 cm
Tail: 19 cm    **1**

**2**

Body: 34 cm
Tail: 42 cm

**3**

Body: 18 cm
Tail: 19 cm

**4**

Body: 22 cm
Tail: 8 cm

Body: 10 cm
Tail: 10 cm    **5**

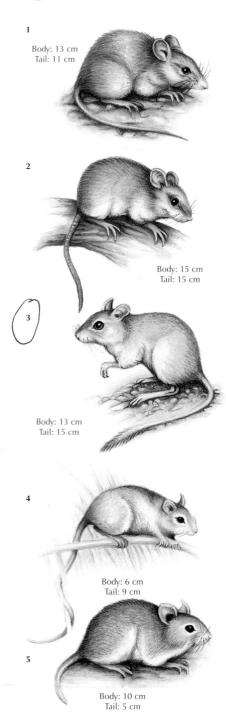

**1**
Body: 13 cm
Tail: 11 cm

**2**
Body: 15 cm
Tail: 15 cm

**3**
Body: 13 cm
Tail: 15 cm

**4**
Body: 6 cm
Tail: 9 cm

**5**
Body: 10 cm
Tail: 5 cm

### 1   MULTIMAMMATE MICE
*Mastomys coucha* and *M. natalensis*

Two species indistinguishable. Grey-brown. **Pale flanks.** Underside greyish. Female has **8 to 12 nipples.** Nocturnal. Up to 20 young born monthly. N and E.
**Similar**
**HOUSE MOUSE  *Mus musculus***
Brown above, paler below. Widespread near human habitation.
**NAMAQUA ROCK MOUSE  *Aethomys namaquensis***
Tail longer than body. White below. Rock outcrops throughout s Africa.
**PYGMY MOUSE  *Mus minutoides***
Much smaller (5 cm plus 5 cm tail). Pure white below. E half of region.
**FAT MOUSE  *Steatomys pratensis***
Feet and underparts white. N and E.
**SPINY MOUSE  *Acomys spinosissimus***
Distinctive spiny coat.

### 2   TREE MOUSE
*Thallomys paedulcus*

Yellowish-grey, lighter on flanks. White underparts. **Eyes ringed with black.** Nocturnal. **Arboreal.** Groups nest in tree holes stuffed with leaves and twigs. N two-thirds of region.

### 3   BUSHVELD GERBIL
*Tatera leucogaster*

Grey-brown. White underparts. **Hindlegs longer, stronger than forelegs.** Tuft of black hair at tip of tail. Nocturnal. Hops rather than walks. N two-thirds of region.
**Similar**
**SHORT-TAILED GERBIL  *Desmodillus auricularis***
Short tail. White patch at base of ears. W half of region.
**HAIRY-FOOTED GERBIL  *Gerbillurus paeba***
Smaller (10 cm plus 11 cm tail). Hair on soles of feet.
**CAPE GERBIL  *Tatera afra***
Long, woolly coat. Extreme SW.
**HIGHVELD GERBIL  *Tatera brantsii***
Tail white near base. Throughout central interior.

### 4   GREY CLIMBING MOUSE
*Dendromus melanoti.*

**Ashy grey. Dark spot on forehead.** Dark stripe down back. Curl tail around stems while climbing. Makes ball-shaped nest in ta grass. Widespread except arid W and Karoo.
**Similar**
**CHESTNUT CLIMBING MOUSE  *D. mystacalis***
Bright chestnut with dark dorsal stripe. NE.
**PYGMY ROCK MOUSE  *Petromyscus collinus***
Larger (9 cm plus 9 cm tail). Yellowish-grey. Rocky areas of Namibia.

### 5   POUCHED MOUSE
*Saccostomus campestr*

Large cheek pouches. Round body. Short tail. Soft, grey coa White underparts. Slow-moving. Nocturnal. Lives in burrow Widespread except arid W and mountainous E.
**Similar**
**WHITE-TAILED MOUSE  *Mystromys albicaudatus***
Short tail plus feet white. Central areas, S and SE.

### LEOPARD     *Panthera pardus*

**Ears small, rounded.** Pale yellow-gold with dark spots, **those on flanks arranged in rosettes**. Legs strongly built. Tail long. Mostly nocturnal, especially in areas of human development. Solitary. Territorial. Male's territory overlaps those of several females. Long-range contact call a rasping cough. Rests in trees, thick cover or caves. Prey (mainly medium-sized mammals) is stalked, rushed from short range and killed by bites to back of neck, skull or throat. Carcasses often hoisted into trees and fed on over several days. Diet also includes mice, birds, reptiles, fish, insects. Usually two or three cubs per litter. Young disperse at 18 months to two years. Widespread except central South Africa and in true desert.

Shoulder: 60 cm

### CHEETAH     *Acinonyx jubatus*

**Head small. Dark "tear stripes" from inside each eye to back of lips. Ears small, rounded.** Fur coarse, buff with black spots. Limbs long, slender. Tail long. Female solitary. Males sometimes in twos or threes. Hunts in cooler part of day by sprinting after prey at speeds up to 100 km/h. Knocks prey down and kills with throat bite. Drags prey to cover; feeds quickly to avoid scavengers. Prey includes medium-sized antelope or the young of larger species; also hares and ground birds. Rarely returns to a kill. Up to six cubs per litter. Mother frequently moves cubs to new refuges to avoid predators. Cubs disperse at 12 months. Savanna woodland and grassland undisturbed by human settlement. N half of region.

Shoulder: 80 cm

### LION     *Panthera leo*

Males' manes range from small ruffs to full capes around head and shoulders. Tawny, sometimes with grey cast. Underparts pale or white. **Black tuft at end of tail.** Cubs have pale spots on limbs and underside. Prides consist of a group of four to 12 related females and one to six males, unrelated to the females. Female group is stable; males are replaced after one to 10 years. Prides are territorial. Intruders are warned off by roaring. Most hunting is by females. Males appropriate kills and cubs get leftovers. Prey includes large and small mammals, birds, reptiles, insects. Female leaves pride to give birth to up to six cubs. Cubs are introduced to pride at about six weeks. Female cubs remain in pride; males leave after two or three years. N half of region, mostly confined to conservation areas.

Shoulder: 1-1,25 m

### SERVAL     *Felis serval*

**Ears large, upright, bluntly pointed.** Buffy brown. Black irregularly shaped spots and bands. Lightly built, long-legged. **Tail short.** Solitary. Nocturnal. Usually seen near water and dense grass or reeds. Eats mice and occasionally birds, insects. Litters of two to three in summer. N and E.

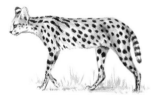

Shoulder: 60 cm

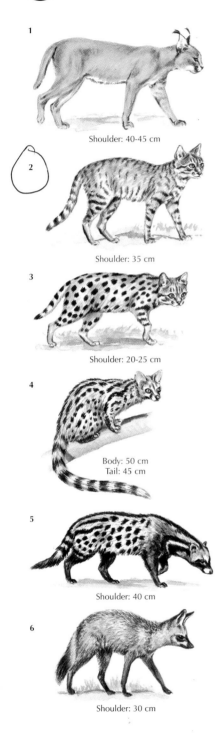

1
Shoulder: 40-45 cm

2
Shoulder: 35 cm

3
Shoulder: 20-25 cm

4
Body: 50 cm
Tail: 45 cm

5
Shoulder: 40 cm

6
Shoulder: 30 cm

### 1   CARACAL                                    *Felis caraca*

Face marked with black and white around eyes and sides of shor
muzzle. Back of ears black sprinkled with white, with **long black
tassels on tips**. Body and limbs uniform russet above, white o
buff on underside. Legs strongly built. Paws large. **Tail short**. Soli
tary. Usually nocturnal, especially where persecuted. Eats mam
mals up to impala size, birds, reptiles, invertebrates. Litters of up
to four in summer. Favours woodland and scrub throughout
Africa.

### 2   AFRICAN WILD CAT                           *Felis lybica*

Similar to a tabby domestic cat but **legs longer, back of ears rich
orange-red.** Hybridises with domestic cat. Markings on body
sometimes very indistinct. Solitary. Nocturnal. Terrestrial but ca
climb well. Sleeps in dense cover, rock crevices or holes i.
ground. Eats mammals up to size of rabbits, young of small ante
lope, reptiles, birds, invertebrates. Litters of two to five in summe
Widespread except in desert.

### 3   SMALL SPOTTED (BLACKFOOTED) CAT      *Felis nigripe*

**Back of ears same colour as body. Pale tawny with distinct spots**
Dark stripes on throat, shoulders, upper limbs. **Tail short.** Solitary
Nocturnal, secretive. Terrestrial but can climb well. Sleeps i
dense cover, rock crevices or holes in ground. Eats mice, inverte
brates. Litters of about three in summer. Open scrub in dry cen
tral areas.

### 4   SMALL-SPOTTED GENET                     *Genetta genett.*

Pointed muzzle. Striking black bars in front of eyes. Large round
ed ears. Pale grey or buff with **small black or rusty spots**. Look
like a long, slim cat. **Legs dark**. Tail long and slightly bushy, wit
**black bands and white tip**. Solitary. Nocturnal. Arboreal; ver
agile climber. Eats small vertebrates, arthropods, fruit. Litters of u
to five in summer. Widespread except moist areas E of Draken
berg.
**Similar**
**LARGE-SPOTTED GENET  *G. tigrina***
Spots larger. Legs pale. Tail tip black. E and S.

### 5   AFRICAN CIVET                            *Civettictis civett*

"Bandit's mask" markings on face. Neck and body striped are
spotted black on grey. Tail banded. Limbs black. Solitary. Noctu
nal. Terrestrial. Eats invertebrates, fruit, small vertebrates, carrio
takes distasteful foods such as millipedes, frogs. Often scavenge
around camp sites. Litters of up to four in summer. Woodland ar
forest wherever water is available. N and NE.
**Similar**
**TREE CIVET  *Nandinia binotata***
Brown with small dark spots. Arboreal. Only in forests in extrem
NE.

### 6   BAT-EARED FOX                           *Otocyon megalo*

Muzzle black with white band across forehead. **Ears very larg**
Hair long and fluffy, grizzled grey. Limbs slender, black. T.
bushy with broad black tip. Active day or night but avoids daytin
heat. Often in pairs or families. Sleeps in holes in ground. Detec
insect prey by sound, digging for buried larvae. Eats insects, esp
cially termites, beetle larvae. Up to six young born in summ
Favours dry, open country. W two-thirds of region, extendi
down Limpopo valley into Kruger National Park.

### BLACK-BACKED JACKAL — *Canis mesomelas*

Muzzle long, pointed. Ears upright, pointed. Lips, chin and throat white. Mantle of black flecked with white on back of neck, shoulders, back, upper flanks. Sides of neck, lower flanks and limbs buffy to rich reddish-brown. Tail bushy with **black tip**. Active day or night in undisturbed country; nocturnal in developed areas. Forages singly but lives in pairs or small family groups. Long-range contact call a distinctive, high, drawn out "nyaaaa-aa-aa-aa". Omnivorous. Litters of up to six in spring. Both parents and sometimes older siblings help to raise young. Widespread except extreme NE.

Similar

**SIDE-STRIPED JACKAL  *C. adustus***
Less distinctly marked. Tip of tail white. N and E.
**CAPE FOX  *Vulpes chama***
Smaller. Silvery grey. Head light russet. Not in N or E.

Shoulder: 38 cm

### WILD DOG — *Lycaon pictus*

Distinctively patterned with blotches of black, tan and white. Ears large and erect **with rounded tips**. Legs long. Tail slightly bushy. Diurnal. Intimately social. Lives in closely bonded, extended family groups operating over huge home ranges. Hunts cooperatively to run down prey. Shares food by regurgitation. Long-range contact call a musical "hoo-hoo"; high-pitched twittering during friendly interactions. Eats mammals up to wildebeest size but mostly medium-sized antelope. Only one pair in pack breeds. Litters usually about 12 pups, cared for by all pack members. Botswana, Zimbabwe, Mozambique, Kruger National Park and KwaZulu-Natal parks. Seriously endangered.

Shoulder: 75 cm

### AARDWOLF — *Proteles cristatus*

Muzzle broad, **black, hairless. Ears erect, bluntly pointed**. Pale buff with black stripes on body and legs. Hair long. Tail bushy. Nocturnal. Lives in pairs, forages alone. Diet almost exclusively harvester termites licked from soil surface. Litters of up to four in summer. Prefers open habitats wherever termites are available. Widespread except in forest.

Shoulder: 50 cm

### SPOTTED HYAENA — *Crocuta crocuta*

Muzzle dark brown, blunt, very strong. Ears **rounded**. Hair on neck and body **short**, pale brown-grey with scattered dark spots. Spots less distinct in older animals. Forequarters more powerful than hindquarters, giving sloping line to back. Tail short, bushy, dark-tipped. Female has false penis and scrotum. Nocturnal. Lives and hunts in clans. Long-range contact call is distinctive rising "whoooo-oop"; they also chatter and giggle in close groups. Hunts medium to large prey or scavenges other predators' kills. Twins born at any time and cared for only by mother, not weaned until 18 months old. N half of region.

Shoulder: 80 cm

### BROWN HYAENA — *Hyaena brunnea*

Muzzle and face black. Ears upright, **pointed. Pale mantle of long hair on neck and shoulders**. Body dark brown. Legs striped. Long hair on tail. General appearance like large shaggy dog. Lives in groups but forages alone. Territorial but ranges widely, sometimes entering urban localities. Scavenges carrion, eggs, insects; eats melons for water. Nomadic males mate with territorial females. Litters of up to four born at any time; cared for by group. Prefers arid habitats in central areas and NW.

Shoulder: 80 cm

Body: 36 cm
Tail: 26 cm

Body: 30 cm
Tail: 16 cm

Body: 73 cm
Tail: 22 cm

1,25 m

1 m

1,6 m

### 1   STRIPED POLECAT *Ictonyx striatus*

Pointed snout. **White patches on forehead and cheeks.** Black with four striking white stripes along body. Long hair. Bushy tail mostly white. Solitary. Nocturnal. Defends itself with spray of stinking secretion from anal glands. Largely insectivorous. Frequently seen killed on roads. Up to three young born in summer. Throughout s Africa.
**Similar**
**2   STRIPED WEASEL** *Poecilogale albinucha*
Cheeks black. Forehead and neck all-white. Elongated body.

### 3   HONEY BADGER *Mellivora capensis*

Ears and eyes small. Solidly built. **Black with white or grey back.** Legs short and strong with long claws. Solitary; occasionally in pairs or small groups. Mainly nocturnal. Raids beehives for honey; digs up rodents, spiders. Very aggressive. Twins born in summer. Widespread except Namib desert, central areas and SE.

### 4   CAPE CLAWLESS OTTER *Aonyx capensis*

Muzzle short, blunt. Ears very small. Brown with **white chin, throat, neck and chest.** Sleek, lithe. **Nails (not claws) on fingers and toes.** Hindfeet webbed. Tail thick at base, tapering to short point. Found in sea or freshwater. Probably territorial. Solitary or in pairs or families. Eats fish, crustaceans, molluscs, birds, insects. Crushes crab shells, unlike water mongoose. Twins born at any time. E half of region and extreme N, along Orange River and S coast.
**Similar**
**SPOTTED-NECKED OTTER** *Lutra maculicollis*
Throat and chest mottled pale cream. Feet have claws.

### 5   PANGOLIN *Manis temminckii*

No external ears. **Upperparts covered in scales.** Forefeet have heavy claws. Solitary. Nocturnal. Walks on hindlegs. Rips open termite nests and licks up insects. If molested rolls up with head protected by tail. Single young born in midwinter; rides crossways on mother's back. Widespread except in S and in forest or desert.

### 6   AARDVARK *Orycteropus afer*

Long, pig-like snout. Long, pointed ears. Pale buff-grey skin shows through sparse hair. Hunched posture. Limbs strong and heavy with thick claws. Tail thick, tapered. Solitary. Strictly nocturnal. Sleeps by day in one of several large, self-dug burrows. Ant and termite nests are clawed open and insects licked out. Single young born in early spring. Widespread except in desert and forest.

**1    SURICATE**                            *Suricata suricatta*

**Black "bandit's mask" around eyes.** Light brown with darker
stripes across back. Legs longer than in other small mongooses.
Long claws. Tail thin with black tip. Diurnal. Forages in soil and
litter. **Highly social** in family groups. Sentinels keep watch for
predators. Only one pair in each group breeds; litters cared for by
whole group. W half of region.
Similar
GROUND SQUIRREL see p. 170

**2    YELLOW MONGOOSE**                    *Cynictis penicillata*

Tip of nose black. Body brownish or reddish-yellow in S, tending
to grey in N. **Tail bushy with white tip.** Diurnal. Lives in groups
in communal burrow but forages singly. Flees with tail arched up.
Eats mostly invertebrates; occasionally succulent plants for mois-
ture. Litters of up to five in summer. W half of region except
Namib desert.
Similar
WHITE-TAILED MONGOOSE *Ichneumia albicauda*
Legs long, black. Tail white except base. N and E.
SELOUS' MONGOOSE *Paracynictis selousi*
Dark face and lower limbs. White tail tip. NE.

**3    SLENDER MONGOOSE**                    *Galerella sanguinea*

Tip of nose red. Colour varies from orange to dark grey. Long,
low-slung. Tail thin with **black tip.** Solitary. Diurnal. Hunts along
paths and roads for invertebrates, fruit, carrion. Flees with tail
horizontal; flicks it up when reaching cover. One or two young
born in summer. N of Orange and Tugela rivers.
Similar
SMALL GREY MONGOOSE *G. pulverulenta*
Grizzled grey. Tail tip only slightly darker. SW.

**4    WATER MONGOOSE**                      *Atilax paludinosus*

Head larger than in other mongooses. Dark reddish-brown to
black. Hair long, coarse. Tail bushy at base, tapering to thin tip.
Toes not webbed as in otters. Crepuscular in vegetation close to
water. Solitary or with young. Eats small waterside animals leaving crab shells whole. One or two young born in summer. S and
and along Orange River.
Similar
LARGE GREY MONGOOSE *Herpestes ichneumon*
Tail slender with black tip. Diurnal. Small family groups.

**BANDED MONGOOSE**                          *Mungos mungo*

Brownish-grey with **narrow dark stripes on rear half of body.**
Diurnal. **Groups up to 30** forage in soil and litter; sleep together
in burrows. Chatter frequently. Eats mainly insects, fruit. All
females in group breed and suckle each other's young. Open
woodland in N and E.

**DWARF MONGOOSE**                           *Helogale parvula*

Very dark brown. Legs short. Diurnal. Territorial. **Highly social** in
family groups. Sentinels watch for predators. Forages in soil and
litter. Sleeps in burrows often in termite mounds. Only one pair in
group breeds; litters cared for by whole group. Dry open woodland and grassland in N and NE.

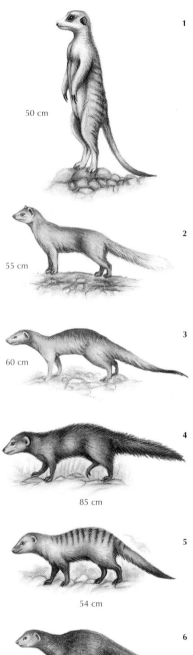

1

50 cm

2

55 cm

3

60 cm

4

85 cm

5

54 cm

6

38 cm

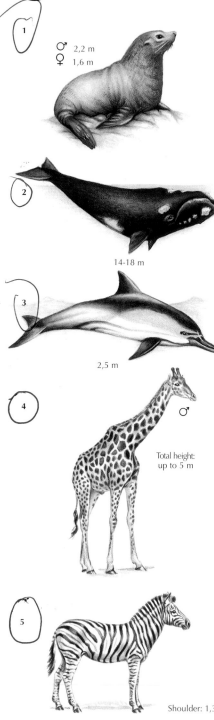

♂ 2,2 m
♀ 1,6 m

14-18 m

2,5 m

♂

Total height:
up to 5 m

Shoulder: 1,3 m

**1   CAPE FUR SEAL**               *Arctocephalus pusillus*

**Muzzle pointed**. Whiskers long, thick. Neck thick, especially in males. **Limbs modified into flippers.** Brown fur short, dense. More aquatic than terrestrial. Feeds on fish, octopus, crayfish at sea. Rests and breeds on land. Male defends harem of females in breeding colony. Single pup born in summer. Breeding colonies on W coast and offshore islands. Found in inshore waters of W and S coast as far E as East London.

**2   SOUTHERN RIGHT WHALE**           *Eubalaena australis*

Head large with small eyes. No external ears. Nostrils form blow hole on top of head. Mouth very large, arched. Pale callosities on head are different on each whale. Front limbs modified to flippers. No hindlimbs. Horizontal tail fins. Filter-feeds on plankton. Swims slowly near surface, sometimes rolling, splashing, leaping. Migrates from Antarctic Ocean to Cape inshore waters in June and returns in December. Single calf born off Cape S coast around August.

**3   COMMON DOLPHIN**               *Delphinus delphis*

Elongated, pointed beak. Body streamlined; neck and head indistinguishable. Dark grey above, pale below. **Hourglass pattern on sides; front half brown-grey, rear half pale grey.** Prominent fin. Flippers sharply pointed. No hindlimbs. Horizontal tail flukes. Strong, agile swimmer, frequently jumping clear of water. Feeds cooperatively by surrounding fish shoals. Throughout s African waters.
**Similar**
**BOTTLENOSED DOLPHIN** *Tursiops aduncus*
Plain grey, slightly paler below. Wide, rounded beak.

**4   GIRAFFE**                    *Giraffa camelopardalis*

Tallest living animal; unmistakable. Long neck and legs. Covered with dark brown blotches on buffy background. Pair of blunt "horns" on top of head. Back slopes from shoulders to rump. Tail has long, black hairs at tip. Females and young in small herds; bulls solitary. Bulls fight by swinging their heads at each other. Browses on trees, bushes. Single calf born at any time. Savanna woodland in N.

**5   BURCHELL'S ZEBRA**              *Equus burchelli*

Muzzle black. Rest of animal striped black and white; **stripes extend under belly. Stripes on lower legs faint.** Usually pale chestnut shadow stripes on rump. **No dewlap.** Breeding groups of up to about 5 mares held by one stallion. Young males form bachelor herds. Breeding group flees predators in a tight bunch with stallion as rearguard. Alarm call a sharp yelp "kwa-ha-ha". Grazes on short grass in grassland and open woodland where water available. Single foal born at any time. N and E.
**Similar**
**CAPE MOUNTAIN ZEBRA** *E. zebra zebra*
White belly. Legs boldly striped. Lateral stripes on rump. No shadow stripes. Dewlap under throat. Confined to conservation areas in S.
**HARTMANN'S MOUNTAIN ZEBRA** *E.z. hartmannae*
Mountains of Namibia.

## 1　ELEPHANT　　　　　*Loxodonta africana*

Largest land mammal; unmistakable. Nose and upper lip elongated into trunk. Usually has a pair of tusks growing down and forwards from upper lip. Ears very large. Almost hairless with rough grey skin, often coloured by dust or mud. Limbs massive. Females and young live in family herds. Males solitary or in small groups. Complex social life. Drinks daily if possible, fond of bathing and wallowing. Eats about 170 kg (up to 300 kg) of vegetation per day. Single calf born at four- to five-year intervals. Confined to large conservation areas except in NE and extreme N.

## 2　WHITE RHINOCEROS　　　　*Ceratotherium simum*

**Upper lip broad**. Two horns on nose. **Ears bluntly pointed**. Eyes small. Neck thick and powerful with **hump at shoulders**. Three toes on each foot, showing bare grey skin. Cows and young bulls in groups. Breeding bulls solitary, territorial. Single calf born at two- to four-year intervals. Calf runs **in front of** mother. **Grazes grass**. Confined to conservation areas.

**Similar**

**BLACK RHINOCEROS** *Diceros bicornis*

Upper lip pointed. Ears rounded. Solitary. Calf runs **behind** mother. Browses trees, shrubs. Endangered.

## 3　HIPPOPOTAMUS　　　　*Hippopotamus amphibius*

Massive head with very wide muzzle. Huge mouth armed with tusks. Eyes and ears small, high on head. Short thick neck. Barrel-shaped body. Thick legs. Short, flattened tail with fringe of stiff bristles. Almost hairless skin brownish-grey with pinkish folds. Spends most of day in water with eyes, ears and nostrils exposed. Can submerge for up to six minutes. Grazes at night, sometimes travelling long distances. Single calf born at any time, sometimes in water. N and NE.

## 　BUSHPIG　　　　*Potamochoerus porcus*

Blunt muscular snout. Small eyes. Pointed, tufted ears. Similar to domestic pig but has coarse reddish to dark brown hair. **Long white hairs along back, on sides of face and ears. Tusks not conspicuous**. Social in sounders of up to 12. Nocturnal. **Runs with tail down**. Omnivorous; diet includes carrion, newborn lambs, roots, crops. Litters of three or four born in large nests in summer. Forests and dense vegetation in NE and along SE coast.

## 　WARTHOG　　　　*Phacochoerus aethiopicus*

Blunt muscular snout. **Large tusks emerge from mouth, curve upwards and inwards. Large "warts" on sides of face. Coarse dark mane on neck and back**. Rest of body sparsely bristly. Thin tail. Diurnal. Small family groups. Sleeps in holes. Fond of wallowing. **Runs with tail held straight up**. Omnivorous, mainly grazing. Litters of up to six born in holes in summer. N half of region.

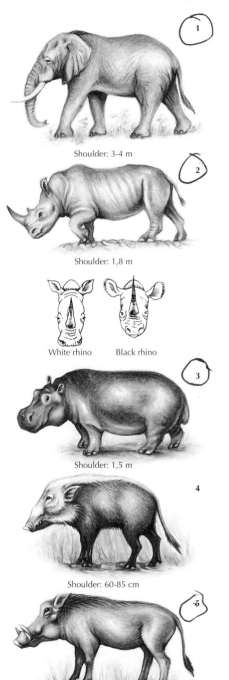

Shoulder: 3-4 m

Shoulder: 1,8 m

White rhino　　Black rhino

Shoulder: 1,5 m

Shoulder: 60-85 cm

Shoulder: 60-70 cm

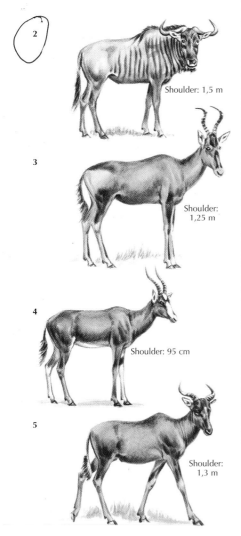

Shoulder: 1,4 m

Shoulder: 1,5 m

Shoulder: 1,25 m

Shoulder: 95 cm

Shoulder: 1,3 m

**1   BUFFALO**                          *Syncerus caffer*
Curved horns on both sexes rise from heavy bosses, spread out
and downwards, then curve up and inwards. Brownish-grey, darkening with age. Hair sparse in old bulls. Herds of up to thousands.
Old bulls solitary or in small groups. Grazes grass; occasionally
browses on small trees, shrubs. Single calf born in summer. Inhabits grassland where water and shade is available in N and E.

**2   BLUE WILDEBEEST**            *Connochaetes taurinus*
Face black. Horns on both sexes spread **outwards, then up and
inwards**. Black mane on neck and shoulders. Long hair hanging
from chin and throat. Adult grey with silvery sheen and faint darker stripes on upper body. **Tail black**. Calf buff. Females and bachelor herds of up to 30, sometimes aggregations of thousands.
Breeding bulls territorial. Migratory in some areas. Eats grass. Single calf born in November or December. Open woodland within
15 km of drinking water in north-central areas and NE.
**Similar**
**BLACK WILDEBEEST  *C. gnou***
Horns spread forwards and upwards. Tail white. Stiff hair on muzzle. South-central highveld grassland.

**3   RED HARTEBEEST**              *Alcelaphus buselaphus*
Head long, narrow. Black on top of muzzle. Horns set high on
head, rise straight up, curve forwards then sharply backwards.
Back slopes from hump on shoulders. **Brick-red with black on
shoulders and legs**. Pale upper rump. Female less distinctly
marked. Herds of up to 20, sometimes aggregations of hundreds.
Breeding bulls territorial. Grazes on grass; will browse if grass in
short supply. Young born in early summer. Grassland and savan-
na in dry central areas and NW.
**Similar**
**LICHTENSTEIN'S HARTEBEEST  *Sigmoceros lichtensteinii***
Yellowish with no black markings. NE.

**4   BLESBOK**                    *Damaliscus dorcas phillipsi*
White blaze on muzzle and forehead **broken by dark bar
between eyes**. Horns on both sexes rise straight up, spread sideways and back, then forwards and inwards, ridged for most of
length. Body dark red-brown. Belly white. **Pale on rump**. Small
herds. Ram marks territory with dung heap. Grazes or browses if
grass unavailable. Young born around December. Central South
Africa.
**Similar**
**BONTEBOK  *D.d. dorcas***
White blaze not broken by dark bar between eyes. Rump and
lower legs white. Sw Cape.

**5   TSESSEBE**                        *Damaliscus lunatus*
Narrow muzzle. Front of face dark. Horns on both sexes spread
outwards, then back, then slightly upwards. Body red-brown **with
purplish sheen**. Darker patches on front of shoulders, upper limbs
and in narrow stripe down forelegs. Yellow on belly and inside
legs. Small herds. Breeding bulls territorial. Grazes on tall or
freshly sprouted grass. Young born around October. Woodland-
grassland edges where water is accessible in N and NE. Patchy
distribution.

### 1  SPRINGBOK   *Antidorcas marsupialis*

White face. Black band through eye along side of face. Horns on both sexes rise upwards, then out and backwards, then forwards and in. Cinnamon above. White below, on rump and inside of legs. Dark chocolate stripe along flanks. Small herds. Rarely congregates in thousands. Breeding rams territorial. Migratory in some areas. Can live without drinking water. Displays by leaping vertically on all four legs ("pronking"). Grazes or browses; also eats roots, melons for moisture. Breeds in rainy season. Open grassland, Karoo and scrub in dry W.

### 2  IMPALA   *Aepyceros melampus melampus*

Black spot on top of head. Top of muzzle dark brown. Horns on males only, ridged and forming graceful lyre shape. Reddish-brown, paler on lower flanks. White underparts. Black stripes on rump either side of white haunches and down centre of tail. **Black patches above hind ankles.** Herds of six to 20; up to 100 in dry season. Males territorial during winter rutting, driving other males away from harem by roaring and fighting. Single lamb born in spring. Dependent on water daily. Browses and grazes. Open woodland where water is available in NE; widely translocated.

**Similar**

**BLACK-FACED IMPALA  *A.m. petersi***
Black blaze on muzzle. N Namibia.

### 3  WATERBUCK   *Kobus ellipsiprymnus*

White **"eyebrows"**. Horns on males only, long, ridged, sweeping outwards and slightly back in wide arc. White throat. **White ring on rump**. Coat shaggy, grey-brown. Small herds of 12 or more females and young or bachelors. Breeding males solitary, territorial. Young born in summer. Grazes in grassland and dense cover close to water. NE; widely translocated in areas with good rainfall.

### 4  RED LECHWE   *Kobus leche*

Horns on males only, long, ridged, sweeping slightly backwards and upwards in smooth arc. Rich yellow-red. White underparts. **Black down front of forelegs**. Rump distinctly higher than shoulders. Tail tip black. Herds of up to 30, sometimes aggregations of thousands. Enters water freely. Runs through shallows with bounding action. Swims well. Males hold small territories for breeding. Young born in summer. Grazes on waterside grasses. Okavango swamp and Chobe floodplain.

**Similar**

**PUKU  *K. vardonii***
Horns shorter, thicker. No black on forelegs.

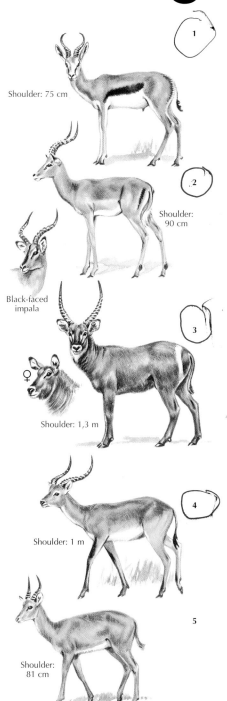

Shoulder: 75 cm

Shoulder: 90 cm

Black-faced impala

Shoulder: 1,3 m

Shoulder: 1 m

Shoulder: 81 cm

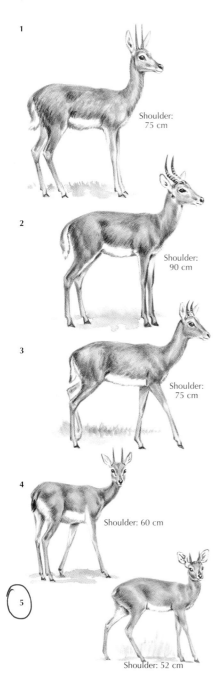

1

Shoulder:
75 cm

2

Shoulder:
90 cm

3

Shoulder:
75 cm

4

Shoulder: 60 cm

5

Shoulder: 52 cm

### 1  GREY RHEBOK
*Pelea capreolus*

**Eyes ringed with white**. Horns on males only, narrow vertical spikes with slight forward curve. Ears tall, narrow. Hair long, woolly. Brownish-grey. Underparts white. Small herds. Rams are territorial. When alarmed flees with rocking-horse action while flashing white underside of tail. Independent of surface water. Single lamb born in summer. Grazes on rocky slopes with grass cover. S and central areas of South Africa.

### 2  REEDBUCK
*Redunca arundinum*

White facial markings and upper throat. Horns on males only, lower portion ridged, curving out and forward. Pale yellow-brown or grey-brown. White underparts. **Dark brown down front of forelegs**. Tail short and bushy with white underside. Pairs or small family groups in tall grass and reeds near water. Avoids thick bush. Rams are territorial. Generally grazes grass. N and E.

### 3  MOUNTAIN REEDBUCK
*Redunca fulvorufula*

Head and neck yellower than greyish-brown body. Horns on males only, short, thick, lower section ridged, upper section curved sharply forward. No dark brown on forelegs. Coat woolly. White underside of tail exposed when fleeing. Herds of about six or more in dry stony areas with grass and scattered bushes. Active mornings and evenings. Mountainous areas in E and S.

### 4  ORIBI
*Ourebia ourebi*

**Pale on sides of face, above eyes and on throat**. Horns on males only, thin, upright with slight forward curve, heavily ridged at base. Glandular patch below ears. Chestnut-buff with white underparts including chest. **Upperside of tail black**. Long, thin neck. Solitary or small family groups. Prefers short or burned grass. Rests on raised ground with head up to watch for danger. Independent of surface water. Selective browser and grazer. Scattered distribution in E and N.

### 5  STEENBOK
*Raphicerus campestris*

**Large ears strikingly marked on inside. Black on top of muzzle**. Horns on males only, upright spikes, ridged at base. Rich brick-red. White underparts. Hooves sharply pointed. Solitary or in pairs. Territorial. Buries its urine and faeces. Active mainly in morning and evening. Independent of water. Selective browser and grazer; digs for roots and tubers in grassland where there is some tree cover. Single lamb born at any time. Widespread except in forest, desert and rocky hills.

### 1 KLIPSPRINGER        *Oreotragus oreotragus*

Head small. Muzzle pointed. Horns on males only, short, straight spikes. Body compact. Grey-yellow speckled with brown or black. **Stands on tips of hooves.** Territorial pairs or parents with young inhabit mountainous or rocky habitat. Agile runner and leaper on steep rocks. Alarm call a piercing whistle. Independent of water. Browses bushes, trees. Single lamb born at any time. Discontinuous but widespread, restricted to rocky areas.

### 2 COMMON DUIKER        *Sylvicapra grimmia*

Dark band on top of muzzle. Glandular slits in sides of face. Spiky tuft of hair between ears. Horns on males only, straight and sharp, ridged at base. Colour varies from grey to red-yellow. Solitary in a variety of habitats that provide cover. Hides if disturbed; dashes off at last moment. Active dawn and evening. Independent of water. Browses and digs for wide range of vegetable food and small invertebrates. Single lamb born at any time. Throughout s Africa.

### 3 GRYSBOK        *Raphicerus melanotis*

Horns on males only, short, smooth and straight, sloping backwards in same plane as face. Large ears. **Rich brick-red, flecked with white. Underparts buffy.** Slightly hunched posture. **False "hooves" above fetlocks of hindlegs.** Solitary or in pairs. Secretive. Nocturnal but may be seen at dawn and dusk. Grazes in fynbos. Single lamb born in early summer. Extreme S and SW.
**Similar**
**SHARPE'S GRYSBOK  R. sharpei**
No false hooves. Only in NE.

### 4 SUNI        *Neotragus moschatus*

Pointed muzzle. Deep glandular slits in sides of face. Horns on males only, **rising from just above eyes**, sloping back in same plane as face, ridged almost to tips. Hindquarters higher than shoulders. Reddish-brown. Pale underparts. Pairs or small groups with territorial male. Secretive in thick forest habitat. Browses or eats fallen leaves. Single lamb born in summer. Extreme N and NE.

### 5 DAMARA DIK-DIK        *Madoqua kirkii*

Muzzle sharply pointed, **swollen just behind tip.** White around eyes. Erects tuft of long hair on forehead when stressed. Horns on males only, short, ridged, backward-sloping. Grizzled yellow-grey. White underparts. Hunched posture. Pairs or families browse in thickets, woodland. Single lamb born in summer. N Namibia.

### 6 BLUE DUIKER        *Philantomba monticola*

Smallest antelope in s Africa. Glandular slits in sides of face. Both sexes have short spike-like horns with tuft of hair between. Colour varies from slate grey to brown with grey sheen. Underparts white. Tail has white fringe. Hunched posture. Secretive. Solitary or in pairs. Browses in dense forest, coastal bush. Single lamb born at any time. One population along SE coast, another in Mozambique.
**Similar**
**RED DUIKER Cephalophus natalensis**
Uniform red above and below. Black and white tail tip. E and NE coast with isolated population in Soutpansberg.

1

Shoulder:
60 cm

2

Shoulder:
50 cm

3

Shoulder:
54 cm

4

Shoulder:
35 cm

5

Shoulder:
40 cm

6

Shoulder: 32 cm

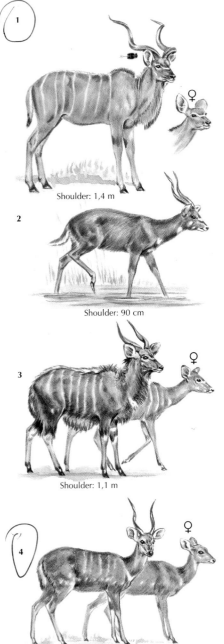

Shoulder: 1,4 m

Shoulder: 90 cm

Shoulder: 1,1 m

Shoulder: 80 cm

### 1 KUDU — *Tragelaphus strepsiceros*

Narrow white bar across face just in front of eyes. Large ears. **Wide spiralling horns** on males only. Mane on shoulders. Male has beard below neck. Pale grey-brown with narrow vertical white stripes over back. Tail brown above, white below. Small herds in woodland and savanna where water is available. Males and females separate except in breeding season. Mainly browses but also grazes fresh grass. Young born mostly in late summer. Throughout s Africa.

### 2 SITATUNGA — *Tragelaphus spekei*

White bar on face between eyes. Shallow spiralling horns on males only. Two white patches on front of neck. Hair long, rough. Male dark brown, female more reddish-brown. White on legs. **Long, splayed hooves.** Rests in reedbeds, moves out at night to graze. Very good swimmer. Single young born in late summer. Only in n Okavango and Chobe.

### 3 NYALA — *Tragelaphus angasii*

White bar in front of eyes, **broken in middle**. White spots on cheeks. Horns on males only, curling out and back, then in and forward. **Horns have distinct white tips**. Male dark grey with about 12 white stripes over back; long black mane, beard and fringe beneath entire body. **Legs yellow.** Female chestnut with narrow white stripes over back. Secretive. Small herds browse in woodland, thickets. Young born mostly in summer. E and NE.

### 4 BUSHBUCK — *Tragelaphus scriptus*

Pale patches in front of eyes. Horns on males only, shallow spirals with spiral ridge. White band on throat and at base of neck. Male chocolate brown, female grey-buff to chestnut. White spots on flanks and four to eight white transverse stripes on back. Secretive. Solitary or in small groups in thick cover near water. Mainly browses. Young born at any time. N and E plus coastal bush in S and E.

## 1  ELAND — *Taurotragus oryx*

Brush of coarse hair on forehead of males only. Horns on both sexes, tightly spiralled with deep spiral ridge. Horns longer and thicker in male. Neck of male enormously thick with bearded dewlap. Body and legs fawn, grey in prime males, especially around neck. Herds of up to about 50; aggregations of thousands in n Kalahari. Bull makes clicking sound as it walks. Browses. Single calf born at any time. Central areas, N and NE plus Drakensberg.

## 2  SABLE — *Hippotragus niger*

Top of muzzle black. **White stripe from in front of each eye extending to mouth**. Black stripe along each cheek. Lower jaw white. Long scimitar-like horns in both sexes, swept backwards over shoulders. Horns much heavier in mature bulls. Ears long, russet-coloured. Mature bulls **glossy black** with long, upstanding mane. Cows and young males brown, darkening with age. **All have white underparts**. Calf russet. Prefers dry grassland with limited bush where water is available. Mostly grazes but will browse if grass is poor. Herds of up to 30 females and young are controlled by an old cow. During breeding a bull will dominate the herd and defend his position aggessively. Single calf born in late summer. NE but historically more widely distributed.

## 3  ROAN — *Hippotragus equinus*

**White patches in front of eyes not reaching white muzzle**. Horns with backward sweep in both sexes. **Ears long with tassels on tips**. Neck has mane and beard of black-tipped hair. Grey-brown tinged reddish. Underparts paler. Tail black-tipped. Herds of about 12. Not territorial. Dominant bull maintains access to female herd by defeating other bulls. Grazes, preferring tall grass. Single calf born at any time. Open woodland with long grass and available water. N and NE.

## 4  GEMSBOK — *Oryx gazella*

**White across forehead between eyes. Black stripe from base of each horn though eye to middle of lower jaw. Horns long and straight** in both sexes. Neck very thick. Grey with black stripe along spine. Black patch on top of rump. Black band low on flanks. Belly white. Legs black and white. Tail black. Small herds of about 15; many more during rains. Also solitary bulls. Single calf born in summer; remains hidden from herd for about a month. Grazes in semi-desert habitats, eating wild melons for moisture. Independent of surface water. Arid central areas and nw half of region.

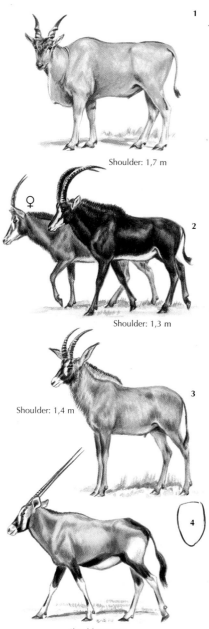

1

Shoulder: 1,7 m

♀

2

Shoulder: 1,3 m

3

Shoulder: 1,4 m

4

Shoulder: 1,2 m

# GRASSES, SEDGES, FERNS & FUNGI

Grasses, sedges, restios, rushes, ferns and fungi are unrelated botanically
but have been included in a single chapter for convenience.

**Grasses** are members of the Gramineae family which have leaf sheaths split lengthwise on the side opposite the blade. The stem is cylindrical, and hollow between nodes. Grasses are wind-pollinated flowering plants bearing various types of inflorescences (see accompanying illustrations). These are useful for identification.

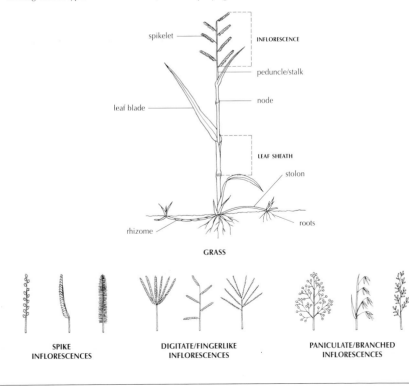

spikelet

INFLORESCENCE

peduncle/stalk

node

leaf blade

LEAF SHEATH

stolon

roots

rhizome

**GRASS**

**SPIKE
INFLORESCENCES**

**DIGITATE/FINGERLIKE
INFLORESCENCES**

**PANICULATE/BRANCHED
INFLORESCENCES**

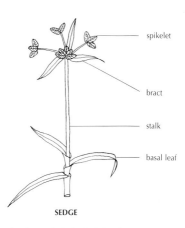

spikelet

bract

stalk

basal leaf

**SEDGE**

**Sedges** are members of the Cyperaceae family in which the leaf sheaths are continuous around the stem, splitting open with age. The stem is solid, and may be cylindrical or triangular. Sedges are found mostly in moist areas.

**Rushes** have small, wind-pollinated flowers (similar to the lily in structure) in dense clusters at the end of slender, cylindrical, hollow stems. Leaves are cylindrical or flat and hard, or reduced to a sheath. Rushes are mostly found in swampy areas.

**Restios** are members of the Restionaceae family. Their stems are solid and jointed, with leaves reduced to dry sheaths at nodes. Restios are largely confined to the winter rainfall area, namely the southern and southwestern Cape. This is one of the three major families that constitute fynbos (along with proteas and ericas), taking the place of grasses in this biome. Restios are wind-pollinated. Male and female flowers occur on separate plants, often with very different appearance.

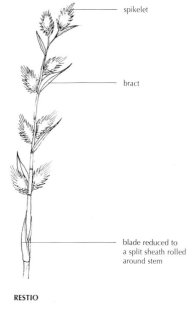

spikelet

bract

blade reduced to
a split sheath rolled
around stem

**RESTIO**

**Ferns** and their allies belong to the group Pteridophyta. They do not bear flowers and seeds, but produce wind-blown spores. These grow into very small green discs or prothalli which carry both male and female organs. The fertilised female puts down roots and a new fern plant develops (the prothallus withers away). Ferns are dependent on moisture for reproduction but some have adapted to dry environments by evolving the ability to wait for water, and, where necessary, to reproduce vegetatively by means of runners. Resurrection ferns generally shrink and curl up in dry periods, unfolding in response to rain or moisture. Other species have a dormant period of a few months. A few species can survive several years without water, and others have drought-resistant spores which can survive up to 20 years without water.

Ferns provide one of the most direct links with prehistoric times. The common ancestors of club mosses (lycopods) and horsetails were most abundant worldwide about 400 million years ago and the ferns were at their height over 100 million years ago. In southern Africa there is an excellent fossil record of this prehistoric flora.

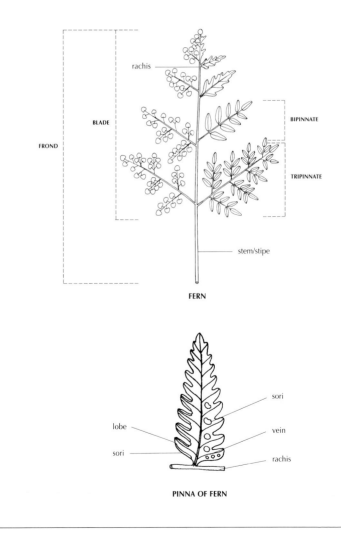

FERN

PINNA OF FERN

**Fungi.** Mushrooms, puffballs and other fleshy fungi are the reproductive or fruiting bodies of the plant. Fungi reproduce by means of spores. These spores grow a long tube (hypha) which branches and re-branches until a web-like mycelium is formed. This is the main body of the fungus, responsible for food and growth. It can reproduce sexually or asexually.

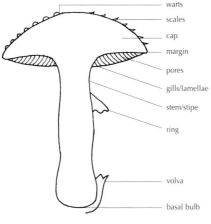

warts
scales
cap
margin
pores
gills/lamellae
stem/stipe
ring
volva
basal bulb

**MUSHROOM**

Unlike other plants, fungi lack chlorophyll and cannot produce their own food. Nourishment is therefore obtained from other organisms in one of three ways:

- Saprobic fungi draw food from dead or rotting plant and animal tissue.
- Parasitic fungi live on live host plants or animals.
- Symbiotic fungi form mutually beneficial associations with algae to form lichens: the algae create food and the fungi keep the algae moist. Symbiotic associations also exist between fungi and wood-destroying termites.

Because fungi do not derive food in the same way as most other plants, some botanists regard them as not belonging to the plant kingdom.

## Scope of this chapter

There are tens of thousands of species of grasses, ferns and fungi, and the descriptions in this chapter are merely a cross-section of the more commonly found species. However, readers will be able to find and identify these species in different parts of the region. It is hoped that this will initiate and encourage a basic interest which may be developed further.

## Dimensions

The first dimension given with each description in this chapter refers to the total height of the mature plant. Other dimensions in the text are for specific parts of the plant and are clearly stated. Only the greatest dimension is given; this usually indicates length but sometimes indicates diameter. Leaf measurements refer to the length of the blade excluding the stalk. The dimensions given either consist of a range or are maximums, with smaller dimensions possible in different specimens. Where two dimensions are given for structures such as leaves or flowers, e.g. 120x140 mm, the first is the length dimension and the second the breadth.

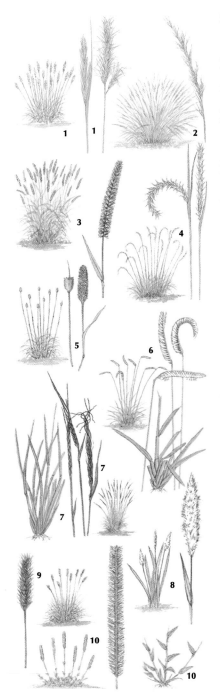

## Grasses with compact, spike-like inflorescence

### 1   TASSEL BRISTLEGRASS                 *Aristida congesta*

Up to 900 mm. Perennial. Conspicuous, compact, white head (Dec-Jun). Widespread in warm dry grassland, particularly in disturbed areas. Throughout region.

### 2   NGONGONI BRISTLEGRASS           *Aristida junciformis*

Up to 900 mm. Perennial. Leaf blade **narrow and wiry**. Inflorescence narrow, up to 200 mm long (Nov-May). Widespread in open grassland, bushveld, fynbos, from SW to N.

### 3   BLUE BUFFALO GRASS                   *Cenchrus ciliaris*

Up to 1,2 m. Perennial. Leaves up to 10 mm wide, **keeled, blue-green**. Inflorescence up to 120 mm long (Aug-Apr). **Bristles come away with seed**, unlike golden bristlegrass (facing page). Common in dry areas, spreading due to cultivation as pasture grass.

### 4   WIRE LEMON GRASS   *Elionurus muticus (=E. argenteus)*

Up to 1 m. Perennial. Leaves **wiry, folded**, curled, coppery with age (bitter lemon taste). Inflorescence up to 120 mm long, curled back when mature (Sept-May). Common in open grassland, on poor rocky soils. E half of region.

### 5   THIMBLE GRASS                  *Fingerhuthia africana*

Up to 900 mm, usually less. Perennial. Leaves up to 400x4 mm. Inflorescence up to 50 mm long (Sept-May). Widespread, on well-drained soils, except in some areas in E.

### 6   CATERPILLAR GRASS                     *Harpochloa falx*

Up to 900 mm. Perennial. Leaves **blunt-tipped**, **rigid**. Inflorescence up to 80 mm long, **curving back with age** (Sept-Apr). Common in open grassland, middle to high altitude, from SW to N.

### 7   SPEAR GRASS                   *Heteropogon contortus*

Up to 700 mm. Perennial. Leaves blunt-tipped. Flowering stem **flattened at base**. Inflorescence up to 70 mm long (Oct-Mar), **seeds barbed**. Open grassland, rocky and disturbed soils. Widespread except in dry NW.

### 8   COTTONWOOL GRASS                  *Imperata cylindrica*

Up to 1,2 m. Perennial. Leaves up to 1 000x12 mm, **sharp tip**. Inflorescence 80-250 mm long (Aug-Jun). Common in poorly drained areas, high rainfall grassland. Widespread.

### 9   COPPER WIRE GRASS               *Merxmuellera disticha*

Up to 700 mm. Perennial. Leaves wiry, short and curved, or longer, up to 400 mm, less curved. Inflorescence up to 100 mm long, **two rows of spikelets** (Oct-May). Common, coast to mountain grassland, from SE to central areas.

### 10  CAT'S TAIL                             *Perotis patens*

Up to 600 mm. Annual. Leaf blade up to 12 mm wide, margin wavy, with rigid hairs. Inflorescence up to 300x25 mm (Nov-Apr). Sandy, poor soils, disturbed areas in NE.

**1 GOLDEN BRISTLEGRASS**     *Setaria sphacelata*
Up to 2 m. Robust perennial. Leaves up to 400x15 mm, flat or folded. Inflorescence up to 300 mm long (Oct-May). Bristles orange, **do not fall off with seeds**. On damp soils in grassland and woodland, from SE coast to interior in N.

**2 RATSTAIL DROPSEED** *Sporobolus africanus (=S. capensis)*
Up to 1,5 m. Perennial. Leaves shiny, blade up to 400x4 mm. Inflorescence **compact, narrow**, up to 450 mm long (Oct-Apr). Disturbed areas, especially coast and more arid areas, also watercourses, from SW, E to N.
Similar
**BUSHVELD DROP-SEED** *S. fimbriatus*
Stems bright yellow at base. Inflorescence whorled, **open**.

**3 COMMON CARROT-SEED GRASS**     *Tragus berteronianus*
Up to 300 mm. Annual. Leaves short, blade up to 5 mm wide, flattened. Inflorescence up to 100 mm long (Nov-May), **spikelets covered with hooked spines**. Common (weed) in disturbed areas. Widespread except SW.

**4 CENTIPEDE GRASS**     *Urelytrum agropyroides*
       *(=U. squarrosum)*
Up to 1,6 m. Perennial. Leaves up to 300x6 mm, waxy bloom when young, bitter taste. Inflorescence up to 250 mm long, **awns flattened**, up to 120 mm long, **bend outwards when ripe** (Oct-Jun). Grassland, stony hillsides, from E coast areas to N, NW.

**Grasses with digitate (fingerlike) inflorescence**

**5 RHODES GRASS**     *Chloris gayana*
Up to 1,5 m. Perennial (annual). Inflorescence with up to 20 stalks (Nov-May). Moist areas, on disturbed ground, grassland. Widespread from S, E to N.

**6 FEATHERED CHLORIS**     *Chloris virgata*
Up to 900 mm. Perennial (annual). Leaf up to 10 mm wide. Inflorescence with 4-15 erect stalks (Dec-Jun). Disturbed soils, almost throughout region except in fynbos.

**7 FINGER GRASS**     *Digitaria eriantha*
Up to 1 m. Perennial. Inflorescence up to 200 mm long with up to 15 stalks (Jan-Apr). Widespread.

**8 VELVET SIGNAL GRASS**     *Brachiaria serrata*
Up to 900 mm. Perennial. Leaves up to 10 mm wide, hairy, with sharp tip. Each flowering stalk up to 25 mm long (Oct-May). Open grassland, bushveld, usually on rocky ground. Widespread from SE to N.

**9 BASKET GRASS**     *Oplismenus hirtellus*
150-800 mm. Perennial with rambling stems. Leaves up to 20 mm wide. Inflorescence up to 100 mm long, 3-7 stalks up to 30 mm long (Jan-Jun). In dense shade of forest, coast to mountains, from SE to N.

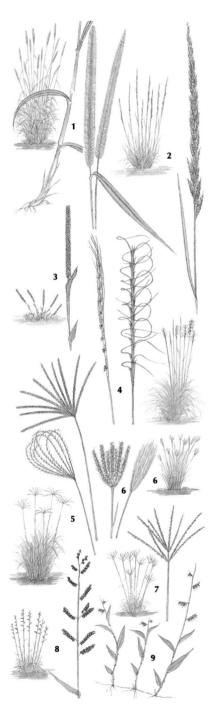

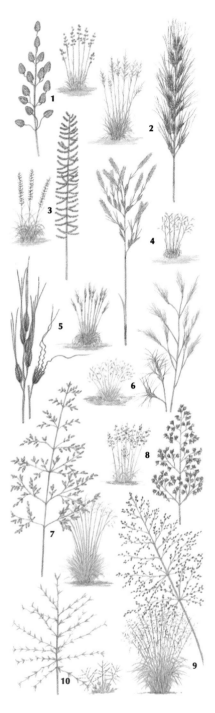

## Grasses with paniculate (branched) inflorescence

**1  HEARTSEED LOVEGRASS**        *Eragrostis capensis*

Up to 900 mm. Perennial. Leaf blade up to 100 mm long, shiny, rolled inwards. Inflorescence up to 150 mm long (Sept-Apr). Common in grassland on shallow soils, also in damp or disturbed areas, from SW to tropical Africa.

**2  COMMON RUSSET GRASS**        *Loudetia simplex*

Up to 1,2 m. Perennial. Leaves flat or rolled. Nodes **ringed with hairs.** Inflorescence up to 300 mm long, awn up to 50 mm long (Nov-Jan). Open grassland, poor sandy soils in high rainfall areas, from E to NE.

**3  HERRINGBONE GRASS**        *Pogonarthria squarrosa*

800 mm. Perennial. Leaves wiry. Inflorescence up to 300 mm long (Oct-May). Common on disturbed ground, scattered in grassland. Widespread from E to NW.

**4  SMALL BUSHMAN GRASS**        *Stipagrostis obtusa*

Up to 600 mm. Perennial. Leaves in basal cushion, 20-200 mm long, curved, **nodes black.** Inflorescence up to 200 mm long, awns up to 30 mm long (Jul-May). Widespread in Karoo and Namibia, valuable grazing.
**Similar**
**TALL BUSHMAN GRASS** *S. ciliata*
Taller. **Ring of white hairs at nodes.**

**5  HAIRY TRIDENT GRASS**        *Tristachya leucothrix*
        *(=T. hispida, Apochaete hispida)*

Up to 900 mm. Perennial. Leaves up to 6 mm wide, flattened, **hairy, curled.** Inflorescence with **hairy spikelets** up to 40 mm long, awn up to 100 mm long (Oct-Mar). Open grassland, common in highland sourveld. Widespread in summer rainfall areas.

**6  WHITE STICK GRASS**        *Aristida congesta*
        **subsp. *barbicollis***

Up to 600 mm. Perennial (annual). Leaves small. **Much-branched flowering stems,** inflorescence up to 200 mm long (Oct-May). Widespread in dry grassland, particularly in disturbed areas. Summer rainfall areas.

**7  WEEPING LOVEGRASS**        *Eragrostis curvula*

Up to 1,5 m. Perennial. Variable colour and growth forms. Leaves up to 600 mm long, narrow, rough, drooping (weeping) with age. Inflorescence much-branched, up to 300 mm long (Oct-Dec). Common in disturbed and high rainfall areas. Almost throughout region.

**8  NATAL RED TOP**        *Melinis repens*
        *(=Rhynchelytrum repens)*

Up to 1 m. Annual. Leaves up to 11 mm wide, rough. Inflorescence up to 200 mm long (Oct-Jun). Disturbed areas, common on roadsides. Widespread.

**9  GUINEA GRASS**        *Panicum maximum*

Up to 2,5 m. Perennial. Leaves up to 30 mm wide, leaf sheath **densely hairy.** Inflorescence up to 400 mm long (Nov-Jul). Open woodland and damp places. Widespread except very arid areas.

**10  SMALL TUMBLE GRASS**        *Trichoneura grandiglumis*

Up to 400 mm. Perennial. Leaves short, up to 7 mm wide, flattened. Inflorescence stiff, up to 250 mm long by 300 mm wide (Dec-Jan). Open grassland, disturbed ground. Widespread in summer rainfall areas in E, NW.

**1  COMMON WILD SORGHUM**          *Sorghum bicolor*
                                          *(=S. verticilliflorum)*

Up to 2,5 m. Annual. Leaf blade up to 30 mm wide. Inflorescence up to 400 mm long (Jan-Jun). Savanna, grassland, watercourses, disturbed areas, from NW to NE, tropical Africa to Australia.

**2  BROAD-LEAVED BRISTLEGRASS**          *Setaria megaphylla*
                                              *(=S. chevalieri)*

Up to 2 m. Perennial, in large clumps. Leaf blade up to 100 mm wide, pleated, margin rough. Inflorescence up to 600 mm long (Sept-Jun). Shade, moist areas, from SE to Zimbabwe.

**3  SNOWFLAKE GRASS**          *Andropogon eucomus*

Up to 900 mm. Perennial. Lower leaves flattened. Inflorescence branched, with **silvery hairs** (Nov-May). Wet areas, roadsides, from SW to Botswana and Namibia.

**4  BROAD-LEAVED TURPENTINE GRASS**          *Cymbopogon*
                                                  *excavatus*

Up to 1,5 m. Perennial, in clumps. Leaves **blue-green** with waxy coating, up to 14 mm wide, broader at base. Inflorescence up to 300 mm long. Aromatic, tasting strongly of turpentine. Widespread in open grassland, from SE to N and Botswana, Namibia.
**Similar**
**NARROW-LEAVED TURPENTINE GRASS  *C. plurinodis***
**Narrow leaf blades.** Widespread including S.
**GIANT TURPENTINE GRASS  *C. validus***
Taller (up to 2,4 m). Robust perennial, in large clumps. Leaves up to 600 mm long by 10 mm wide with **pale mid-vein**. Inflorescence up to 400 mm long. Grassland, rocky mountainsides in high rainfall areas, from SE to N.

**5  COMMON THATCH GRASS**          *Hyparrhenia hirta*

Up to 1 m. Perennial, in dense clumps. Leaf keeled. Flowering stems woody, inflorescence up to 300 mm long, awns up to 35 mm long (Sept-Mar), reddish with age. Open grassland, stony soil, near rivers, disturbed areas. Widespread except in NW and far N.

**6  RED GRASS**          *Themeda triandra*

300 mm to 1,8 m. Perennial. Leaves green to blue-green, **reddish-brown** when dry, blade up to 8 mm wide, folded, basal leaf sheaths flattened. Flowers Oct-Jul. Most common in **undisturbed grassland**. Widespread except parts of NW.

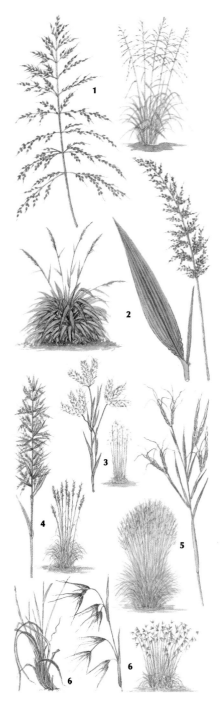

## Sedges

**1**  *Cyperus obtusiflorus*

Up to 450 mm. Perennial herb, from rhizome. Leaves up to 200 mm long. Inflorescence up to 20 mm diam (Oct-Feb). Widespread in grassland up to 1 370 m, common in coastal areas.
**Similar**
**2**  *C. sphaerocephalus*
Yellow spikelets. Found at higher altitudes.

**3**  *Cyperus dives (=C. immensus)*

Up to 2 m. Leaves stiff. Flowering stem three-angled, edges sharp. Inflorescence up to 200 mm wide (midsummer). In large colonies in wet areas, coast to mountains.

**4**  *Cyperus rupestris*

Up to 300 mm. Tufted. Leaves erect, fine, narrow, with sharp tip. Inflorescence has narrow spikes up to 20 mm long (midsummer). Roots form dense mats on rock or shallow soils. Widespread.

**5**  *Kyllinga alba*

Up to 400 mm. Slender perennial. **Inflorescence white.** Widespread in **dry woodland**, from NE to tropical Africa.
**Similar**
*K. alata*
Inflorescence greenish-yellow. Moist areas in grassland.

**6**  *Mariscus congestus*

Up to 1,3 m. Stems three-angled. Leaves up to 10 mm wide at base. Branched inflorescence (summer). Grassland, moist areas. Widespread.

## Restios: male and female flowers on separate, often very different-looking plants

**7**  *Elegia capensis*

Up to 2,5 m. Tussocks. **Spathes drop off.** In dense stands along streams and wet areas in fynbos.

**8**  *Elegia persistens*

Up to 500 mm. Tussocks. Fynbos.

**9  CAPE REED**  *Thamnochortus spicigerus*

Up to 2 m. In dense clumps (Jun-Aug). Sandy flats, from SW to SE.
**Similar**
**COMMON REED  Phragmites australis** and **P. mauritianus**
Up to 3 m. Leaves long, flat. Panicle large, fluffy. Covering large areas of wetland, banks and shallows. Belongs to grass family, not restios. Throughout region.

**10**  *Cannomois virgata*

Up to 4 m. Tussocks, branching. Inflorescence up to 300 mm long. Streams and damp areas. Fynbos.

## Rushes

**11**  *Juncus kraussii*

Up to 1,5 m. Rounded clumps. **Leaves, stems tough, ending in sharp spike.** Marshy areas near coast, from SE to Mozambique.
**Similar**
**BULRUSH  Typha capensis**
Up to 3 m. Long fleshy leaves. Inflorescence with velvety, chocolate-coloured female flowers with male spike above on same stem. Throughout region.

## Ferns

**1  CLUB MOSS**  *Lycopodium cernuum*
Up to 850 mm. Main stem prostrate, secondary branches erect. Tips of branches hang downwards. Common in moist areas, in light shade and full sun, from SW to tropical Africa.

**2  SPREADING CLUB MOSS**  *Selaginella kraussiana*
Prostrate, mat-forming. High rainfall and mist forest, in shade, coast to 2 500 m. From S to tropical Africa.

**3  PITTED POTATO FERN**  *Marattia fraxinea*
Up to 2 m. Large main stem up to 1 m. Leaf stalk up to 1 m long, base swollen, blade up to 3x1,5 m, bipinnate (twice divided), (tree ferns *Cyathea* are tripinnate). Leaflets up to 170x14 mm. **Sori are capsules**. Deep shade, flowing streams, evergreen mist forest, from S to Zimbabwe and Mozambique.

**4  ROYAL FERN**  *Osmunda regalis*
Up to 1,5 m. Sturdy main stem up to 300 mm tall. Fronds up to 1 300x450 mm, bipinnate. Sterile leaflets up to 80x20 mm. Fertile leaflets much smaller, up to 30x3 mm. Near flowing water. Common in low altitude, warm areas, sea level to 2 000 m. From SW to Zimbabwe. Worldwide in cool, wet areas.

**5  CREEPING/CORAL FERN**  *Gleichenia polypodioides*
Up to 800 mm. Creeping rhizome, up to 5 mm thick, fronds widely spaced. Leaf blade **divided, partly incised**. Disturbed high rainfall areas, common weed in Cape, less common further north, coast to 2 000 m. From S to Tanzania.
**Similar**
*G. umbraculifera*
**Silvery beneath**, leaflets longer, larger, **not incised.**
*Dicranopteris linearis*
Lower leaf stalks bare, more robust plant.

**6  SCENTED FERN**  *Mohria caffrorum*
Up to 800 mm. Fronds soft, erect, tufted. Leaf blade up to 460x70 mm. Aromatic turpentine scent when crushed. Grassland, forest margins, common in wet and dry areas, coast to mountains over 2 300 m. Widespread in Africa.

**7  FALSE BRACKEN**  *Hypolepis sparsisora*
1-3 m. Fronds erect, widely spaced. Leaf stalk up to 1 m long, pale brown. Blade up to 1 000x800 mm. Evergreen mist forest. Along coast from SW to NE, interior in N and into tropical Africa.
**Similar**
**BRACKEN** *Pteridium aquilinum*
**Fronds rough, hard**. Leaf stalk pale green. Very large communities in grassland. Common worldwide.

**8  BOOTLACE FERN**  *Vittaria isoetifolia*
Fronds hanging, up to 900x3 mm. Creeping rhizome. **Leaf stalk green**. Sori in continuous line inside edge of blade. Epiphyte on old trees or on rocks in mistbelt and forests in S. From SW to Zimbabwe and Mozambique.

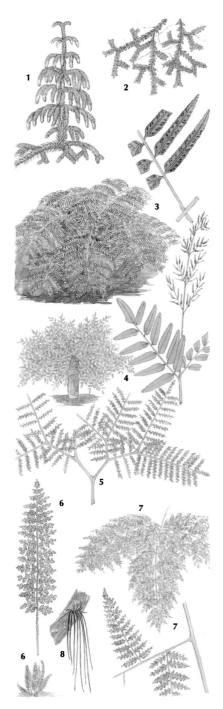

**1   MAIDENHAIR FERN**            *Adiantum capillus-veneris*
Fronds up to 400 mm long. Stalk **shiny black**. Blade up to
200x180 mm. In damp areas at low altitudes, coast to 1 800 m.
Widespread in Africa and the world.

**2**                              *Cheilanthes eckloniana*
Up to 450 mm tall. Fronds erect. Leaf stalk **shiny brown**. Widespread in summer rainfall areas, sea level to 2 300 m.

**3   COMMON LIP FERN**            *Cheilanthes viridis*
Up to 900 mm. Leaf stalk up to 400 mm long, dark brown. Blade
up to 500x240 mm. Variable. Forest, rocky areas, woodland, sea
level to 2 000 m. Widespread.
Similar
**COASTAL COMMON LIP FERN** *C.v.* var. *macrophylla*
**Very large leaflets.** Always in moist shady areas.

**4   GERANIUM FERN**              *Doryopteris concolor*
Up to 250 mm. **Blade horizontal**, up to 130x120 mm. Sori in
almost continuous line along edge. Moist shade in rocky areas,
forest, woodland, coast to up to 1 650 m. From SE to N and NE.

**5   LADDERBRAKE**                *Pteris vittata*
Up to 1,2 m. Large tufted fronds. Stalk pale brown, blade up to
1 150x400 mm, leaflets up to 200x13 mm. Sori continuous, marginal. Damp soil near water in warm N half of region.

**6   HARD FERN**                  *Pellaea calomelanos*
Up to 550 mm. Fronds tufted. Stalk shiny black, blade up to
300x400 mm, leaflets more or less triangular, thick, grey-green.
Rock outcrops, coast to 1 800 m. Widespread.

**7**                              *Polypodium polypodioides*
Up to 330 mm. Creeping rhizome, scales dark brown. Fronds
erect or arching. Blade up to 205x65 mm, **covered with scales
beneath**. Epiphytic on trees, also on large boulders, 200-1 700 m.
Widespread in cool, moist areas. Withstands drought.
Similar
**COMMON POLYPODY** *P. vulgare*
Blade smooth on both surfaces.

**8   SMOOTH LANCE FERN**          *Pleopeltis schraderi*
Up to 400 mm. Leaf stalk up to 60 mm long, creeping rhizome,
black. Fronds closely spaced, blade up to 340x29 mm, evergreen.
**Sori in upper half to third of blade.** High rainfall areas, epiphytic
or lithophytic in evergreen forest or scrub, coast to 2 300 m. From
S to Zimbabwe, Mozambique and tropical Africa.
Similar
*Microgramma lycopodioides*
Sori extend to base of blade.

**9   OAK LEAF FERN**              *Microsorium scolopendrium*
                                   *(=Phymatodes scolopendria)*
Up to 900 mm. Creeping rhizome up to 10 mm thick, fronds
widely spaced. Stalk light brown, blade up to 450x300 mm, lobes
up to 30 mm wide, fertile frond lobes much narrower. Dune and
coastal forest, low altitude woodland, riverine forest, from SE
coast to Zimbabwe and tropical Africa.

**10**                             *Microsorium punctatum*
Up to 1,5 m. Large clumps. Stalk short, blade up to 1 500x800
mm, sori small, scattered. Usually in shade, in low altitude forest
from coast to 1 000 m. From SE coast to e Zimbabwe and into
tropics. (Resembles bird's nest fern *Asplenium nidus* from
Asia/Indian Ocean.)

**1   BROAD-LEAVED MOTHER FERN** *Asplenium gemmiferum*
Up to 1 m. Fronds erect. Blade up to 1 m. Up to 12 pairs leaflets, **base asymmetric, margin entire to crenate**. Bud on tip of fronds develops into young plant. Among rocks in deep shade in forest, below 1 600 m. From S to N and NE.
**Similar**
*A. boltonii*
More leaflets, narrower.

**2   CARROT FERN**   *Asplenium rutifolium*
Up to 480 mm. Tufted. Blade up to 300x100 mm. Epiphyte, occasional lithophyte in damp evergreen forests, coast to 2 000 m. Widespread from SW through E to Zimbabwe, Mozambique.

**3   SCALY FERN**   *Ceterach cordatum*
Up to 250 mm. Tufted. Leaf stalk short, black. Blade up to 240x85 mm. **Dense, flat, shiny, pale brown scales beneath frond**. Size variable, largest in driest areas. Semi-desert to woodland, coastal forest to mountain grassland. Widespread.

**4   BOG FERN/SCALY LADY FERN**   *Thelypteris confluens*
Up to 900 mm. Slender underground rhizome. Stalk pale to dark brown. Blade up to 450x150 mm, thin, soft, **leaflets not reducing in size**. Large colonies in **marshy areas in full sun** or light shade. Widespread except in arid W from sea level to 2 060 m.

**5   DOWNY WOOD FERN**   *Thelypteris dentata*
Up to 1,8 m. Rhizome **short, creeping, up to 10 mm thick**. Blade up to 1 600x540 mm, **lower leaflets reducing in size**. Warm, damp areas along streams, forest margins 350-1 600 m in SE and E.

**6**   *Elaphoglossum acrostichoides*
Up to 500 mm. **Closely spaced fronds**. Blade up to 360x36 mm. Fertile frond with longer stalk and smaller blade, sori covering whole undersurface except midrib. Epiphytic and in grassland, near streams and in scrub, sea level to 2 800 m. Widespread.

**7   LOPLOBED WOOD FERN**   *Dryopteris inaequalis*
Up to 1,5 m. Fronds arching, **subterranean rhizome. Stalk has brown scales at base**. Blade 250-1 000x200-400 mm, leaflet margins crenate. Along streams, in forest, sea level to 2 200 m. Widespread from Cape Peninsula through E to tropical Africa.

**8   KNYSNA FERN**   *Rumohra adiantiformis*
Up to 900 mm. **Creeping rhizome above soil,** reddish-brown scales. **Thick, shiny, leathery fronds**. Blade up to 500x350 mm. Shade of forest, scrub, also rocky mountain grassland, common in cool southern forests, sea level to 2 160 m. From SW through E to Zimbabwe. Widespread in s hemisphere.

**9   GIANT HARD FERN**   *Blechnum attenuatum*
Up to 1,5 m. **Tufted fronds**. Blade up to 1 800x360 mm, leaflets with prominent veins, margins entire. **Fertile fronds narrower**. New fronds coppery pink. Terrestrial or lithophytic, on stream banks in grassland, evergreen forest, spray zone of waterfalls, 100-2 000 m. Common from S to E, less frequent in Zimbabwe.

**10**   *Stenochlaena tenuifolia*
Fronds up to 3 m long. Terrestrial and epiphytic, **creeping rhizome up to 20 mm thick**. Fronds arching, stem shiny light brown. Sterile blade up to 2 m by 700 mm, leaflets up to 350x38 mm, **stiff, shiny above. Fertile blade very narrow (3 mm), covered in sori**. Swamp forest, humid coastal areas in E. Rare in NE.

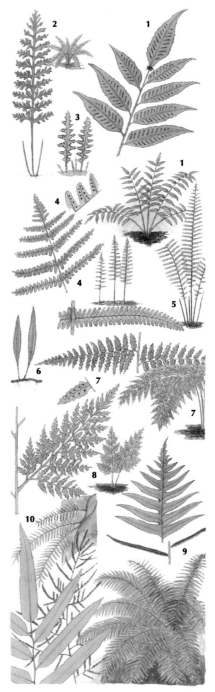

## Fungi

### 1 FLY AGARIC
*Amanita muscaria*

Up to 200 mm diam. Singly or in groups in shade. Cap has white warts, sticky when young. Stem 90-200x10-30 mm, white to yellowish, broader at base, ring soft, white. Summer and autumn. Under pine and oak trees. Widespread. POISONOUS.

### 2 FUNNEL WOODCAP
*Lentinus sajor-caju*

Up to 160 mm diam. Singly or in groups on dead wood. Cap softly leathery but with age becoming hard, convex to cup- or funnel-shaped, surface cracking, margin inrolled, wavy, white to cream or brown. Stem solid, short, 30x15 mm. Early summer. From S to NE.

### 3 PARASOL MUSHROOM
*Macrolepiota zeyheri*

100-250 mm diam. Scattered in grassland. Cap soft, white, with pale brown scales. Stem 100-200x10-20 mm, slender, broader base. Ring large, loose, double, soft, creamy white. After good rain, late summer to early winter. Fairly common. From SW to tropical Africa.

### 4 I'KOWE
*Termitomyces umkowaani*

Up to 250 mm diam. Singly or scattered. Cap fleshy, surface smooth. Stem smooth, white, up to 150x20 mm, **broader at base**. After rains Oct-Mar. **Always associated with termitaria**. From SE to N.

### 5 ORANGE TUFT
*Gymnopilus junonius*
*(=Pholiota spectabilis)*

Up to 150 mm diam. Dense clusters. Cap surface smooth with small orange scales. Stem up to 200x40 mm, swollen lower down, smooth or scaly. Ring papery. Late autumn. On stumps or base of unhealthy hardwood trees. From SW to E.

### 6 FIELD MUSHROOM
*Agaricus campestris*

Up to 120 mm diam. Singly or in groups. Cap smooth. Stem up to 100x25 mm, firm. Ring halfway or above, disappearing with age, **pink lamella**. After spring rain or late autumn rain. Grassland. Widespread in high rainfall areas.
**Similar**
**EDIBLE HORSE MUSHROOM** *A. arvensis*
More robust (up to 200 mm diam). Stem widens **slightly** at base; **lamella white, turning brown. Aniseed odour.** Lawns, pastures after good rain in autumn.

### 7 YELLOW-STAINING MUSHROOM
*Agaricus xanthodermus*

70-130 mm diam. In groups. Cap bell-shaped to large flattened/convex top, **staining yellow when touched/bruised.** Stem 60-120x8-15 mm, **slender with bulbous base**; lamella white turning greyish-pink then black (Mar-Jul). **Smells of carbolic.** In grassy areas, open woodland. From SW to N. POISONOUS.

**1  SHAGGY INK CAP**  *Coprinus comatus*
Up to 50 mm diam. Clusters. Cap up to 150 mm high. Stem up to 220x20 mm with movable ring. Cap rolls back to release spores, releasing a black liquid. After good rain in summer or autumn. Grassland. Widespread.

**2  SULPHUR TUFT**  *Hypholoma fasciculare*
Up to 70 mm diam. Dense clusters on dead hardwood trees. Cap margin wavy. Stem 50-200x2-10 mm, joined to other stems at base; lamellae yellow to dark brown. From SE to NE.

**3  CEP**  *Boletus edulis*
Up to 200 mm diam. Robust. Cap smooth, glossy pale to dark reddish-brown. **Stem large, swollen towards base,** up to 120x60 mm, white to pale brown, **upper section with raised white threads.** Late autumn to early winter in winter rainfall areas, early summer to late autumn in summer rainfall areas. Oak and pine plantations throughout region.
**Similar**
**OAK BOLETUS  *B. aestivalis***
Pale cap, stem not so large, brown, with network of brown threads all over.

**4  ORANGE-BROWN LACQUERED BRACKET**  *Ganoderma lucidum*
Up to 500 mm diam. Singly or in groups. Cap up to 50 mm thick. Corky when young, maturing woody; upper surface shiny. Summer-autumn. On trunks of broadleaved trees. From SW through E to Zimbabwe.

**5  SULPHUR SHELF**  *Laetiporus sulphureus*
Up to 300 mm wide. Large overlapping clusters. Cap velvety; flesh juicy when young, brittle with age. Late summer-autumn. Smells of chicken. Parasitic on dead hardwoods, living oak and gum trees, causing heart rot. From SW to NE.

**6  EDIBLE BRACKET**  *Lenzites elegans (=L. palisoti)*
Up to 350 mm wide and 15 mm thick. Singly or in groups. Cap leathery to woody; white to cream, smooth. Summer-autumn. Fragrant spicy smell. On dead hardwood trees. From S to Zimbabwe and tropical Africa.

**7  TROPICAL CINNABAR BRACKET**  *Pycnoporus sanguineus*
Up to 75x40 mm and 5 mm thick. Singly or clustered. Cap leathery to hard; upper surface velvety to smooth and shiny. On dead wood of broadleaved and pine trees. Widespread to tropical Africa.

**8  GEM-STUDDED PUFF-BALL**  *Lycoperdon perlatum (=L. gemmatum)*
Up to 50 mm high and 30 mm diam. Singly or clustered. Covered with tiny warts leaving depressions, narrowing to stalk-like base. Late summer-autumn. Among fallen leaves of broadleaved trees. From S to NE.

**9  DYE BALL**  *Pisolithus tinctorius*
Up to 200 mm high and 170 mm diam. Singly or clustered. Shape variable. Midsummer to late autumn. Associated with gum and wattle trees. Common and widespread.

# WILD FLOWERS

Wild flowers are here defined as any flowering plants that are not included
in the definition of trees or grasses in other chapters.

The flowering plants are divided into two classes, the monocotyledons (with single seed-leaf, parallel veins and flower parts in threes or multiples of three) and dicotyledons (two seed-leaves, net veins and flower parts in fours, fives or multiples of these).

Monocotyledons include the bulbous plants: lilies, gladioli, watsonias, the amaryllis family and orchids — some of the most beautiful and sought-after flowers.

Dicotyledons represent the larger group, with great variety in flower shape and size. Some well-known examples are pelargoniums, mesembryanthemums, succulents including the ground aloes, crassulas, kalanchoes and euphorbias; over 600 species of ericas, the foul-smelling stapelias; helichrysums and the Barberton daisy, a beautiful single red daisy now bred into large, multicoloured horticultural varieties.

All flowers have the organs shown in the accompanying illustration of a typical flower but care is needed when identifying species of different shapes.

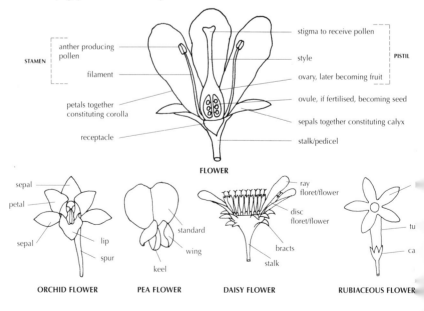

STAMEN

anther producing pollen

filament

petals together constituting corolla

receptacle

stigma to receive pollen

style

ovary, later becoming fruit

PISTIL

ovule, if fertilised, becoming seed

sepals together constituting calyx

stalk/pedicel

**FLOWER**

sepal

petal

sepal

lip

spur

**ORCHID FLOWER**

standard

wing

keel

**PEA FLOWER**

ray floret/flower

disc floret/flower

bracts

stalk

**DAISY FLOWER**

tu

ca

**RUBIACEOUS FLOWER**

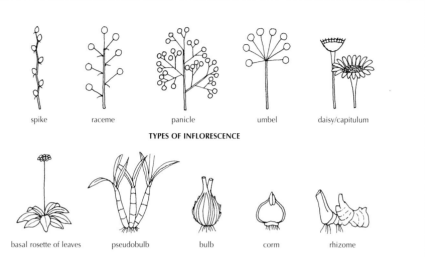

spike   raceme   panicle   umbel   daisy/capitulum

**TYPES OF INFLORESCENCE**

basal rosette of leaves   pseudobulb   bulb   corm   rhizome

**PARTS OF PLANTS**

There is often more plant mass beneath the soil than above it. This hidden resource is well known and understood by the herbalists and subsistence farmers of the subcontinent. The roots, tubers, bulbs and corms, together with the leaves, stems, bark, flowers and fruits, provide a wide range of traditional medicines, cures and magical potions that have been used for centuries and continue to support and minister to the majority of people of the region.

## Scope of this chapter

Altogether some 24 000 species of flowering plants are estimated to be found in the region. The 400 that have been selected for this chapter represent those that are most commonly seen. They include examples of all the major families, and it will be unusual for the reader not to be able to identify at least the genus of a specimen found in the veld. Regional floral guides will need to be referred to for greater precision.

## Distribution

The flowers described in this chapter are widely dispersed in many different habitats, but the southern African region is most famous for the fynbos biome. Known as the Cape floral kingdom, this is one of only six floral kingdoms in the world. The smallest by far, it is confined to the southern tip of Africa, and comprises only 3,5% of the land mass — and yet 41% of the whole continent's plant species are to be found here, including about 6 000 endemics.

Other regions and habitats are also rich in floral diversity. One of the most spectacular natural events to be seen is the annual blossoming of flowers in the semi-desert Namaqualand, known as the succulent Karoo. Second only to fynbos in the number of endemics, this area experiences an extraordinary metamorphosis in spring when the arid landscape is transformed into fields of flowers.

The desert itself has a sparse but fascinating flora, mostly succulents.

In grassland areas, healthy veld will invariably include a wide range of spring and autumn flowers interspersed among the grass. Many of these species are adapted to surviving fire and in burnt areas the flowers often appear before the recovery of grass species.

## Dimensions

The first dimension given with each description in this chapter refers to the total height of a large, mature plant. Other dimensions in the text refer to specific parts of the plant and are clearly stated. Only the greatest dimension is given; this usually indicates length but sometimes indicates diameter. Leaf measurements refer to the length of the blade excluding the stalk. The dimensions given either consist of a range or are maximums, with smaller dimensions possible in different specimens.

**1 ARUM LILY** *Zantedeschia aethiopica*

300-600 mm (up to 1,5 m in shade). Leaves soft, blade up to 300 mm long, stems spongy, up to 600 mm long. Male and female flowers clustered on central yellow spadix, spathe cream-white, up to 200 mm long (Aug-Jan). Well known worldwide as a garden plant. Evergreen, survives frost and snow, sometimes deciduous. Marshy areas, sea level to mountains, often in large communities. Widespread.

**2 YELLOW ARUM** *Zantedeschia pentlandii*

Up to 700 mm. **Leaves dark green.** Flower spathe up to 180 mm long (Nov-Jan) with **deep purple patch in centre.** Deciduous. Marshy areas in NE.
**Similar**
**SPOTTED-LEAF ARUM** *Z. albomaculata*
**Leaves spotted.** Spathe white to yellow with deep purple patch in centre. Three subspecies. Marshes, rocky areas, mountains, mist-belt, from SE to Zimbabwe.

**3 PINK ARUM** *Zantedeschia rehmannii*

Up to 450 mm. Leaf **tapering at both ends.** Spathe up to 100 mm long, greenish-white to deep pink (Nov-Jan). Deciduous. Mountains, grassland, from E to N.

**4 WANDERING JEW** *Commelina erecta*

Up to 200 mm. Low-growing, spreading, perennial herb. Flowers 15 mm diam, produced **from within folded spathe** (spring-summer). Most species have bluish flowers. Widespread except at high altitudes.
**Similar**
**5 YELLOW COMMELINA** *C. africana*
**Flowers yellow.** Widespread.
**Genus** *Aneilema*
Flowers **free** (**not** within spathe).

**6 DOLL'S POWDERPUFF** *Cyanotis speciosa*

Up to 250 mm. Leaves clustered at base. Dies back in winter. Inflorescence erect, **feathery stamens** (spring-summer). Widespread in damp, grassy or rocky areas.

**7 FLAME LILY** *Gloriosa superba*

Up to 2 m. Stems branching, climbing with tendril leaf tips. Flowers up to 100 mm diam, pale green, yellow, to red and yellow, very variable (Nov-Mar). Plants die back after flowering. Red seeds. White tuber. Coastal dunes, woodland, from SE to tropical Africa.

**8 BUTTER LILY** *Littonia modesta*

Up to 2 m. Climbing with tendril leaf tips, leaves **narrow, whorled.** Flowers up to 30 mm long (Oct-Jan). Widespread from coast to 1 450 m. From SE to N.

**9 CHRISTMAS BELLS** *Sandersonia aurantiaca*

Up to 750 mm. Leaves small (sometimes ending in a tendril). Stem unbranched. Flowers up to 35 mm long (Dec-Jan). Grassland, forest margins at higher altitudes, from SE to N.

**10 PYJAMA FLOWER** *Androcymbium melanthoides*

Up to 300 mm. Few leaves, up to 300 mm long. Flowers small, hidden within white to pinkish bracts (Dec-Jan). Grassland, rocky areas, Karoo, E and N. Variable, three subspecies.

**1   KAFFERTJIE**                    *Wurmbea spicata*

Up to 200 mm. Low-growing corm. Leaves up to 200 mm long.
Flowers scented at night (Aug-Nov). Widespread in winter rainfall
areas.

**2   SLANGKOP**                    *Ornithoglossum viride*

Up to 200 mm. Low-growing corm. Leaves sheathing base. Flowers up to 25 mm diam, on long stalks (Jun-Sept). Widespread on
sandy flats, lower slopes, from S to Namaqualand.

**3   CAT'S TAIL**                    *Bulbinella latifolia*

Up to 750 mm. Leaves up to 200 mm long, slender, grooved,
brown fibres at base. Inflorescence up to 120 mm long (Jul-Oct).
Marshy winter rainfall areas.

**4   BULBINE**                    *Bulbine abyssinica*

Up to 650 mm. Leaves fleshy, cylindrical, up to 150 mm long, in
basal rosette. Flowers up to 20 mm diam with **feathery stamens**
(Oct-Apr), sometimes orange. Widespread in grassy and rocky
areas.
**Similar**
**BROADLEAVED BULBINE  *B. latifolia***
Leaves up to 300 mm long, up to 110 mm wide at base, pale
bright green. Dry, rocky areas. Widespread.

**5**                    *Chlorophytum bowkeri*

Up to 1 m. Rosette of leaves, recurved, 300x20 mm. Unbranched
flowering stem up to 1 m high. Flowers 25 mm diam (summer).
Widespread (summer rainfall), damp grassland, rocky and shady
areas.
**Similar**
**HEN-AND-CHICKENS  *C. comosum***
Forest floor, in large colonies. Well-known garden plant, espe-
cially the white-striped-leaf variety. Flowering stem with tuft of
leaves on top, eventually bending over and rooting.
***C. krookianum***
Leaves 1 000x80 mm. Flowering stem up to 2 m high, branched.

**6   RED-HOT POKER**                    *Kniphofia linearifolia*

Up to 1,5 m. Leaves 600-1 400 mm long and 28 mm wide, keeled,
bending over. Inflorescence up to 160x65 mm, tapering to tip,
colour varies (Jan-Apr). In colonies. Hilly grassland, marsh,
stream banks. Widespread from SE to Zimbabwe.
**Similar**
**RED-HOT POKER  *K. praecox***
Well known worldwide as a garden plant. Inflorescence dense,
robust, up to 300x70 mm. Origins in the wild obscure.

**GIANT POKER**                    *Kniphofia multiflora*

Up to 2 m. Robust, leaves broad. Inflorescence **long, narrow**,
flowers open **upwards**. Marshes, usually at high altitude.

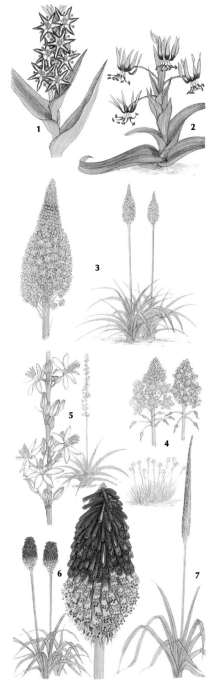

**1**            *Aloe aculeata*

Up to 1,5 m. Leaves 600 mm long and 80-120 mm wide, forming rosette, spiny on both surfaces. Inflorescence up to 600x70 mm (May-Jul). **Not** in dense groups. Hot, dry, rocky areas in N.

**2**   **GUINEAFOWL ALOE**      *Aloe aristata*

Up to 700 mm. Leaves 100x15 mm, **long dry tips, spots forming hard white protuberances.** Inflorescence 200x150 mm (Nov). Compact groups. Hot, dry, sandy flats, rocky mountain slopes, grassy hillsides, from Karoo to Lesotho, Drakensberg.

**3**            *Aloe boylei*

Up to 800 mm. Leaves 600x80 mm, **flat, broad for most of length**, soft white teeth. Inflorescence **flat**, 120 mm diam, flowers 40 mm long (Dec-Jan). Small groups, grassland, from E to N.
Similar
*A. cooperi*
**Leaves in fan** (rosette in older plants), **narrow, distinctly keeled Inflorescence pyramidal.**
*A. ecklonis*
Leaves more flatly spreading, smaller flowers.

**4**   **KANONAALWYN**      *Aloe claviflora*

Up to 300 mm. Leaves rough, margins with sharp brown teeth. Inflorescence **angled** (Aug-Sept). Hot, dry central areas to NW.

**5**            *Aloe kraussii*

Up to 400 mm. Leaves 400x35 mm, **in a fan** (rosettes in old plants), tiny white teeth on margin. 1-3 flowering stems (Nov-Feb). Sandy, stony or damp soil in E.
Similar
**GRASS ALOE** *A. ecklonis*
**Much broader leaves**, **in rosette**, **prominent teeth** on margins. Flowers yellow to red. Widely distributed, coast to 2 000 m.

**6**   **CORAL ALOE**      *Aloe striata*

Up to 1 m. Leaves 500x200 mm, spreading, incurved smooth margin. Inflorescence 60x60 mm (Jul-Oct). Large colonies on rocky slopes in hot, dry areas. Widespread from SW to SE. Subsp. *karasbergensis*: inflorescence pyramidal (Jan-Mar). From W to NW.

**7**   **SOAP ALOE**      *Aloe maculata (=A. saponaria*

600 mm to 1 m. Leaves up to 300 mm long and 80-120 mm wide, tip dry, twisted. Hard brown teeth on margins. **Inflorescence compact, flat-topped**, 120x160 mm (throughout the year). Singly or in large communities. Grassland, rocky slopes, sea level to 2 000 m in winter and summer rainfall areas. Widespread.

**8**   **KLEINAALWYN**      *Aloe greatheadii (=A. davyana*

Up to 1,5 m. Leaves spreading, 200 mm long, hard edge with brown teeth, no spots beneath. Inflorescence up to 300x80 mm (Jun-Jul). Scattered or in colonies in grassland, bushveld. Widespread from central areas to N, Zimbabwe, Mozambique.

**9**   **CHABAUD'S ALOE**      *Aloe chabaudii*

800 mm to 1 m. Leaves greyish, 500x100 mm. Inflorescence 160x100 mm (Jun-Jul). Large groups. Hot, dry, frost-free area from E to Malawi.

**10 FENCE ALOE**      *Aloe tenuior*

Up to 3 m. Scrambler. Leaves blue-green, 150x15 mm, sheathing stem, in terminal rosettes. Inflorescence 160x40 mm, flowers yellow to orange/red (Aug-May). Thicket, forest margins, from SE to east-central areas.

**1 AGAPANTHUS** *Agapanthus praecox*

Up to 1,5 m. Evergreen perennial. Leaves up to 600x50 mm. Inflorescence up to 200 mm diam, up to 100 flowers in a head, **not drooping, lobes curved back,** pale blue/mauve (Dec-Jan). Dense clumps, rocky hillsides in SE and E. Three subspecies.
Similar
**A. campanulatus**
Deciduous perennial. **Not as robust as** *A. praecox*. Flowers deep blue. Damp places, grassland, rocky areas over 2 400 m. Widespread.
**DWARF AGAPANTHUS A. africanus**
Smaller (up to 600 mm). **Evergreen.** Fewer leaves up to 250x12 mm. Up to 18 deep blue flowers in **smaller head.** Rocky mountainsides in S.

**2 DROOPING AGAPANTHUS** *Agapanthus inapertus*

Up to 1,8 m. **Deciduous.** Leaves up to 500 mm long. **Flowers drooping, lobes not spreading, deep blue** (summer). In clumps, grassland, mountains in E and N.

**3 WILD GARLIC** *Tulbaghia acutiloba*

Up to 300 mm. Leaves up to 250x8 mm, usually after flowers. Flowers up to 15 mm diam (Aug-Sept). Faint garlic scent. Scattered in grassland. Widespread, from SE to N.

**4 WILD GARLIC** *Tulbaghia simmleri*

Up to 450 mm. Strap-shaped leaves up to 450 mm long. Inflorescence up to 70 mm diam (Jun-Jan), **sweetly scented.** In clumps in damp areas in NE.
Similar
**. violacea**
Powerful garlic scent. Widespread.

**SLYMUINTJIE** *Albuca setosa* (=A. pachychlamys)

Up to 400 mm. Bulb with fibrous top. Leaves **after** flowers, up to 200 mm long, narrow. Flowers **erect**, up to 20 mm long, white to yellow or green (Jul-Jan). Grassland, open rocky slopes over 2 400 m. Widespread.

**GREEN BELLS** *Dipcadi viride*

Up to 1 m. Bulb. Leaves slender, up to 600 mm long, narrow, keeled. **Flowers open in same direction** (Oct-Apr). Grassland, rocky areas, coast to mountains. Widespread.

**BLUE SQUILL** *Scilla natalensis*

Up to 1 m. Large bulb with papery tips. Rosette of smooth, broad leaves, erect, up to 500 mm long, developing after flowers. Inflorescence up to 300x100 mm, flowers pale blue to deep purplish-blue (Jul-Nov). In colonies. Damp grassland, rocky slopes, coast to mountains. Widespread, from SE to N.

**WILD SQUILL** *Scilla nervosa*

Up to 400 mm. Bulb with fibrous tips. Leaves up to 300 mm long, narrow, stiff, erect, twisted, appear **with flowers.** Flowers small, white, with emerald green spot at base of tepals, stalks lengthening with age (Sept-Jan). Small rounded clumps, scattered in grassland, coast to 2 000 m. Widespread.

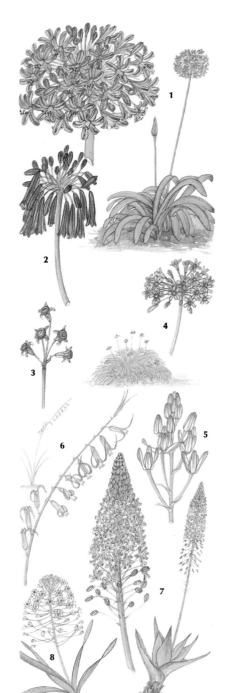

**1 PINEAPPLE LILY** *Eucomis autumnalis*

Up to 600 mm. Large bulb. Leaves **unspotted with wavy margins**. Inflorescence **with terminal tuft of leaf-like bracts** (Dec-Apr). Damp grassland, coast to mountains over 2 450 m. Widespread from SE to N.

**Similar**

*E. bicolor*

Larger (up to 1 m). Leaves and flowers edged purple.

*E. comosa*

Leaves and flowering stem spotted purple. **Flowers creamy white, ovary purple** (summer). Moist grassland.

**2 CHINCHERINCHEE** *Ornithogalum thyrsoides*

Up to 500 mm. Bulb. Leaves erect, up to 350 mm long. Flower up to 50 mm diam (Sept-Dec). Sandy flats and slopes, from SW to Namaqualand.

**Similar**

**3 SNAKE FLOWER** *O. maculatum*

Orange flowers (Sept-Oct).

**4** *Ornithogalum seiner*

Up to 300 mm. Leaves slender. Flowers up to 15 mm diam (Oct-Nov). Large colonies in dry grassland, from N to NW.

**5 FOREST LILY** *Veltheimia bracteat*

Up to 500 mm. Bulb. Leaves up to 450x70 mm. Flowers Jul-Sep. **Fruit an inflated capsule**. Colonies in light shade, coastal bush in SE.

**6 CAPE COWSLIP** *Lachenalia aloide*

Up to 300 mm. Bulb. Leaves variable in size, up to 170 mm long, spotted. Flowers up to 30 mm long (Jul-Nov). In clumps. Rock outcrops in mountains in S. Three subspecies.

**Similar**

**7** *L. mutabilis*

Up to 170 mm. Single leaf. **Flowers small** (Jul-Sept).

**8 MOTHER-IN-LAW'S TONGUE** *Sansevieria hyacinthoide*

Flowering stem up to 450 mm high. Leaves up to 600x80 mm, **smooth, flat**, fibrous. Flowers open at night (Dec-Mar), scented. Fruit up to 8 mm diam. Large colonies, in dry sandy or rock areas, from SE to N.

**Similar**

*S. aethiopica*

Leaves **V-shaped, rough**. Occurs in S, N and NW.

**9** *Sansevieria pearson*

Flowering stem up to 1 m high. Leaves cylindrical, up to 1 m high, with sharp tips. From E to NW.

**10 ASPARAGUS FERN** *Asparagus plumos*

Up to 2 m. Twining climber. Leaves up to 5 mm long, **flattene** branchlets, leaves on one plane. Flowers up to 7 mm diam, whi scattered (summer). Dune forest, forest margins, scrub, from SE N.

**11 FOXTAIL** *Asparagus densiflor*

Up to 450 mm. Multistemmed with short, curved spines. Leav up to 15x2 mm. Flowers clustered or singly, scented (summe Fruit up to 10 mm diam. Widespread, from SE to NE.

**12 SMILAX** *Myrsiphyllum asparagoid* *(=Asparagus asparagoide*

Up to 2 m. Scrambling, stems twisting, wiry. Leaves up to 40x. mm. Flowers up to 10 mm long, sweetly scented (Jul-Sept). Fr 10 mm diam. Widespread in forest, bushveld.

**1 BLOOD ROOT** *Wachendorfia thyrsiflora*

Up to 1,8 m. Tuberous red root. Leaves in fan, pleated, up to 800x80 mm. Inflorescence up to 450 mm long, each flower up to 30 mm diam. Swamps, stream banks, coastal areas, from S to SE.

**2 BLOOD FLOWER** *Haemanthus coccineus*

Up to 400 mm. Bulb. Leaves up to 450x150 mm in the middle, sometimes barred with purple markings on undersurface, smooth or softly hairy, after flowers. Flowers Feb-Apr. Fruit soft, white to pink. Singly or in large communities, usually in shade. Widespread in winter rainfall areas, sea level to 1 200 m.

**3 APRIL FOOL** *Haemanthus albiflos*

Flowering stem up to 350 mm long. **Evergreen**. Leaves erect, firm, up to 400x115 mm, sometimes with white spots, smooth or hairy, margin hairy. Inflorescence up to 70 mm diam (Jan-Oct, **Apr-Aug**). Fruit oval, 10 mm diam, white to red. Singly or in large colonies. Widespread in woodland, valley bushveld, from S to E along coastal belt.
Similar
*H. deformis*
Evergreen. Leaves flat, **roundish**, up to 260x250 mm, smooth or hairy. Flowering stem **short**. Occurs in E.

**4 SNAKE LILY** *Scadoxus multiflorus*

Up to 900 mm. Bulb. Rolled leaf bases form a false stem, spotted at base. Inflorescence up to 200 mm diam (Oct-Jan). Shiny red fruit. Grassland and woodland, low to high altitude. Widespread, from E to N.
Similar
**CATHERINE WHEEL** *S.m. subsp. katherinae*
Up to 1,2 m. Large, deep pink flower head (Jan-Feb). Damp, **warm** forests, from SE to Zimbabwe.

**5 BLOOD LILY** *Scadoxus puniceus*

Up to 900 mm. Leaves up to 600 mm long, with or after flowers. Inflorescence up to 150 mm diam (Jul-Nov). Light or deep shade, widespread in summer rainfall areas.

**6 TUMBLEWEED** *Boophane disticha*

Inflorescence up to 200 mm diam. Bulb **protruding well above ground**. Leaves up to 300 mm long, in a fan. Flower stalks lengthen to 300 mm with seed enclosed terminally. Large dry fruiting head up to 600 mm diam, breaks loose, rolling in the wind. Grassland. Widespread.

**7 CLIVIA** *Clivia miniata*

Up to 800 mm. Leaves strap-shaped, up to 600 mm long. Inflorescence up to 300 mm diam, flowers up to 80x60 mm, scented (Aug-Oct). Large red fruit. A pale yellow variety rare in the wild. Forest, from SE to NE.

**8 DROOPING CLIVIA** *Clivia nobilis*

Up to 800 mm. Leaves up to 1 m long, with **rough** edge, tip rounded or indented. Up to 30 **tubular** flowers, **drooping** (Jun-Oct). Forest, rock faces, from SE to E.
Similar
*C. gardenii*
Fewer flowers, leaf tip pointed, margin faintly rough. E forests.
*C. caulescens*
Develops a **stem**. N forests.

### 1 RIBBON-LEAVED NERINE — *Nerine angustifolia*

Up to 500 mm. Bulb. Leaves appear with flowers; **narrow**, up to 250 mm long, with **groove** on upper surface. Flowers 50 mm long (Feb). Marshy grassland, mountains, from SE to N.

### 2 RED NERINE — *Nerine sarniensis*

Up to 450 mm. Bulb. Leaves after flowers, strap-like up to 450x28 mm. Flowers up to 40 mm long, sparkling with gold dust (Mar-May). Rocky mountainsides in SW.

### 3 BELLADONNA LILY — *Amaryllis belladonna*

Up to 900 mm. Bulb. Leaves after flowers, strap-shaped, arched, up to 600x40 mm. Flowers up to 130x80 mm (Feb-Mar), fragrantly scented. Occurs in SW.

### 4 CANDELABRA FLOWER — *Brunsvigia natalensis*

Up to 700 mm. Bulb. Leaves erect, margins undulating or not. Inflorescence up to 450 mm wide, flowers up to 50 mm long (Nov-Jan). Flower stalks double in length, fruit developing on tips, drying out to form a tumbleweed. Grassland, marshy areas at higher altitudes. Widespread in summer rainfall areas.

### 5 RIVER CRINUM — *Crinum macowanii*

Up to 800 mm. Bulb. Leaves up to 1 000x100 mm. Inflorescence held erect, up to 50 flowers. Flowers **wide open**, up to 200 mm long, **pollen black**, old flowers brown (Oct-Dec), fragrantly scented. **Fruit beaked.** Grassland, marshy areas. Widespread, from SE to Zimbabwe.
**Similar**
*C. bulbispermum*
Sheathing base of leaves forming "stem" up to 300 mm long. Flowers narrow, **drying pink or red, pollen grey/brown. Fruit no beaked.**

### 6 MOORE'S CRINUM — *Crinum moorei*

Up to 1 m. **Bulb with neck or stem up to 300 mm long.** Leaves up to 900x90 mm. 2-10 flowers, pink to white. Successive flowering stems produced over extended flowering period (Oct-Mar).
**Similar**
### 7 *C. delagoense*
Leaves broad, lying fairly **flat on the ground.** Dark pink striped flowers, petals curling back. Fruit spectacular. Grassland, sandy soils, NE.

### 8 GROUND LILY — *Ammocharis coranica*

Up to 300 mm. Bulb. Leaves strap-like, up to 450x40 mm. Inflorescence with up to 20 flowers, up to 40 mm long (Nov-Jan). Large communities, grassland. Widespread.

**1 YELLOW FIRE-LILY**      *Cyrtanthus breviflorus*
Up to 200 mm. Bulb. Leaves after flowering, up to 370x30 mm.
Flowers up to 30 mm long (Sept-Oct), scented. Grassland, coast
to mountains, first to appear after fire. Widespread.

**2 FIRE-LILY**      *Cyrtanthus contractus*
Up to 400 mm. Bulb. Flowers up to 80 mm long (Aug-Oct). Best
seen on recently burnt veld. Grassland. Widespread.

**3 INANDA LILY**      *Cyrtanthus sanguineus*
Up to 450 mm. Bulb. Leaves up to 250x13 mm, appearing with
flowers. Flowers 110x100 mm (Jan-Apr). Coastal forest, thicket,
rocky areas near water, from SE to NE.

**4 STAR FLOWER**      *Hypoxis hemerocallidea (=H. rooperi)*
Up to 250 mm. Bulb with fibrous outer layer. Leaves **in three
ranks**. Flowers up to 50 mm diam (Sept-Jan). Grassland. Widespread.
**Similar**

**5 SMALL YELLOW STAR**   *H. argentea*
Up to 60 mm. Leaves narrow. Widespread in grassland.

**6 RED STAR**      *Rhodohypoxis baurii*
Up to 100 mm. Bulb. Flowers up to 25 mm diam, white to deep
pink (Oct-Jan). Widespread in damp areas in mountains.

**7 STARS**      *Spiloxene capensis*
Up to 300 mm. Leaves broad, spirally twisted. Flowers up to 60
mm diam, colour and markings vary considerably. SW.

**8 BOBBEJAANSTERT**      *Xerophyta retinervis*
Up to 2 m. **Fibrous black stems.** Grass-like leaves up to 250 mm
long. Flowers up to 50 mm long, scented (Aug-Oct). Hot, dry
areas, on rocky hillsides, widespread from E coast northwards.

**9 YELLOW TULP**      *Moraea alticola*
Up to 1 m. In clumps. Corm. **Fibrous network sheathing stem and
leaf at base. Flowers large**, outer tepals up to 88 mm long, inner
erect, up to 70 mm long (Oct-Mar). Drakensberg and Lesotho
above 2 200 m.
**Similar**
*M. spathulata*
Flowers smaller, **outer tepals up to 50 mm long, inner up to 40
mm long**. Forest margins, grassland, among rocks. **Widespread.**
*M. huttonii*
Dark, bright blotch on each crest. Near running water, mountains.

**10 DAINTY MORAEA**      *Moraea tripetala*
Up to 150 mm. Leaves long, narrow, bent to trailing. Flower outer
tepals up to 35 mm long (Aug-Dec). Widespread in both high
rainfall and arid areas in SW.

**11 PEACOCK FLOWER**      *Moraea villosa*
Up to 400 mm. Single long, slender leaf with velvety white down.
Flower outer tepals broad, up to 40 mm long, purple, lilac, pink
or orange, rarely creamy white (Aug-Sept). Lower mountain
slopes, flats in SW.

**12 WILD IRIS**      *Dietes grandiflora*
Up to 1 m. Evergreen. Leaves up to 1 000x10 mm. Flowers up to
110 mm diam (summer). In clumps, in shade of forest, thicket,
from SE to E.

**13 SPIDER FLOWER**      *Ferraria divaricata*
Up to 450 mm. Corm. Leaves sheath base. Flowers up to 55 mm
diam. Sand or shale, from Namaqualand to Namibia.

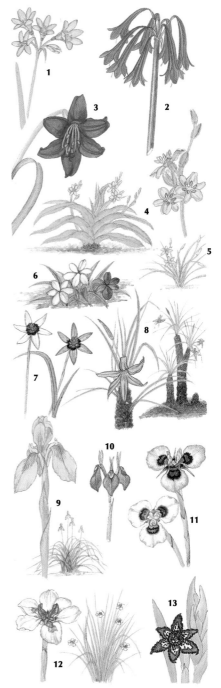

**1  RED TULIP**                    *Homeria miniata*

Up to 600 mm. Corm. Stems branching. Two leaves, longer than stem. Flowers yellow to salmon pink, up to 45 mm diam, cup-shaped, scented (Aug-Sept). In sandy soil. Namaqualand and Clanwilliam.

**2  ARISTEA**                      *Aristea woodii*

Up to 900 mm. Perennial. Leaves up to 450x13 mm. Inflorescence up to 180 mm long, flowers 20 mm diam (Dec-Feb), closing in early afternoon. Forest margins, grassland, marshy areas. Widespread.

**3  TALL ARISTEA**                 *Aristea major*

Up to 1,7 m. Leaves rigid, up to 1 000x25 mm. Inflorescence up to 230 mm, flowers up to 35 mm diam (Oct-Nov). Lower hill slopes, from SW to SE.

**4  RIVER LILY**                   *Schizostylis coccinea*

Up to 600 mm. Rhizome. Leaves up to 250x10 mm. Flowers up to 60 mm diam (Dec-Mar). In clumps on banks of rivers and streams in mountains, from SE to N.

**5  WINE-CUPS**                    *Geissorhiza radians*

Up to 150 mm. Small corm. Leaves narrow, ribbed. Flowers up to 35 mm diam (Sept). S.

**6  PINK SATIN FLOWER**            *Geissorhiza ovata*

Up to 150 mm. Two broad, oval leaves at base. Flower tube up to 27 mm long (Aug-Oct). Coastal flats, mountain slopes in S.

**7  YELLOW IXIA**                  *Ixia maculata*

Up to 450 mm. Corm. Leaves up to 250x5 mm, sharp-tipped. Flowering stem slender, erect. Up to 9 flowers in a head, each flower base with papery bracts up to 10 mm long. Flowers up to 40 mm diam, only opening in sunlight (Sept-Oct). Coastal areas in S.
**Similar**
**GREEN IXIA** *I. viridiflora*
Up to 600 mm high. Inflorescence up to 210 mm long, flowers up to 35 mm diam, **green**. Rare.

**8  HAREBELL**                     *Dierama igneum*

Up to 1,35 m. Forms small clumps. Corm. Leaves up to 900x mm. Flowers up to 30 mm long (spring-summer). Grassland, coast to 1 500 m. From SE to E.

**9  PENCILLED TRITONIA**           *Tritonia lineata*

Up to 450 mm. Leaves 150x18 mm. Flowers Oct-Feb. Savanna, grassland. Widespread, from SE to N.

**10  FALLING STARS**               *Crocosmia aurea*

Up to 90 mm. Leaves up to 450x13 mm. Flowers up to 70 mm diam (Feb-Mar). Scattered or in large communities. Forest margins, from SE to N.
**Similar**
**11  PLEATED LEAVES** *C. paniculata*
Leaves up to 1 000x30 mm, pleated. Flowers in zigzag spike, branched (Jan-Feb). Large colonies in moist grassland in mountains, E and N.

**WINE-CUP BABIANA**     *Babiana rubrocyanea*
Up to 180 mm. Corm. Leaves in a fan.Flowers 30 mm diam, sweetly scented (Jul-Oct).Winter rainfall areas in SW.

**DWARF BABIANA**     *Babiana hypogea*
Up to 200 mm. Leaves up to 300 mm long. Flowers up to 50 mm diam, clustered at ground level, sweetly scented (Jan/Mar/Jul). Edge of vleis, from west-central areas to Zimbabwe.

**RAT'S TAIL**     *Babiana ringens (=Antholyza plicata)*
Up to 450 mm. Leaves up to 300 mm long, **pleated**. Flowering stem branched, flowers up to 55 mm long, in dense spike (Jul-Oct). Sandy flats near coast, from SW to Namaqualand.

**KALKOENTJIE**     *Gladiolus alatus*
Up to 300 mm. Leaves 180x10 mm, curved. Flowers 50 mm long, variable (Sept-Oct). Sandy flats and hill slopes in SW.

**LARGE PAINTED LADY**     *Gladiolus carneus*
Up to 450 mm. Flowers 80 mm long, white, cream or pink (Oct-Nov). Sandy or marshy areas below 1 200 m in SW.

**HONEY FLOWER**     *Gladiolus longicollis*
Up to 800 mm. One leaf sheathing stem. Usually single flower (Oct-Dec). Tube up to 60 mm long, tepals up to 40 mm long. Grassland, coast to mountains. Widespread.

**NATAL LILY**     *Gladiolus dalenii*
Up to 1,2 m. Up to 25 flowers, up to 100x50 mm. Colour greenish-orange to orange flecked with brown or red and yellow. Grassland. Widespread.

    *Gladiolus scullyii*
Up to 300 mm. Leaves grass-like. Flowers 40 mm (Sept). S.

    *Gladiolus saundersii*
Up to 900 mm. **Erect. Leaves stiff, 600x26 mm, margins thickened, in fan**. Flowers 60 mm diam, **downward-facing** (Jan-Mar). Rocky hillsides 1 700-3 000 m, from SE to s Drakensberg.
Similar
**G. cruentus**
Plants hanging. Flowers **not drooping**. Wet cliffs **near E coast**.
**G. flanaganii**
Leaves short, stiff. **Flowers rather closed**, dark red with narrow white flashes. Wet cliffs. **High on Drakensberg escarpment**.

**SPRINGBOK PAINTED PETALS**     *Lapeirousia silenoides*
Corm. Single basal leaf up to 100 mm long. Flower tube up to 50 mm long (spring). Sandy and rocky areas in Namaqualand.

    *Watsonia pulchra*
Up to 1,2 m. **In small clumps**. Leaves **30 mm wide**, margin thickened, **mid-vein not**. Bracts brown, flowers 50 mm wide, pink (Dec-Mar). Grassland, from E coast to escarpment.
Similar
**NATAL WATSONIA**  **W. densiflora**
Large clumps. Leaves up to 15 mm wide, **mid-vein thickened**, up to 42 flowers. From E coast inland to 1 000 m.

**WOODLAND PAINTED PETALS**     *Anomatheca laxa*
Up to 300 mm. Leaves up to 450x13 mm. Flowers up to 35 mm across, red or pale lilac (summer). Common in shade. Summer rainfall areas in E.
Similar
**A. grandiflora**
Up to 600 mm. Flowers 60 mm diam. E, NE and N.

### 1 CRANE FLOWER *Strelitzia regina*

Up to 1,5 m. Flowering stems longer than leaves. Up to six flowers enclosed within a spathe up to 200 mm long. Large clumps on rocky slopes near rivers and coast, from SE to E.

### 2 SPIDER ORCHID *Bartholina burmanniana*

Up to 220 mm. Single leaf up to 18 mm diam. Lip divided into many narrow lobes up to 32 mm long (Aug-Nov). Fynbos or restioveld, flowering after fire, sea level to 1 200 m in SW and S.

### 3 *Bonatea speciosa*

Up to 1 m. Robust. Leaves up to 130x40 mm. Large inflorescence Flowers up to 80 mm long, trilobed lip, each lobe up to 30 mm long, spur up to 45 mm long. Coastal scrub, forest margins, scrub sea level to 1 200 m. From SW to N.

### 4 *Satyrium coriifolia*

Up to 770 mm. Leaves thick, up to 150 mm long. Inflorescence up to 300 mm long, up to 45 flowers, sepals up to 13 mm long spurs up to 9 mm long (Aug-Dec). Coastal areas, from SW to SE.

### 5 *Satyrium longicauda*

Up to 800 mm. Leaves up to 200 mm long, prostrate or partly erect, separate from flowering stem. Up to 60 flowers, sepals up to 11 mm, spur up to 46 mm long, white to pink, scented (Oct Apr). Very variable. Widespread in summer rainfall areas from coast to mountains.

### 6 *Disa cornuta*

Up to 1 m. Robust. Leaves sheathing base, up to 160 mm long margins wavy. Inflorescence dense, sepals up to 18 mm long, spur up to 20 mm long (Sept-Feb). Grassland in summer rainfall areas mountains and sandy flats in S. Widespread in e half of region.

### 7 *Disa crassicornis*

Up to 1 m. Robust. Inflorescence with up to 25 flowers, sweetly scented, sepals up to 40 mm long, spur up to 40 mm long (Nov Mar). Grassland, damp places. Midlands and mountains, from S to E.

### 8 *Disa nervosa*

Up to 800 mm. Robust. Dense inflorescence, sepals up to 25 mm long, spur up to 20 mm long (Jan-Feb). Rocky grassland. Wide spread from SE to N.

### 9 *Disa uniflora*

Up to 600 mm. Flower spur up to 15 mm, lateral sepals up to 6 mm long (Jan-Mar). Common along streams in SW and S, 100 1 200 m.

### 10 *Disa woodii*

Up to 700 mm. Cylindrical inflorescence up to 160 mm long Sepals up to 7 mm, slender spur up to 1,5 mm (Sept-Nov). Wide spread in damp grassland, from SE to N.

### 11 *Herschelianthe baurii (=Herschelia baurii*

Up to 400 mm. Leaves appear after flowers. Inflorescence with 2 14 flowers, sepals up to 11 mm long, spur up to 6 mm long, l beard-like (Aug-Nov). Grassland from coast to mountains, from S to N and NE.

**1 GRANNY BONNET**         *Disperis fanniniae*

Up to 450 mm. Leaves up to 80x30 mm. Flower hood up to 20 mm, lateral sepals up to 14 mm (Jan-Apr). Forests, plantations, 200-2 000 m. From SE to N.

**2**         *Polystachya ottoniana*

Up to 80 mm. Epiphyte. Pseudobulbs up to 25x15 mm, forming long chains. Leaves up to 60x10 mm. Inflorescence from new growth, 1-5 flowers, variable in size and colour (Aug-Dec). Common on rocks and trees in forest. From SE to N, coast to 1 800 m.

**3**         *Ceratandra grandiflora*

Up to 430 mm. Robust. Leaves up to 80 mm long. Dense inflorescence, flowers up to 30 mm wide (Oct-Dec). Marshes from sea level to 450 m in S.

**4 LEOPARD ORCHID**         *Ansellia africana*

Up to 1,5 m. Robust epiphyte forming large clumps in trees. Pseudobulbous stems up to 1 m long and 30 mm diam. Leaves up to 300x40 mm. Inflorescence branched, up to 1 m long, flowers up to 40 mm diam, lightly scented (Jun-Sept-Nov). Scrub, bushveld, sand forest, from E coast to tropical Africa.

**5**         *Eulophia clavicornis*

Up to 900 mm. Slender. Leaves up to 200 mm long. Flowers up to 40 mm wide (Aug-Sept). Widespread in grassland. Sea level to mountains, from S to N. Three subspecies.

**6**         *Eulophia angolensis*

Up to 1,4 m. Robust. Leaves up to 900x50 mm. Flowers up to 50 mm wide (Oct-Apr). Clumps in marshy areas, grassland. Coast and inland, from E coast to tropical Africa.

**7**         *Eulophia cucullata*

Up to 500 mm. Slender. Leaves up to 300x10 mm, appear after flowering. Flowers up to 30 mm long (Oct-Nov). Grassland, edge of marshes, from E coast to tropical Africa.

**8 PURPLE VLEI ORCHID**         *Eulophia horsfallii*

Up to 2 m. Robust. Leaves up to 150x90 mm, pleated. Flowers up to 60 mm wide, petals longer, broader (Sept-Mar). Marshy areas, edge of forest, from E coast to tropical Africa.

**9**         *Eulophia speciosa*

Up to 900 mm. Robust. Leaves up to 600x20 mm. Flower sepals up to 20 mm long, petals longer, broader (Oct-Jan). Widespread, from S to N.

**10**         *Eulophia welwitschii*

Up to 900 mm. Leaves pleated, stiffly erect, up to 700x20 mm. Dense inflorescence, flowers up to 45 mm long (Nov-Jan). Widespread in grassland, marshy areas, sea level to mountains, from SE to tropical Africa.

**11**         *Cyrtorchis arcuata*

Stems up to 400 mm long. Epiphyte. Leaves up to 160x30 mm, tip unequally bilobed. Several flowering stems. Flowers up to 50 mm wide, spurs up to 60 mm long. Sweetly scented at night (Jan-May). On trees and rock faces. Common. Forest, sea level to 1 000 m, from SE to tropical Africa.

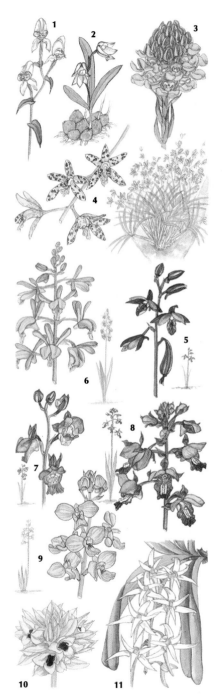

**1   BEARDED SERRURIA**            *Serruria barbigera*

Up to 500 mm. Very variable growth form. 3-4 flower heads, up to 38 mm diam (winter-summer). Low to high altitudes in S (Caledon district).

**2   ROOISTOMPIES**            *Mimetes cucullatus*

500 mm to 1,5 m. Erect stems from base. Leaves up to 35x12 mm changing colour towards top of stems in flowering season. 4-8 flower heads **shorter** than red-tipped leaves (Jul-Nov). On well drained soils. Widespread in S and SW.

**3**            *Protea witzenbergiana*

Up to 500 mm. Low growing, forming clumps. Leaves up to 600x85 mm, stalk 10-100 mm long. Flower heads up to 120 mm diam (Sept-Dec). Strong, yeasty scent. Plants very variable. Widespread, particularly in mountains of S and SW.

**4   LIGHTED MATCHES**            *Tapinanthus rubromarginatus*
            *(=Loranthus rubromarginatus)*

Up to 1 m tall. Semi-parasite **forming large clumps** in trees. Leaves deciduous, up to 40x15 mm. Flowers up to 50 mm long (Sept-Dec). Fruit up to 10 mm diam, red. Widespread in NE and N.

**5   LIGHTED MATCHES**            *Moquinella rubra*
            *(=Loranthus elegans)*

Up to 900 mm diam. Semi-parasite, in large clumps. Leaves up to 40x10 mm long. Flowers up to 40 mm long (Apr-Aug). Widespread in S.

**6   MISTLETOE**   *Erianthemum dregei (=Loranthus dregei)*

Up to 1 m. Large clumps, branches hanging down. Young leaves velvety, smooth when mature. Flowers up to 50 mm long (Jun-Dec). Fruit up to 12 mm long. Widespread in woodland. Summer rainfall areas.

**7   SNAKE ROOT**            *Persicaria serrulata*
            *(=Polygonum salicifolium)*

Up to 1 m. Slender herb. Leaves up to 150 mm long. Arching inflorescence (summer). Marshy areas. Widespread.

**8**            *Persicaria senegalensis*

Up to 1 m. Branched. Leaves large, up to 250x60 mm. Flowers pink (Sept-May). Widespread in marshy areas, from SE to N.

**9**            *Commicarpus pentandrus*

150-900 mm. Prostrate/scrambling herb. Flower head erect, flowers up to 15 mm diam (summer). Widespread in dry areas.

**1   HOTTENTOT'S FIG**     *Carpobrotus quadrifidus*

Up to 150 mm diam. Triangular-sided leaves up to 130x20 mm.
Long trailing stems. Flowers white to cerise (Aug-Oct). Large, edible, juicy fruit. Coastal, from SW to Namaqualand.
**Similar**
**SOUR FIG   *C. edulis***
Flower heads yellow, up to 120 mm diam (Aug-Oct). At low altitudes.
**NATAL CREEPING FIG   *C. dimidiatus***
Leaves 80 mm long. Flower heads up to 120 mm diam, magenta.
Coastal dunes, from SE to Mozambique.

**2   T'NOUTSIAMA**     *Cheiridopsis candidissima*

Up to 150 mm. In small clumps. Leaves up to 110 mm long.
Flower heads up to 70 mm diam, on long stalks (Aug-Oct). In
sand. Namaqualand, Richtersveld.

**3   PIG'S ROOT**     *Conicosia pugioniformis*

Up to 180 mm. Succulent, low-growing plant. Flower heads 80-130 mm diam, held on long stalks above leaves (Aug-Sept). Found
singly or in large colonies. From SW to Namaqualand and
Namibia.

**4   HIGHVELD WHITE VYGIE**     *Delosperma herbeum*

Up to 150 mm. Spreading succulent herb, up to 150 mm high.
Flower heads up to 12 mm diam, white (Sept-Mar). Grassland.
Widespread.

**5   SAND VYGIE**     *Dorotheanthus oculatus*

Up to 80 mm. Annual. Leaves flat, shiny green, turning red.
Flower heads up to 60 mm diam, on long stalks, colour variable
(Jul-Sept). Fruit soft with five valves. Sandy soil, from SW to
Namaqualand.

**6   BI-COLOURED ICE PLANT**     *Drosanthemum bicolor*

Up to 600x600 mm. Succulent shrublet. Leaves cylindrical.
Flower heads up to 40 mm diam (Aug-Sept). SW.

**7   DEW PLANTS**     *Drosanthemum hispidum*

Up to 200 mm. Leaves cylindrical, glistening, up to 20 mm long.
Flower heads up to 30 mm diam, on short stalks (Sept). Fruit a
five-valved flat hard capsule. Flat, dry, sandy places, from S to
Namibia.

**8**     *Drosanthemum speciosum*

Up to 300 mm high and 600 mm wide. Wiry stems, branches
spreading, woody at base. Flower heads up to 50 mm diam,
colour varies from orange to red (spring). From SW to Namaqualand.

### 1 DORINGVY
*Eberlanzia ferox*

Up to 450 mm. Much-branched, flowering stems spiny, spines up to 50 mm long. Leaves succulent, less than 20 mm long. Flower heads up to 10 mm diam (after rain). Fruit woody. Very common in arid areas, usually on shallow soils. Karoo, Namibia.

### 2 GOLDEN VYGIE
*Lampranthus aureus*

Up to 600x600 mm. Branches brown. Leaves with paler dots. Flower heads up to 40 mm diam (Aug-Sept). SW.

### 3 VYGIEBOS
*Lampranthus suavissimus*

Up to 1 m. Shrub. Leaves up to 35 mm long. Flower heads up to 55 mm diam (Aug-Sept). Near coast, Namaqualand.

### 4 TRANSVAAL STONE PLANT
*Lithops lesliei*

Singly or in clumps. Two "leaves" joined at base. Flower head up to 10 mm diam (Mar-Apr). Widespread in N (only representative of this genus in N of South Africa; *Lithops* usually found in arid W).

**Similar**

### 5 *Conophytum pellucidum*
Found in arid W.

### 6 ASBOS
*Psilocaulon junceum*

Up to 1 m. Succulent shrub. Small, succulent leaves fall early, leaving scar. Flower heads up to 10 mm diam, white to pink (Oct-Nov). Common in arid areas. Ash from plant used to make soap. Karoo.

### 7 OSBOSSIE
*Talinum caffrum*

Up to 200 mm. Herb with carrot-like root. Leaves up to 35 mm long, succulent. Flowers up to 15 mm diam (Nov-Mar). Dry and rocky areas. Widespread.

### 8
*Anacampseros lanceolata*

Up to 60 mm. Leaves up to 30 mm long. Flowers up to 20 mm diam (summer). Clumps on stony soils in Karoo, Namaqualand.

### 9 GUNPOWDER PLANT
*Silene burchellii*

Up to 500 mm. Slender herb. Calyx up to 20 mm long, flowers up to 10 mm diam (Nov-Jan). Much-branched. Grassland. Widespread.

### 10 GUNPOWDER PLANT
*Silene undulata (=S. capensis)*

Up to 500 mm. Leaves in basal rosette, covered in sticky hairs. Flowers up to 25 mm diam (Jul/Oct/Apr). Widespread in grassland, in high rainfall areas or near water, from SW to N.

### 11 WILD PINK
*Dianthus mooiensis*

Up to 600 mm. Perennial herb. Flowers up to 35 mm diam (Sept-Nov). Widespread in grassland.

**1   SMALL YELLOW WATER LILY**      *Nymphoides indica*

Flower up to 30 mm diam. Aquatic. Leaves usually smaller than those of *Nymphaea* species. Widespread in watercourses, from S to tropical Africa.

**2   WATER LILY**      *Nymphaea nouchali (=N. capensis)*

Flower up to 110 mm diam. Aquatic. Leaves up to 250 mm diam. Flower petals up to 50 mm long, held above water, colour varies from deep to pale blue or pink (summer). Lovely scent. Widespread in slow-flowing rivers, lakes, pools.

**3   NATAL ANEMONE**      *Anemone fanninii*

Up to 1,5 m. Large leaves up to 600 mm wide, developing to full size **after** flowering. Flowers up to 90 mm diam (Sept-Dec). Widespread in damp areas in mountains, from SE to NE and central areas.
**Similar**
**CAPE ANEMONE  *A. tenuifolia***
Smaller (up to 600 mm). Leaves up to 200 mm long, deeply incised, sharp-tipped. Flowers up to 100 mm diam (Jun-Feb). Common after fires, from SW to SE.

**4   TRAVELLER'S JOY**      *Clematis brachiata*

Up to 5 m. Deciduous climber, no tendrils. Slender woody stems. Flowers up to 10 mm diam, sweetly scented (Mar-Apr). Seed heads up to 50 mm diam. Coast to mountains, in open woodland and on forest margins. Widespread.

**5   BUSH CLEMATIS**      *Clematopsis scabiosifolia*

Up to 2 m. Shrub. Leaves and stems covered in soft hairs. Flowers up to 50 mm diam, in terminal branched inflorescences (Jan-Feb). Seed heads very similar to (4) above. Dry grassland, rocky areas in NW, Zimbabwe.

**6   BLUE FLAX**      *Heliophila coronopifolia*

Up to 600 mm. Leaves up to 130 mm long. Flowers up to 12 mm diam (spring). From SW to Namaqualand.

**7**      *Cleome angustifolia*

Up to 1,6 m. Annual. Flowers clustered terminally (Nov-Jun). In hot dry areas. N half of region.

**8**      *Cleome hirta*

Up to 1,5 m. Annual, rounded bush. Leaves sticky. Inflorescence up to 300 mm long (Jan-May). Dry areas. N half of region.

**9   SPRAWLING SUNDEW**      *Drosera hilaris*

Up to 250 mm long. Insectivorous. Leaves up to 70 mm long, in basal rosette. Flowers up to 20 mm diam (Sept-Nov). Damp areas, mountain slopes in S.

**10   SUNDEW**      *Drosera cistiflora*

Up to 200 mm long. Leaves up to 30 mm long. Flowers large (Aug-Sept). Colour very variable. In sandy damp areas, from Namaqualand to SE.

**1 PIG'S EARS**       *Cotyledon orbiculata*

Up to 1 m. Robust succulent. **Very variable**. Leaves up to 150 mm long, round or pencil-shaped, clustered at base. Flowering stem up to 450 mm long, flowers up to 25 mm long, pink to orange (winter). Leaves and flowers have waxy bloom. Widespread.

**2 RED CRASSULA**       *Crassula coccinea*

Up to 600 mm. Succulent. Stems branch near base. Leaves up to 25x15 mm. Flowers in terminal clusters (Dec-Jan). Mountains in SW.

**3**       *Crassula pyramidalis*

Up to 80 mm. Dies after flowering (Aug-Sept). Widespread in arid areas in SW, Karoo and Namaqualand.

**4**       *Crassula acinaciformis*

Up to 2 m. Robust succulent maturing over 3-4 years, dying off after flowering. Inflorescence up to 400 mm diam, flat, with masses of creamy white flowers (Jan-Jun). Open woodland, from E to N.

**5**       *Kalanchoe thyrsiflora*

Up to 1 m. Robust succulent maturing over 3-4 years, dying off after flowering. Large leaves at base up to 150x60 mm. Inflorescence up to 150 mm long (Feb-Jul). Grassland, rock outcrops, from SE to N.

**6 KALANCHOE**       *Kalanchoe rotundifolia*

Up to 800 mm. Succulent. Singly or in large communities. Small inflorescence (May-Aug). Widespread, from SE to N.

**7 STOMPIE**       *Brunia nodiflora*

Up to 900 mm. Shrub, from woody base. Leaves up to 3 mm long. Flower heads up to 10 mm diam (Mar-Jun). Common on mountain slopes in S.

**8 DUIKERWORTEL**       *Grielum humifusum*

Stems up to 350 mm long. Prostrate herb. Flowers up to 50 mm diam. Flat sandy areas, in large patches, from SW to Namaqualand.

**9 BRAMBLE**       *Rubus rigidus*

Up to 2 m. Scrambling shrub. Stems have **recurved prickles**. Leaves have 3-5 leaflets, **velvety white beneath**. Flower petals shorter than sepals (Oct-Jan). Fruit orange, ripening black. Thicket, forest margins, from SE to Zimbabwe.
**Similar**
**AMERICAN BRAMBLE** *R. cuneifolius*
White flowers. Seriously invasive alien in high rainfall areas.

**10 CREEPING BAUHINIA**       *Tylosema fassoglensis*

Stems 3-6 m long. Prostrate creeper with enormous tuber. Stems have tendrils. Leaves bilobed, up to 150 mm wide. Flower petals up to 30 mm long (Oct-Jan). Woody pods with 2-3 seeds. Seeds and tuber edible, leaves browsed. Widespread, from N of region to Sudan.

**1 FISHBONE CASSIA** *Chamaecrista mimosoides*
*(=Cassia mimosoides)*

Up to 300 mm. Herb. Erect or prostrate, **without woody rootstock. Up to 65 pairs leaflets,** leaves touch-sensitive. Flowers up to 20 mm diam, sepals brownish-red (Jan-Apr). Grassland, disturbed ground. Widespread.
**Similar**
*C. comosa*
Larger (up to 600 mm), with **woody rootstock. 15-35 pairs leaflets.** Flowers up to 35 mm diam (spring-summer). Widespread in grassland.

**2 HONEY TEA** *Cyclopia genistoides*

Up to 700 mm. Rounded shrublet, densely branched. Leaflet margins rolled back. Flowers up to 15 mm long (Jul-Dec). Tea made from young leaf tips. Widespread on flats and lower slopes in SW.

**3** *Lotononis corymbosa*

Up to 200 mm. Low-growing herb. Flowers Nov-Jan. Common in grassland, from SE to N.

**4** *Lotononis lotononoides*
*(=Buchenroedera lotononoides)*

Up to 700 mm. Herbaceous shrublet. Flowers Dec-Jan. Common in Drakensberg mountains.

**5** *Pearsonia sessilifolia*

Up to 500 mm. Small shrublet, herbaceous from woody base. Leaflets silvery, usually stalkless. Narrow- and broader-leaved forms. Flowers small, in terminal heads, yellow becoming orange with age (Oct-Jan). Widespread in grassland, rocky areas, from E to N.
**Similar**
**6** *P. aristata*
Larger leaflets. Flowers in lax terminal head (Nov-Mar). Pods flat.

**7** *Aspalathus carnosa*

Up to 2 m. Shrub. Leaves needle-like, up to 10 mm long. Flowers up to 25 mm long, in terminal clusters (spring-summer). Sandy and rocky areas. Common in SW.
**Similar**
*A. spinosa*
Spines longer than leaves. Flowers Aug-Apr. Very variable. Most widespread species, mainly at lower altitudes, from SW to E.

**8 MOUNTAIN DAHLIA** *Liparia splendens*

Up to 1 m. Spreading shrub. Leaves up to 50 mm long. Terminal inflorescences up to 80 mm diam (throughout year). SW.

**9** *Crotalaria globifera*

Up to 900 mm. Shrublet. Leaflets up to 30x10 mm, finely hairy. Inflorescence up to 160 mm long, flowers turn coppery with age (Sept-Mar). Small, round, **inflated pod,** up to 13x7 mm. Common in grassland, from SE to NE.

**10** *Argyrolobium speciosum*

Up to 400 mm. Perennial herb. Terminal inflorescences (Oct-Dec). From SE to NE.

**1** *Indigofera hedyantha*

Up to 300 mm. Low shrublet, 600 mm wide. 2-4 pairs leaflets, folded upwards from midrib, silky hairs beneath. Compact inflorescence, **longer than leaves**. Flower up to 12 mm long, **buds with dark brown hairs**, scented (Oct-Dec). Widespread in grassland, on rocky ground, from SE to Zimbabwe.

**2** *Tephrosia grandiflora*

Up to 1 m. Much-branched. Leaves greyish-green, 3-5 leaflets. Flowers up to 30 mm long, terminally borne (Aug-Dec). Woodland, common along roadsides, from SE to N.

**3 BALLOON PEA** *Sutherlandia frutescens*

Up to 1,8 m. Soft shrub. Many-stemmed from base. Up to 17 leaflets of 18 mm long. Flowers up to 50 mm long (Aug-Dec). Fruit inflated. Widespread, usually in dry areas.

**4 LUCKY BEAN CREEPER** *Abrus precatorius*

Up to 2 m. Climber. Up to 10 pairs of leaflets. Flowers up to 10 mm long, mauve (Oct-Dec). Pods hairy when young, up to 30 mm long. Widespread in woodland throughout summer rainfall areas.

**5 BUFFALO BEAN** *Mucuna coriacea*

Up to 2 m. Scrambling climber. Inflorescence up to 80 mm diam (Jan-May). Pods up to 80 mm long, velvety. Golden hairs on calyx and pods extremely irritating: **dangerous to touch!** Thicket, grassland and on disturbed soil in N.

**6** *Eriosema cordatum*

Up to 150 mm. Prostrate herb with spreading stems. Leaflets up to 70 mm long, variable. Inflorescence held erect, above leaves (spring-summer). Widespread in grassland.
**Similar**
*E. psoraleoides*
Single-stemmed shrub up to 1,5 m tall, branching high up. Velvety leaves and stems, leaflets up to 60 mm long, blunt-tipped. Flowers pale yellow (Dec-Mar). Rounded pods up to 15 mm long. Grassland. Widespread, from E to N.

**7 WILD SWEETPEA** *Sphenostylis angustifolia*

Up to 400 mm. Low-growing shrub. Flowers on stem held above leaves, scented (Oct-Jan). On rocky hillsides, grassland. Widespread, from central areas northwards.

**8 CARPET GERANIUM** *Geranium incanum*

Up to 300 mm. Low-growing herb. Flower up to 30 mm diam, petals dented at top, held above leaves, variable in colour (Oct-Dec). Popular garden plant. Widespread in damp areas in S.

**9 NAALDBOSSIE** *Monsonia burkeana*

Up to 150 mm. Perennial herb. Leaves toothed. Petals up to 24 mm long with conspicuous veins, white, mauve to blue (spring). In grassland on sandy soils, rocky areas. Widespread.

## 1 CANDLE BUSH — *Sarcocaulon crassicaule*

Up to 400 mm. Low, succulent shrub. Stems thick, covered in spines. Stems contain large quantities of resin, highly flammable. Flowers up to 30 mm diam, white to yellow (after rain). Widespread in arid areas, from S to Namibia.

## 2 WILD MALVA — *Pelargonium cucullatum*

Up to 2 m. Stems up to 50 mm thick, slightly woody at base. Leaves up to 45x60 mm, cup-shaped, margin slightly to angularly incised. Inflorescence with 4-10 flowers, pink to dark purple, flowers up to 50 mm diam (throughout year). Faintly scented. SW coast.

**Similar**

**P. inquinans**

1-2 m. Rounded shrub. Leaves velvety, up to 120 mm diam. Scarlet flowers (spring) on 80-200 mm stems. SE.

## 3 WAVING PELARGONIUM — *Pelargonium luridum*

Inflorescence 600 mm to 1 m high. Herbaceous. Cluster of leaves at base. Leaves up to 270 mm diam, stalks up to 300 mm long, **margins ranging from entire to deeply incised**, fernlike, often on the same plant (entire leaves appear first). Up to 60 flowers, cream, yellow to pink (Sept-Apr). Widespread in grassland, from SE to Zimbabwe.

**Similar**

**HORSESHOE GERANIUM  P. zonale**

1-2 m. Shrub. Leaves up to 75 mm diam, with purplish horseshoe mark on surface. Pink flowers (Aug-Sept). Forest edge and thicket. SE.

**NAMAQUALAND BEAUTY  P. incrassatum**

Up to 300 mm. In clusters. Leaves 140 mm, lobed and scalloped, with silvery hairs. Flowers in tight heads 75 mm diam, pink to purple (Jul-Oct). Namaqualand.

## 4 IVY-LEAVED GERANIUM — *Pelargonium peltatum*

Leaves up to 70 mm diam. Climbing or trailing perennial. Leaves succulent, **peltate** (stalk inserted in middle of leaf), usually hairless. Inflorescence with up to nine flowers, white to pink, mauve (spring or throughout year). Coastal or succulent bush, from S to SE.

**Similar**

**P. capitatum**

300-500 mm. Straggling low shrub. Leaves velvety. Flowers in dense heads, pinkish-red (all year). SW, S and SE coast.

## 5 SORREL — *Oxalis pescapra*

Up to 400 mm. Perennial herb. Leaves in basal rosette, stalks up to 120 mm long. Flowering stem up to 200 mm long, up to 20 flowers, petals up to 25 mm long (May-Sept). Widespread, becoming a weed in places, from SW to Namibia.

## 6 SORREL — *Oxalis semiloba*

Up to 150 mm. Perennial herb. Leaf size variable, depending on moisture. Flowers up to 25 mm diam (Mar-Jun). Widespread, coast to mountains, from SE to Zimbabwe.

## 7 TORTOISE BUSH — *Zygophyllum morgsana*

Up to 1,5 m. Shrub. Succulent leaves, divided in two, unpleasant scent when crushed. Flowers in pairs, at end of branches (Aug). Large winged fruit. Sandy and rocky places in arid areas, from S to Namibia.

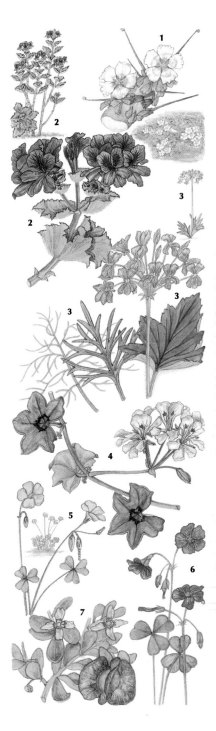

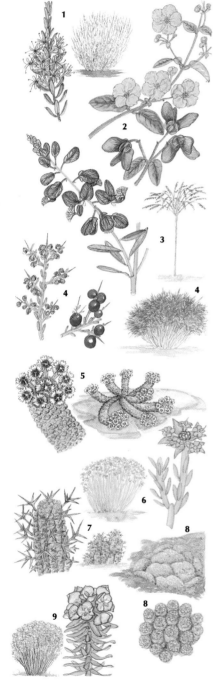

**1   FALSE BUCHU**                    *Agathosma ovata*

200 mm to 1,2 m. Low-growing shrub. Leaves small, aromatic. Flowers Apr-Oct. Grassy mountain slopes, from S to E.

**2   CANARY NETTLE**          *Sphedamnocarpus pruriens*

Stems up to 3 m long. Slender climber. Leaves up to 50 mm long. Flowers up to 25 mm diam, in clusters (Dec-Mar). Winged fruit, wing up to 15 mm long, rust-coloured, with itchy hairs. Scrub and woodland. Widespread, from E to Zimbabwe.

**3   PURPLE BROOM**                    *Polygala virgata*

Up to 2 m. Herbaceus main stem, branching in upper third. Leaves narrow, up to 60 mm long. Flowers up to 20 mm wide, in drooping terminal spikes up to 250 mm long. Widespread on forest margins, in grassland, from SE to Zimbabwe.
**Similar**
**SKAAPERTJIE  *P. leptophylla***
Smaller (up to 300 mm). Leaves up to 20x2 mm. Flowers up to 8 mm long, greenish-pink. Rocky areas on mountain slopes. Widespread in arid areas, from S to Namibia.

**4   SKILPADBESSIE**                    *Nylandtia spinosa*

Up to 1x1 m. Much-branched shrub. Branches spine-tipped. Flowers up to 5 mm long (late winter to early spring). Edible berries. Sandy flats and rocky slopes. Widespread in S, also Namibia.

**5   MEDUSA'S HEAD**          *Euphorbia caputmedusa*

Radiating branches up to 300 mm long. Dwarf succulent, robust. Flowers Jul-Sept. Rock outcrops in SW.

**6   GIFMELKBOS**                    *Euphorbia mauritanica*

Up to 1 m. Much-branched shrub. Spineless, cylindrical branches. Leaves drop early. Inflorescences clustered at ends of stems. Widespread in arid areas of S, E and NW.

**7   STARRY-SPINED EUPHORBIA**     *Euphorbia stellaespina*

Up to 450 mm diam. Clumps, each branch up to 75 mm thick, with 10-16 angles, covered in 3-5 branched spines. Shallow, stony ground in Karoo, Namaqualand.

**8   LION SPOOR**                    *Euphorbia clavarioides*

Up to 300x600 mm. Large, succulent "cushions". On rock outcrops, mountains, from SE to N.

**9   PISGOEDBOSSIE**                    *Euphorbia epicyparissias*

Up to 1,2 m. Stems **red**. Leaves up to 40 mm long. Flowers in terminal clusters up to 80 mm diam (Jul-Feb). Often in large communities. Common in moist areas in mountains, from SE to N.

**1   HONEY FLOWER**                    *Melianthus major*

Up to 2 m. Soft-stemmed shrub. Leaves up to 750 mm long, unpleasant smell when crushed. Terminal inflorescence up to 300 mm long. Flowers up to 25 mm long, heavily nectar-laden. Inflated pods. In S.
**Similar**
**2   *M. comosa***
Inflorescences among leaves. Widespread except SE.

**3   WILD BALSAM        *Impatiens hochstetteri* (=*I. duthiae*)**

Up to 400 mm. Soft herb. Leaves up to 80 mm long, stalk up to 50 mm long. Flowers in clusters of 1-3 (Dec-Feb). In damp conditions in forest. Widespread, from East London to Zimbabwe.

**4   FEATHERHEAD**                    *Phylica pubescens*

Up to 2 m. Branched shrub. Branches and young leaves with silky hairs. Mature leaves up to 35 mm long, pale beneath, sometimes rolled under. Inflorescence up to 50 mm diam (May-Aug). Lower mountain slopes in SW.

**5**                                *Cissus quadrangularis*

Up to 3 m. Succulent creeper/climber. Stem four-angled, up to 50 mm diam with tendrils. Deeply lobed leaves occasionally present on new growth. Inflorescence up to 100 mm long (Oct-Nov). Fruit up to 8 mm diam, red. Widespread in woodland in dry areas.

**6   WILD HOLLYHOCK**              *Sparrmannia africana*

2-6 m. Large woody shrub. Leaves up to 200 mm long, soft. Flowers up to 40 mm diam, in terminal clusters (Jun-Nov). Moist areas on forest margins in SE.

**7   PINK MALLOW**                 *Anisodontea scabrosa*

Up to 2 m. Shrub. Leaves up to 75 mm long. Flowers up to 30 mm diam (summer). Coastal areas, from SW to E.

**8   WILD HIBISCUS**                *Hibiscus calyphyllus*

Up to 2 m. Scrambling shrub. Leaves up to 120 mm long, stalk up to 50 mm long, soft, velvety. Flowers up to 90 mm diam (Nov-Apr). Grassland, thicket, often in shade. Widespread in summer rainfall areas.

**9   DWARF RED HIBISCUS**           *Hibiscus praeteritus*

Up to 1,5 m. Soft shrub. Flowers up to 2,5 mm diam (summer). Arid areas, from N to NW.

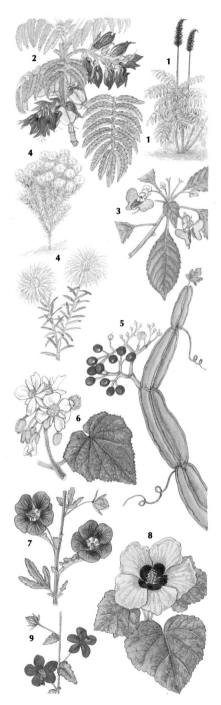

**1 BROODBOS** *Hermannia cuneifolia*

Up to 600 mm. Low shrublet. Leaves up to 20 mm long, scalloped at tip. Flowers up to 10 mm long, yellow to red (after rain). Widespread in drier areas, from S to Namibia.

**2 LION'S EYE** *Tricliceras longipedunculatum*
*(=Wormskioldia longipedunculata)*

Up to 450 mm. Perennial herb. Flowers up to 30 mm diam (Nov-Feb). Grassland. Widespread in N.

**3 WILD BEGONIA** *Begonia sutherlandii*

Up to 1 m. Succulent herb. Forms colonies. Stems fleshy, green or red. Leaves up to 250x150 mm, usually much less, stalk up to 150 mm long. Terminal inflorescence, flowers up to 35 mm diam (Nov-Mar). Fruit three-winged. Damp places in forest, from SE to central Africa.

**4 VLIEËBOS** *Saltera sarcocolla*

Up to 1 m. Shrub. Leaves leathery, rounded, overlapping. Terminal inflorescence with 1-6 flowers, sticky bracts (throughout year). Coastal areas, from Cape Peninsula to Bredasdorp.

**5 YELLOWHEAD** *Gnidia kraussii*
*(=Lasiosiphon kraussiana)*

Up to 300 mm. Low shrublet. Leaves up to 25 mm long. Terminal inflorescence up to 40 mm diam (Aug-Nov), scented. Grassland. Widespread in summer rainfall areas.

**6 ROYAL DISSOTIS** *Dissotis princeps*

Up to 2 m. Shrub. Stems four-angled. **Leaves large,** velvety. **Flowers large, purple,** 50 mm diam (Jan-Mar). Marshy areas inland. Widespread, from E to Zimbabwe.
**Similar**
**WILD LASIANDRA *D. canescens***
Leaves smaller. **Flowers up to 25 mm diam, bright magenta**.

**7 RED HAIRY ERICA** *Erica cerinthoides*

Up to 1 m. Shrub. Leaves up to 6 mm long. Flowers up to 35 mm long, hairy, sticky, drooping downwards (Jul-Nov). Widespread, from S to N.

**8 MASSON'S HEATH** *Erica massonii*

Up to 1 m. Shrub, spreading with age. Leaves up to 10 mm long, long hairs on margins. Flowers sticky, inflorescence with up to 22 flowers (Oct-May). Sandy and rocky areas over 1 000 m in SW.

**9** *Erica viscaria*

Up to 600 mm. Branches straight, sturdy. Flowers large (throughout year). Damp areas in SW.

**10** *Erica sessiliflora*

Up to 2 m. Shrub. Leaves up to 4 mm long. Flowers with **fleshy sepals which swell around fruits, turning red and persisting on plant for years** (Apr-Sept). Widespread in damp areas along coast and inland in S.

**1** *Erica mammosa*

Up to 1,2 m. Shrub. Leaves up to 10 mm long. Flowers white to orange, pink, purple, green or red (Dec-Apr). **Four dents at base of corolla tube.** Widespread in S.

**2 WAX HEATH** *Erica ventricosa*

Up to 2 m. Branches stout. Flowers in dense terminal clusters (Sept-Apr). Mountains in SW.

**3** *Erica plukenetii*

Up to 600 mm. Erect shrub. Leaves up to 20 mm long. Flowers up to 18 mm long, white to reddish-purple (throughout year). Widespread on flats and mountains, from Namaqualand to SE.

**4 PLUMBAGO** *Plumbago auriculata*

Up to 2 m. Scrambling shrub. Leaves up to 50 mm long. Terminal inflorescence up to 100 mm long, flowers up to 25 mm diam, **calyx sticky** (summer). Widespread in hot, dry scrub and forest, from SE to N.

**5 WILD JASMINE** *Jasminum multipartitum*

Up to 3 m. Shrub. **Leaves shiny**, up to 35 mm long, very variable. Flowers up to 40 mm diam (summer), lovely scent. Berries up to 10 mm diam. Thicket, woodland, rocky slopes in drier areas, from SE to N and NE.
**Similar**
*J. stenolobum*
Scrambling shrub, **covered in soft hairs.**

**6 TRANSVAAL CHIRONIA** *Chironia palustris*

Up to 700 mm. Perennial herb. Flowers up to 25 mm diam (Oct-Mar). Widespread in marshy areas, from SE to Zimbabwe.
**Similar**
**CHRISTMAS BERRY** *C. baccifera*
Small, **bright red berries.**

**7 IMPALA LILY** *Adenium multiflorum*

Up to 2 m. Deciduous succulent shrub. Stems smooth, grey, swollen. Leaves up to 100 mm long, shiny, bright green. Flowers up to 50 mm diam (May-Sept). Twin pod with winged seeds. Hot, dry woodland, from NE to tropical Africa.
**Similar**
**SUMMER IMPALA LILY** *A. swazicum*
Much smaller (up to 300 mm). **Flowers plain pink, appearing with leaves** (Jan-May). From E to N.
*A. boehmianum*
Smaller (up to 1,5 m). **Flowers pink, with leaves. Namibia to Angola.**

**8 KUDU LILY** *Pachypodium saundersii*

Up to 1,5 m. Deciduous. Large swollen stem, **long sharp spines**. Leaves up to 70 mm long. Flowers up to 40 mm diam (Apr-Jun). Dry, rocky mountains, from E to N and NE.
**Similar**
*P. succulentum*
Smaller (up to 300 mm). **Flowers deep pink and white.** Arid, rocky places, from central areas to S.

**9 CORKSCREW FLOWER** *Strophanthus speciosus*

Up to 3 m. Scrambling shrub. Leaves three-whorled, up to 100x25 mm. Flower tube up to 10 mm, lobes up to 30 mm long (Sept-Dec), sweetly scented. Paired pods up to 180x15 mm. Forest margins, from SE to N.

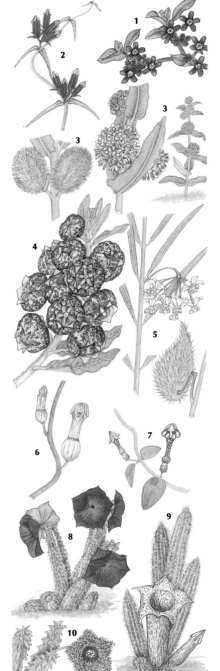

**1  KHADI-ROOT**                    *Raphionacme hirsuta*

Up to 150 mm. Large tuber. Leaves velvety, up to 20 mm long. Flowers up to 10 mm diam (Jul-Nov). Widespread in grassland, coast to highveld, throughout summer rainfall areas.

**2  WAX CREEPER**                    *Microloma sagittatum*

Up to 1,8 m. Slender creeper. Leaves fleshy, slightly hairy, up to 25 mm long. Flower clusters of 3-9, flowers up to 7 mm long (Jul-Sept). Common, from S to Namaqualand.

**3  BITTERHOUT**                    *Xysmalobium undulatum*

Up to 1 m. Perennial. Leaves up to 200 mm long, with wavy margins. Inflorescence up to 50 mm diam, flowers cream to pink (Oct-Feb). Inflated fruit up to 100 mm long. Widespread in grassland throughout summer rainfall areas.

**4**                    *Pachycarpus grandiflorus*

Up to 450 mm. Robust herb. Up to three stems, leaves thick, rough. Flowers up to 50 mm diam, usually less (Nov-Mar). Slightly winged pod up to 90x25 mm. Grassland, from SE to N.

**5  MILKWEED**                    *Asclepias fruticosa*

Up to 1,5 m. Slender, erect shrub. Inflorescence hanging, up to 10 flowers (Dec-Mar). Large inflated pod up to 40x20 mm. Common in grassland and on disturbed ground throughout region.

**6  BUSHMAN'S PIPE**                    *Ceropegia ampliata*

Flower up to 50 mm long. Succulent twining climber. Tiny leaves drop early. Flowers Dec-Apr. Dry thicket, rocky areas, from SE to Zimbabwe.

**7  WHITE-BANDED CEROPEGIA**                    *Ceropegia nilotica*

Flower up to 50 mm long. Slender creeper. Leaves up to 80x60 mm. Flowers very variable. Widespread, from N of region to tropical Africa.

**8  GORDON'S HOODIA**                    *Hoodia gordonii*

Up to 450 mm. Stems up to 50 mm diam, with 12-17 angles and brown spines. Flowers up to 100 mm diam. From W to Namibia and Botswana.

**9**                    *Tavaresia grandiflora (=Decabalone grandiflora)*

Flower tube up to 75 mm long. Resembles a cactus but the flowers identify it as a member of Asclepiadaceae. Unpleasant scent (summer). From central areas northwards.

**10  PORCUPINE HUERNIA**                    *Huernia hystrix*

Up to 100 mm. Low-growing, spreading succulent. Five-angled stems. Flowers up to 50 mm diam (summer). Widespread in dry areas, from SE to Zimbabwe.

**1   GIANT CARRION-FLOWER**          *Stapelia gigantea*

Up to 200 mm. Succulent, branching at base. Flowers up to 400 mm diam, unpleasant odour (Jan-May). Velvety twin pods up to 200 mm long. Large clumps in arid areas, from NE to N.

**2   YELLOW CARRION-FLOWER**          *Orbeopsis lutea*
                                      *(=Caralluma lutea)*

Up to 120 mm. Stems erect. Up to 17 flowers in clusters, colour reddish-brown to yellow, unpleasant odour (Jan-May). Widespread in scrub, grassland in n half of region.

**3**                          *Merremia kentrocaulos*

Flower up to 80 mm diam. Twining stems climb to canopy or form spreading, prostrate mats. Leaves very variable. Flowers close by afternoon (Dec-Apr). Bushveld and savanna in N.
**Similar**
*M. tridentata*
Prostrate. **Smaller, yellow flowers**.

**4   WILD MORNING GLORY**          *Ipomoea cairica*

Flower up to 60 mm diam. Prolific twining climber. Leaves up to 100 mm diam. Flowers Feb-Apr. Widespread at lower altitudes, especially riverine areas, from SE to N and NE.

**5**                              *Turbina oblongata*

Flower up to 70 mm diam. Prostrate or scrambling creeper. Leaves up to 100x50 mm, **yellowish hairs**, held erect. Flowers Nov-Feb. Fruit does not split open. Widespread in summer rainfall areas, frequently on roadsides.
**Similar**
*Ipomoea crassipes*
Fruit splits open.

**6   PRICKLY BUSH**                  *Codon royeni*

Up to 1,5 m. Shrub, covered in long spines. Flowers up to 30 mm long, 20 mm diam. Sandy and rocky areas in Namaqualand, Richtersveld and Namibia.

**7   CHOCOLATE BELLS**          *Trichodesma physaloides*

Up to 600 mm. Shrublet. Leaves up to 60 mm long. Flowers turn brown when touched (Aug-Oct, or after veld fires). Widespread in grassland, from E to Zimbabwe.

**8   EIGHT-DAY HEALING BUSH**          *Lobostemon fruticosus*

Up to 1 m. Much-branched shrub. Leaves up to 60x12 mm. Flowers hairy, up to 25 mm long, pink to blue (Aug-Oct). Sandy areas, from SW to Namaqualand.

**9**                          *Chascanum hederaceum*

Up to 300 mm high. Leaves up to 70 mm long, clustered on ground. Flowers 10 mm wide (Aug-Dec). Rocky areas and grassland, from E to Zimbabwe.

**10**                          *Clerodendrum triphyllum*

Up to 600 mm. Shrublet. Leaves up to 40 mm long. Flowers up to 15 mm long (Aug-Mar). Grassland. Widespread in summer rainfall areas.

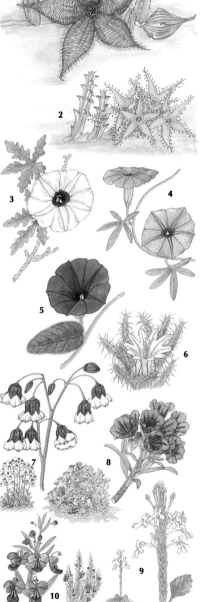

### 1  BUGLE-WEED　　　　　　　*Ajuga ophrydis*

Up to 250 mm. Perennial herb. Leaves thick, up to 80x40 mm. Inflorescence up to 200 mm long, flowers up to 12 mm long (Sept-Apr). Grassland. Widespread in summer rainfall areas.

### 2  WILD DAGGA　　　　　　　*Leonotis ocymifolia*
　　　　　　　　　　　　　　　　　　　*(=L. dysophylla)*

Up to 3 m. Shrub. Leaves up to 150x85 mm, velvety, stalks up to 100 mm long. Inflorescence with flower clusters up to 70 mm diam, flowers up to 45 mm long, held horizontally, **dull orange** (Feb-May). Grassland, rock outcrops, forest margins. Widespread. Variable, three subspecies.
**Similar**
***L. leonurus***
**Leaves narrow, up to** 100x20 mm, **flowers held erect, bright orange**.

### 3  WILD SAGE　　　　　　　*Salvia africana-lutea*

Up to 2 m. Much-branched shrub. Leaves aromatic, up to 35 mm long, hairy. Flowers up to 50 mm long (Jun-Dec). Coastal areas, from SE to Namaqualand.

### 4  HEDGEHOG BUSH　　　　*Pycnostachys urticifolia*

Up to 3 m. Shrub. Leaves up to 120x70 mm, stalk up to 50 mm long. Inflorescence up to 100x30 mm, flowers up to 20 mm long, deep bright blue (Apr-Jun). Marshy areas, forest margins, from N of region to Tanzania.
**Similar**
***P. reticulata***
**Leaves narrow, without stalks.** Flowers pale blue. Widespread in summer rainfall areas up to Tanzania.

### 5  EDGING SPUR-FLOWER　　*Plectranthus saccatus*

Up to 1,25 m. Succulent shrublet. Leaves up to 70x50 mm. Inflorescence up to 120 mm long with **few but large flowers,** up to 30x12 mm (Jan-Apr). Forest margins, from SE to NE.

### 6  PURPLE SPUR-FLOWER　　*Plectranthus ecklonii*

Up to 2 m. Soft shrub. Leaves large, aromatic, up to 170x100 mm. Inflorescence up to 250 mm long, flowers up to 20 mm long (Mar-Apr). Forest, from SE to NE.

### 7  PINK PLUME　　　　　*Syncolostemon densiflorus*

Up to 2 m. Shrub. Stems woody at base, woolly, white. Leaves up to 15x10 mm. Inflorescence up to 160x65 mm, flowers up to 30 mm long (Nov-Apr). Widespread in grassland, forest margins, from SE to NE.

### 8  CAT'S WHISKERS　　*Becium grandiflorum (=B. obovatum)*

Up to 300 mm. Perennial herb. Leaves up to 40 mm long. Flowers up to 17 mm long (Aug-Nov). Grassland. Widespread in summer rainfall areas in E, from SE to tropical Africa.

**1   POISON APPLE**                    *Solanum panduriforme*

Up to 1 m. Shrublet. Stems and leaves with prickles. Flowers up
to 25 mm diam (Nov-Jan). Fruit up to 20 mm diam. Widespread,
especially on disturbed soil.

**2   KAROO VIOLET**              *Aptosimum procumbens*
                                                *(=A. depressum)*

Up to 1 m diam "carpet". Prostrate perennial. Flowers up to 20
mm long (Sept-Mar, after rain). Arid areas, from Namaqualand to
Karoo, central areas and Botswana.

**3**                                          *Diascia barberae*

Up to 400 mm. Herb. Flowers up to 15 mm diam (summer).
Damp, rocky areas at high altitude, from SE to Lesotho and
escarpment.
**Similar**
*D. integerrima*
Smaller (up to 150 mm). Flowers up to 20 mm diam (throughout
summer).

**4   TWINSPUR**                      *Diascia longicornis*

Up to 400 mm. Annual herb. Leaves up to 50x12 mm. Single
flowers, up to 20 mm diam (spring), spurs up to 20 mm long.
Namaqualand.

**5   NEMESIA**                        *Nemesia fruticans*

Up to 250 mm. Herb. Flowers small, colour variable (summer).
Widespread in grassland.

**6   LEEUBEKKIE**                    *Nemesia versicolor*

Up to 600 mm. Annual herb. Leaves up to 43x15 mm. Flowers up
to 11 mm diam, white and yellow, pink or blue, upper and lower
petals sometimes the same colour (Jul-Nov). Sandy areas, from
Namaqualand to SE.

**7   CAPE JEWELS**                    *Nemesia strumosa*

Up to 250 mm. Annual herb. **Flowers up to 25 mm diam**, white,
pink, orange, red (Sept-Oct). Well-known horticultural species.
Sandveld in SW.

**8   RIVERBELL**                      *Phygelius aequalis*

Up to 1 m. Soft shrub. Angled stems. Leaves up to 100 mm long.
Loose inflorescences with hanging flowers up to 40 mm long
(Oct-Jan). On edge of streams at high altitudes. Widespread.
**Similar**
**CAPE FUCHSIA** *P. capensis*
Inflorescence more spread out. Flowers **brighter coral red**.

**9**                                          *Sutera burkeana*

Up to 1 m. Perennial herb. Tiny leaves in tufts. Flowers up to 12
mm diam (Sept-Mar). Rocky areas, grassland, from NE to N.

**10   SUTERA**                        *Sutera grandiflora*

Up to 1 m. Perennial. Leaves up to 30 mm long. Leaves and stems
sticky to touch. Flowers up to 20 mm diam (Jan-Jun). Rocky areas
in mountains, from E to NE.

**11**                                        *Sutera tristis*

Up to 400 mm. Annual. Leaves up to 60x30 mm. Flowers up to
14 mm diam, strongly scented at night (Aug-Dec). Widespread in
dry, sandy areas, from SE to Namibia.

**1 DRUMSTICKS** *Zaluzianskya pachyrrhiza (=Z. maritima)*
Up to 450 mm. Perennial herb with carrot-like root. Leaves up to 70x19 mm. Flowers up to 50 mm long (lobes 10 mm), open at night and on overcast days, scented at night (Oct-Apr). Sandy grassland, mostly coastal areas, from SE to NE.

**2** *Zaluzianskya villosa*
Up to 300 mm. Annual herb. Leaves fleshy, up to 35 mm long. Flower tube up to 20 mm long (Jun-Nov). Flat sandy areas. Widespread in S, Karoo, Namaqualand.

**3** *Hebenstreitia dura*
Up to 600 mm. Multistemmed herb. Leaves up to 30 mm long. Inflorescence up to 50 mm long (throughout year). Grassland and rocky areas. Widespread in summer rainfall areas.
Similar
**H. comosa**
Leaves up to 60 mm long. Inflorescence elongated, up to 120 mm long, flowers heavily scented.

**4 BLUE HAZE** *Selago serrata*
Up to 900 mm. Shrub. Leaves up to 25x10 mm. Flowers in dense heads up to 100 mm diam (Oct-Feb). Widespread in mountains, from SW to SE.

**5** *Walafrida geniculata*
Up to 400 mm. Low-growing shrub. Leaves up to 10 mm long. Inflorescence up to 50 mm long, flowers small, white to pink, blue, purple. Low-lying ground and hills, from Namaqualand to SE and central areas.

**6 WILD PENSTEMON** *Graderia scabra*
Up to 600 mm. Low-growing shrub. Leaves up to 30 mm long. Flowers up to 30 mm diam (Sept-Nov). Grassland, rock outcrops, marshy areas, coast to mountains. Widespread in summer rainfall areas.

**7** *Sopubia simplex*
Up to 500 mm. Semi-parasitic herb. Inflorescence up to 120 mm long (almost throughout year). Marshy areas, grassland. Widespread, from SE to Botswana.
Similar
**S. cana**
Leaves and stems covered in grey hairs.

**8 VLEI INK-PLANT** *Cycnium tubulosum*
Up to 750 mm. Slender semi-parasite. Leaves up to 80 mm, margin toothed. Flowers 40 mm diam (summer), turning black with age or damage. Marshy ground in summer rainfall area.

**9 INK-FLOWER** *Harveya speciosa*
Up to 700 mm. Robust parasite. **Leaves bract-like, yellow or reddish.** Flowers 75 mm (Oct-Feb), turning black. Grassland. SE to N.
Similar
**INK-PLANT** *Cycnium adonense*
100-200 mm. Semi-parasite. **Leaves up to 70 mm.** Flowers white, turning black, 50 mm (Dec-Jan). Grassland. N and NE.

**10 PORT ST JOHN'S CREEPER** *Podranaea ricasoliana*
Flower tube up to 50 mm long. Climber, up to canopy. Flowers in terminal clusters, in profusion (Apr-Jun). Well-known garden plant from Port St John's area in SE.
Similar
**ZIMBABWE CREEPER** *P. brycei*
Smaller, darker, more hairy flowers. Zimbabwe.

**1 WILD FOXGLOVE** *Ceratotheca triloba*

Up to 1,5 m. Bi-annual herbaceous shrub. Leaves up to 50 mm long, aromatic. Flowers up to 75 mm long (Oct-May). Common, especially on disturbed ground, from SE to Zimbabwe.

**2 DEVIL THORN** *Dicerocaryum eriocarpum*
*(= D. zanguebarium)*

Stems up to 1 m long. Prostrate, trailing herb. Flowers up to 35 mm long (Nov-Jan). Fruit flat with two sharp, hard spines. Widespread on sandy or rocky grassland, from E to N and NW.

**3 STREPTOCARPUS** *Streptocarpus primulifolius*

Up to 180 mm. Perennial herb. **Rosette of leaves**, up to 100x40 mm. Flowers up to 50 mm wide (Dec-Apr). Capsules twisted, up to 180x2 mm. Thicket, forest, south-facing slopes on damp soils, rock faces, from SE to NE.
**Similar**
**S. cyaneus**
Leaves up to 300 mm, partly erect. 1-6 flowers, 35-50 mm, mauve, yellow on floor of tube (Oct-Feb). E and NE.
**S. gardenii**
Leaves up to 300 mm, purple beneath, 1-6 flowers up to 50 mm, pale violet, tube greenish (Nov-Apr). E and SE.

**4 RED NODDING-BELLS** *Streptocarpus dunnii*

Up to 150 mm. **Single, very large leaf**, up to 600 mm long. Dense inflorescence. Flowers up to 30 mm long (Nov-Feb). Damp rocky areas at high altitude in E.
**Similar**
**S. vandeleurii**
Single leaf up to 400 mm, tip dying back, margin not lobed. Flowers white. Quartzite ridges in central area.
**S. polyanthus**
1-3 leaves up to 240 mm. Flowers open a few at a time, pale violet, "keyhole"-shaped throat opening (Jul-Feb). E and NE.
**S. confusus**
Single leaf, purplish beneath. Flowers 25 mm, pale violet (Oct-Mar). E and NE.
**S. daviesii**
Single large leaf with small leaf at base. Flowers 45 mm, violet, calyx bell-like (Dec-Mar). E.

**5 BLACK-EYED SUSAN** *Thunbergia alata*

Up to 3 m. Creeper. Leaves slightly hairy. Flowers up to 40 mm diam, colour varies, cream to orange (summer). Damp areas, thicket, forest margins, from SE to tropical Africa.

**6 DWARF THUNBERGIA** *Thunbergia natalensis*

Up to 600 mm. Erect herb. Flowers up to 50 mm long (Aug-Mar). Forest margins, grassland, from SE to Zimbabwe.

**7** *Thunbergia atriplicifolia*

Up to 400 mm. Flowers pale creamy yellow (summer). Common in grassland.

**8 BUSH VIOLET** *Barleria obtusa*

Up to 2 m. Scrambling shrub. Flowers up to 25 mm diam (Mar-Jun). Grassland, scrub, from SE to N.

**9 GREY BARLERIA** *Barleria albostellata*

Up to 1,5 m. Woody shrub, covered in white hairs. Large grey-green leaves. Dense, robust inflorescence (Jan-Mar). Woodland in N.

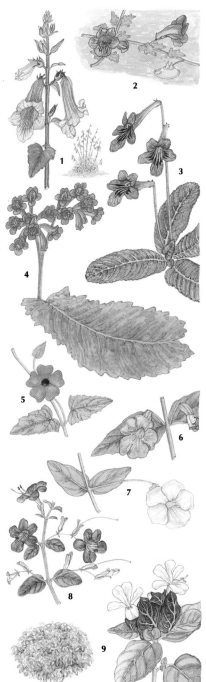

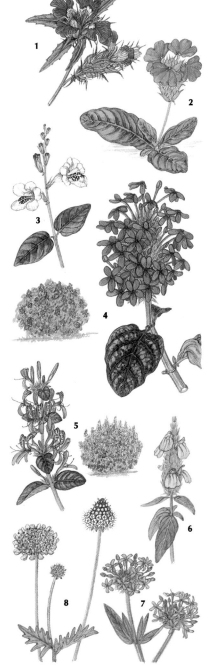

**1**                           *Blepharis subvolubilis*
Up to 300 mm. Low-growing, spiny, perennial herb. Leaves up to 50 mm long, spine-tipped. Flowers up to 20 mm long, bracts spine-tipped (Oct-Jan). Grassland, from E to central areas and N.

**2   CROSSANDRA**               *Crossandra zuluensis*
Up to 300 mm. Perennial herb. Leaves up to 100 mm long, **stalk-less**. Flowers up to 40 mm wide, **bracts** up to 30 mm, **hairless, margins spiny** (Oct-Jan). Bushveld, rocky grassland, from E to Zimbabwe.
**Similar**
*C. greenstockii*
Smaller flowers, **hairy bracts, often entire.**

**3   CREEPING FOXGLOVE**       *Asystasia gangetica*
Up to 500 mm. Spreading, low-growing perennial, sometimes scrambling. Leaves up to 65x30 mm. Flowers up to 20 mm wide (summer). Widespread, grassland, forest margins, disturbed areas, from SE to Botswana, Namibia.

**4   RED RUSPOLIA**       *Ruspolia hypocrateriformis*
Up to 1,5 m. Soft, spreading shrub. Flowers up to 20 mm diam (Feb-May). Forest margins, dry woodland, rocky hillsides in N.

**5   RIBBON BUSH**           *Hypoestes aristata*
Up to 1,5 m. Softly woody perennial shrub. Leaves up to 50 mm long. Terminal inflorescences, flowers up to 25 mm long (May-Jul). Forest margins, dry rocky hillsides, from SE to Zimbabwe.

**6**                                *Justicia flava*
Up to 500 mm. Perennial herb. Summer-flowering. Grassland, bushveld, from E to Zimbabwe.

**7**                       *Pentanisia prunelloides*
Up to 400 mm. Perennial herb. Inflorescence up to 35 mm diam (Aug-Dec, especially after fires). Widespread in summer rainfall areas.

**8   WILD SCABIOSE**         *Scabiosa columbaria*
Up to 800 mm. Perennial. Rosette of leaves at base, leaves very variable, incised or not, up to 100 mm long. Inflorescence up to 50 mm diam (Aug-Mar). Grassland. Widespread, from SW to Zimbabwe.

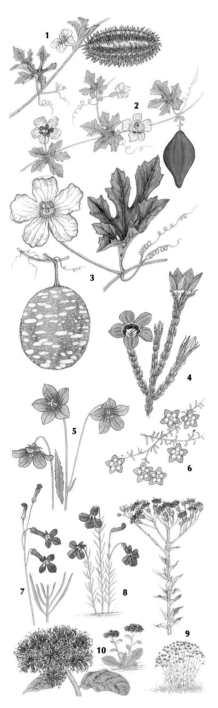

**1 WILD CUCUMBER**           *Cucumis africanus*

Fruit up to 90x50 mm. Annual, prostrate creeper. Leaves up to 100 mm long. Fruit yellow when ripe, hairless (summer). Widespread on floodplains and disturbed areas in Namaqualand, Karoo, Botswana.

**2**           *Momordica balsamina (=M. involucrata)*

Up to 1,5 m. Perennial, herbaceous creeper with tendrils. Leaves 60-90 mm long. Separate male and female flowers, lobes up to 24 mm long (summer), unpleasant scent. Fruit up to 50x30 mm. Widespread.

**3**           *Lagenaria sphaerica (=L. mascarena)*

Fruit up to 100 mm long. Strong climber, to canopy. Leaves thick, up to 180 mm long. Separate male and female plants. Flowers up to 80 mm diam (Feb-Apr). Hard green fruits. Riverine vegetation, from SE to tropical Africa.

**4**           *Roella ciliata*

Up to 400 mm. Sparsely branched. Flowers up to 50 mm diam (summer). Mountain slopes, coastal areas in SW.

**5 GIANT BELL FLOWER**       *Wahlenbergia undulata*

Up to 600 mm. Herb. Leaves up to 35 mm long. Flowers up to 40 mm diam (Nov-Apr). Grassland. Widespread.
**Similar**
**6 *W. prostrata***

Smaller (up to 200 mm). Leaves up to 14 mm long. Flowers up to 20 mm diam (Aug-Sept). Common in Namaqualand.

**7 WILD LOBELIA**           *Lobelia coronopifolia*

Up to 450 mm. Much-branched herb. Flowers up to 25 mm long (throughout year, mostly summer). Widespread in grassland, on moist soils, from SW to N.

**8 BUTTERFLY LOBELIA**      *Monopsis decipiens*
                             *(=Lobelia decipiens)*

Up to 350 mm. Sparsely branched herb. Leaves narrow, up to 10 mm long. Flowers up to 20 mm long (summer, after rain). Grassland, marshy areas. Widespread.

**9**           *Vernonia oligocephala*

Up to 1 m. Perennial herb. Leaves up to 40x25 mm, **silky silvery beneath**. Flower heads up to 10 mm wide, in flat inflorescence (summer). In grassland throughout region.

**10 WILD HELIOTROPE**        *Vernonia hirsuta*

Up to 1 m. Perennial herb. Leaves 80x50 mm or more, **upper surface rough, woolly white beneath**. Large, flattened inflorescences (Aug-Dec). Grassland, scrub, forest margins above 1 900 m. Widespread.

**1   KINGFISHER DAISY**                *Felicia bergerana*

Up to 200 mm. Annual herb. Leaves up to 30x6 mm. Flower head up to 40 mm diam (after rain). Common in Namaqualand.

**2   WILD ASTER**                      *Felicia filifolia*

Up to 1 m. Much-branched perennial. Leaves needle-like, in tufts, up to 25 mm long. Flower head up to 20 mm diam. Common on boulder beds in mountains, rocky and disturbed areas. Widespread.

**3   PINK EVERLASTING**                *Phaenocoma prolifera*

Up to 600 mm. Woody, erect shrub. Tiny leaves. Flower heads with shiny pink or white bracts (Sept-Apr). Fynbos in SW.

**4   STRAWBERRY EVERLASTING**          *Syncarpha eximia*
                                        *(=Helipterum eximium)*

Up to 2 m. Leaves and stems velvety. Flowers midsummer-March. Widespread on south-facing mountain slopes, from S to Tsitsikamma.

**5   FELTED EVERLASTING**              *Syncarpha vestita*
                                        *(=Helichrysum vestitum)*

Up to 1 m. Woolly shrub, much-branched. Leaves up to 800 mm long at base of bush, smaller closer to flower heads. Flower heads up to 50 mm diam (Nov-Jan). From SW to Knysna.

**6   PINK EVERLASTING**                *Helichrysum adenocarpum*

Up to 500 mm. Perennial. Leaves in basal rosette, leaves up to 40 mm long. Flower heads up to 35 mm diam (Jan-Apr). Widespread in grassland, from SE to Zimbabwe.

**7**                                   *Helichrysum cooperi*

Up to 750 mm. Erect annual. Branched inflorescence (summer). Widespread in grassland and on disturbed ground in summer rainfall areas.

**8   MONKEY TAIL EVERLASTING**   *Helichrysum herbaceum*

Up to 250 mm. Herb. Leaves grey-green. Flower heads shiny golden yellow (throughout year). Grassy mountain slopes, coast and inland, from S to Zimbabwe.

**9**                                   *Helichrysum pilosellum*

Up to 600 mm long. Leaves large, in basal rosette. Flowers Aug-Jan. Grassland. Widespread, from SE to Zimbabwe.

**10  BUSH TEA**                        *Athrixia phylicoides*

Up to 1 m. Much-branched. Leaves up to 30 mm long, shiny dark green above, woolly white beneath. Flower heads up to 15 mm diam (May-Nov). Scrub, woodland, grassland. Widespread, from SE to Zimbabwe.

**11  OX-EYE DAISY**                    *Callilepis laureola*

Stems up to 400 mm long. Multistemmed perennial. Leaves up to 60 mm long. Flower heads up to 60 mm diam (Sept-Dec, or after fires). Widespread in grassland in summer rainfall areas.

**1 WILD ROSEMARY** *Eriocephalus africanus*

Up to 1 m. Shrub. Leaves alternate, aromatic. Flower heads up to 10 mm diam (May-Sept). Widespread in rocky areas, mainly near coast, from S to Namaqualand.
Similar
**KAPOKBOS** *E. ericoides*
Leaves opposite, up to 3 mm long. Seeds covered in white wool. Widespread in S, central areas and Namibia.

**2 COULTER BUSH** *Hymenolepis parviflora (=Athanasia parviflora)*

Up to 1,3 m. Sturdy shrub. Leaves up to 70 mm long. Inflorescence up to 100 mm diam, strongly scented (Nov-Dec). Widespread, from Namaqualand to SE.

**3 BUTTON FLOWERS** *Cotula barbata*

Up to 180 mm. Annual herb. Leaves up to 40 mm long. Flower heads up to 10 mm diam (Jul-Sept). Sandy areas, from SW coast to Namaqualand.

**4 GANSKOS** *Cenia turbinata (=Cotula turbinata)*

Up to 400 mm. Annual. Leaves soft, velvety. Flower heads up to 30 mm diam, stalk up to 90 mm long (Jun-Dec). **Flower head depressed in centre**, small rays sometimes present. Widespread in S.

**5 ANCHOR KAROO/KAROOBOSSIE** *Pentzia incana*

500 mm to 1 m. Densely branched shrub. Leaves up to 6 mm long, bitter smelling. Flower heads up to 8 mm diam. Widespread in arid and rocky areas.

**6 SUCCULENT BUSH SENECIO** *Senecio barbertonicus*

Up to 2 m. Scrambling, succulent shrub. Leaves cylindrical up to 80x8 mm, stems shiny yellowish. Flowers sweetly scented (Jul-Sept). Rocky grassland, bushveld, from E to Zimbabwe.

**7 WILD CINERARIA** *Senecio elegans*

Up to 1 m. Annual herb. Leaves up to 75 mm long, fleshy near coast. Flower heads up to 25 mm diam (Jul-Mar). Sandy coastal areas, lower mountain slopes, from Namaqualand to SE.
**Similar**
*S. speciosa*
Found in summer rainfall areas, **rosette of very large** fleshy leaves at base.

**8 CANARY CREEPER** *Senecio tamoides*

Up to 20 m (canopy). Succulent creeper. Leaves up to 70 mm long. Inflorescence up to 130 mm diam. Flower head up to 20 mm diam (Apr-Jul). Forest, from SE to Zimbabwe.
**Similar**
*S. macroglossus*
**Large**, daisy-like flower heads up to 35 mm diam, **not in large inflorescence.**

**9 POM-POM** *Kleinia fulgens (=Senecio fulgens)*

Up to 300 mm. Succulent herb. Leaves clustered towards base, glaucous grey to green. Flower head up to 30 mm diam (winter). Bushveld, rocky hillsides, from E to N.

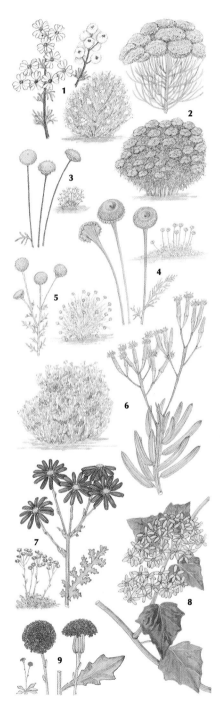

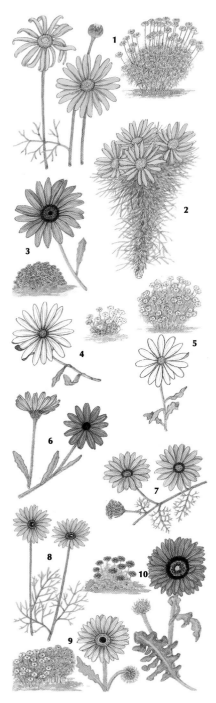

**1  CLANWILLIAM DAISY**          *Euryops speciosissimus*
Up to 1 m. Branched shrub. Leaves up to 140 mm long. Flower heads up to 80 mm diam (spring). SW.

**2  GEEL MAGRIET**          *Euryops abrotanifolius*
Up to 2 m. Single-stemmed shrub. Leaves up to 90x1,5 mm, crowded towards top of stem. Flower heads up to 50 mm diam, sometimes clustered (Jan-Dec, after fires). Sandy and rocky areas, coast to mountain slopes in SW.

**3  NAMAQUALAND DAISY**          *Dimorphotheca sinuata*
Up to 300 mm. Annual herb. Leaves up to 50 mm long. Flower heads 50-80 mm diam, singly (Jul-Sept). Widespread in sandy areas, from Clanwilliam to Namibia.

**4  RAIN DAISY**          *Dimorphotheca pluvialis*
Up to 300 mm. Annual herb, branching from base. Leaves up to 70 mm long. Flower heads up to 70 mm diam, singly (Jul-Sept). From SW to Namaqualand and Namibia.

**5  BRIDE'S BOUQUET**          *Dimorphotheca cuneata*
Up to 1 m. Perennial rounded bush. Leaves up to 20 mm long, clustered towards tops of stems, aromatic. **Ray florets coppery beneath**; flower heads close at night, reopening next day (Jul-Sept). From S to central areas and Botswana.

**6  BERGBIETOU**          *Osteospermum jucundum*
Up to 450 mm. Spreading herb. Leaves up to 60 mm long. Flower head up to 50 mm diam (Aug-Mar). Rocky grassland. Widespread in summer rainfall areas.

**7**          *Osteospermum pinnatum*
Up to 400 mm. Annual herb, erect or spreading. Leaves up to 30 mm long. Flower head up to 50 mm diam (Jul-Sept). Sandy areas in Namaqualand, Karoo, Namibia.

**8**          *Ursinia cakilefolia*
Up to 250 mm. Annual herb. Leaves up to 60 mm long. Flower heads up to 35 mm diam (Jul-Sept). SW.
**Similar**
**U. sericea**
Larger (up to 600 mm). Leaves grey-green. Flowers Sept-Feb.

**9**          *Arctotis diffusa (=A. canescens)*
Up to 550 mm. Bushy annual herb. Flower heads up to 50 mm diam, white to yellow or pale orange (Jul-Sept). Sandy areas in Namaqualand.

**10**          *Arctotis fastuosa*
Up to 600 mm. Annual herb. Leaves up to 150 mm long. Flower heads singly, up to 60 mm diam (Jul-Sept). Widespread in sandy areas, from Namaqualand to Namibia.

**1 BOTTERGOUSBLOM** *Arctotis gumbletonii*

Up to 250 mm. Perennial herb. Leaves up to 160 mm long, with silvery hairs. Flower head up to 55 mm diam (Jul-Sept). Namaqualand.

**2 BEETLE DAISY** *Gorteria diffusa*

Up to 300 mm. Prostrate annual. Leaves up to 50 mm long. Flower heads singly, up to 35 mm diam (Jul-Sept). Arid areas, from SW to Namaqualand.

**3 BOTTERBLOM** *Gazania krebsiana*

Up to 150 mm. Perennial herb. Leaves up to 160 mm long, woolly white beneath, shape simple to lobed. Flower head up to 60 mm diam, singly, colour varies (Jul-Sept). Widespread, from S to Botswana.

**4** *Gazania lichtensteinii*

Up to 200 mm. Annual herb. Leaves up to 40 mm long. Flower heads up to 40 mm diam (Jul-Sept). S, N and Namibia.

**5** *Berkheya zeyheri*

Up to 900 mm. Leaves up to 80 mm long. Flower head up to 90 mm diam (Oct-Jan). Grassland. Widespread in summer rainfall areas.

**6 PERDEBOS** *Didelta spinosa*

Up to 2 m. Shrub. Leaves up to 70x60 mm, slightly succulent. Flower head 40-70 mm diam (Jul-Sept). Sandy and rocky areas, from Namaqualand to Namibia.

**7 DICOMA** *Dicoma zeyheri*

Up to 300 mm. Perennial shrublet. Leaves up to 120 mm long, woolly white beneath. Flower heads up to 50 mm diam (Dec-May). Rocky, hilly areas, from E to N.

**8 BARBERTON DAISY** *Gerbera jamesonii*

Up to 400 mm. Perennial herb. Leaves up to 300 mm long. Flower head up to 80 mm diam (Aug-Dec). Well-known garden plant with many horticultural varieties. Rocky areas in N.

Similar

**HILTON DAISY** *G. aurantiaca*

Midlands in E.

**9** *Gerbera ambigua (=G. kraussii)*

Up to 300 mm. Perennial herb. Leaves up to 80 mm long. Flower heads up to 60 mm diam (Aug-Nov). Widespread in grassland in summer rainfall areas.

# TREES

Trees are woody plants over 2 m tall and with a stem over 100 mm in diameter.
They include plants from many different groups and classifications, e.g. ferns, gymnosperms such
as cycads and yellowwoods and flowering plants, both monocotyledons and dicotyledons.

In order to identify trees, consideration may have to be given to the leaf, the flower, the fruit, the bark and the overall shape of the tree. Leaf structures and terminology are shown in the accompanying illustrations. Where pertinent to identification, fruit and flowers are illustrated with the descriptions.

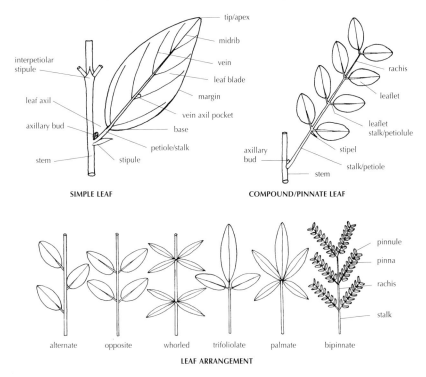

SIMPLE LEAF

COMPOUND/PINNATE LEAF

LEAF ARRANGEMENT

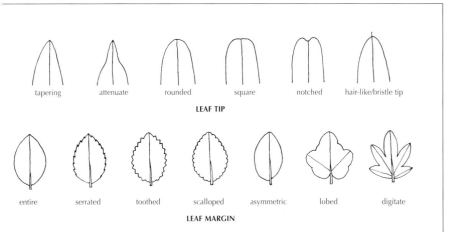

LEAF TIP: tapering, attenuate, rounded, square, notched, hair-like/bristle tip

LEAF MARGIN: entire, serrated, toothed, scalloped, asymmetric, lobed, digitate

## Scope of this chapter

Southern Africa has almost 1 500 species of trees. Many of these are insignificant and would only be of interest to the ardent botanist. They, together with other rare or sparsely distributed species, have been omitted. The chapter contains descriptions of 465 species that are most likely to be seen.

## Distribution

The trees in this chapter are representative of a wide range of habitats and climatic conditions (see map on p. 3):

» **Coastal bush.** Typical trees are the white milkwood *Sideroxylon inerme* and coastal red milkwood *Mimusops caffra*.

**Forest.** Evergreen forests are sometimes referred to as "yellowwood forests", the most conspicuous trees usually being the yellowwoods *Podocarpus* spp. The diversity of species increases in the northerly forests where a more tropical, equatorial flora is encountered. Much of the forest in southern Africa has been stripped of its biggest trees by the timber cutters of earlier times. Today it is threatened by cut-and-burn agricultural encroachment.

**Woodland.** The northern parts of southern Africa are dominated by woodland of various types. In Zimbabwe and Mozambique tall, broadleaved woodland occurs (called miombo). Bushveld refers to a mixed woodland characteristic of the northern areas of South Africa. Acacia woodland, with trees widely spaced on highly seasonal grassland plains, is typical of Botswana and eastern Namibia.

**Grassland** has few indigenous trees although stands of exotics such as bluegums and wattles have become established in most areas.

**Desert** and semi-desert (Karoo) support a sparse tree population of only very specialised, mostly succulent forms.

**Fynbos** also has very specialised trees, generally of the protea family, although evergreen forests occur within the fynbos floral region. Fynbos has become seriously infested with invasive introduced species.

**Mangroves.** This habitat with its specialised trees has been much reduced in extent.

## Dimensions

The first dimension given with each description in this chapter refers to the full height of a mature tree. Since the full size of trees varies considerably under different growing conditions, this measurement is only a rough indicator. Other measurements in the text are of leaves, flowers, pods, etc. Only the greatest dimension is given; this usually indicates length but in the case of flowers and fruit may indicate diameter. Leaf measurements refer to the length of the blade excluding the stalk. The dimensions given either consist of a range or are maximums, with smaller dimensions possible in different specimens.

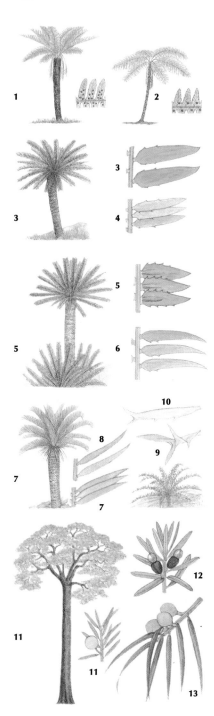

**1 COMMON TREE FERN**                    *Cyathea dregei*
2-5 m. **Sturdy** main stem. Leaves 2-3 m, **leaflet margins entire.
Sori in two rows.** In full sun. Moist savanna from coast to mountains (forest in Zimbabwe).

**2 FOREST TREE FERN**                    *Cyathea capensis*
2-4 m. Slender main stem, **leaflet margins finely serrated. Sori
singly.** Tangled hairlike mass at base of fronds. Deep forest.

**3 NATAL CYCAD**                    *Encephalartos natalensis*
3-6 m. Main stem usually erect. Leaves 1,5-3 m. **Leaflets widely
spaced, lower leaflets reduced to spines. New leaves and cones
coated with brown wool.** Rocky slopes along e escarpment.
Similar
**EASTERN CAPE CYCAD  E. altensteinii**
Leaves 3,5 m. No spines at stalk base. No wool on crown.
**4 LEBOMBO CYCAD  E. lebomboensis**
Often reclining. **Leaves overlap downwards.** Spines at leaf base.
**WATERBERG CYCAD  E. eugene-maraisii**
Leaves 1,3 m. Bluish. Leaflet teeth small or absent.
**TONGALAND CYCAD  E. ferox**
Short stem. Leaflets dark green, **lobed teeth.** Maputaland.
**POOR MAN'S CYCAD  E. villosus**
**Underground stem.** Leaves 3 m. Leaflets toothed, spines at base.
**DRAKENSBERG CYCAD  E. ghellinckii**
Leaflets needle-like. Wool covers new leaves. E escarpment.

**5 MODJADJI CYCAD**                    *Encephalartos transvenosus*
5-13 m. Main stem erect. Leaves 2,5 m. **Yellow** stalk. Leaflets
**closely spaced, overlap upwards,** toothed. Up to four large golden-brown cones. Soutpansberg and Letaba districts.
Similar
**6 BARBERTON CYCAD  E. paucidentatus**
Leaflets widely spaced. Fewer teeth, usually on lower edge. Barberton district.

**7 KEI CYCAD**                    *Encephalartos princeps*
Up to 5 m. Stems sucker from base. Leaves 1-1,3 m, **tip of leaf
stalk curves downwards. Leaflets overlap in upper half.** 1-3
cones, olive-green. Rock outcrops in Kei River catchment.
Similar
**8 KAROO CYCAD  E. lehmannii**
Leaflets **well spaced.** Sundays and Groot River catchment.

**9 EASTERN CAPE BLUE CYCAD**                    *Encephalartos horridus*
No stem. Leaves bluish-grey, top third recurved. **Leaflets deeply
lobed and twisted.** Port Elizabeth and Uitenhage district.
Similar
**10 BUSHMAN'S RIVER CYCAD  E. trispinosus**
Leaves green, **not recurved.** Leaflets **lobed only in top third** of
leaf.

**11 COMMON YELLOWWOOD**                    *Podocarpus falcatus*
10-60 m. **Bark dark purplish-brown, flaking in rough roundish
patches** on mature trees. Leaves 15-100 mm, **with twist at base.
Seeds yellow, flesh-covered** (Dec-Jun). E forest.
Similar
**12 REAL YELLOWWOOD  P. latifolius**
**Bark longitudinally fissured, peeling in strips.** Forest in S and E.
**13 HENKEL'S YELLOWWOOD  P. henkelii**
Bark **greyish**-brown, flaking in strips, **red underbark.** Leaves long,
drooping, tapering gradually. Inland forest along e escarpment.

**1 WELWITSCHIA** *Welwitschia mirabilis*
Leaves up to 3 m. Usually **flattened woody hump protruding just above ground, producing two leaves in lifetime of plant**. Stem up to 2 m above ground, 2-3 m below ground before start of tap root. Leaves grow continuously, becoming torn and tangled. Flowers cone-like, male and female on separate plants. Namib desert.

**2 WILD DATE PALM** *Phoenix reclinata*
3-10 m. Main stem often reclining, forming dense clumps. Leaves 2-4 m. **Long spines at base.** Fruit orange to brown, edible. Along watercourses, in grassland at low altitudes from SE through Africa.
**Similar**
**RAPHIA PALM** *Raphia australis*
Larger (up to 24 m). Single-stemmed. Leaves 6-10 m with red midrib. Kosi Bay area. Naturalised at Mtunzini.

**3 LALA PALM** *Hyphaene coriacea (= H. natalensis)*
3-7 m. Main stem erect or reclining, suckering from base. Leaves 2 m including stalk. **Leaf base asymmetric.** Fruit brown, 60 mm, edible. Stem tapped to make wine, leaves used for basketware. Low-lying, sandy areas in E.
**Similar**
**REAL FAN PALM** *H. petersiana (= H. ventricosa)*
Larger (up to 20 m). **Not clustering**. N Namibia, Botswana, Zimbabwe.

**4 BORASSUS PALM** *Borassus aethiopum*
Up to 20 m. Erect main stem with swelling in upper half. Leaves 4 m including stalk, **symmetric at base**. Fruit 180 mm, yellowish-orange. Mozambique and NE of region.

**5 KRANTZ ALOE** *Aloe arborescens*
Up to 3,5 m. Much-branched. Leaves grey-green, reddish in dry conditions. Flower spikes 300 mm, 2-4 per stem, sometimes yellow or orange (May-Jul). Used for fencing. Rocky hillsides, fynbos, moist and arid savanna, grassland. Widespread, from S eastwards through region.

**6 TREE ALOE** *Aloe barberiae (=A. bainesii)*
10-18 m. Main stem up to 1 m diam, bark smooth, grey. Leaves 900 mm. Flowering spikes 300 mm. Flowers pink, tipped green (Apr-Jun). Thickets, kloofs and savanna in E of region, from SE to Mozambique.

**7 QUIVER TREE** *Aloe dichotoma*
-7 m. Main stem tapering, up to 1 m diam at base, branches **spreading**. Leaves held **erect**, 350 mm. Flower spikes yellow, 300 mm, **emerging above leaves** (Jun-Jul). Hot, dry, rocky desert and semi-desert in n Cape and Namibia.
**Similar**
**GIANT QUIVER TREE** *A. pillansii*
Taller, more slender. Branches erect. Leaves curve **downwards**, lower heads **hang below leaves**. Richtersveld.

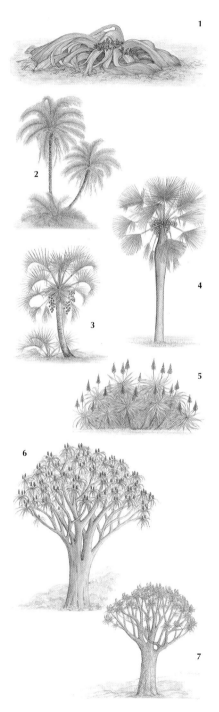

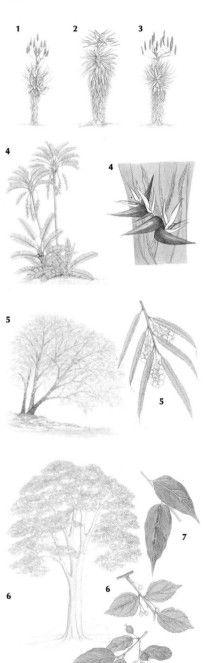

### 1 MOPANE ALOE *Aloe littoralis*

Up to 3,5 m. Leaves **erect**. Flower heads branched, flower spikes held erect. Woodland and arid savanna in N.

### 2 MOUNTAIN ALOE *Aloe marlothii*

2-5 m. Leaves 1,5 m, spines on both sides. Single, branched flower head, **spikes held horizontally, flowers along upper stalk only.** Flowers orange to red, tipped purple (May-Jul). Rocky slopes, woodland, savanna and grassland in N and E.
**Similar**
**NATAL ALOE  A. spectabilis**
1-3 flower heads, **semi-erect**, flowers all around stalk. E.
**ZIMBABWE ALOE  A. excelsa**
**Recurved leaves**. Many flower heads. S Zimbabwe and Mozambique.

### 3 BITTER ALOE  A. ferox

Up to nine erect red flower spikes. **Leaves straight.** Widespread on rocky slopes in SE.
**FAN ALOE  A. plicatilis**
Much-branched. **Grey leaves in upright "fans".** Fynbos in SW and S.
**LEBOMBO ALOE  A. spicata (=A. sessiliflora)**
Up to five yellow flower spikes. **Leaves reddish.** N and E.
**TILT-HEAD ALOE  A. speciosa**
Leaves in tilted spirals. **Red and white** flower spikes. SE.
**STRAND ALOE  A. thraskii**
**Leaves curve down.** Few yellow flower spikes. Coastal dunes from SE northwards.

### 4 NATAL WILD BANANA *Strelitzia nicolai*

3-12 m. Palm-like, in clumps. Stems smooth, marked with leaf scars. Leaves 2 m. White and blue flowers within **tiered blue sheaths.** Black seed with woolly orange cover. E coastal bush.
**Similar**
**WHITE STRELITZIA  S. alba**
Pure white flowers. S forest.
**TRANSVAAL STRELITZIA  S. caudata**
White and blue flowers in **single** blue sheaths.

### 5 WILD WILLOW *Salix mucronata*

Up to 15 m. Bark deeply fissured. Leaves hairless or silver-haired, vary from dark green to grey-green. Young stems green to reddish. Male and female trees. Woolly seeds. Alongside water throughout region.

### 6 WHITE STINKWOOD *Celtis africana*

Up to 30 m. Deciduous. Tall in forest; spreading crown in open. Bark smooth, pale grey. Leaves alternate, size variable: 20-100 mm, **strongly three-veined from asymmetric base, margin serrated in upper half, tapering abruptly to long tip.** Fruit 4 mm on 1 mm stalk (Oct-Dec). Throughout Africa.
**Similar**
**7 FALSE WHITE STINKWOOD  C. durandii**
Larger leaf tapers to long drip tip. Margin seldom serrated.
**8 NATAL WHITE STINKWOOD  C. mildbraedii**
Leaves stiff, shiny, with rounded or no serrations. Fruit 12 mm.

## 1 PIGEONWOOD — *Trema orientalis*

5-15 m. Bark smooth, grey, with raised white dots. Alternate leaves 50-100 mm, **three-veined from asymmetric base, serrations along full length of margin.** Fruit 6 mm, **in bunches on very short stalks** (Feb-Nov). Common pioneer tree, widely distributed in warm, fairly high rainfall areas. Savanna and grassland, from SE to Zimbabwe and Namibia.

## 2 THORNY ELM — *Chaetachme aristata*

5-15 m. Single or multistemmed. Bark pale grey. Zigzag branches sometimes have single or paired straight spines. Leaves leathery, with **bristle tip**, 20-100 mm, margin entire or **deeply serrated on young or coppice leaves.** Fruit 15 mm, in abundance (Apr-Dec). Forest, thicket, savanna, grassland. Common along E coast, also to Zimbabwe and Mozambique.

## 3 NAMAQUA FIG — *Ficus cordata*

Up to 10 m. Spreading crown. Bark smooth, pale grey. Rock-splitter with pale roots spreading over rock faces. Leaves 110 mm, base lobed or square. Figs 12 mm, velvety, brownish-purple, **stalkless, in pairs.** Dry, rocky areas in nw Cape and Namibia. Similar

## 4 WONDERBOOM *F.c.* subsp. *salicifolia*

Bark rough, brownish-grey (mature specimens). Leaves 80-120 mm. Figs 8 mm, red with white flecks, **on short stalks, crowded in leaf axils** towards ends of stems. Rock outcrops, woodland, savanna and grassland, from E to Botswana and Zimbabwe.

## 5 RED-LEAVED FIG — *Ficus ingens*

3-12 m. Main stem usually straggling, on rock faces. Occasionally free-standing in open country and forest. Spectacular **spring flush of coppery red leaves.** Leaves 60-150 mm, **yellow veins protrude beneath**, shape variable. Figs 13 mm in pairs in leaf axils. Savanna and grassland. Resembles (4), which has smaller figs, no red spring leaves.

## GIANT-LEAVED FIG — *Ficus lutea*

10-25 m. Huge buttressed main stems, dark grey bark. Leaves 130-400 mm, **yellowish veins, bud sheaths silvery.** Furry, stalkless, yellow figs 26 mm, **crowded in leaf axils towards ends of branches.** Forest at low altitude in N and E. Similar

## SWAMP FIG *F. trichopoda*

Smaller (5-12 m). Only tree in region with **stilt roots**, an adaptation to swampy conditions. Leaves heart-shaped with **whitish veins, tinged red.** Rose-red bud sheaths. Figs smaller, red, singly or in pairs, on short stalks. Coastal and swamp forest along E coast.

### 1 SYCAMORE FIG                *Ficus sycomorus*

10-35 m. Huge buttressed trunk. Bark powdery yellowish-orange. Leaves **rough**, 50-200 mm. Figs 30 mm, in **large branched bunches off main stems**. Riverine vegetation in NE and Namibia.
**Similar**

### 2 CAPE CLUSTER FIG   *F. sur*

Bark smooth, white to grey. Leaves **smooth**, irregularly toothed, **narrower** than in (1). **Flush of coppery new leaves in spring.** Moist savanna.

### 3 COMMON WILD FIG            *Ficus thonningii*

10-20 m. Smoothish grey bark. **Strangler.** Aerial roots. Spreading crown. Leaves very variable, 50-100 mm, shiny. **Long stalk** 45 mm. Figs 10 mm, **finely hairy, stalkless.** Widespread in woodland, rocky hillsides and forest in N and E.
**Similar**

### 4 NATAL FIG   *F. natalensis*

Leaves with rounded tip and **short stalk**, 4-20 mm. **Figs 7 mm, hairless, on stalks.** E coast forest.

### 5 FOREST FIG   *F. craterostoma*

**Blunt to concave-tipped leaves** with semi-persistent bud sheaths. **Figs without stalks.** Forest.

### 6 LARGE-LEAVED ROCK FIG        *Ficus abutilifolia*

2-10 m. **Rock-splitter.** Bark smooth, white. Conspicuous white roots. **Thick twigs.** Leaves large, 160 mm, **both surfaces sometimes woolly**, long stalk, conspicuous veins, margins wavy. Figs 16 mm, singly or in pairs, in leaf axils on terminal twigs. Rocky hills and grassland in N and E.

### 7 MOUNTAIN FIG                *Ficus glumosa*

Rock-splitter or medium tree. Bark pale, flaky, yellowish-grey. **Young leaves, leaf stalks, shoots covered in long golden hairs.** Mature leaves thick, shiny, without hairs on upper surface, 30-120 mm. Figs 15 mm, **clustered towards ends of branches.** N and E.

### 8 TRANSVAAL BEECH             *Faurea saligna*

6-10 m. Bark dark grey-black, rough. New stems red. Leaves 50-150 mm, **narrow, drooping, with pink stalk.** Spring and autumn leaves red. Flowers in drooping, **slender** spikes 150 mm (Oct-Jan). Nutlets with silvery hairs. Rocky hillsides and woodland. Inland in N and E.
**Similar**

**FOREST BEECH** *F. galpinii*
Leaves slightly broader than in (8). High altitude forest in mountains in NE.

### 9 TERBLANS   *F. macnaughtonii*

Larger (25 m). Leaves more elliptical than in (8), 70 mm, wavy margins. Forest in S and E.

### 10 BROAD-LEAVED BEECH   *Faurea rochetiana* (=*F. speciosa*)

3-5 m. Leaves 80-130 mm, **densely hairy. Veins conspicuous on both surfaces, side veins join in continuous line along wavy margin.** Autumn leaves red. E woodland and hilly grassland.
**Similar**

**MANICA BEECHWOOD** *F. rubriflora*
Flowers red. High altitude forest in Zimbabwe and Mozambique.

**1 SILVER TREE**  *Leucadendron argenteum*

Up to 10 m. Bark smooth, grey, with conspicuous leaf scars. Leaves silvery, 180 mm, clustered towards ends of branches. Male and female flowers on separate trees, surrounded by silvery bracts. Female flowers cone-like. Only on Table Mountain.

**2 DUNE YELLOWBUSH**  *Leucadendron coniferum*

Up to 4 m. Much-branched, rounded. Narrow leaves bristle-tipped, twisted 90°, clustered at ends of sturdy branches. Female cones redden seven months after flowering. Fynbos in SW.
**Similar**
**3 TALL YELLOWBUSH**  *L. eucalyptifolium*
Up to 5 m. Leaves long, narrow, 105 mm, twisted 90°, tips pointed. Tree turns yellow during long flowering season (winter-spring). Fynbos in s mountains, from Montagu to Grahamstown.
**4 ROSE COCKADE**  *L. tinctum*
Smaller (1,3 m). Shrub with stout branches. Leaves large, broad with rounded tip. **Terminal leaves yellow in flowering season.** Cones have spicy smell. Fynbos in SW.

**5 COMMON PINCUSHION**  *Leucospermum cuneiforme*

3-6 m. Usually **multistemmed shrub.** Bark rough, grey-brown, with **warty lumps at base of stems.** Leaves 110 mm with **flattened, notched, toothed tip.** Flower heads 90 mm (mostly summer). S and E coast and inland to 1 000 m.
**Similar**
**6 GREY TREE PINCUSHION**  *L. conocarpodendron*
Bark thick, dark grey. **Gnarled branches.** Subsp. *conocarpodendron* (N and W of Table Mountain): leaves hairy, **grey-green;** subsp. *viridum* (sw Cape): leaves smooth, **dark green.**
**7 NODDING PINCUSHION**  *L. cordifolium*
Smaller (2 m). Spreading shrub. Flower heads 100 mm, orange to red (autumn-spring). Fynbos in SW.

**8 ROCKET PINCUSHION**  *Leucospermum reflexum*

Up to 3 m. Spreading shrub. Stems sturdy, erect. Small, grey leaves. Common in gardens. Cedarberg fynbos.
**Similar**
**9 FIRE-WHEEL PINCUSHION**  *L. tottum*
Flower heads large, **flattened** (Sept-Jan). Fynbos in SW.

**10 COMMON SUGARBUSH**  *Protea caffra*

Up to 6 m. Stem gnarled, bark thick, fissured, black. Young stems pink. Leaves narrow, 80-150 mm. Flower heads 80 mm. Bracts pink, red to green (Oct-Jan). Widespread in grassland in summer rainfall areas.
**Similar**
**WAGON TREE**  *P. nitida*
Main stem dark, showing pale underbark. **Grey-green leaves. Flowers creamy white.** Widespread in **winter rainfall fynbos.**

**11 AFRICAN WHITE SUGARBUSH**  *Protea gaguedi*

7 m. Thick, corky, pale brown bark. Silvery hairs on young leaves. Flowers hairy, pinkish-white, 70 mm (Jan-Mar). Central and e areas.

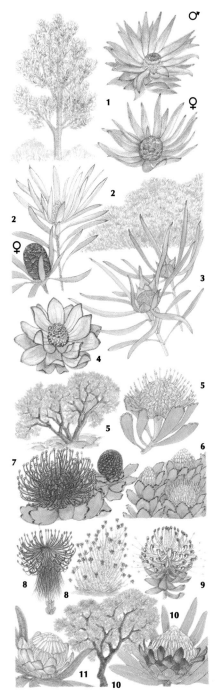

### 1 BLUE SUGARBUSH
*Protea neriifolia*

Up to 4 m. Much-branched. Bark dark grey. Leaves 150 mm, **stalkless**, usually bright green. Flower heads on short stalks within leaves (Apr-Sept). Upper flower bracts pale to deep pink, beard white to purplish-black; lower bracts curve back like wood-shavings. Coastal areas in S and E, from sea level to 1 300 m.
**Similar**
**LAUREL SUGARBUSH** *P. laurifolia*
Leaves broader, greyish, with distinct **leaf stalk**. Confined to SW.

### 2 REAL SUGARBUSH
*Protea repens*

Up to 5 m. Erect, greyish-brown stems. Leaves narrow, 130 mm, stalkless, yellow to bluish-green. Flower heads slender, bracts white to deep pink, sticky or shiny (Dec-Jun). Copious nectar a traditional source of sugar. From SW to SE.

### 3 SILVER SUGARBUSH
*Protea roupelliae*

Up to 7 m. Bark thick, black, fissured. Leaves **bluish** with silvery hairs or hairless, 160 mm, **held erect, in terminal rosettes**. Flower heads large, within rosette of leaves, inner bracts **spoon-shaped, bracts longer than densely hairy flowers** (Apr-Jun). Forms protea woodland with *P. caffra*. Summer rainfall grassland, from SE to N.

### 4 LIP-FLOWER BUSH
*Protea subvestita*

Up to 4 m. Bark smooth, grey. Leaves 80 mm in dense terminal rosettes. Young leaves and stems covered in woolly white hairs which rub off – absent on mature leaves. Flower heads small, bracts whitish to deep pink (Dec-Mar). **Tips of inner bracts curve back** to form "lip". Montane grassland above 1 200 m, often in groves.
**Similar**
**CLUSTER-HEAD SUGARBUSH** *P. welwitschii*
Flower heads in groups of 2-4. Grassland and savanna.

### 5 BEARDED SUGARBUSH
*Protea magnifica*

Up to 3 m. Leaves broad, 100 mm. Flower heads large, 120 mm, very variable, bracts yellow to deep pink, woolly tips white to purplish-brown (Jun-Jan). SW, usually above 1 200 m.

### 6 PEACH PROTEA
*Protea grandiceps*

Up to 2 m. Rounded. Leaves broad, 130 mm, blue-green. Flower heads conspicuous, bracts vary in colour, beard white to purple (Sept-Jan). From S to SE, usually above 1 200 m.

### 7 KING PROTEA
*Protea cynaroides*

Up to 2 m. Stems erect, from woody rootstock. Leaves roundish on **long red stalks**, 300 mm. Flower heads 300 mm, bracts usually pale pink, with or without soft white hairs (throughout year). Very variable. From SW to SE, coast to 1 000 m.

**1 SOURPLUM** *Ximenia caffra*

Up to 6 m. Short, slender main stem, branching low down. Bark dark, rough. Twigs end in spines. Leaves smooth, 30-80 mm. Flowers small, green (Aug-Jan). Fruit 40 mm. Savanna and grassland from E to N and NW.
**Similar**
**BLUE SOURPLUM** *X. americana*
Leaves bluish grey-green. Fruit orange.

**2 SPEKBOOM/PORKBUSH** *Portulacaria afra*

Up to 5 m. Succulent. Bark shiny grey or reddish-brown. Leaves opposite, 10-30 mm. Flowers in massed sprays on ends of branchlets (Jun-Oct). Winged seeds. Rocky hillsides, hot dry areas and moist savanna. From SE to N.

**3 WILD CUSTARD-APPLE** *Annona senegalensis*

Up to 4 m. Bark dark grey. Leaves **roundish**, 180 mm, brownish hairs on veins beneath. Flowers white, 30 mm. Fruit 50 mm, ripening orange (Sept-Mar). Woodland on sandy soils, savanna and grassland. From E to NE.

**4 STINKWOOD** *Ocotea bullata*

10-25 m. Main stem up to 1,6 m diam. Bark smooth, grey or pink when young, rough, dark when mature. Leaves alternate, large, 70-120 mm, **two or more raised bubbles in axils of lower veins.** Fruit 20 mm (Feb-Jun). Widespread in evergreen forest in S, SW and E.
**Similar**
**BASTARD STINKWOOD** *O. kenyensis*
No pockets in axils of veins.

**5 SHEPHERD'S TREE** *Boscia albitrunca*

Up to 7 m. Main stem sturdy, twisted, whitish. Compact, rounded crown. Leaves 10-50 mm, tough, velvety, in clusters, alternate on young stems. Flowers small, **no petals**, in profusion, honey-scented. Fruit 15 mm, smooth (Jan-Mar). Widespread except in S and SE where it is replaced by *B. oleoides* (**flowers with petals**).
**Similar**
**6 STINK-BUSH** *B. foetida*
Bark light brown, branches angular. **Leaves very small**, 10-25 mm. **Flowers and wood have unpleasant scent.**
**ROUGH-LEAVED SHEPHERD'S TREE** *B. angustifolia*
Densely hairy beneath leaves. Savanna in N.
**WILLOW-LEAVED BOSCIA** *B. salicifolia*
Leaves long, narrow. Savanna in N.

**7 BLACK STORM** *Cadaba aphylla*

Up to 3 m. Bark brown. Branches blue-green, ending in spiny tip. **No leaves** except on very young stems. Flowers 30 mm, in bunches on twigs. Fruit 90 mm, rough, with sticky glands (Aug-Dec). Widespread in dry interior.
**Similar**
**8 NATAL WORM BUSH** *C. natalensis*
Bark grey with raised dots. Leaves thin, 40 mm, with sharp tip. Flowers mauve. Fruit 50 mm. Woodland, from SE to Zimbabwe.
**PINK CADABA** *C. termitaria*
Bark blackish, **young stems hairy.** Savanna in N and NE.

**9 WOOLLY CAPER BUSH** *Capparis tomentosa*

Up to 10 m. Robust climber or straggling shrub. Young parts covered in velvety hairs. **Short, paired, hooked spines.** Leaves 30-80 mm, stalks velvety. Flowers in terminal clusters (Aug-Nov). Fruit 40 mm. Widespread from SE to Zimbabwe and n Botswana.

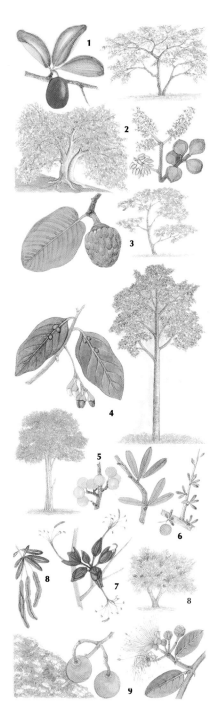

### 1 BEAD-BEAN TREE  *Maerua angolensis*

3-10 m. Bark greyish, young stems brown with raised white dots. Leaves shiny, thin, 25-70 mm, with **hairlike tip, drooping on long stalk, thickened towards leaf blade.** Flowers sweetly scented, a mass of creamy white stamens, 40 mm long, turning yellow (Aug-Oct). Pod 160 mm. Widespread in woodland and savanna, from E to N.

**Similar**

**RINGWOOD TREE**  *M. schinzii*

Leaves velvety. Along watercourses. Only in Namibia.

### 2 COMMON BUSH-CHERRY  *M. cafra*

3-5 leaflets, leathery, 100 mm, size variable. Fruit 45 mm, hanging on stout stalk. Coast to mountains. Moist savanna and grassland, from SE to N.

**FOREST BUSH-CHERRY**  *M. racemulosa*

Flowers small, stamens 10 mm long. From SE to E.

**NEEDLE-LEAVED BUSH-CHERRY**  *M. rosmarinoides*

Leaves trifoliolate, very narrow, needle-like tip. E areas.

### 3 BUTTER TREE  *Tylecodon paniculatus*

Up to 3 m. Dwarf succulent tree. Main stem fleshy; green. Peeling, yellow papery bark. Leaves fleshy, 75 mm. Flowers yellowish, hanging on slender branched stalks (Dec-Jan). Dry rocky hillsides in succulent Karoo, fynbos.

**Similar**

**PHANTOM TREE**  *Moringa ovalifolia*

Larger (up to 7 m). Stem squat, swollen. Bark smooth, shiny, pale white to copper. Leaves compound, clustered towards ends of branches. Flowers small, white, in large branched sprays (Nov-Feb). Flattish pod 400 mm. Namibia.

### 4 CHEESEWOOD  *Pittosporum viridiflorum*

3-15 m. Bark dark, rough; tastes, smells like liquorice. Leaves alternate or clustered, variable in size and shape, 100 mm. **Triangle of three small dots clearly visible in broken-off leaf stalk.** Flowers in scented terminal clusters (Sept-Nov). Fruit 10 mm, in profusion, brown when ripe, splitting to expose shiny, sticky red seeds. Widespread in S, E and NE.

### 5 RED ALDER  *Cunonia capensis*

5-18 m. Bark dark, fissured, rough in mature trees, pale and flaky when young. 3-5 pairs glossy leaflets, 70-100 mm, pink veins. **Leaf buds enclosed in large spoon-shaped flat stipules.** Flowers in spikes 200 mm (Feb-May). Fruit small, two-horned capsule, tiny sticky seeds (May-Jul). Forest, from coast to mountains in S and E.

### 6 OLDWOOD/OUHOUT  *Leucosidea sericea*

2-9 m. Bark very rough, flaky, reddish-brown. Leaves aromatic, silky white beneath, 2-3 pairs leaflets and occasional smaller pairs in between, **silky stipules.** Small flowers with silky calyx, in terminal spikes 80 mm (May-Aug). Grassland at high altitudes in E.

### 7 MOBOLA PLUM  *Parinari curatellifolia*

Up to 13 m. Spreading. Bark rough, dark grey, young stems covered in yellowish hairs. Leaves 80 mm, leathery, velvety greyish-yellow beneath. Flowers small, white, scented, in short branched heads 60 mm. Fruit 50 mm, edible (Oct-Jan). Woodland and on sandy soils in N.

**1  RED STINKWOOD**  *Prunus africana*

10-20 m. Rather weeping habit. Bark rough, dark brown. Leaves alternate, smooth, shiny, 50-150 mm, **pink stalk**. Flowers small, singly or in sprays 70 mm. Fruit 10 mm (Sept-Nov). Evergreen forest, from SE to N.

**2  FLAT-CROWN**  *Albizia adianthifolia*

10-25 m. Bark pale brown. Leaves 400 mm, 4-7 pinna pairs, leaflets 20 mm. Leaf stalk and rachis covered in rusty velvety hairs. **Large fat gland at base of leaf stalk.** Flower heads held above new leaves (Aug-Dec). Cream, papery pods 125 mm, in profusion. Coastal forest and woodland.
Similar
**BITTER FALSE-THORN  A. amara**
Very fine leaflets, golden velvety hairs. Moist and arid savanna in N.
**PURPLE-LEAVED FALSE-THORN  A. antunesiana**
Can be confused with *Burkea africana* (p. 252). **Leaflets pale beneath.** Moist and arid savanna in N.
**BROAD-POD FALSE-THORN  A. forbesii**
Very fine leaflets. Broad, flat, woody, reddish-brown pods 140 mm. Moist savanna in NE.
**COMMON FALSE-THORN  A. harveyi**
Leaflets small, narrow, **sickle-shaped with pointed tip**. Moist and arid savanna in NW to NE.

**3  WORM-BARK FALSE-THORN  A. anthelmintica**
Smaller (3-10 m). Multistemmed. **Twigs sometimes end in spike.** Leaves 80 mm, 2-4 pinna pairs, leaflets shiny. **Completely covered in white flower heads** before leaves in spring (Aug-Sept). Pale cream pods 100 mm. Savanna, from NE to NW.

**4  PAPERBARK FALSE-THORN  A. tanganyicensis**
Thin red papery peeling bark reveals smooth, shiny, creamy-grey underbark. Pods dark brown, 300 mm (Sept-Dec). Rocky areas in savanna in N.

**5  LARGE-LEAVED FALSE-THORN**  *Albizia versicolor*

7-20 m. Bark dark grey, rough in mature specimens. Leaves 300 mm, 1-3 pinna pairs, leaflets 55 mm, shiny above, **greyish beneath, with rusty velvety hairs.** New leaves reddish-brown. Flower heads large, white (Oct-Dec). Pods thin, yellowish to deep red or pale brown, 200 mm. Woodland in N and NE.

**6  ANA TREE**  *Faidherbia albida*

Up to 30 m. Often **leafless in summer**, coming into flower and leaf in autumn. Bark grey-brown, smoothish. **Young stems white.** Thorns straight, 20 mm. Leaves 130 mm, leaflets small. Flowers in **spikes 170 mm.** Pods 150 mm, in bunches (Mar-Aug). Woodland, riverine vegetation and savanna, NE to NW.

**7  FLAME THORN**  *Acacia ataxacantha*

Up to 10 m. Tree or scrambler. Bark light brown, flaking, with longitudinal fissures. Thorns short, hooked, scattered along stems. Leaves 140 mm, leaflets 5 mm, **dark green, with large, paired, triangular stipules. Creamy-yellow flower spikes** 100 mm (Sept-Feb). Pods 80 mm (Dec-Jun). Watercourses in savanna in N and E.
Similar
**PRICKLY THORN  A. brevispica**
Thorns on **pale longitudinal ridges**. Leaves yellowish-green, velvety beneath. Flowers pale **yellow balls. Brown pods covered in velvety hairs.** Drier areas, from SE to E.
**RIVER CLIMBING THORN  A. schweinfurthii**
Thorns, in rows, on dark ridges. **Leaves dark green.** Flowers **creamy-white balls**. Riverine vegetation in E and N.
**COAST CLIMBING THORN  A. kraussiana**
Only *Acacia* with **tendrils**. Large leaflets. Flowers **creamy-white balls.** E to NE coast.

## 1 COMMON HOOK-THORN   *Acacia caffra*

Up to 12 m. Twisting main stem, **drooping foliage. Bark rough, grey-brown.** Thorns in **hooked pairs.** Leaves 230 mm, **leaflets 7 mm.** Leaf stalk with prickles beneath. Flower spikes 140 mm (Sept-Nov). Pods 160 mm. Woodland and grassland in SE, E and N within South Africa.

**Similar**

**BLUE THORN  *A. erubescens***

Papery bark. Bluish hooked thorns. Fine blue-green leaflets. Arid savanna and grassland in N.

**PLATE THORN  *A. fleckii***

Very thorny. Blue-green leaflets. Forms thickets. Arid savanna in N.

## 2 MONKEY THORN   *Acacia galpinii*

18-35 m. Main stem straight, branches massive, flattish crown. Bark yellow, flaky, maturing dark grey, fissured. Thorns hooked, dark brown. Leaves 150 mm, leaflets 4-11 mm. Flower spikes 90 mm (Sept-Oct). Pods 280 mm, woody. Woodland, near water, and grassland in N and NE.

## 3 RED THORN   *Acacia gerrardii*

Up to 8 m. Main stem straight, branching high up. Crown flattish, not very spreading. Bark dark grey, fissured, red in the grooves. **Young stems orange.** Thorns **straight or slightly curved.** Leaves 100 mm, leaflets 7 mm. **Young leaves, branchlets, pods covered in velvety grey hairs.** Flowers **massed among leaves.** Pods red to grey-brown, 160 mm (Dec-May). Widespread in woodland and grassland in N and E.

## 4 CAMEL THORN   *Acacia erioloba*

Up to 11 m. Spreading crown. Bark rough, fissured, grey to brown. Thorns straight, 60 mm. Leaves grey-green, 100 mm, leaflets 13 mm. Scented flowers (Jul-Sept). Pods woody, **velvety**, 130 mm long and **25 mm thick.** Dry central and w areas.

**Similar**

**GREY CAMEL THORN  *A. haematoxylon***

Tiny leaflets with velvety hairs. Long, slender, velvety grey pods. W areas and Kalahari.

**CANDLE THORN  *A. hebeclada***

Woody, swollen pods, **held erect.** Arid central and w savanna.

## 5 SWEET THORN   *Acacia karroo*

4-10 m, up to 20 m. **Very variable growth form.** Spreading, rounded crown. Thorns 70 mm. Leaves 10-100 mm, leaflets 3-10 mm. Scented flowers in clusters **on ends of branchlets** (Oct-Feb). Pods **sickle-shaped**, 260 mm, in clusters. Widespread except Botswana.

**Similar**

**FALSE UMBRELLA THORN  *A. luederitzii***

Multistemmed, much-branched, forming thickets. Var. *luederitzii:* spines **not enlarged**; Namibia and Botswana. Var. *retinens:* spines **abnormally enlarged**; NE.

**BLACK THORN  *A. mellifera***

Branches rigid, blackish. Thorns hooked. Only 1-4 pairs **grey-green leaflets.** Stubby pods, 70 mm. Arid central and nw savanna.

## 6 KNOB THORN   *Acacia nigrescens*

7-20 m. Bark rough with **spine-tipped knobs**, sometimes absent on older trees. Thorns small, hooked. Leaves 80 mm, **leaflets in 1-2 pairs, large**, 30 mm. Leafless tree covered in pink buds, then scented, creamy spikes (Aug-Sept). Pods thin, 110-140 mm. Savanna in NE.

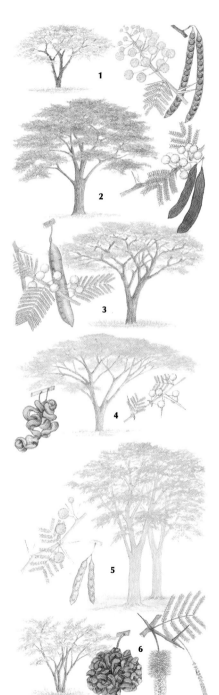

### 1  SCENTED THORN · *Acacia nilotica*

Up to 6 m. Bark rough, fissured, blackish. Thorns **white, straight,** 90 mm. Leaves 40 mm, six pinna pairs, leaflets 4 mm. Flowers scented, **up to eight per node, on new growth** (Sept-Jan). Pods **beaded**, 200 mm, drying sticky black. Central, e and n savanna.

**Similar**

Members of the *Acacia* genus are the typical thorn trees of Africa, with compound leaves and a variety of spines. They differ in growth patterns and other respects.

**WHITE THORN  A. polyacantha**

Up to 20 m. Bark **pale** with peeling, corky flakes. Hooked thorns. Flowers in white spikes. Zimbabwe and ne South Africa.

**THREE-HOOK THORN  A. senegal**

2-5 m. Single or multistemmed. Bark greyish-yellow, papery. **Hooked thorns in threes: two up, one down.** Small leaves, 40-55 mm. White flower spikes. Pods thin, short, broad, 70 mm. Savanna in E, N and W.

### 2  SPLENDID ACACIA · *Acacia robusta*

6-20 m. Dense, spreading crown. Bark rough, grey-black. Thorns straight, 110 mm, sometimes absent. Leaves **dark green**, 90 mm, 2-6 pinna pairs, leaflets 12 mm. **Flowers among leaves**, scented (Jul-Oct). Pods **woody**, 70-160 mm. Often near watercourses. Central, e and n savanna.

### 3  PAPERBARK THORN · *Acacia sieberiana*

7-15 m. Bark **conspicuous, rough, peeling, grey-yellow.** Thorns **straight, white,** 50 mm. Leaves 100 mm, 3-20 pinna pairs, leaflets 6 mm. Branchlets, leaves and flower stalks can be covered in dense golden hairs. Flowers scented (Sept-Nov). Pods woody, grey-brown, 200 mm. Central, e and n grassland and savanna.

### 4  UMBRELLA THORN · *Acacia tortilis*

5-20 m. **Flat crown.** Bark rough, grey-black. **Thorns in pairs: hooked, 15 mm long; or straight and thin, 90 mm long; or one hooked, one straight.** Leaves small, 30 mm, 4-10 pinna pairs, leaflets 2 mm. **Flowers small, white balls**, in clusters on old wood (Oct-Feb). Pods in curled clusters. Central, e and n dry woodland.

### 5  FEVER TREE · *Acacia xanthophloea*

10-25 m. Bark smooth with yellow powdery surface. Thorns **straight,** 110 mm. Leaves 100 mm, 2-9 pinna pairs, leaflets 8 mm. Flowers scented (Aug-Nov). Pods in bunches, papery, flat, straight, 130 mm. Low-lying areas near water, sometimes forming forest stands. NE.

### 6  SICKLE BUSH · *Dichrostachys cinerea*

2-7 m. Multistemmed shrub. Stems light brown to greyish, deeply grooved. **Woody, spine-tipped twigs.** Leaves 250 mm, up to eight pinna pairs, leaflets grey to olive-green, 3-11 mm. Flowers bicoloured, 60 mm (Oct-Jan). Pods in **curled clusters**, 100 mm diam. Subspecies differ mainly in size. Forms thickets in overgrazed areas. Central, e and n woodland.

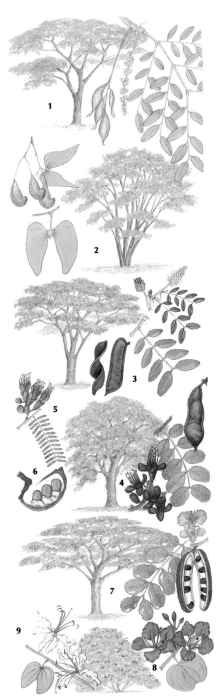

### 1 WILD SYRINGA — *Burkea africana*

5-15 m. Bark rough, flaking, dark grey. **Tips of young branches velvety, reddish-brown.** Leaves 400 mm, clustered at ends of branches, 2-4 pinna pairs, 5-11 leaflets per pinna, 60 mm. Flowers hang in spikes of 240 mm towards ends of branchlets (Sept-Nov). Pods thin, flat, 80 mm. Savanna in n half of region.

### 2 MOPANE — *Colophospermum mopane*

4-18 m. **Bark deeply fissured, flaking,** greyish-white to blackish. **"Butterfly" leaves,** drooping, each lobe 45-100 mm, stalk 40 mm. Flowers small, in short hanging sprays. Pods leathery, 50 mm, in clusters, **not** splitting on tree. Single seed **covered with red sticky dots.** N.

**Similar**

**LARGE FALSE MOPANE** *Guibourtia coleosperma*
Leaflets **sickle-shaped**, with **short stalks**. Extreme N.

**SMALL FALSE MOPANE** *Guibourtia conjugata*
**Bark smooth.** Leaflets with **rounded tips, very short stalks.** Pods split open on tree. Extreme N and NE.

### 3 MSASA — *Brachystegia spiciformis*

8-18 m. Bark dark grey, rough and fissured, smooth when young. Leaves 200 mm, hanging, **four pairs leaflets, terminal pair largest**, 25-80 mm. **Pinkish-red flush of new leaves.** Flowers scented (Aug-Nov). Pods woody, 140 mm, **hidden among leaves.** Woodland in N and NE.

**Similar**

**MUNONDO** *Julbernardia globiflora*
Six pairs leaflets, largest in middle; pods velvety, held above leaves. NE.

### 4 WEEPING BOER-BEAN — *Schotia brachypetala*

3-22 m. Bark rough, grey-brown. Leaves 180 mm, **4-6 pairs leaflets**, 25-80 mm, base asymmetric, leaf stalk sometimes winged. New leaves coppery. Flowers in dense clusters **on old wood, petals absent, stamens joined at base** (Aug-Nov). Pods woody, 60-160 mm, splitting on tree. Near termite mounds and watercourses in woodland in E and NE.

**Similar**

### 5 KAROO BOER-BEAN — *S. afra*

Smaller (up to 5 m). Leaves **fine, clustered on side shoots, 6-18 pairs leaflets**, 25 mm. **Flowers with petals.** S coast and Namaqualand.

### 6 DWARF BOER-BEAN — *S. capitata*

Smaller (up to 5 m). Multistemmed or **scrambling shrub.** Leaves smaller than in (4). **Flowers have well-developed petals (throughout summer).** Lowlands in E and NE.

### 7 POD MAHOGANY — *Afzelia quanzensis*

10-20 m. Bark grey, smooth with flaky patches. Leaves drooping, 350 mm, 4-7 pairs leaflets, 90 mm, twist in leaflet stalk. Flowers held above leaves (Oct-Dec). **Large, woody pods**, 100-170 mm. Woodland and dry forest in NE.

### 8 PRIDE-OF-DE KAAP — *Bauhinia galpinii*

2-5 m. Scrambling shrub. Leaves 70 mm, **deeply notched.** Flowers 80 mm, in branched clusters (throughout summer). Pods hard, 80 mm. Woodland in NE.

**Similar**

### 9 COFFEE NEAT'S FOOT — *B. petersiana*

**Leaves bilobed, notched almost half the length.** Central and n areas.

**BUSH NEAT'S FOOT** *B. tomentosa*
Leaves joined about halfway. **Flowers yellow, bell-shaped.** NE.

**1  SJAMBOK POD**                    *Cassia abbreviata*

3-6 m. Bark rough, dark brown. Leaves 300 mm, 5-12 pairs
leaflets, 30-60 mm. Flowers scented, 40 mm, massed in large
clusters on ends of twigs (spring), with or without new leaves
(Aug-Oct). **Pods long, cylindrical, hanging,** 900 mm, velvety
when young. Open woodland near watercourses and termite
mounds in NE.

**2  AFRICAN WATTLE**            *Peltophorum africanum*

4-8 m. Often multistemmed, branching low down, with spreading
crown. Bark smooth when young, becoming rough grey-brown.
Leaves 200 mm, 4-7 pinna pairs, 10-23 pairs leaflets, 7 mm,
asymmetric base. Young leaves, flower buds and young pods covered in fine rusty hairs. Flowers 20 mm with crinkly petals, in
erect, terminal sprays 150 mm (Sept-Apr). Pods flat, leathery, 50-
100 mm, in hanging bunches. Open woodland in n half of region.

**3  WILD LABURNUM**                 *Calpurnia aurea*

3-9 m. Often multistemmed, bark pale brown, darker with age.
Leaves 200 mm, drooping, up to 15 pairs leaflets plus terminal
one, 25-40 mm, soft, grey beneath. Flowers 25 mm, in hanging
bunches 250 mm long (throughout summer). Pods 100 mm,
papery, in hanging bunches. Forest, bushveld, forest margins and
grassland in E and SE.

**4  BLOSSOM TREE (KEURBOOM)**       *Virgilia oroboides*

Up to 9 m. Crown sparse, spreading. Bark smooth, light grey
when young; rough, dark grey when mature. Leaves 200 mm, 5-
20 pairs leaflets plus terminal one, 25 mm. Flowers 13 mm, white
to deep pink, in dense sprays 100 mm, scented (Aug-Jan). Velvety
pods 80 mm. Forest margins and watercourses along S and SW
coast.

**5  TREE WISTARIA**             *Bolusanthus speciosus*

4-10 m. Crown narrow, with drooping foliage. Bark blackish,
rough and deeply grooved. Leaves 300 mm, 3-7 pairs leaflets plus
terminal one, 70 mm, base asymmetric. Flowers pale blue to violet, in hanging bunches 200 mm (Sept-Nov). Pods narrow, 100
mm, papery, in hanging clusters. Wooded grassland, on heavy
soils near water along escarpment in N and E, plus N-central
areas.

**6  CAPE RATTLE-POD**              *Crotalaria capensis*

2-5 m. Main stem slender, bark light brown, fissured. Leaves 100
mm, leaflets thin, blue-green beneath, 60 mm, with bristle tip.
**Two leaf-like stipules at base of leaf stalk.** Flowers 25 mm, in
sprays 200 mm (Oct-Apr). Inflated pods 80 mm, rattle in wind
when ripe. Forest margins and fynbos along S, SE and E coast and
escarpment.

**7  WATER BLOSSOM PEA**          *Podalyria calyptrata*

2-4 m. Leaves 45 mm. Flowers mauve to pink, 25 mm (Jul-Sept),
sweetly scented. Pods flat, furry, 40 mm. Forest margins and along
streams in mountains in SW.

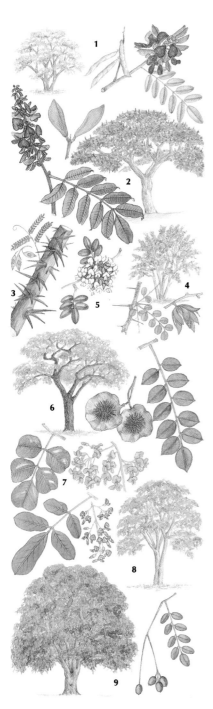

### 1 CORK BUSH  *Mundulea sericea*

1,5-4 m. **Bark corky, pale brown, deeply grooved.** Leaves covered in **silvery hairs**, 4-10 pairs leaflets plus terminal one, 20-60 mm. Flowers 20 mm, in bunches 140 mm (Oct-Feb). Pods velvety, 75-100 mm. On sandy soils in open woodland in N and NE.

### 2 UMZIMBEET  *Millettia grandis*

10-25 m. **Bark light grey-brown, flaking.** Leaves 250 mm, 3-4 pairs leaflets plus terminal one, 20-50 mm, **side veins parallel, evenly spaced. Stipel at base of each leaflet.** Flower heads 250 mm (Nov-Mar) and velvety pods, 150 mm, **held erect above leaves.** Forest along E coast.
**Similar**
**GIANT UMZIMBEET  M. sutherlandii**
Bark smooth. Leaflets smaller, rounder. Flowers in lax sprays. Pods hang down.

### 3 THORNY ROPE  *Dalbergia armata*

Up to 30 m. Robust climber. **Woody spines** 100 mm. Leaves fine, 80 mm, 10-20 pairs leaflets plus terminal one, 6-11 mm, pale beneath. Flowers small, creamy white, in clusters of 100 mm **towards ends of horizontal branches** (Oct-Nov). Pods flat, papery, 50 mm. Forest in E.

### 4 ZEBRAWOOD  *Dalbergia melanoxylon*

Up to 7 m. Straggling shrub. Stem and branches with spines. Leaves clustered on side branchlets, 8-13 leaflets, alternate. White flowers in sprays 100 mm. Pods 70 mm. Woodland in N and NE.
**Similar**
### 5 GLOSSY FLAT-BEAN  D. nitidula
Robust. **No spines.** 4-7 pairs leaflets plus terminal one.
**CLIMBING FLAT-BEAN  D. obovata**
Robust climber or tree. **Young twigs twine. Large leaflets blue-grey beneath, wavy margins.** E coast.

### 6 KIAAT  *Pterocarpus angolensis*

5-16 m. Bark dark grey, rough. Leaves 300 mm, 5-9 pairs leaflets plus terminal one, 25-70 mm, bristle-tipped. Flowers 20 mm, in hanging bunches 200 mm (Dec-Feb). Pods 100 mm diam. Woodland in N and NE.
**Similar**
### 7 ROUND-LEAVED KIAAT  P. rotundifolius
**1-3 pairs rounded leaflets** plus terminal one, 150-300 mm, **parallel side veins, wavy margins.** Flowers conspicuous, with crinkly petals. Pods **without bristles over seed case.**

### 8 APPLE-LEAF  *Lonchocarpus capassa*

5-15 m. Bark pale grey-brown, flaky. Leaves 200 mm, 1-3 pairs leaflets, 40-100 mm, plus large terminal one, 150 mm. Shiny above, velvety grey-green beneath. Flowers in sprays 150 mm (Oct-Nov). Pods 120 mm. Woodland in N and NE.

### 9 NYALA TREE  *Xanthocercis zambesiaca*

Up to 30 m. Bark rough, dark brown. Leaves 150 mm, up to seven pairs alternate leaflets plus terminal one, 55 mm. Crushed leaves have unpleasant smell. Flowers small, in sprays 50-100 mm (Sept-Dec). Fruit 25 mm. Riverine vegetation in NE.

## 1 COMMON CORAL TREE — *Erythrina lysistemon*

3-10 m. Bark pale grey-brown with scattered thorns. Leaves 220 mm, terminal leaflet 125 mm, stalk 160 mm, main vein with prickles. Two long glands at base of leaflets. Flowers in **slender, erect heads** 90 mm, standard petal **narrow, enclosing** stamens (Jun-Oct). Pods 200 mm. Central, e and ne woodland.
Similar
## 2 COAST CORAL TREE — *E. caffra*
**No prickles** on leaf stalk. Flowers in **dense, broad heads.** Standard petal **curved back** to display stamens. Coastal forest in S and E.

## 3 BROAD-LEAVED CORAL TREE — *Erythrina latissima*

4-12 m. **Bark rough, corky, grey. Leaves very large, leathery,** terminal leaflet 250 mm. Compact flower heads 250 mm, stalk 300 mm, **held horizontally** (Aug-Sept). Calyx brownish-red. **Large, cylindrical pods** 300 mm. Woodland in E and NE.
Similar
## RED-HOT-POKER TREE — *E. abyssinica*
**Leaves smaller,** terminal leaflet 140 mm. Flower heads **held erect. Calyx scarlet.** Zimbabwe.
## NAMIB CORAL TREE — *E. decora*
Terminal leaflet roundish, 180 mm. Flower buds covered in white hairs. N Namibia.

## 4 SMALL KNOBWOOD — *Zanthoxylum capense*

2-15 m. Bark dark grey with **cone-shaped knobs tipped with short straight spines.** Leaves in clusters, 40-200 mm, **leaflets small,** 4-10 pairs plus terminal one, 10-60 mm, **margin finely scalloped, base with two small hard lobes,** covered in clear gland dots (against the light). **Citrus-scented when crushed.** Flowers small, in short sprays (Oct-Feb). Fruit 5 mm. Woodland in E and NE.
Similar
## 5 KNOBWOOD — *Z. davyi*
Larger (10-24 m). **Large, woody knobs**, 60 mm, with **upward-curving spines. Leaflets larger,** 20-100 mm. Forest.

## 6 CAPE CHESTNUT — *Calodendrum capense*

8-25 m. Bark smooth, pale grey, stem buttressed in older specimens. Leaves 60-220 mm, **scattered gland dots (clear against sun).** Flowers 60 mm, in sprays 200 mm (spring). Large woody fruit 60 mm, splitting into five lobes. Large black seeds. Forest, scrub, coast to mountains, from S to Zimbabwe.

## 7 WHITE IRONWOOD — *Vepris lanceolata*

5-20 m. Bark smooth, light grey. Leaves leathery, leaflets 50-120 mm, shiny, **stalkless, gland-dotted.** Leaf stalk 150 mm. Lemon-scented when crushed. Flowers, fruit in **branched, terminal heads** 120 mm (Dec-Jan). Fruit four-lobed, 5 mm, **ripens black.** Forest and thicket in E and SE.
Similar
## 8 BUSHVELD WHITE IRONWOOD — *V. reflexa*
Smaller (2-6 m). Leaflets with stalks, leaves drooping. Fruit 12 mm, ripens red. Woodland in NE.

## 9 HORSEWOOD — *Clausena anisata*

3-10 m. Leaves clustered towards ends of branches, 300 mm, up to 17 leaflets, 10-60 mm, gland-dotted, margins scalloped, **asymmetric at base, lowest leaflets much smaller. Crushed leaves have strong, unpleasant smell (aniseed).** Flowers creamy yellow, in sprays 160 mm (May-Aug). Fruit 7 mm. Thicket and forest in S and SE.

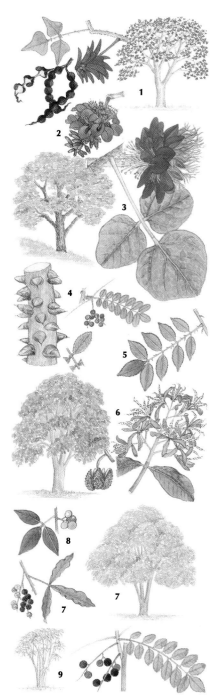

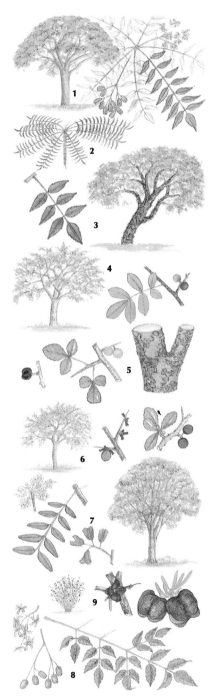

### 1 WHITE SYRINGA                      *Kirkia acuminata*

6-15 m. Bark smooth to flaky grey. Leaves clustered towards ends of branches, sticky when young, **6-10 pairs large leaflets** plus terminal one, 20-80 mm, **base asymmetric**, margin serrated. Stalk 30-100 mm. Beautiful autumn colours. Flowers Oct-Nov. Fruit 15 mm, splitting into four. Woodland and rocky hillsides in NE.
**Similar**

### 2 MOUNTAIN SYRINGA  *K. wilmsii*
**10-15 pairs smaller leaflets**, 15 mm. Coppery in autumn. Confined to n South Africa.

### 3 RED-STEM CORKWOOD            *Commiphora harveyi*

5-15 m. **Bark dark green, with large, papery, coppery pieces peeling off. No spines.** Leaves 200 mm, three pairs leaflets plus terminal one, 50-70 mm. Seed with **four-lobed** pseudaril. Hot, rocky valleys along E coast and escarpment.
**Similar**
**FOREST CORKWOOD  *C. woodii***
Bark **not** peeling. Forest along E coast and escarpment.
**PAPERBARK CORKWOOD  *C. marlothii***
Bark green, with **large, yellow, papery sheets peeling off.** Woodland and arid rocky areas in N.
**ZEBRA-BARK CORKWOOD  *C. merkeri***
Grey-green bark with horizontal blackish stripes. Arid savanna in N.
**HAIRY CORKWOOD  *C. africana***
Bark **not** peeling. **Branchlets spine-tipped.** Leaflets velvety. Savanna in N and NE.
**SAND CORKWOOD  *C. angolensis***
**Branchlets not spine-tipped.** Trifoliolate or four pairs velvety leaflets. On Kalahari sands in central, n and nw areas.

### 4 VELVET CORKWOOD                  *Commiphora mollis*

Up to 8 m. Bark grey or green, **flaking.** Leaves 300 mm, 2-6 pairs leaflets plus terminal one, 60 mm, velvety hairs beneath. Fruit velvety. Dry woodland in N.

### 5 GREEN-STEM CORKWOOD        *Commiphora neglecta*

3-5 m. Usually multistemmed with arching branches. Pale, papery, flaking outer bark over dark green underbark. Spine-tipped branchlets. Bushveld in N and E within South Africa.

### 6 TALL COMMON CORKWOOD   *Commiphora glandulosa*

Up to 8 m. Bark grey-green, peeling in small papery flakes. Branchlets end in spines. Leaves usually simple, leaflets 75 mm. **Fruit oval.** Central and n savanna.
**Similar**
**COMMON CORKWOOD  *C. pyracanthoides***
Smaller (1-3 m). Bark grey reddish-green. Leaves clustered on spine-tipped branchlets.

### 7 SNEEZEWOOD                      *Ptaeroxylon obliquum*

7-20 m. Bark rough, fissured and flaking (smooth grey when young). Leaves 250 mm, 3-7 pairs leaflets, 13-50 mm. Unpleasant scent when crushed. Flowers in bunches (Aug-Nov). Fruit bilobed capsule, reddish-brown, 20 mm, seeds winged. E forest.

### 8 SYRINGA                              *Melia azederach*

Widespread in disturbed areas and riverine vegetation. Introduced from India; invasive.

### 9 CHINESE LANTERNS                *Nymania capensis*

Up to 4 m. Bark dark grey. Leaves in clusters on short side shoots. Flowers 30 mm (from Jul). **Inflated, papery pods** 40 mm. Hot, dry areas in SW.

## 1 WILD HONEYSUCKLE TREE     *Turraea floribunda*

3-10 m. Bark grey or brown. **Branches horizontal.** Young stems and leaves velvety. Leaves 25-150 mm, **conspicuous herringbone veins**. Flowers 55 mm (Sept-Feb), strongly scented. Fruit shiny, woody, 25 mm, splitting to reveal red seeds. Forest and woodland in E and NE.
Similar
## 2 SMALL HONEYSUCKLE TREE   *T. obtusifolia*

Smaller (1-3 m). Bark with rusty spots. Leaves clustered, 50 mm, **slightly lobed towards tip**. Flowers **unscented**. Coastal forest and central, e and ne woodland.

**LOWVELD HONEYSUCKLE TREE   *T. nilotica***
Leaves large, 160 mm, hairy beneath, tip rounded. Ne savanna.

## 3 CAPE ASH     *Ekebergia capensis*

10-35 m. Main stem sometimes fluted. Bark grey-brown, rough, flaking. Leaves hanging, arranged spirally towards ends of branchlets, 3-5 pairs leaflets, without stalks except terminal one, 150 mm. Flowers small, in spays 80 mm (Aug-Dec). Fruit 20 mm. Forest, riverine woodland and savanna, from coast to about 1 500 m in e half of region.
Similar
**WILD PLUM  *Harpephyllum caffrum***
See p. 260. **Whorled** leaves, not hanging.
**ROCK ASH  *E. pterophylla***
Botanically similar but smaller (up to 5 m). 1-2 pairs leaflets with rounded tips. **Winged stalk between leaflets.** Forest margins, rock outcrops and along e escarpment, from E to N.

## 4 NATAL MAHOGANY     *Trichilia emetica*

8-20 m. Bark smooth, dark grey or brown. 3-5 pairs leaflets plus terminal one, 150 mm, **brownish hairs beneath, rounded tip.** Flowers silvery green, velvety, 16 mm, in dense bunches (Sept-Nov). Fruit 25 mm with **distinct neck, pointed tip**, velvety, splitting into three segments. Six black seeds with red cover. Woodland, riverine vegetation and savanna at low altitudes in E.
Similar
## 5 FOREST MAHOGANY   *T. dregeana*

Larger (10-35 m). Leaves very dark green, almost hairless beneath, tips of leaflets pointed. **Fruit with indented tip, no neck.** Evergreen forest.

## 6 SEPTEMBER BUSH     *Polygala myrtifolia*

1-3 m. Slender, much-branched. Leaves 20-50 mm, soft with **bristle tip**. Flowers have keeled petals with **feathery crest** (throughout year). Fruit a slightly winged capsule. Forest margins, dune bush and open hillsides in S and E.

## 7 VIOLET BUSH     *Securidaca longepedunculata*

Up to 6 m. Slender. Bark smooth, greyish-white. Leaves 10-50 mm, sometimes needle-like. Flowers in short bunches 70 mm (Aug-Nov), strong violet scent. Seeds with wing, 40 mm. Woodland and arid savanna on sandy soils in NE.

## 8 COMMON PHEASANT-BERRY   *Margaritaria discoidea*

5-15 m. Bark **rough, flaking**, grey or brown. **Branches horizontal on young trees. Leaves produced on one plane**, 20-100 mm, with herringbone veins. Flowers small (Sept-Nov). Fruit small trilobed capsule, 10 mm. Coastal and riverine forest in E and NE.
Similar
**POTATO BUSH  *Phyllanthus reticulatus***
Scrambling shrub. Leaves small, alternate, on side twigs; compound in appearance. Round fruit 6 mm, reddish-brown to black. Characteristic **potato smell** given off by flowers, especially in evening. Thicket and riverine vegetation in warm lowland areas. E coast, NE and N.

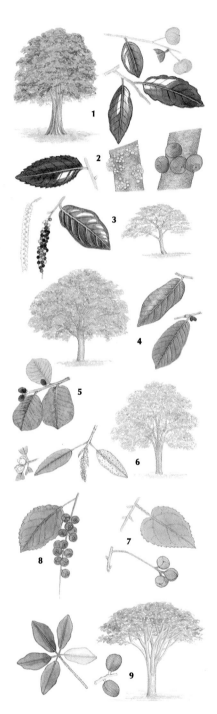

**1 FOREST IRONPLUM**                          *Drypetes gerrardii*

6-20 m. Main stem **fluted, buttressed**, bark grey. **Branches at right angles to trunk.** Branchlets square with **dense orange hairs.** Leaves 40-150 mm, **brownish-orange hairs on stalk.** Flowers Sept-Nov. Fruit 13 mm, softly hairy. Forest, woodland and savanna on e escarpment.

Similar

**2 NATAL IRONPLUM** *D. natalensis*

Smaller (3-10 m). Leaves stiff, **held on one plane, margin with spine-tipped serrations.** Flowers and fruit on old stems, fruit 25 mm. Forest along E coast.

**3 TASSEL BERRY**                          *Antidesma venosum*

3-7 m. Bark flaky. Leaves 25-150 mm, velvety brownish hairs beneath. **Conspicuous veins looping along margins.** Flowers in dangling spikes (Jan-May), male and female on separate trees. Fruit 10 mm, fleshy, in dangling bunches 120 mm. Forest margins and wooded grassland in E, NE and N.

**4 MITZEERI**                          *Bridelia micrantha*

7-15 m. Leaves arranged symmetrically, 60-100 mm, smooth **herringbone veins run to margin.** Red-gold in autumn, spring flush coppery red. Flowers very small (Aug-Oct). Fruit 10 mm. Forest and woodland in low-lying areas in E and NE.

Similar

**5 VELVET SWEETBERRY** *B. mollis*

Sparse crown. Bark dark grey, flaking. Leaves broad, 25-130 mm, **covered in soft hairs.** Rocky areas and arid savanna in N.

**BLUE SWEETBERRY** *B. cathartica*

Scrambling shrub or tree. Leaves small, **bluish-grey beneath.** Riverine thicket in NE and N.

**6 LAVENDER FEVER-BERRY**                          *Croton gratissimus*

2-15 m. Bark rough. Young stems shiny, silvery yellow with brown dots. Leaves 25-90 mm, shiny above, silvery with **dense orange speckles beneath.** Stalk 30 mm. Flowers on dangling spikes 100 mm (throughout summer). Fruit three-chambered silver capsule, 12 mm, with orange speckles. Bushveld, rock outcrops and savanna in n half of region.

Similar

**7 LARGE FEVER-BERRY** *C. megalobotrys*

Bark smooth. Dense crown. Leaves 25-180 mm. Fruit 35 mm. Riverine vegetation and savanna in N.

**8 FOREST FEVER-BERRY** *C. sylvaticus*

Tall, straight main stem 1 m diam. Leaves 60-150 mm, two knob-like glands where stalk and leaf blade meet. Fruit soft, 13 mm. Forest and woodland in E.

**9 MANKETTI TREE**                          *Schinziophyton (=Ricinodendron) rautanenii*

10-20 m. Bark smooth. 5-7 leaflets, 60-110 mm, pale grey beneath, hairy. Stalk 150 mm, covered with rusty hairs. Flowers yellow, in sprays 120 mm (Oct-Nov). Fruit 35 mm, velvety, enclosing single, hard seed. On Kalahari sands, woodland and arid savanna in N.

**1 TAMBOTI** *Spirostachys africana*

5-10 m. Main stem tall, straight. **Bark black, rough, thick, cracked in rectangular blocks.** Thick white sap. Twigs sometimes end in spines. Leaves alternate, 35-70 mm, **scalloped margins.** Autumn colours yellow to red. Flower spikes 30 mm (Jul-Sept). Fruit capsule 10 mm, often infested with larvae which cause the "beans" to jump 300 mm in the air. Woodland, watercourses and savanna, often in groves, in n and e lowlands and n Namibia.

**2 TREE EUPHORBIA** *Euphorbia ingens*

7-10 m. Main stem short, angled. Massive **single crown.** Bark textured, grey. Side branches with four wing-like angles. Spines paired, 2 mm, **do not form continuous ridge.** Flowers yellow, in groups on margins of wings. Fruit **round,** 13 mm capsule, on stalk 45 mm, reddish. Woodland and savanna on E coast, in N and NE.

**3 RUBBER EUPHORBIA** *Euphorbia tirucalli*

6-9 m. Main stem round, rough, with spreading roundish crown. Branchlets green, **cylindrical,** 8 mm diam. **No spines.** Fruit round, 8 mm. Bushveld, rocky hillsides and savanna, from E coast to NE.

**4 LEBOMBO EUPHORBIA** *Euphorbia confinalis*

3-10 m. Main stem tall, often branched, each large branch with crown of **four-winged** branchlets 70 mm diam. Spines 5 mm. Rocky slopes, riverine vegetation and savanna in NE.

**5 TRANSVAAL CANDELABRA TREE** *Euphorbia cooperi*

4-6 m. **Side branches die off each year, leaving main stem bare for up to 3 m.** Bark rough, grey; candelabra-shaped crown. Side branches curve upwards with large 5/6-angled segments 150 mm. Short thorns 5-15 mm. Flowers in groups above thorns (Jul-Sept). Fruit trilobed capsule, maroon-red. Bushveld, rock outcrops and savanna in E and N.

**6 VALLEY-BUSH EUPHORBIA** *Euphorbia grandidens*

7-12 m. One or more round or angled branching main stems topped with fine, **candelabra-like crowns** 1 m diam. Lower side branches die off. **Branchlets slender, 10-20 mm diam, not segmented, wavy margins with warty cushions. Spines short, with two tiny prickles above them.** Dry forest, in hot valleys and on rock outcrops along E and SE coast.
Similar

**7 LOWVELD EUPHORBIA** *E. evansii*

Smaller (2-6 m). No prickles above thorns. Restricted to E.

**8 RIVER EUPHORBIA** *Euphorbia triangularis*

4-8 m. Main stem round, branching. Yellowish-green branchlets curve upwards, forming crowns 2 m diam. **Branchlets have 3-5 angles, divided into segments 75-300 mm. Spines small, paired, on continuous ridge along margins.** Fruit 8 mm. Dry rocky hillsides in valleys, usually in groves, also with (6); from SE to NE coast.

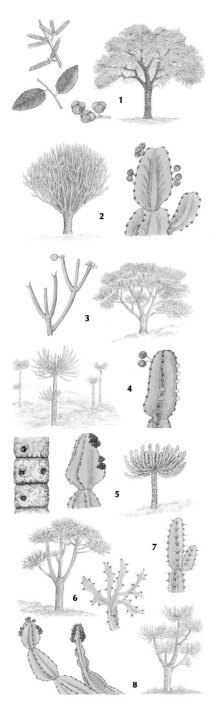

### 1 MARULA                        *Sclerocarya birrea*

7-17 m. Bark flaking in round patches. **Branchlets thick-tipped, rounded.** 3-7 pairs leaflets plus terminal one, 30-100 mm. Young leaf margin serrated. New leaves coppery. Male and female flowers on separate trees; male: drooping sprays 80 mm long; female: single, on 30 mm stalk (Sept-Nov). Fruit 40 mm, ripening yellow once fallen. Woodland and forest margins in N and NE.

### 2 WILD PLUM                  *Harpephyllum caffrum*

10-20 m. Main stem buttressed. Bark rough, dark brown when mature. Branches on young trees candelabra-like. Leaves arranged spirally, **firm, not drooping**, 4-8 pairs leaflets plus terminal one, 50-100 mm, leathery, very short stalks except on terminal leaflet. Margin wavy. **Scattered red leaves always on tree.** Flowers small, in sprays (Nov-Feb). Fruit 25 mm. Low-altitude forest, from SE to E.

### 3 LIVE-LONG TREE                  *Lannea discolor*

6-10 m. Bark dark grey, roughish. **Tips of twigs thick.** 3-5 pairs leaflets plus terminal one, 30-100 mm, **velvety grey-white beneath.** Young leaves velvety. Flowers small, yellow, in narrow sprays 140 mm (Oct-Nov). Fruit 10 mm. Woodland and rocky areas in N and NE.
**Similar**
### 4 FALSE MARULA  *L. schweinfurthii*
**Twigs thin, stiff.** 1-3 pairs leaflets plus terminal one, 20-90 mm. Woodland in NE.

### 5 RED BEECH                    *Protorhus longifolia*

10-25 m. Bark smooth, brown. Milky sap. Leaves opposite, 80-150 mm, side veins parallel, forking near margins. **Scattered red leaves always on tree.** Flowers in dense terminal sprays 150 mm (Jul-Sept). Fruit 12 mm. Forest, rock outcrops and riverine vegetation at low altitudes, from SE and E to NE.

### 6 COMMON RESIN TREE          *Ozoroa paniculosa*

3-5 m. Bark thick, rough, grey. Branchlets reddish-brown. Leaves alternate or whorled, 40-120 mm, silvery beneath, midrib and side veins protruding, **margins slightly wavy, almost scalloped, short hard tip.** Flowers small, in short terminal heads 40 mm (Aug-Feb). Fruit 7 mm. Wooded grassland in n half of region.
**Similar**
### 7 BROAD-LEAVED RESIN TREE  *O. obovata*
Twigs greyish-yellow with raised dots. Leaves obovate, 25-120 mm. **Stalk short, flat**, 20 mm. Coastal and lowveld bush in E and NE.
### 8 NAMIBIAN RESIN TREE  *O. crassinervia*
Leaves 25-110 mm, thickly velvety beneath, conspicuous net veining. Inland Namibia.
### 9 AFRICAN RESIN TREE  *O. insignis*
Leaves 170 mm. Thick, rusty, yellowish hairs beneath, conspicuous net veining, margin thickened. Zimbabwe.
### 10 CURRANT RESIN TREE  *O. sphaerocarpa*
Leaves densely velvety beneath, leathery, margin thick, wavy, incurled, rough-edged, with short spike-like tip. Fruit **round.** NE within South Africa.

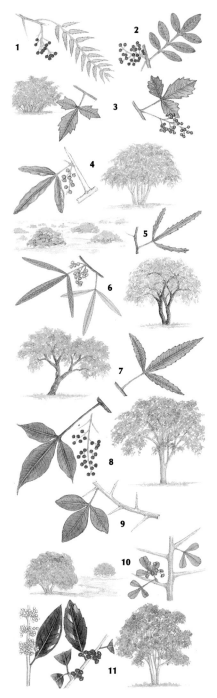

**1  PEPPER TREE**                    *Schinus molle*

Up to 15 m. Main stem short. Sparse, weeping crown. Leaves 250 mm, leaflets 10-40 mm. Introduced from South America.
**Similar**
**2  BRAZILIAN PEPPER TREE  *S. terebinthifolius***
Leaflets oval, 2-5 pairs plus terminal one. Invasive on E coast.

**3  NANA-BERRY**                    *Rhus dentata*

1-5 m. **Leaves vary** in size, usually hairy, margins toothed. Terminal leaflet 10-40 mm. Young leaves coppery. Flowers small, yellow, in terminal sprays 140 mm (Aug-Nov). Fruit 4 mm. Forest margins, rock outcrops and scrub in e third of region.
**Similar**
**DRAKENSBERG KARREE  *R. montana***
**3-7 leaflets**, terminal one 27-68 mm. Parchment-like. Drakensberg.

**4  THORNY KARREE**                 *Rhus gueinzii*

3-8 m. Bark fissured, sometimes with spines, branches arching. Terminal leaflet 13-100 mm, margin wavy. Flowers in **protruding** sprays 80 mm (Sept-Feb). Fruit 4 mm. Woodland, from E to N.

**5  BROOM KARREE**                  *Rhus erosa*

Up to 3 m. Much-branched, bark grey, branchlets orange-brown. Terminal leaflet 25-90 mm. Flowers in loose heads, 100 mm (Oct-Dec). Fruit 5 mm. Rocky slopes in central and se South Africa.

**6  KARREE**                        *Rhus lancea*

2-8 m. Bark dark brown, rough. Terminal leaflet 90-120 mm, leathery. Flowers in dense terminal clusters 60 mm (Jul-Sept). Fruit 5 mm. Woodland and riverine vegetation, central areas.
**Similar**
**WHITE KARREE  *R. pendulina***
Leaves pale, margins entire. Spines often on branches. Karoo.

**7  MOUNTAIN KARREE**               *Rhus leptodictya*

Up to 4 m. Bark rough, dark brown. Terminal leaflet 40-140 mm. Flower heads 150 mm. Fruit flattened, brown or orange. Woodland and rocky ground in central and n areas.

**8  RED CURRANT**                   *Rhus chirindensis*

3-20 m. Young stems with woody spines. Terminal leaflet 60-130 mm, midrib and stalk pink. Flower sprays 200 mm (Aug-Jan). Fruit 6 mm. Forest, rocky hillsides, from S, SE and E to N.

**9  COMMON WILD CURRANT**           *Rhus pyroides*

1-6 m. Growth form very variable. Bark smooth, grey, occasionally with spines. Terminal leaflet 6-85 mm, leathery, hairy, margin entire. Flowers in hanging bunches 100 mm (Aug-Mar). Fruit 5 mm, yellowish-red. E half of region and n Namibia.

**10  THORNY CURRANT**               *Rhus longispina*

Up to 4 m. Densely branched. Bark on main stems rough. Long spines **conspicuous, pale yellowish.** Terminal leaflet 10-40 mm. Flower bunches 50 mm. Fruit 65 mm. Se Karoo.
**Similar**
**KUNI-BUSH  *R. undulata***
Spiny. Aromatic. Leaves shiny when young, margin wavy, stalk **winged**. SW to s Namibia.

**11  HOLLY**                        *Ilex mitis*

8-20 m. Branchlets white. Young stems reddish with raised dots. Leaves 70-130 mm, midrib sunken on upper surface, raised beneath. Young leaves serrated. Stalk red, 10 mm. Flowers small (Oct-Feb). Fruit 7 mm. Forest in S and E.

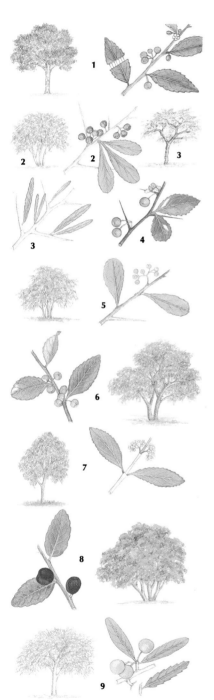

**1 SILKY BARK** *Maytenus acuminata*

2-6 m. Bark mottled brown with white and orange patches. Young stalks angular, purplish. **No spines.** Leaves 13-120 mm, thinly leathery, margin reddish. **Stalk short, red. Fine silvery threads in broken leaf.** Flowers Nov-Mar. Fruit bi- or trilobed capsule, 10 mm. Forest and rock outcrops in S and E.

**2 COMMON SPIKE-THORN** *Maytenus heterophylla*

2-6 m. Single or multistemmed. Bark sometimes deeply grooved. Spines 13-50 mm. Leaves in **clusters or alternate**, 10-90 mm. Margin serrated in **upper third**. Flowers 7 mm, in clusters (Aug-Mar), unpleasant scent. Fruit trilobed capsule. Throughout region.

**3 NARROW-LEAVED SPIKE-THORN** *Gymnosporia linearis*
*(=Maytenus linearis)*

Up to 5 m. Branches long, slender. Spines 50 mm. Leaves 20-90 mm, leathery. Flowers yellow, in small clusters (Aug-Sept). Fruit 7 mm, seed with partial yellow cover. Arid Karoo in S and W.

**4 BLACK FOREST SPIKE-THORN** *Gymnosporia mossambicensis (=Maytenus mossambicensis)*

2-5 m. Bark smooth, reddish-grey. **Slender spines** 80 mm. Leaves 10-65 mm, **thin**. Flowers small, whitish-pink (Oct-Mar). Fruit trilobed capsule 13 mm, on long stalk. Forest understorey in E.

**5 RED SPIKE-THORN** *Gymnosporia senegalensis*
*(=Maytenus senegalensis)*

1,5-4 m. Young stems red. Spines 50-100 mm. Leaves 20-120 mm, thick, leathery, midrib hairy, **margin with fine, rounded serrations**. Flowers creamy green (Jun-Oct). Fruit bilobed capsule 6 mm. Widespread except S-central interior.

**6 KOKO TREE** *Maytenus undata*

2-15 m. Bark dark grey, flaking with pinkish-brown underbark. New growth angular, purplish. **No spines.** Leaves **alternate**, 20-130 mm, often with **white bloom beneath** and spiny tip. Flowers pinkish or white (Sept-May). Fruit trilobed, seed shiny yellow. Forest and watercourses in S, E and NE.
**Similar**
CAPE BLACKWOOD *M. peduncularis*
Branches drooping. Flower and fruit on **long** stalk, 25 mm.

**7 BUSHMAN'S TEA** *Catha edulis*

2-7 m. Bark light grey, becoming cracked. Leaves 55-110 mm, hanging, **side veins swept sharply forward**. Flower clusters 20 mm diam (Aug-Nov). Fruit reddish-brown, narrow, trilobed, 10 mm, with winged seeds. Woodland, mostly inland, in E and NE.

**8 KOOBOO-BERRY** *Cassine aethiopica*

3-15 m. Bark roughish, smooth in forest. Leaves 20-120 mm, leathery, veins yellow, margin softly serrated, sometimes velvety beneath. Flowers small (Oct-Dec). Fruit 10-20 mm, smooth or hairy. Forest and woodland in SE, E and NE.

**9 TRANSVAAL SAFFRON** *Cassine transvaalensis*

2-6 m. Bark smooth. **Rigid, arching stems. Twigs smooth, white, blunt.** Leaves 20-70 mm, **usually in threes. Young leaves with sharp serrations.** Flowers small (Dec-Apr). Fruit 25 mm. Woodland and thicket in N and NE.
**Similar**
WHITE SILKY BARK *C. eucleiformis*
Latex threads in snapped leaf. E and NE.
CAPE SAFFRON *C. peragua*
Leaves almost circular. Fynbos in S and E.
COMMON SAFFRON *C. papillosa*
Yellow underbark. Leaves with stiff, spine-tipped serrations.

**1 WHITE PEAR** *Apodytes dimidiata*

5-15 m. Main stem fluted. Bark smooth, grey with white patches, conspicuous white horizontal bands at coast. Leaves 20-150 mm, **margin slightly wavy**, rolled under. **Pinkish-red stalk** 20 mm. Thin, elastic, connecting thread when leaf broken. Flowers in terminal bunches 110 mm diam (Sept-Apr). Fruit 6 mm, shiny scarlet pseudaril. Forest, rock outcrops, coastal bush and woodland in S, E and NE.

**2 JACKET-PLUM** *Pappea capensis*

4-10 m. Bark pale grey-brown, smooth or peeling. **Crown intricately branched, impenetrable mass.** Leaves variable, 70-170 mm, much smaller in dry areas, leathery, rough, midrib and parallel side veins yellow, conspicuous on both surfaces. **Young leaf margins sharply serrated.** Flowers in spike-like heads 25-160 mm (Sept-Mar). Fruit 20 mm. Black seed covered in shiny, red jelly. Woodland, scrub and termitaria. Widespread except NW.

**3 SAND OLIVE** *Dodonaea angustifolia*

2-7 m. Multistemmed, branching low down. Bark grey, finely fissured, branchlets reddish, twigs sticky. Leaves 100 mm, drooping, sometimes sticky. Flowers small, green (Apr-Jul). Fruit 2/3-winged capsule 19 mm. Forest margins, coastal dunes, woodland and lowlands, from S, SE and E to NE.

**4 NATAL BOTTLEBRUSH** *Greyia sutherlandii*

2-7 m. Bark rough, dark grey-brown. Young stems smooth, reddish-grey. Leaves clustered at ends of branchlets, 100 mm, rough, **smooth pale green beneath**. Stalk **almost sheathing stem**. Flowers 20 mm, in **erect terminal heads** 120 mm (Aug-Oct). Fruit cylindrical capsule 20 mm. Mountain slopes on e escarpment.
**Similar**
**5 TRANSVAAL BOTTLEBRUSH** *G. radlkoferi*
Leaves **velvety white beneath**. N Drakensberg.
**KEI BOTTLEBRUSH** *G. flanaganii*
**Few, hanging** flower heads. SE.

**6 BUFFALO-THORN** *Ziziphus mucronata*

3-10 m. Bark grey, rough, cracked. **Thorns in pairs, one straight, one hooked.** Leaves 30-90 mm, **three-veined from asymmetric base**. Flowers small (Oct-Jan). Fruit 15 mm, smooth leathery skin. Woodland and grassland. Widespread except SW.

**7 BROWN IVORY** *Berchemia discolor*

4-12 m. Bark grey, roughly fissured. Leaves 50-140 mm, **veins in neat herringbone pattern ending at margin**. Flowers small (Nov-Jan). Fruit 20 mm. Riverine forest and woodland at low altitudes in N and NE.

**8 RED IVORY** *Berchemia zeyheri*

3-12 m. Bark smooth, becoming cracked. Leaves 25-60 mm, thin. Flowers small (Sept-Jan). Fruit 13 mm, fleshy, on long stalks. Woodland, near watercourses, in central and e areas.

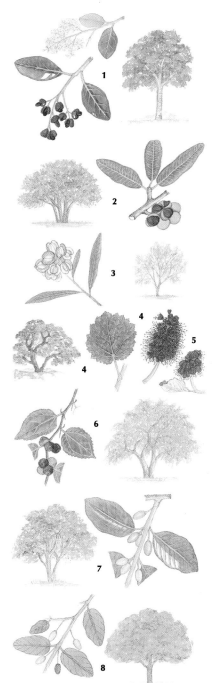

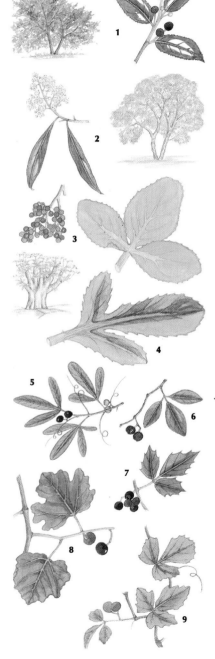

### 1 DOGWOOD
*Rhamnus prinoides*

2-6 m. Slender main stem, smooth grey-brown bark. Leaves 30-100 mm, **conspicuously shiny, very dark green**, margin serrated. Flowers on slender stalks (Nov-Jan). Fruit 5 mm, fleshy. Forest margins, streambanks, **inland**, from S to NE.

### 2 LAVENDER TREE
*Heteropyxis natalensis*

4-10 m. Bark pale greyish-white. Leaves hanging, 30-140 mm, shiny above, dull, paler beneath. **Lavender scent when crushed.** Flowers tiny (Sept-Mar). Fruit shiny brown, **oval**, 4 mm, in dense clusters. Woodland and rocky hillsides in NE-central and e areas.

### 3 BLUE COBAS
*Cyphostemma juttae*

2-4 m. **Dwarf** succulent tree. Bark pale green, peeling with creamy papery flakes. **Leaves** deeply lobed, trifoliolate when mature. Leaflets 120-350 mm, midrib with scattered prickles. Flowers in flat-topped, spreading heads (Nov). Fruit 12 mm. Namib desert.

**Similar**

### 4 COBAS *C. currorii*

Larger **tree** (up to 7 m). Bark **yellowish-brown, peeling to pinkish-white underbark.** Leaflets 300 mm, velvety when young. Rocky areas in desert.

### 5 BABOON GRAPE
*Rhoicissus digitata*

Up to 15 m. Climber. Young stems covered in russet hairs. **3-5 leaflets**, 35-90 mm, **very short stalks**, smooth above, **fine russet hairs beneath.** Stalk 25 mm long. Conspicuous in new russet leaf. Flowers small, yellowish-green, in drooping branched heads (Jan-Apr). Fruit 15 mm, fleshy. Common on coastal dunes. Grassland, thicket, forest margins and fynbos in S, E and N.

**Similar**

### 6 BITTER FOREST GRAPE *R. revoilii*

**Only three leaflets**, each with stalk 20 mm long. Leaf margins rarely lobed. NE.

### 7 GLOSSY FOREST GRAPE *R. rhomboidea*

Main stem dark brown. Leaves 50-120 mm, **side leaflets asymmetric with short stalks** (1-4 mm), glossy above, pale russet hairs beneath, margin irregularly toothed with hairlike tip to each tooth. Leaf stalk 25 mm. Forest margins, from SE to N.

### 8 COMMON FOREST GRAPE *R. tomentosa*

Scrambling shrub or canopy climber. Broad woody main stem with rough bark. Young stems covered with velvety russet hairs, tendrils hairy. Leaves **simple**, 90-200 mm, three-veined from base, **margin lobed**. Stalk 60 mm, velvety. Dense flower heads covered in russet velvety hairs (Nov-Jan). Fruit 20 mm. Forest, from SW coast to E and N.

### 9 BUSHMAN'S GRAPE *R. tridentata*

Scrambling shrub. Main stem crooked when free-standing. Bark light brown. Young stems with velvety greyish or rusty hairs. **Leaf size variable, side leaflets usually asymmetric, with short stalks or none**, 50-90 mm. Leaf stalk 40 mm. Leaves turn red in autumn. Widespread in coastal dunes, coastal forest, forest margins, rocky hillsides and moist savanna in e half of region.

**1 SILVER RAISIN**                 *Grewia monticola*

2-10 m. Bark rough, grey-brown. Arching branches, weeping habit. Young branchlets with dense russet hairs. Leaves asymmetric at base, 25-90 mm, young leaves reddish. Flowers yellow, 13 mm (Oct-Jan). Fruit single or bilobed, each lobe 8 mm. Woodland and mountainsides in E and NE.

**Similar**

**2 WHITE RAISIN** *G. bicolor*

Young stems hairless. Leaves densely **velvety white** beneath, held horizontally or drooping, **base rounded** to slightly asymmetric. Woodland and savanna in N and NE.

**3 VELVET RAISIN** *G. flava*

2-4 m. **Leaves upright, base symmetric.** Woodland, grassland and arid savanna in central and nw areas.

**4 SANDPAPER RAISIN** *G. flavescens*

1-3 m. Main stem square, **young branches with rough hairs.** Leaves 40-120 mm, rough hairs on both sides. N and NE.

**5 CROSS-BERRY**             *Grewia occidentalis*

1-10 m. Scrambling shrub. Leaves 25-75 mm, **tapering to slender tip.** Flowers **pink**, 35 mm (Oct-Jan). Fruit four-lobed, each lobe 25 mm. Forest, forest margins and woodland in s and e half of region.

**Similar**

Members of the *Grewia* genus usually have fairly similar leaves but different growth patterns.

**CLIMBING RAISIN** *G. caffra*

Scrambling shrub. **Stems square**. Yellow flowers. Riverine vegetation and savanna in E and NE.

**FALSE SANDPAPER RAISIN** *G. retinervis*

Leaves stiff, harshly hairy. Flowers yellow. Fruit single, 9 mm. Arid savanna in N and NW.

**MALLOW RAISIN** *G. villosa*

Leaves **roundish**, 60-120 mm, thick, rough. Yellow flowers do not open fully. Fruit four-lobed. Woodland in N and NE.

**FOREST RAISIN** *G. lasiocarpa*

Leaves **large,** 40-120 mm, roundish, thick, rough. **Large** pink flowers, 50 mm. Forest in E.

**6 WILD COTTON TREE**         *Hibiscus tiliaceus*

4-9 m. Multistemmed. Bark grey-brown, smooth or with small raised dots. Leaves large, 260 mm, velvety white beneath. Flowers 120 mm, turning coppery, dropping after a day (Aug-May). Fruit oval, 25 mm, covered in golden hairs. Fringing rivers along E coast.

**7 SNOT APPLE**                 *Azanza garckeana*

3-10 m. Bark rough, brown, branchlets with woolly hairs. Leaves 3-5 lobes, 200 mm, hairy. Stalk 130 mm. Flowers 60 mm (Dec-May). Fruit woody capsule 40 mm. Woodland in NE.

**8 BAOBAB**                   *Adansonia digitata*

10-25 m. Main stem up to 10 m diam, bark smooth, folded, pinkish-grey. Leaves clustered towards ends of twigs, 3-9 leaflets, 50-150 mm. Leaf stalk 120 mm. Flowers 200 mm (Oct-Dec). Fruit 240 mm, hard shell covered with velvety hairs. Arid savanna in N.

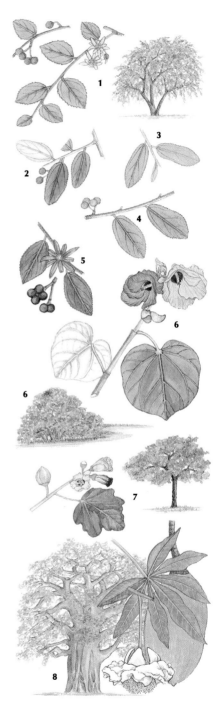

### 1 COMMON WILD PEAR — *Dombeya rotundifolia*

3-5 m. Bark rough, fissured. Leaves 30-150 mm, **thick, rough.** Flowers white or pink, 20 mm, in profusion on bare tree (Jul-Sept). Fruit small capsule within old flowers which turn brown and papery. Open woodland and hillsides in N and NE.

**Similar**

### 2 PINK WILD PEAR *D. burgessiae*

Multistemmed shrub. **Leaves very large, lobed, softly hairy,** 50-180 mm. Flowers pink or white with pink veins, 50 mm (Apr-Aug). Forest margins and rock outcrops in E and NE.

### 3 NATAL WILD PEAR *D. cymosa*

**Bark pale grey.** Leaves **small**, usually 45 mm, thin. Flowers **small**, 13 mm (Mar-May). Forest margins and coastal bush in E.

### 4 COMMON STAR-CHESTNUT — *Sterculia rogersii*

3-6 m. Bark grey, peeling, with shiny cream or pink underbark. Leaves **small**, 30-60 mm, **soft, thin. Stalk slender**, 20 mm. Flowers on short twigs and mature stems, 20 mm (Jul-Jan). Fruit 3-5 lobes, each 80 mm, velvety, resembling a peach. Seeds dark grey with stinging hairs. Woodland and rock outcrops in NE.

**Similar**

**AFRICAN STAR-CHESTNUT** *S. africana*

Larger (5-12 m). Bark smooth, silvery white to greenish, flaking, with marbled underbark. Leaves **large**. Flowers in **spikes** 90 mm. Fruit lobes 150 mm. Exposed seeds resemble ticks. N.

### 5 LOWVELD CHESTNUT — *Sterculia murex*

Up to 10 m. Bark rough. 5-7 leaflets 150 mm, hairy. Stalk 230 mm. Flowers 25 mm, in sprays 100 mm (Jul-Oct). Fruit 2-5 lobes, each 200 mm. Dry rocky areas. Only in Mpumalanga lowveld.

### 6 CAPE PLANE — *Ochna arborea*

3-8 m. **Smooth, marbled bark**, flaking, **cool to touch.** Leaves 70-230 mm, **leathery**, margin sometimes wavy, serrated or entire. Flowers 20 mm (Aug-Nov). Sepals **red**, 1-5 berry-like drupes, each 10 mm. Forest margins in SE, E and NE.

**Similar**

### 7 RED IRONWOOD *O. holstii*

**Bark rough, not flaking. Branches, leaves horizontal.** Leaves with **narrow base, short stalk.** Mistbelt forest in E and NE.

### 8 NATAL PLANE *O. natalitia*

**Bark flaking in thin strips, brown.** Small gall resembling tiny *Protea* in leaf axil. Forest in SE, E and NE.

### 9 PEELING PLANE — *Ochna pulchra*

3-8 m. Bark peeling, grey-brown, underbark smooth, cream. Flowers **small, in spikes**. Sepals **pink**. Woodland and rocky ground in N.

**Similar**

**BRICK-RED OCHNA** *O. schweinfurthiana*

Bark thick, cracked, dark grey. Extreme NE.

**SMALL-LEAVED PLANE** *O. serrulata*

Bark smooth, brown. Branchlets densely covered in raised white dots. Leaves small, 25-50 mm, margin with sharp, fine serrations. S, E and N within South Africa.

## 1 CURRY BUSH
*Hypericum revolutum*

1-3 m. Multistemmed. Bark scaly, reddish-brown. **Resinous juice**. Leaves opposite, 20 mm, soft, with **scattered oblong black dots**, base **clasping stem**. Flowers 50 mm (throughout year). Fruit reddish-brown capsule. **Curry-like scent**. Forest margins, rock outcrops, grassy mountainsides and streambanks in N and NE.
**Similar**
**LARGE-LEAVED ST JOHN'S WORT** *H. roeperianum*
Larger leaves, 80 mm. NE.

## 2 FOREST GARCINIA
*Garcinia gerrardii*

4-10 m. Main stem straight, **branches angled, winged by clasping leaf stalks. Watery yellowish-brown sap**. Leaves 40-100 mm, margin rolled under, tip recurved. New leaves red. Flowers 15 mm, in terminal clusters 60 mm (Oct-Jan). Fruit 25 mm. Forest and rock outcrops in E.

## 3 LOWVELD MANGOSTEEN
*Garcinia livingstonei*

3-8 m. Main stem short, sturdy, with angular, much-branched crown. Bark rough dark grey, smooth pale grey on young stems. Branches short, thick, in threes or opposite pairs. **Yellow sap**. **Leaves in threes**, 40-140 mm, **stiff, blue-green**, pale midrib and veins. Young leaves soft, red. Flowers small, in clusters (Aug-Sept). Fruit 35 mm, thin skin with sticky latex, edible firm pulp. Woodland and coastal grassland in NE.

## 4 WILD TAMARISK
*Tamarix usneoides*

Up to 9 m. Bark pale to dark brown, peeling in strips. Leaves reduced, scale-like, overlapping. Flowers in sprays (Jan-Apr). Desert and arid Karoo in W.

## 5 FOREST PEACH
*Rawsonia lucida*

6-15 m. Main stem straight, slender. Bark smooth, flaking in grey strips revealing orange patches. Branches long, drooping, smooth with raised dots. Leaves 70-160 mm, glossy, paler beneath, **margin with spiny, incurving serrations**. Stalk 12 mm. Flowers 20 mm (Sept-Nov). Fruit **fleshy capsule** 40 mm, splitting into five segments when dry. Forest understorey in SE, E and NE.

## 6 SNUFFBOX-TREE
*Oncoba spinosa*

3-10 m. Young branches dark reddish-brown with raised white dots. **Single spines slender, sharp**, 50 mm. Leaves alternate, 30-120 mm, thin, shiny. New leaves coppery pink. Flowers 80 mm, 20 petals (Sept-Jan). Fruit 60 mm, with hard shell and pointed tip, turning blackish-brown. Woodland and riverine forest in E and NE.

## 7 AFRICAN DOG-ROSE
*Xylotheca kraussiana*

1-7 m. Bark smooth. No spines. Leaves 60-100 mm, shiny or velvety dark green above, paler beneath, tip tapering, rounded. Flowers 70 mm (throughout summer). Fruit woody capsule, smooth or ridged, splitting into eight segments. Seeds black with sticky **red cover**. Woodland and dune forest along E coast.
**Similar**
**NORTHERN AFRICAN DOG-ROSE** *X. tettensis*
Seeds without sticky cover. Extreme NE.

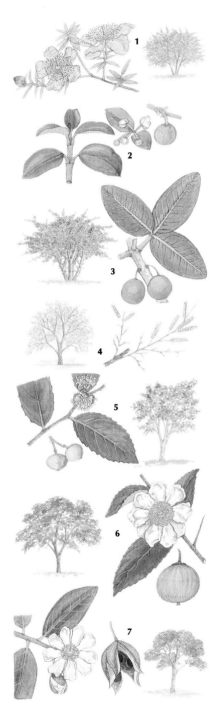

**TREES**

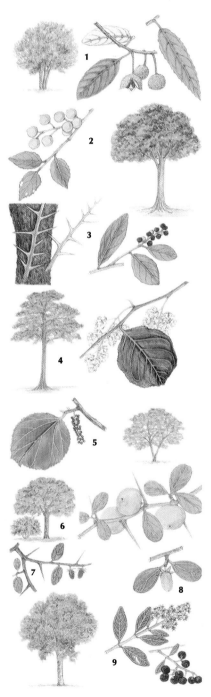

**1 WILD PEACH**  *Kiggelaria africana*

4-13 m. Bark smooth, pale brown, becoming darker, flaky and fissured. Young branches yellowish, hairy. Leaves 35-120 mm, **hairy pockets in axils of veins (small bumps on upper surface).** Young leaves large, margin serrated. Flowers small, yellow (Aug-Jan). Fruit rough, warty, 20 mm, splitting into four valves. Shiny black seeds with sticky, bright red coating. Forest, fynbos and rock outcrops in s and e half of region.

**2 RED PEAR**  *Scolopia mundii*

10-35 m. Main stem sometimes fluted. Bark smooth grey-brown, becoming rough, flaky. Coppice shoots with spines 20 mm. Leaves 35-70 mm, rigid, **margin sharply serrated.** Stalk **pink.** Young leaves large, shiny. Flowers in small clusters 20 mm diam (May-Aug). Fruit 10 mm, with sharp tip. Forest, forest margins and mountainsides, usually at high altitudes, in S and E.

**3 THORN PEAR**  *Scolopia zeyheri*

3-15 m. Bark smooth, grey, becoming soft, flaky. **Large woody spines** 200 mm, sometimes massed at base. Leaves 20-80 mm, leathery. Stalk pinkish. **Bent leaf shows thin, white waxy layer.** Flowers creamy white, in clusters 30 mm (Apr-Sept). Fruit 5-10 mm. Forest margins and termitaria in e half of region.

**4 BROWN IRONWOOD**  *Homalium dentatum*

10-30 m. Main stem fluted, buttressed in mature specimens. **Branches horizontal.** Leaves 40-130 mm, thin, shiny. Flowers small, in heads 100 mm (Jan-May). Fruit tiny capsule. Evergreen and scrub forest in E and NE.

**5 WILD MULBERRY**  *Trimeria grandifolia*

4-10 m. Bark flaky, new twigs purplish-brown with raised pale dots. Leaves round, 130 mm, **5-9 veins from base.** Flowers small (Aug-Feb). Fruit small capsule, 5 mm. Forest margins in E and NE.

**6 KEI-APPLE**  *Dovyalis caffra*

3-8 m. Bark smooth, silvery grey, maturing rough, fissured, dark grey. Spines 50 mm. Leaves in **clusters on short side twigs,** 20-55 mm, leathery. Flowers small, creamy green (Nov-Jan). Fruit **round,** velvety, 40 mm, edible pulp. Woodland in NE-central, e and se areas.

**Similar**

**7 COMMON SOURBERRY**  *D. rhamnoides*

Slender spines 80 mm. Leaves **arranged horizontally,** 13-30 mm. Fruit red, 13 mm. Forest and scrub in SE, E and N within South Africa.

**GLOSSY SOURBERRY**  *D. lucida*

No spines. Fruit **round,** orange, hairy. Forest in SE, E and NE.

**8 WILD APRICOT**  *D. zeyheri*

Spines 30 mm, or spineless. **Leaves alternate or clustered,** 15-70 mm, young leaves velvety. Fruit **oval,** 20 mm, smooth. Woodland, forest margins and rocky places in NE-central and e areas.

**9 MOUNTAIN HARD PEAR**  *Olinia emarginata*

10-15 m. Upward-growing branches. Bark pale brownish-yellow, flaking. **Young twigs square, branchlets smooth, pale creamy white.** Leaves 20-50 mm, tip rounded, **notched.** Stalk pinkish-red. Flowers small, in hanging sprays 30 mm (Oct-Nov). Fruit 10 mm. Forest, streambanks and rock outcrops in E and NE.

## 1 POMPON TREE — *Dais cotinifolia*

2-7 m. Bark grey, branchlets flattened at nodes. Leaves 70-90 mm, smooth. Flowers tubular, in terminal clusters 40 mm diam (Nov-Feb). Fruit small nutlet. Forest margins, riverine vegetation and rocky valleys in E and NE.

## 2 TRANSVAAL PRIVET — *Galpinia transvaalica*

3-10 m. Bark rough, cracked. Young stems shiny red-brown. Leaves 25-90 mm, leathery, **midrib ends in raised dot** (gland) **before recurved tip**. Flowers in large sprays towards ends of branches (Dec-Apr). Fruit 4 mm, reddish-brown, in clusters. Woodland and thicket in lowveld in NE.

## 3 POWDER-PUFF TREE — *Barringtonia racemosa*

4-10 m. Bark smooth with raised dots, greyish-brown mottled white. Leaves 80-350 mm, thick. Stalk purple. Scattered coppery red leaves on tree. Flowers 35 mm, in hanging racemes 1 m long, unpleasantly scented (Nov-Jun). Fruit 40 mm. Fringing swamps and estuaries along E and NE coast.

## 4 RED MANGROVE — *Rhizophora mucronata*

2-5 m. Bark fissured, dark reddish-brown. **Branched stilt roots** up to 2 m. Leaves 76-150 mm, thick, **narrowing to short sharp tip.** Flowers creamy white, 25 mm diam, in small clusters (Nov-May). Fruit develops to 300 mm pod, falling into mud when mature. Estuaries along E coast.

## 5 BLACK MANGROVE — *Bruguiera gymnorrhiza*

2-5 m. Main stem buttresses extend 800 mm, emerging as **knee-roots (aerial breathing roots)**. Bark rough, red-brown, branches smooth, yellowish-grey. Leaves 76-120 mm, **tapering to tip**. Flowers 40 mm, singly (throughout year), calyx with 16 lobes. Fruit develops to 150 mm ridged pod. Seaward side of mangrove swamps along E coast.

## 6 RED BUSHWILLOW — *Combretum apiculatum*

3-6 m. Bark grey to blackish, cracked, flaking with age. Leaves 30-130 mm, **tip twisted at right angles to leaf blade. New leaves sticky, shiny.** Flowers creamy yellow, in spikes 70 mm (Sept-Feb). Fruit four-winged, 28 mm, shiny, **slightly sticky at centre.** Woodland and rocky hillsides in N and NE.

## 7 RIVER BUSHWILLOW — *Combretum erythrophyllum*

5-10 m. Bark cream to pale greyish-brown, mottled, flaking. Leaves on short side twigs, 50-100 mm, thin, **6-10 pairs side veins, margin fringed with hairs. Flush of white leaves in spring.** Flowers greenish-white, in spikes 25 mm (Sept-Nov). Fruit 14 mm, yellowish-green. Rivers and watercourses in e half of region and along Orange River.

**Similar**

## CAPE BUSHWILLOW — *C. caffrum*

Leaves **longer, narrower, darker green above, 4-7 pairs side veins**. Flowers brownish-green. Fruit with reddish wings. E Cape only.

## 8 FOREST BUSHWILLOW — *C. kraussii*

Spring flush of white leaves. Leaves reddish-purple in autumn. Flowers creamy white, in heads 60 mm long. Fruit small, 20 mm. Forest in E and NE within South Africa.

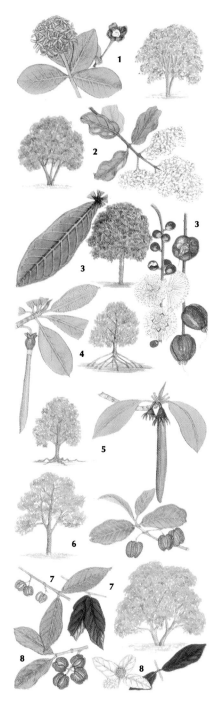

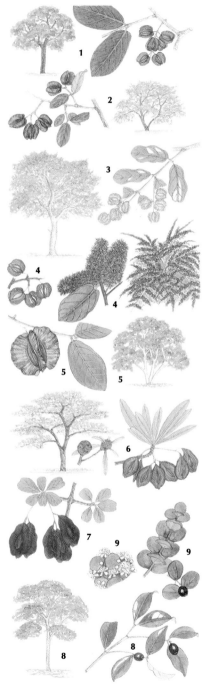

### 1 VELVET BUSHWILLOW — *Combretum molle*

4-8 m. Bark rough, brownish-black. Leaves 60-100 mm, **thick, rough, hairy. Young leaves densely velvety.** Flowers yellow, in spikes 40-90 mm (Sept-Nov). Fruit 20 mm. Woodland and grassland in e half of region.

### 2 RUSSET BUSHWILLOW — *Combretum hereroense*

2-6 m. Bark thick, corky, greyish-black. Leaves *small*, 20-70 mm, short recurved tip. Young leaves with velvety brown hairs beneath. Flowers white, in spikes 30 mm (Sept-Nov). Fruit small, 23 mm. Woodland and drainage lines. Widespread in N.

### 3 LEADWOOD — *Combretum imberbe*

7-12 m. Bark rough, cracked into irregular blocks. **New growth straight, opposite twigs, often spine-tipped.** Leaves 25-80 mm, midrib orange-red, hairlike tip. New leaves silvery grey. Flower spikes 40-60 mm (Nov-Mar). Fruit 15 mm. Woodland and watercourses in n half of region.

### 4 FLAME CREEPER — *Combretum microphyllum*

Scrambling climber, reaching canopy at 20 m. Bark brown, flaking. Woody spines, singly or in pairs, 25 mm. Leaves 40-100 mm. Flowers bright red, in horizontal heads 80 mm long (Aug-Oct). Fruit 20 mm. Riverine vegetation in NE.
**Similar**
HICCUP NUT *C. bracteosum*
Red flowers in round heads, 40 mm. Fruit **not winged**. SE and E.

### 5 LARGE-FRUITED BUSHWILLOW — *Combretum zeyheri*

3-6 m. Bark smooth, whitish, branches arching. Leaves 70-140 mm, margin wavy. Flower spikes 70 mm (Sept-Nov). Fruit **large**, four-winged, 60 mm. Open woodland and grassland in N and NE.

### 6 SILVER CLUSTER-LEAF — *Terminalia sericea*

4-8 m. **Branches horizontal.** Bark blackish-grey, deeply fissured. Leaves 55-120 mm, covered in silvery hairs. **Characteristic round galls.** Flowers small, cream, in spikes 160 mm (Nov-Jan). Fruit single-winged, 35 mm. Woodland in central, n and ne areas.
**Similar**
### 7 LOWVELD CLUSTER-LEAF *T. prunioides*
Branches low down. Bark striated, dark grey-brown. Leaves on short, hard, spike-like side twigs, 20-30 mm, tip rounded or notched. Buds red, opening white (Oct-Jan). Fruit 40-60 mm. Woodland, near watercourses or rocky hills, in N and NE.

### 8 COMMON FOREST MYRTLE — *Eugenia natalitia*

5-10 m. Bark smooth or flaking, pale brown. Leaves 25-80 mm, **midrib slightly sunken above,** protruding below, **aromatic when crushed.** Flowers white, with **mass of stamens** (Jun-Dec). Fruit 13 mm. Forest in SE and E.
**Similar**
### 9 DUNE MYRTLE *E. capensis*
Leaves **round** to oval, 10-40 mm, **thick**, leathery, **main vein often not reaching tip**, stalkless. Coastal dunes along SE and E coast.

**1 WATER BERRY** *Syzygium cordatum*

5-12 m. Bark rough, corky, grey. Twigs square. Leaves 25-100 mm, thick, leathery, smooth, **base clasping stem**. Flowers 25 mm, in heads 100 mm diam (throughout summer). Fruit 20 mm. Along watercourses in se and e half of region and extreme N.

**2 WATER PEAR** *Syzygium guineense*

10-15 m. Bark smooth, mottled, greyish-brown. Leaves 35-150 mm, paler beneath with clear gland dots, narrow and tapering to tip. **Stalk 20 mm.** Flowers in large terminal heads (Oct-May). Riverine vegetation in N, NE and E.
**Similar**
**FOREST WATERWOOD** *S. gerrardii*
Main stem buttressed. Leaves smaller, 55 mm, **abruptly tapering to long narrow tip**. Forest in E.

**3 NATAL ROCK CABBAGE TREE** *Cussonia natalensis*

4-6 m. Bark corky, brown. Leaves **3-5 deep lobes**, 50-150 mm, margin bluntly serrated. Stalk 300 mm. Flowers in up to 12 cylindrical racemes, 150 mm (Feb-May). Fruit purplish, 6 mm, crowded on spikes. Woodland and rocky hillsides in E and NE.

**4 COMMON CABBAGE TREE** *Cussonia spicata*

4-10 m. Bark thick, corky, fissured, grey. Leaves 700 mm, clustered at ends of branches, 5-9 leaflets, deeply lobed, **sometimes to midrib**, 70-150 mm. Leaf stalk up to 1 m. Flowers densely packed in 8-12 spikes, 50-150 mm, forming **erect, candelabralike inflorescence** (Apr-Jun). Fruit purple, 6 mm, clustered on spikes. Forest margins, scrub, woodland and rock outcrops in s and e half of region.
**Similar**
**5 MOUNTAIN CABBAGE TREE** *C. paniculata*
7-9 leaflets, 100-300 mm, entire to deeply lobed, **never cut to midrib**, margin broadly serrated. Leaf stalk 300 mm. Subsp. *sinuata* (5a): leaf margins wavy, deeply lobed; subsp. *paniculata* (5b): leaf margins entire or sparsely serrated. Flowers and fruit clustered in large, much-branched heads. Rock outcrops, woodland and mountains in e half of South Africa.

**6 NATAL FOREST CABBAGE TREE** *Cussonia sphaerocephala*

15-25 m. Bark dark grey. Leaves 400 mm, 6-12 leaflets fan out from end of 900 mm stalk. Flowers on short thick spikes 80-140 mm (Mar-Jun). Fruit purplish, small, clustered on spikes. Forest in E and SE within South Africa.

**7 FALSE CABBAGE TREE** *Schefflera umbellifera*

-20 m. Bark fissured, greyish-brown. 3-5 leaflets, 75-150 mm, leathery, margin very wavy, pointed or notched tip. Leaf stalk 200 mm. Flowers small, yellow, in terminal heads 180 mm (Jan-May). Fruit red, 3 mm. Forest along coast and inland, from SE to E and NE.

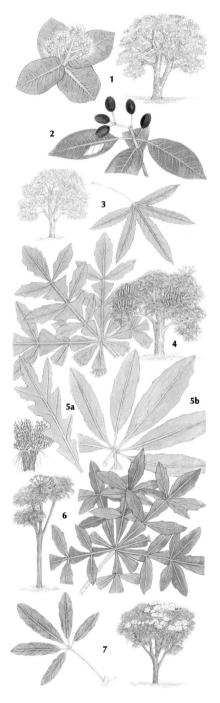

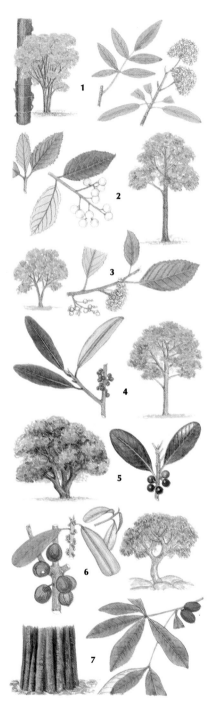

### 1 PARSLEY TREE *Heteromorpha trifoliata*

2-6 m. **Bark satiny-smooth** on new stems, **peeling horizontally in coppery brown flakes.** Older stems segmented. **Simple leaves:** in drier areas drooping, margin entire. **Compound leaves:** 3-7 leaflets varying in shape, 60-100 mm, margin entire or toothed. Terminal leaflet stalk 20 mm, side leaflets stalkless. **Leaf stalk clasping stem.** Flower heads 50 mm diam (Jan-Apr). Fruit small, bilobed. Forest margins and rock outcrops in S and E.

### 2 ASSEGAI *Curtisia dentata*

7-15 m. Bark deeply fissured, dark brown, young stems smooth. Leaves **opposite,** 25-100 mm, leathery, grey-green beneath, veins covered with velvety hairs, margin wavy, coarsely serrated. Young leaves covered in bronze hairs. Coppice leaves longer, more deeply serrated. Flowers cream, in sprays 120 mm (Dec-Feb). Fruit white to red, 10 mm. Evergreen forest, from S and E coast to 1 800 m and into Zimbabwe.

### 3 FALSE ASSEGAI *Maesa lanceolata*

3-5 m. Bark rough, greyish red-brown. Young stems smooth or covered in rusty velvety hairs. **Leaves alternate,** 40-170 mm, leathery, thick, veins prominent beneath, often with rusty hairs. Flowers in heads 100 mm (Nov-Aug). Fruit 6 mm. Drainage lines and forest margins in E and NE.

### 4 CAPE BEECH *Rapanea melanophloeos*

3-10 m. Main stem sometimes fluted in forest. Bark smooth, pinkish-grey with raised dots on young stems, rough, grey-brown on mature stems. Leaves 50-130 mm, thick, gland dots visible when held to light, paler beneath. Stalk yellow or purplish-red. Flowers in small clusters (May-Jul). Fruit 5 mm, clustered close to stems. Forest in S, SW, E and NE.

### 5 WHITE MILKWOOD *Sideroxylon inerme*

4-15 m. Bark grey-brown to black, rough. Leaves **oblong,** 40-120 mm, leathery, smooth; paler, dull beneath with fine rusty hairs when young. Margin entire, rolled under. **White latex in broken leaf or stalk.** Flowers small (Nov-Apr). Fruit 12 mm. Coastal forest, woodland and termitaria in coastal lowland in SW, S, E and NE.

### 6 TRANSVAAL MILKPLUM (STAMVRUG) *Englerophytum (=Bequaertiodendron) magalismontanum*

2-10 m. Bark grey, slightly scaly. Young twigs with rusty hairs. Leaves 70-140 mm, crowded towards ends of branchlets, leathery, shiny above, **fine silvery brown hairs beneath**, margin entire, rolled under. Flowers 10 mm, pinkish, buds covered in rusty hairs, in clusters (Jun-Oct). Fruit 25 mm, on old wood. Rocky mountainsides in N-central and ne areas.
**Similar**

### 7 NATAL MILKPLUM *E. (=B.) natalense*

Main stem often fluted, with **horizontal branches.** Bark smooth, grey. Leaves 60-150 mm, smooth, **silvery grey silky hairs beneath.** Flowers creamy white, in small groups (Nov-Feb). Fruit 25 mm. Forest understorey along SE and E coast.

**1 TRANSVAAL RED MILKWOOD**      *Mimusops zeyheri*

3-15 m. Bark pale to dark grey, deeply grooved, cracked. Leaves 40-110 mm, leathery, margin wavy, slightly thickened. Young leaves covered in rusty hairs. Flowers creamy white, 10 mm, in small clusters, on stalks 30 mm (Oct-Feb). Fruit yellow, 35 mm. Wooded hillsides, riverine vegetation in N and NE.
**Similar**

**2 COASTAL RED MILKWOOD**   *M. caffra*

4-10 m. Leaves 30-70 mm, leathery, paler with whitish hairs beneath, margin rolled under. Flowers Jun-Oct. Fruit red, 20 mm. Coastal forest and dunes along E coast.

**3 RED MILKWOOD**   *M. obovata*

4-20 m. Leaves 20-70 mm, thinly leathery. Flowers Sept-Dec. Fruit red, 35 mm. Forest, woodland, from SE and E coast to 1 200 m.

**4 LOWVELD MILKBERRY**      *Manilkara mochisia*

4-10 m. Bark dark, rough or smooth. Twigs thick, zigzag. **Leaves** 15-60 mm, in **dense rosettes**, hard, smooth. Flowers small, yellow, in dense clusters (Sept-Dec). Fruit 12 mm. Open woodland, usually on heavy clay soils, in N and NE.
**Similar**

**5 FOREST MILKBERRY**   *M. discolor*

Young stems covered in reddish hairs. Leaves 35-100 mm, towards ends of branchlets, fine silvery hairs beneath. Flowers 7 mm (Sept-Dec). Coastal forest in E and NE.

**6 MAGIC GUARRI**      *Euclea divinorum*

3-8 m. Bark grey-brown, rough, cracked. **Leaves opposite,** 35-80 mm, hard, leathery, **margin very wavy.** Flowers in small round heads, 1-3 per leaf axil (Aug-Dec). Fruit 7 mm. Woodland in N and NE.
**Similar**

**7 KAROO GUARRI**   *E. crispa*

**Young branchlets with rusty scales.** Leaves 15-50 mm, **hard, leathery,** margin wavy or flat. Flowers in **branched sprays** 30 mm (Dec-May). Fruit 5 mm. Forest margins, woodland and rocky hillsides in e half of region.

**8 TONGA GUARRI**   *E. natalensis*

Branchlets covered in fine rusty hairs. Leaves 30-100 mm, **velvety rusty hairs beneath, veins prominent on upper surface.** Flowers creamy white, in **branched heads**, 35 mm diam (Jun-Oct). Fruit 10 mm, in clusters 35 mm long. Forest and open woodland in NE and E, and along SE coast.

**9 BUSH GUARRI**   *E. schimperi*

Leaves without hairs, margin wavy or not. Flowers in **unbranched sprays**, 50 mm long (Nov-Apr). Coastal forest, woodland in SW, SE, E and NE.

**10 COMMON GUARRI**   *E. undulata*

3-6 m. Neat, rounded canopy. Leaves 20-30 mm, margin wavy or flat. Flowers in short, unbranched, **single heads** (Oct-Jan). Woodland, thicket, rock outcrops and arid areas in Namibia and South Africa except SE and extreme W.

**MOUNTAIN GUARRI**   *E. coriacea*

Leaf margin **very wavy**. Fruit 15 mm. Rocky mountain slopes along upper Orange and Caledon rivers.

**11 EBONY TREE**      *Euclea pseudebenus*

5-10 m. Bark rough, dark. Leaves 13-50 mm, leathery. Flowers greenish-yellow (Aug-Sept). Fruit 8 mm, black. Arid areas, dry river courses in W and NW.

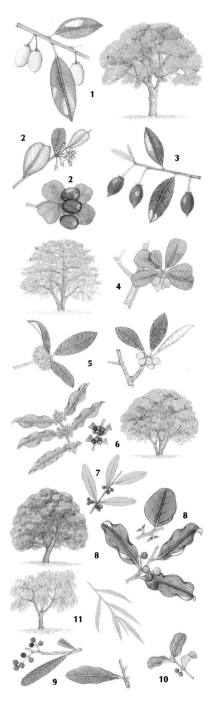

### 1 BLUEBUSH — *Diospyros lycioides*

2-7 m. Multistemmed. Bark grey. Leaves 15-110 mm, towards ends of twigs, usually hairy. Flowers 15 mm on stalks 30 mm (Sept-Dec). Fruit 20 mm. Widespread except in SW and desert.

### 2 JACKAL-BERRY — *Diospyros mespiliformis*

10-15 m. Bark rough, grey. Leaves 45-140 mm, shiny. Flowers cream, 12 mm (Oct-Nov). Fruit 25 mm. Woodland, termite mounds and riverine vegetation in N and NE.

### 3 SMALL-LEAVED JACKAL-BERRY — *Diospyros natalensis*

6-10 m. Main stem tall, with horizontal branches. Bark smooth. Leaves 10-36 mm. Flowers white (Oct-Dec). Fruit 12 mm. Sand and coastal forest along SE and E coast and in NE.

### 4 BLADDER-NUT — *Diospyros whyteana*

4-7 m. Multistemmed. Bark almost black. Leaves 25-40 mm, **wavy**, fringed with soft hairs. Flowers creamy yellow, 10 mm (Jul-Oct). Fruit 20 mm, **enclosed in inflated, papery calyx**. Forest, scrub and rock outcrops in S and E.

### 5 WILD JASMINE — *Schrebera alata*

4-8 m. Bark cracked or flaking. 1-2 pairs leaflets plus larger terminal one, 30-80 mm, smooth or velvety, stalk with broad wings clasping stem. Flowers 15 mm, in clusters 110 mm (Oct-Feb). Fruit capsule 30 mm, splitting on tree. Forest and rocky hillsides in E and NE.

### 6 WILD OLIVE — *Olea europaea*

5-10 m. Bark rough. **Young stems square**. Leaves 20-100 mm, leathery, shiny above, **greyish-brown scales beneath, veins indistinct**, margin rolled under. Flower heads 60 mm, **in leaf axils** (Oct-Dec). Fruit 10 mm. Widespread except central and w desert.

### 7 FALSE IRONWOOD — *Olea capensis*

4-30 m. Bark longitudinally fissured. Leaves 40-100 mm, thick, leathery. Flower heads 80 mm (Nov-Feb). Fruit 20 mm. Subsp. *enervis* (7a): leaves 50 mm, **midrib raised in bottom half only**. Fruit **round**, 10 mm. Forest along SW to E coast and inland in NE.

### 8 TRANSVAAL MUSTARD TREE — *Salvadora australis* (=*S. angustifolia*)

3-7 m. Leaves 20-70 mm, **soft, almost fleshy**, velvety grey hairs. Flowers **among leaves** (Aug-Sept). Fruit 10 mm, velvety. Thicket and floodplains in NE.

**Similar**

**MUSTARD TREE *S. persica***

Leaves oblong to circular, 50 mm. **Flowers in terminal sprays longer than leaves**. Arid savanna in NW and NE.

### 9 NEEDLE BUSH — *Azima tetracantha*

Scrambling shrub. **Spines four-whorled**. Leaves 13-55 mm. Flowers in clusters 30 mm diam (Oct-Nov). Fruit 10 mm. Open woodland in S, E and NE.

### 10 CAPE TEAK — *Strychnos decussata*

3-10 m. Leaves 15-50 mm, hard, shiny, blade curved upwards. Flowers cream, in clusters (Oct-Dec). Fruit 17 mm, asymmetric with sharp tip, 1-2 **flat seeds**. Riverine and sand forest in SE, E and NE.

**1  BLACK MONKEY ORANGE**  *Strychnos madagascariensis*
3-8 m. Short, hard side twigs. Leaves clustered, 20-80 mm, **thick, velvety**. 3-5 veins from base. Flowers in clusters (Oct-Dec). Fruit 80-100 mm, grey-green ripening orange, woody shell. Woodland and thicket in E and NE.

**2  GREEN MONKEY ORANGE**  *Strychnos spinosa*
3-7 m. **Paired spines**. Leaves 15-90 mm. Flowers Sept-Feb. Fruit 70-120 mm, yellowish-brown when ripe. Woodland along SE and E coast and inland in NE.
**Similar**
**CORKY-BARK MONKEY ORANGE  S. cocculoides**
Bark corky, **fissured. Curved spines.** Fruit dark green with white speckles, ripening yellow. Arid savanna in N.
**SPINE-LEAVED MONKEY ORANGE  S. pungens**
Leaf tip **spinelike**. Fruit bluish-green, ripening yellow.

**3  COMMON WILD ELDER**  *Nuxia congesta*
3-10 m. Bark fissured. **Leaves three-whorled**, 10-80 mm. **Stalk short.** Flowers in **dense terminal heads** (May-Jul). Forest and rock outcrops in SE, E and NE.
**Similar**
**4  FOREST ELDER  N. floribunda**
Bark rough, flaking. Leaves 50-150 mm, **long stalks,** 45 mm. Flowers in **loose heads** 300 mm (May-Sept). Forest and along seepage lines.
**5  WATER ELDER  N. oppositifolia**
Smaller (2-5 m). Bark fissured, peeling in narrow strips. Leaves in opposite pairs, 45-90 mm, thin. Flowers tiny, in much-branched heads. Riverine bush in E, NE and N.

**6  FALSE OLIVE**  *Buddleja saligna*
2-7 m. Bark pale grey, fissured, flaking. Twigs square. Leaves 15-100 mm, whitish beneath, side veins form continuous line close to margin, margin rolled under. Flowers cream, in heads 120 mm diam (Aug-Jan). Scrub, woodland and margins of dry forest in e half of region.

**7  WEEPING SAGE**  *Buddleja auriculata*
2-4 m. Branches arching, willow-like. Twigs covered in dense whitish-grey hairs. Leaves 30-120 mm, drooping, thin, papery, velvety white beneath. Flowers in sprays 60 mm (May-Aug). Forest margins and mountain slopes along escarpment in SE and E.

**8  SAGEWOOD**  *Buddleja salviifolia*
4-8 m. Bark stringy, twigs square, woolly. Leaves 30-140 mm, soft, heavily textured above, velvety beneath, margin finely scalloped, thickened. **Stalk absent.** Flowers in terminal heads 120 mm (Aug-Oct). Forest margins, rock outcrops and watercourses in e half of region.

**9  COMMON POISON-BUSH**  *Acokanthera oppositifolia*
2-7 m. Upright branches. Leaves 50-100 mm, thick, leathery, **side veins distinct**, margin rolled under, sharp tip. Flower tube 11 mm (Jun-Oct). Fruit red, ripening black, 20 mm. Riverine vegetation and rock outcrops in e half of region.
**Similar**
**DUNE POISON-BUSH  A. oblongifolia**
Side veins obscure. Along SE and E coast.
**ROUND-LEAVED POISON-BUSH  A. rotundata**
Leaves roundish, sandpapery. Fruit round. NE.

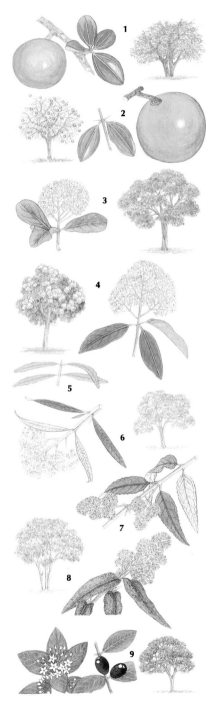

**1 FOREST NUM-NUM** *Carissa bispinosa*

1-4 m. **Spines forked or twice forked,** 45 mm. Milky sap. Leaves 10-70 mm, leathery. Flowers 10 mm, in **terminal clusters** (Aug-Jan). Fruit 16 mm. Dry woodland and forest understorey in e of region and n Namibia.
Similar

**2 BIG NUM-NUM** *C. macrocarpa*

Spines woody, 50 mm. Leaves 20-60 mm, bristle tip. Flowers 35 mm (throughout year). Fruit 50 mm. Dune forest along SE and E coast.

**CLIMBING NUM-NUM** *C. edulis*

**Spines simple, straight.** Fruit 11 mm, purplish-black. Woodland in N and NE.

**3 HORN-POD TREE** *Diplorhynchus condylocarpon*

4-10 m. Leaves 30-70 mm, drooping. Flowers white, 10 mm (Sept-Dec). Each fruit lobe 50 mm, splitting to release **winged seeds.** Woodland in N.

**4 TOAD TREE** *Tabernaemontana elegans*

3-10 m. **Bark corky,** deeply cracked. Milky sap. Leaves 90-200 mm. Stalk 25 mm. Flowers white, 15 mm, petals narrow (Nov-Mar). Each fruit lobe 70 mm, splitting on tree when ripe, seeds covered with orange pulp. Margins of riverine forest at low altitudes in NE.
Similar

**5 FOREST TOAD TREE** *T. ventricosa*

**Bark smoothish.** Flowers 25 mm, petals **broader.** Fruit **smooth.** Forest understorey in E and NE.

**6 QUININE TREE** *Rauvolfia caffra*

7-15 m. Bark thinly corky, yellowish-brown. Milky sap. Leaves in whorls, 120-280 mm, **translucent veins.** Flowers white, in terminal heads 200 mm diam (May-Oct). Fruit ripening wrinkled black, 15 mm. Forest, usually near water, in E and NE.

**7 ELEPHANT'S TRUNK** *Pachypodium namaquanum*

1,5-3 m. Succulent. Stem covered in spine-tipped protuberances. Head tilts towards N. Leaves 80-120 mm, grey-green, velvety, margin wavy. Rocky hillsides in Richtersveld and s Namibia.

**8 BOTTLE TREE** *Pachypodium lealii*

Up to 7 m. Bark smooth, greyish-green, branches reddish-brown. Spines 30 mm. Leaves clustered near tips of branchlets or singly on main stems, 25-80 mm, velvety, margin wavy. Flowers white, 60 mm diam (Jul-Aug). Rocky hillsides in n Namibia.

**9 SEPTEE TREE** *Cordia caffra*

2-12 m. Bark conspicuous, **smooth, mottled,** creamy brown to pink with large dry flaking pieces. Leaves drooping, 50-100 mm, thin, shiny. **Stalk slender,** 50 mm. Flowers cream, 10 mm, in terminal clusters (Sept-Oct). Fruit 12 mm, sharp tip. Coastal forest in SE, E and NE within South Africa.
Similar

**10 SNOTBERRY CORDIA** *C. monoica*

Leaves 50-80 mm, **sandpapery above** with softer hairs beneath. Fruit 20 mm. Riverine vegetation from n South Africa northwards.

**1  SANDPAPER BUSH**                    *Ehretia obtusifolia*

2-5 m. Arching branches. Bark smooth, light grey-brown. Leaves 40-110 mm, thick, **rough**, hairy, upper margin often widely serrated. Flowers 6 mm, in terminal clusters (Oct-Feb). Fruit 7 mm. Drainage lines and sand forest in NE.

**2  PUZZLE BUSH**                        *Ehretia rigida*

2-6 m. Multistemmed with tangled **branches arching downwards.** Bark smooth, pale grey. Leaves in clusters, on short side twigs, 13-50 mm. Flowers 7 mm, in terminal clusters (Jul-Nov). Fruit orange, ripening black, 7 mm. Forest margins and woodland throughout region.

**3  PIPE-STEM TREE**                     *Vitex rehmannii*

Up to 7 m. Bark light grey, cracked. Usually five leaflets, 50-110 mm, leathery, hairy beneath, **leaflet stalks short** or absent. Flowers 8 mm (Nov-Jan). Fruit black, pear-shaped, 6 mm, with **persistent, five-lobed papery calyx**. Woodland and rocky hillsides in NE within South Africa.

**4  TINDERWOOD**                    *Clerodendrum glabrum*

2-10 m. Bark pale, rough, lightly flaky. Branchlets with raised white dots. Leaves three-whorled or opposite pairs, 20-100 mm, sometimes velvety beneath, drooping, pungent smell when crushed. Flowers 10 mm, in heads 50 mm (Dec-Jun). Fruit whitish, 10 mm. Widespread in e half of region.
**Similar**
**5  BLUE-FLOWERED TINDERWOOD  C. myricoides**
Branchlets purplish-brown with raised white dots. Leaves 15-95 mm, soft, finely hairy. Flowers 20 mm diam (Oct-Jan). Fruit 2-4 lobes, 10 mm diam. Rocky hillsides and bush in E and NE.

**6  WHITE MANGROVE**                    *Avicennia marina*

3-11 m. Bark pale yellowish-green with raised dots, flaking. Breathing roots 90 mm, sticking up out of mud. Leaves 30-100 mm, thick, leathery, dense grey hairs beneath. Flowers cream, small (Oct-May). Fruit 25 mm. Estuaries and intertidal zone along SE and E coast.

**7  GINGER BUSH**                        *Tetradenia riparia*

Up to 3 m. Succulent. Bark grey, smooth. Leaves 70-90 mm, soft, finely hairy. Flowers white to mauve, in heads 200 mm (Jul-Sept). Forest margins and rocky hillsides in E and NE, also n Namibia.

**8  HONEY-THORN**                       *Lycium oxycarpum*

2-4 m. Bark pale brown, rough, peeling. Leaves on spiny side shoots, 13-50 mm, appear after rain. Flower tube 20 mm (Feb-May). Fruit 9 mm. Karoo.

**9  HEALING-LEAF TREE**                *Solanum giganteum*

2-5 m. Bark grey with short, **almost straight spines.** Young growth has thick white woolly hairs. Leaves 70-300 mm, dense wool beneath. Flowers 10 mm, in large terminal heads (Dec-Apr). Fruit 10 mm, in heads 200 mm. Forest margins and disturbed areas in N-central, s, se and e areas.
**Similar**
**10  GOAT-APPLE  S. aculeastrum**
Bark greyish-brown, with **curved spines** 20 mm. Leaves 45-140 mm, **deeply lobed, spines on midrib**. Flowers 25 mm (Sept-Nov). Fruit 50 mm. Woodland in SE, E and NE.
**11  BUG TREE  S. mauritianum**
No spines. Leaves 400 mm, **large lobes at base of stalk**. Fruit hairy, **yellow.** Introduced from Asia. Invader.

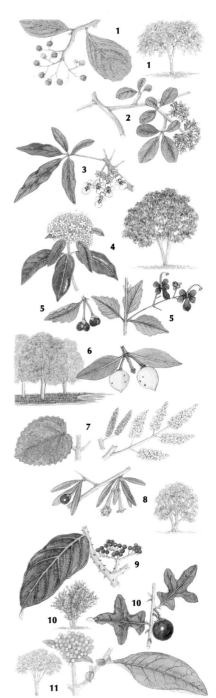

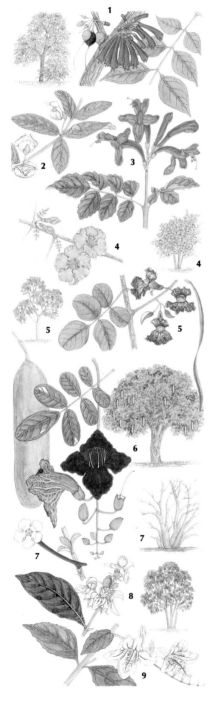

### 1  TREE FUCHSIA
*Halleria lucida*

2-12 m. Bark pale greyish-brown, fissured, flaky. Leaves 25-70 mm. Flower tube 40 mm, **on old wood** (Apr-Aug). Fruit 10 mm. Forest, rock outcrops and near watercourses in S, SE, E and NE.

### 2  NATAL SHELL-FLOWER BUSH
*Bowkeria verticillata*

3-5 m. Bark grey, branchlets reddish, twigs with raised white dots. Leaves three-whorled, 25-130 mm, corrugated above with **sunken veins**, velvety beneath. Flowers 20 mm, sticky calyx (Nov-Jan). Fruit trilobed capsule 16 mm. Forest margins, along streams and in mountains on escarpment in SE.

### 3  CAPE HONEYSUCKLE
*Tecomaria capensis*

Up to 4 m. Multistemmed. Bark brown with raised pale dots. Up to five pairs leaflets plus terminal one, 10-45 mm. Flowers 50 mm (Jun-Nov). Pod 130 mm, splitting to release winged seeds. Forest margins and thicket. Widespread in SE and E.

### 4  MOPANE POMEGRANATE
*Rhigozum zambesiacum*

Up to 4 m. Branches at right angles, **spine-tipped.** Leaves small, 2-4 pairs leaflets plus terminal one, 5 mm. Flowers 35 mm diam (Sept-Nov). Fruit pale brown, flat capsule 38 mm. Woodland, thicket and rocky hillsides in NE.

### 5  BELL BEAN TREE
*Markhamia zanzibarica*

Up to 8 m. Bark grey, flaky. 2-3 pairs leaflets plus terminal one, 25-140 mm. Flowers 50 mm, in branched sprays (Sept-Jan). Slender capsule 600 mm. Rocky hillsides and riverine vegetation in N and NE.

### 6  SAUSAGE TREE
*Kigelia africana*

6-15 m. 3-5 pairs leaflets plus terminal one, 100 mm, hard, rough. Flowers 150 mm, velvety inside, in hanging sprays 900 mm (Aug-Oct). Fruit 600 mm, up to 7 kg. Riverine vegetation on floodplains in NE.

### 7  TRANSVAAL SESAME BUSH
*Sesamothamnus lugardii*

Up to 5 m. Succulent. Bark peeling. Hard spines 15 mm. Leaves 45 mm, whitish hairs when young. Flower tube 150 mm, **short spur at base of tube** (Sept-Dec). Fruit flat, woody capsule 50 mm. Winged seeds. Hot dry areas in N.

### 8  PISTOL BUSH
*Duvernoia adhatodoides*

3-10 m. Leaves 150-230 mm. Flowers 25 mm, in sprays 80 mm (Feb-Aug). Fruit club-shaped capsule, 30 mm, splitting with explosive crack. Forest understorey and rock outcrops in E.

### 9  FOREST BELL BUSH
*Mackaya bella*

Up to 4 m. Multistemmed, slender. Leaves 140 mm. Flowers 60 mm, in terminal sprays 150 mm (Aug-Nov). Fruit club-shaped, bivalved capsule 35 mm. Forest understorey, streambanks and moist savanna in E and NE within South Africa.

**1 AFRICAN TEAK**                    *Breonadia salicina*

10-30 m. Bark rough, fissured. Leaves whorled, 120-300 mm, **leathery**, veins pale yellowish-green. Flower heads 40 mm diam on stalks 60 mm (Dec-Mar). Fruit tiny bilobed capsule, clustered in hard, round head. Riverine forest in NE.

**2 NARROW-LEAVED FALSE BRIDE'S BUSH**         *Tarenna supra-axillaris*

Up to 7 m. Much-branched with pale whitish-grey bark. Leaves 30-90 mm, leathery. Flowers 7 mm with protruding stamens, in clusters (Nov-Dec). Fruit 8 mm. Forest, near streams, rock outcrops and coastal dunes in NE.

**3 WILD POMEGRANATE**              *Burchellia bubalina*

3-6 m. Young twigs hairy. Leaves 50-180 mm, quilted above, sometimes hairy. Flower tube 25 mm, softly hairy, in terminal clusters (Sept-Dec). Fruit reddish-green, 15 mm. Forest and rocky hillsides in S, SE, E and NE within South Africa.

**4 THORNY BONE-APPPLE**            *Catunaregam spinosa*

3-7 m. Bark smooth, pale grey with white bands. Young stems with hard, sharp, woody spines 30 mm. Leaves clustered or opposite, 38 mm, shiny above, velvety beneath. Flowers white, aging yellow, 20 mm diam (Aug-Nov). Fruit greenish-brown, 25 mm. Woodland and forest margins in E and NE.

**5 THORNY GARDENIA**            *Hyperacanthus amoenus*

3-8 m. Branches in rigid pairs, at right angles. Twigs often reduced to spines. Leaves opposite or in clusters, 15-70 mm. Young leaves pinkish-red. Flowers **singly**, 50 mm diam (Nov-Mar). Fruit 20 mm. Forest in E and NE within South Africa.

**6 LOWVELD GARDENIA**              *Gardenia volkensii*

Up to 5 m. Bark pale grey, flaking. Branchlets rigid, three-whorled. Leaves three-whorled, 30-50 mm. Young leaves long, narrow, pointed. Flowers 100 mm diam, white aging yellow (Jul-Oct). Fruit 60 mm, with shallow ribbing. Woodland in N and NE.
**Similar**
**WHITE GARDENIA  G. thunbergia**
Flowers do not turn yellow. Fruit **without ribs**. Forest along SE and E coast.

**7 CAPE GARDENIA**              *Rothmannia capensis*

7-15 m. Erect branches, drooping leaves, "hessian"-textured bark. Leaves 75-100 mm, clustered towards ends of branches, leathery, shiny and warty above, small pockets in axils of veins beneath. Flowers bell-shaped, 70 mm diam (Dec-Feb). Fruit 70 mm. Forest, forest margins and rock outcrops in central, s, se and e areas.
**Similar**
**8 BELL GARDENIA/SEPTEMBER BELLS  R. globosa**
Leaves 40-100 mm, veins yellowish to reddish. Flowers bell-shaped, 35 mm diam. Fruit 25 mm, woody. Forest in E and NE within South Africa.

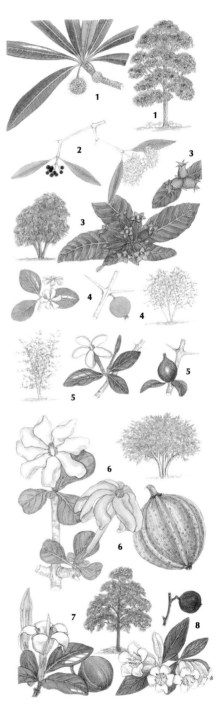

### 1 WILD LOQUAT — *Oxyanthus speciosus*
4-10 m. Main stem slender, with long horizontal branches. Bark smooth. Leaves 75-300 mm, tufts of hairs in axils of veins. Flowers 35 mm (Nov-Feb). Fruit 20-50 mm. Forest, near streams, in E and NE.

### 2 JACKAL-COFFEE — *Tricalysia lanceolata*
3-7 m. Main stem sometimes fluted. Bark yellowish, corky, flaking. Leaves 25-100 mm, thin, **shiny, many pairs veins**, margin wavy. Flowers 13 mm (Jul-Oct). Fruit 5 mm. Forest margins, rock outcrops and streambanks in SE, E and NE within South Africa.

### 3 NATAL FLAME BUSH — *Alberta magna*
5-10 m. Leaves 70-130 mm. Flowers 30 mm, in clusters (Feb-Jun). Fruit with papery wings, 20 mm. Forest margins and rock outcrops, usually near streams, in E.

### 4 WILD MEDLAR — *Vangueria infausta*
3-5 m. Bark smooth, pale grey. Twigs velvety, opposite. Leaves 50-240 mm, **thickly furry**, blade often with small galls on surface. Fruit shiny green to yellowish-brown, 35 mm diam. Woodland and rocky hillsides in e half of region and n Namibia.

### 5 COMMON TURKEY-BERRY — *Canthium inerme*
4-7 m. Bark pale grey becoming soft, flaking. Young stems branching at right angles. **Strong, straight spines**. Leaves 25-75 mm, pockets in axils of veins beneath, margin rolled under. Fruit 13 mm, bilobed, on long stalk. Forest along S and E coast and in NE.
**Similar**
### 6 ROCK ALDER *C. mundianum*
Main stem fluted, branches erect, spreading. Bark pale grey, smooth, with white and darker patches. Leaves 15-70 mm, hairs on veins, pockets of white hairs beneath. S, E and NE.
**HAIRY TURKEY-BERRY *C. ciliatum***
Slender spines. Small leaves, leaf margin **fringed with hairs**.
**CORKY TURKEY-BERRY *C. suberosum***
Bark **corky**. Leaves leathery, no pockets in axils.

### 7 TRANSVAAL QUAR — *Psydrax obovata*
7-12 m. Bark blackish, flaking in strips. Leaves 15-50 mm, pockets in axils of veins beneath. Flowers in dense clusters, **in profusion** (Nov-Jan). Fruit 6 mm. E and NE.

### 8 CLIMBING TURKEY-BERRY — *Keetia gueinzii*
Robust climber. Twigs hairy, no spines. Leaves 40-110 mm, hairs on veins, in pockets in axils of veins. **Neatly paired leaves appear compound**. Flowers in dense clusters (Sept-Nov). Fruit single or bilobed, 10 mm. Forest in E and NE.

### 9 GLAND-LEAF TREE/LEAF-NODULE TREE *Pavetta edentula*
Up to 5 m. Bark corky. Twigs opposite, thick, knobbly. Leaves 200 mm, at ends of branchlets, slightly fleshy, raised yellow midrib and side veins beneath, scattered dark dots. Flowers 20 mm, in dense large heads (Dec-Jan). Fruit 9 mm. Woodland, rocky hillsides and moist savanna in E and NE.
**Similar**
**COMMON BRIDE'S BUSH *P. gardeniifolia***
Twigs flattened. Leaves 25-60 mm, shiny, smooth, tapering abruptly to blunt tip. Woodland and rocky hillsides in central and ne areas.
### 10 WEEPING BRIDE'S BUSH *P. lanceolata*
Bark finely fissured. Leaves 85 mm, hairy pits in axils of veins beneath, **stalk short**. Forest margins in E and NE.

### 1  BLACK BIRD-BERRY          *Psychotria capensis*

3-8 m. Bark pale brown. Leaves 70-150 mm, **leathery**. Flower heads 80 mm (Aug-Jan). Fruit yellow, ripening red or black, 7 mm. Forest and forest margins, from coast to mistbelt in SE, E and NE.

### 2  LOWVELD BITTER-TEA          *Vernonia colorata*

Scrambler up to canopy. Young stems velvety. Leaves 150 mm, sparsely hairy above, thinly woolly beneath, margin finely serrated. Flowers lilac, in large branched terminal heads (Apr-Sept). Riverine thicket in NE.

### 3  COAST SILVER OAK          *Brachylaena discolor*

4-10 m. Bark pale brown, grooved. Twigs woolly white. Leaves 25-110 mm, white felted beneath. Flowers cream, thistle-like, in clusters (Jul-Sept). Coastal forest and thicket along E coast and NE within South Africa.
**Similar**
**NATAL SILVER OAK  *B. uniflora***
Main stem tall, bare. Flowers whitish, inconspicuous. Evergreen forest in E.

### 4  MOUNTAIN SILVER OAK  *B. rotundata*

Leaves densely hairy beneath. Flowers yellow, in dense terminal clusters 150 mm. Woodland and rocky hillsides in N-central area.

### 5  LOWVELD SILVER OAK  *B. huillensis*

Bark dark brown, rough, fissured. Leaves **broadest in middle**, 50-75 mm, white felted beneath, sharp hairlike tip. Woodland, rocky areas and arid savanna in NE.

### 6  WILD CAMPHOR BUSH          *Tarchonanthus camphoratus*

Up to 5 m. Bark deeply striated. Twigs pale cream. Leaves 13-150 mm, velvety beneath, margin entire or finely serrated. Flowers cream, in terminal sprays 90 mm (Mar-Nov). Seed covered in white woolly hairs. Widespread except central and w desert.

### 7  BROAD-LEAVED CAMPHOR BUSH *Tarchonanthus trilobus*

Up to 8 m. Main stem single, with dense crown. Bark grey-brown, rough, fissured, flaking. Leaves 75-200 mm, tips trilobed in S of range. Flowers creamy yellow (Sept-Feb). Rock outcrops, thicket and forest margins in E and NE.

### 8  WHITE BRISTLE BUSH          *Metalasia muricata*

Up to 4 m. Upward-growing branches. Bark whitish-grey. Leaves tiny, 10 mm. Flowers white, pink or purple, in terminal clusters 60 mm diam (throughout year). Coastal dunes, mountains and near streams in SW, SE and E-central areas.

### 9  BUSH-TICK BERRY          *Chrysanthemoides monilifera*

1-6 m. Leaves 15-75 mm, leathery or succulent. Young leaves with white cobwebby hairs. Flowers in profusion (throughout year). Fruit 6 mm, purple when ripe. Coastal dunes, mountains, fynbos and grassland in SW, S, E and NE.

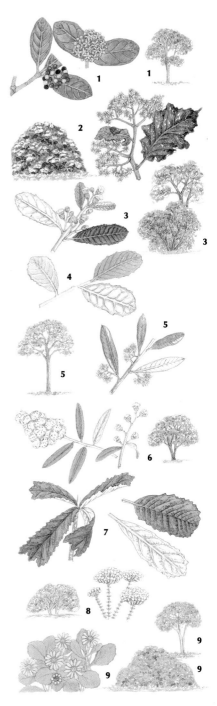

# GLOSSARY

**aggregation:** large collection

**annual:** with life cycle of one year

**apical:** terminal; at the end or top of a structure

**arboreal:** living in trees

**aril:** fleshy outer covering that encloses the seed or part of it and develops from the ovule stalk, often brightly coloured

**arthropods:** invertebrate animals with jointed legs

**asperities:** sharp or rough pimple-like elevations on the skin

**axil:** angle of contact between a leaf or branch and its main stem

**basal:** situated at the base

**bi-annual:** half-yearly

**bolas:** small rounded mass

**boss:** massive protuberance at the base of horns

**bract:** specialised leaf with flower growing in its axil

**buttress:** outgrowth at the base of the trunk of a tree to provide support

**calcareous:** containing calcium; chalky

**callosities:** hard, thick areas of skin

**calyx:** collective term for all sepals of a flower

**carapace:** hard shield covering all or part of the body

**carpel:** cell or chamber within the pistil or ovary of a flower, usually ovule-bearing

**caruncle:** fleshy protuberance

**casque:** helmet-like structure

**cephalothorax:** combined head and thorax

**cere:** soft waxy swelling, containing the nostrils, at the base of the upper mandible in certain birds

**cerci:** sensory appendages at tip of abdomen

**cilia:** hair-like structures

**coppice:** new growth from a stem

**corm:** underground stem base swollen with food deposits and capable of vegetative reproduction

**corolla:** collective term for all petals of flower

**corpulent:** bulky in body

**crenate:** leaves with edges notched with rounded, scalloped teeth

**crepuscular:** active at dawn and dusk

**cryptic:** camouflaged or blending with surroundings

**culmen:** upper ridge of a bird's bill

**deciduous:** shedding all leaves at the end of growing season

**decurved:** curving downwards

**detritus:** disintegrated material or debris

**dewlap:** fold of loose skin hanging from throat

**diurnal:** active during the day

**drupe:** fleshy fruit containing a stone or pip

**echolocation:** determination of the position of an object by measuring the time taken for an echo to return from it, and the direction of the echo

**endemic:** occurring only in a specified region

**epiphyte:** plant that grows on another plant but is not parasitic

**flaccid:** flabby

**fluted:** arranged in waves or grooves

**formic acid:** volatile irritant secreted by certain insects

**fynbos:** vegetation in which dominant plants are heaths, restios and proteas; found on coastal plains and mountains of the southern and south-western Cape

**galls:** rough swellings on plants usually caused by disease or insect damage

**gape:** interior of the mouth; alternatively the line along which the mandibles of a bird close

**gland dot:** translucent or coloured dot in a leaf, visible against the light

**glaucous:** covered with a powdery, usually whitish, bloom

**herb:** non-woody plant that dies or becomes dormant underground after the growing season

**herbaceous:** plants or plant parts that are fleshy rather than woody

**herbivorous:** feeding on plants

**hermaphrodite:** an organism with both male and female reproductive organs

**hybridise:** interbreeding between different species

**imago:** sexually mature stage in insect metamorphosis

**inflorescence:** part of a plant that consists of the flower-bearing stalks

**insectivorous:** feeding on insects

**keel:** narrow, hard ridge

**keeled:** ridged

**lamella:** spore-bearing gill of a mushroom

**lithophytic:** growing on stones or rock

**lobe:** curved or rounded projection or division forming part of a larger structure

**mandible:** either of a pair of mouthparts in insects or arthropods, used for biting and crushing food; alternatively the upper or lower part of a bird's bill

**margin:** edge or outline

**melanistic:** having dark or blackened pigmentation

**midrib:** main, central vein in a leaf

**montane:** mountainous

**morphology:** the form and structure of an animal or plant

**nagana:** sleeping sickness

**necrosis:** decaying of bone or tissue

**nocturnal:** active at night

**node:** point on stem from which leaves or lateral branch grows

**odiferous glands:** glands that secrete an odour

**oestrus:** regularly occurring period of sexual receptivity in female mammals

**omnivorous:** feeding on a wide variety of food including plants and animals

**ovipositor:** egg-laying appendage on female animal

**pedipalp:** either of a second pair of appendages on the cephalothorax of arachnids

**pelagic:** of the open seas

**peltate:** leaf with the stalk attached to its undersurface instead of its base or margin

**perennial:** plant with a life cycle longer than two years

**pheromone:** chemical substance, produced and released, influencing behaviour of other individuals of the same species

**pinna:** leaflet or primary division of a compound leaf or frond

**pinnate:** divided into leaflets

**pioneer plant:** species that is customarily one of the earliest to establish itself on bare or disturbed ground

**prehensile:** capable of grasping

**proboscis:** mouthpart modified to form tubular probe

**pronking:** bouncing vertically on all four feet — peculiar to springbok

**pseudaril:** false covering enclosing seed or fruit

**pseudobulb:** thickened stem or stem base in many of the orchid family

**raceme:** inflorescence in which flowers are borne along main stem, with oldest flowers at base; may be simple or compound

**rachis:** central axis or stem of inflorescence or compound leaf

**radula:** rasp-like tongue

**raptor:** bird of prey

**ray floret:** one of the strap-shaped flowers in the outer ring of a floral head that also bears disc flowers

**recurved:** curving upwards

**restio:** reed-like, wind-pollinated plant; male and female flowers on separate, often very different-looking plants

**rhizome:** horizontal underground stem thickened by deposits of reserve food and possessing buds or nodes for vegetative reproduction

**rootstock:** short underground stem, similar to rhizome but erect

**rosette:** rose-shaped patch of colour; alternatively a circular cluster of leaves growing from the base of a stem, usually at ground level

**rufous:** reddish-brown

**scute:** horny plate on shell of tortoise or enlarged scale on other reptile

**semi-parasite:** plant that contains chlorophyll and is partially self-sustaining, partially parasitic

**sepal:** one of the modified leaves comprising the calyx at the base of a flower — usually green, not coloured like the petals

**sori (singular sorus):** fertile body on underside of fern frond containing a cluster of spores

**sounder:** herd of pigs

**spadix:** floral spike, enclosed in spathe, with fleshy axis bearing many small flowers without stalks

**spathe:** large bract, often coloured, that encloses or supports the inflorescence of certain plants

**speculum:** patch of iridescent colour on the wing of some birds, mainly ducks

**spinneret:** appendage through which silk is extruded (e.g. on abdomen of spider)

**stabilimentum:** band of silk spun across middle of spider web

**stilt root:** root elevated to protrude above water level in swamps or estuaries

**stipel:** minute leaf at the base of the pinna of a compound leaf

**stippling:** dotted area

**stipule:** leaflike outgrowth at base of a leaf or its stalk; scar is left when it falls off

**strangler:** tree that supports its growth by engulfing the trunk of another, ultimately killing it

**striated:** grooved or striped

**stridulation:** sound produced by rubbing together certain appendages, e.g. wings, legs

**succulent:** plant with fleshy, juicy tissues containing water reserves

**sucker:** new shoot growing from the main stem or root of a plant

**tepals:** petals or sepals that are not clearly differentiated

**terminal:** at the tip or end

**termitaria:** termite nests

**trifoliate:** compound, with three leaflets

**truncate:** cut off at the tip

**tuber:** fleshy underground stem or root that stores food and is an organ of vegetative reproduction

**tubercle:** small, rounded nodule

**wattle:** fleshy appendage

# FURTHER READING

## Lower invertebrates

Carruthers, V.C. (ed.) 1982. *The Sandton Field Book: A Guide to the Natural History of the Northern Witwatersrand.* Rivonia: Sandton Nature Conservation Society.

Lawrence, R.F. 1984. *The Centipedes and Millipedes of Southern Africa: A Guide.* Cape Town: A.A. Balkema.

Potgieter, D.J., Du Plessis, P.C. and Skaife, S.H. 1971. *Animal Life in Southern Africa.* Cape Town: NASAU.

## Spiders and other arachnids

Filmer, M.R. 1991. *South African Spiders: An Identification Guide.* Cape Town: Struik.

Prinz, A. and Leroux, V. 1986. *South African Spiders and Scorpions: Identification, First Aid and Medical Treatment.* Cape Town: Anubis Press.

## Insects

Braack, L. 1991. *Leo Braack's Field Guide to Insects of the Kruger National Park. Cape Town:* Struik.

Dickson, C.G.C. and Kroon, D.M. (eds) 1978. *Pennington's Butterflies of Southern Africa.* Johannesburg: Ad. Donker.

Migdoll, I. 1987. *Ivor Migdoll's Field Guide to the Butterflies of Southern Africa.* Cape Town: Struik.

Pinhey, E.C.G. 1975. *Moths of Southern Africa.* Cape Town: Tafelberg.

Scholtz, C.H. and Holm, E. (eds) 1985. *Insects of Southern Africa.* Durban: Butterworths.

Skaife, S.H. in Ledger, J. (ed.) 1979. *African Insect Life.* Revised edition. Cape Town: Struik.

Williams, M. 1994. *Butterflies of Southern Africa: A Field Guide.* Halfway House: Southern Book Publishers.

## Freshwater fishes

Jubb, R.A. 1967. *Freshwater Fishes of Southern Africa.* Cape Town: A.A. Balkema.

Pienaar, U. de V. 1978. *The Freshwater Fishes of the Kruger National Park.* Pretoria: National Parks Board.

Skelton, P.H. 1993. *A Complete Guide to the Freshwater Fishes of Southern Africa.* Halfway House: Southern Book Publishers.

## Frogs

Carruthers, V.C. 1976. *A Guide to the Identification of the Frogs of the Witwatersrand.* Johannesburg: Conservation Press.

Du Preez, L. 1996. *Field Guide and Key to the Frogs and Toads of the Free State.* Bloemfontein: University of the Orange Free State.

Passmore, N.I. and Carruthers, V.C. 1995. *South African Frogs: A Complete Guide.* Revised edition. Halfway House: Southern Book Publishers and Witwatersrand University Press.

Pienaar, U. de V., Passmore, N.I. and Carruthers, V.C. 1976. *The Frogs of the Kruger National Park.* Pretoria: National Parks Board.

Poynton, J.C. 1964. The Amphibia of Southern Africa: A Faunal Study. *Annals of the Natal Museum.* No. 17, pp. 1-334.

Poynton, J.C. and Broadley, D.G. 1985, 1987, 1988, 1991. Amphibia Zambesiaca, 1-5. 2 Ranidae. *Annals of the Natal Museum,* 26(2), 27(1), 28(1), 29(2), 32.

## Reptiles

Boycott, R.C. and Bourquin, O. 1988. *The South African Tortoise Book: A Guide to South African Tortoises, Terrapins and Turtles.* Johannesburg: Southern Book Publishers.

Branch, B. 1988. *Bill Branch's Field Guide to the Snakes and Other Reptiles of Southern Africa.* Cape Town: Struik.

Broadley, D.G. 1962. *FitzSimons' Snakes of Southern Africa.* Johannesburg: Delta Books.

Marais, J. 1992. *A Complete Guide to the Snakes of Southern Africa.* Halfway House: Southern Book Publishers.

Pienaar, U. de V., Haacke, W.D. and Jacobsen, N.H.G. 1978. *The Reptiles of the Kruger National Park.* Pretoria: National Parks Board.

## Birds

Frandsen, J. 1982. *Birds of the South-Western Cape.* Sandton: Sable Publishers.

Ginn, P.J., McIlleron, W.G. and Milstein, P. le S. 1989. *The Complete Book of Southern African Birds.* Cape Town: Struik.

Harris, T. 1988. *Shrikes of Southern Africa.* Cape Town: Struik.

Kemp, A. 1987. *The Owls of Southern Africa.* Cape Town: Struik.

Maclean, G.L. 1993. *Roberts' Birds of Southern Africa.* 6th edition. Cape Town: John Voelcker Bird Book Fund.

Mundy, P. *et al.* 1992. *The Vultures of Africa.* Randburg: Acorn Books.

Newman, K. 1996. *Newman's Birds of Southern Africa.* Green edition. Halfway House: Southern Book Publishers.

Rowan, M.K. 1983. *The Doves, Parrots, Louries and Cuckoos of Southern Africa.* Cape Town: David Philip.

Sinclair, I., Hockey, P. and Tarboton, W. 1993. *Sasol Birds of Southern Africa.* Cape Town: Struik.

Steyn, P. 1982. *Birds of Prey of Southern Africa: Their Identification and Life Histories.* Cape Town: David Philip.

Steyn, P. 1984. *A Delight of Owls: African Owls Observed.* Cape Town: David Philip.

Trendler, R. 1994. *Attracting Birds to your Garden.* Cape Town: Struik.

## Mammals

Apps, P. 1992. *Wild Ways: Field Guide to the Behaviour of Southern African Mammals.* Halfway House: Southern Book Publishers.

Apps, P. (ed.) 1996. *Smithers' Mammals of Southern Africa: A Field Guide.* Halfway House: Southern Book Publishers.

Bonner, W.N. 1980. *Whales.* Dorset: Blandford Press.

De Graaff, G. 1981. *The Rodents of Southern Africa.* Durban: Butterworths.

Estes, R.D. 1993. *The Safari Companion: A Guide to Watching African Mammals.* Halfway House: Russel Friedman Books.

Liebenberg, L. 1990. *A Field Guide to the Animal Tracks of Southern Africa.* Cape Town: David Philip.

Pienaar, U. de V., Rautenbach, I.L. and De Graaff, G. 1980. *The Small Mammals of the Kruger National Park.* Pretoria: National Parks Board.

Rautenbach, I.L. 1982. *Mammals of the Transvaal.* Pretoria: Ecoplan.

Skinner, J.D. and Smithers, R.H.N. 1990. *The Mammals of the Southern African Subregion.* Pretoria: University of Pretoria.

Smuts, G.L. 1982. *Lion.* Johannesburg: Macmillan.

Stuart, C. and T. 1988. *Field Guide to the Mammals of Southern Africa.* Cape Town: Struik.

Stuart, C. and T. 1994. *A Field Guide to the Tracks and Signs of Southern and East African Wildlife.* Halfway House: Southern Book Publishers.

Van Dyk, A. 1991. *The Cheetahs of De Wildt.* Cape Town: Struik.

## Grasses and sedges

Gibbs Russell, G.E. *et al.* 1990. *Grasses of Southern Africa: Memoirs of the Botanical Survey of South Africa.* No. 58. Pretoria: Botanical Research Institute.

Gordon-Gray, K.D. 1995. Cyperaceae in Natal. *Strelitzia 2.* Pretoria: National Botanical Institute.

Lowrey, T.K. and Wright, S. (eds) 1987. *The Flora of the Witwatersrand: 1 The Monocotyledons.* Johannesburg: Witwatersrand University Press.

Meredith, D. (ed.) 1955. *The Grasses and Pastures of South Africa.* Cape Town: Central News Agency.

Muller, M.A.N. 1984. *Grasses of South-west Africa/Namibia.* Windhoek: Department of Agriculture and Nature Conservation.

Roberts, B.R. and Fourie, J.H. 1975. *Common Grasses of the Northern Cape.* Vryburg: Northern Cape Livestock Co-operative.

Tainton, N.M., Bransby, D.I. and Booysen, P. de V. 1976. *Common Veld and Pasture Grasses of Natal.* Pietermaritzburg: Shuter & Shooter.

Van Oudtshoorn, F. 1992. *Guide to the Grasses of South Africa.* Arcadia: Briza Publications.

## Ferns

Burrows, J.E. 1990. *Southern African Ferns and Fern Allies.* Sandton: Frandsen Publishers.

Crouch, N. and Clark, T. 1994. *The Ferns of Ferncliffe: A Rambler's Guide.* Howick: Share-net, Wildlife Society of South Africa.

Hancock, F.D. and Lucas, A. 1973. *Ferns of the Witwatersrand.* Johannesburg: Witwatersrand University Press.

Jacobsen, W.B.G. 1983. *The Ferns and Fern Allies of Southern Africa.* Durban: Butterworths.

Roux, J.P. 1979. *Cape Peninsula Ferns.* Cape Town: National Botanic Gardens of South Africa.

## Fungi

Levin, H. *et al.* 1987. *A Field Guide to the Mushrooms of South Africa.* Cape Town: Struik.

Stephens, E.L. and Kidd, M.M. 1968. *Some South African Edible Fungi.* Cape Town: Longman.

Stephens, E.L. and Kidd, M.M. 1970. *Some South African Poisonous and Inedible Fungi.* Cape Town: Longman.

Van der Westhuizen, G.C.A. and Eicker, A. 1994. *Field Guide: Mushrooms of Southern Africa.* Cape Town: Struik.

## Wild flowers

Batten, A. and Bokkelmann, H. 1966. *Wild Flowers of the Eastern Cape Province*. Cape Town: Books of Africa.

Burman, L. and Bean, A. 1985. *Hottentots Holland to Hermanus: South African Wildflower Guide 5.* Cape Town: Botanical Society of South Africa.

Craven, P. and Marais, C. 1989. *Waterberg Flora: Footpaths In and Around the Camp.* Windhoek: Gamsberg.

Craven, P. and Marais, C. 1986. *Namib Flora: Swakopmund to the Giant Welwitschia via Goanikontes.* Windhoek: Gamsberg.

Eliovson, S. 1980. *Wild Flowers of Southern Africa.* Johannesburg: Macmillan.

Fabian, A. and Germishuizen, G. 1982. *Transvaal Wild Flowers.* Johannesburg: Macmillan.

Gledhill, E. 1981. *Eastern Cape Veld Flowers.* Cape Town: Department of Nature and Environmental Conservation of the Cape Provincial Administration.

Hobson, N.K. 1970. *Karoo Plant Wealth.* Pearston: Pearston Publications.

Joffe, P. 1993. *The Gardener's Guide to South African Plants.* Cape Town: Delos.

Kidd, M.M. 1983. *Cape Peninsula: South African Wildflower Guide 3.* Cape Town: Botanical Society of South Africa.

Killick, D. 1990. *Field Guide to the Flora of the Natal Drakensberg.* Johannesburg: Jonathan Ball and Ad. Donker.

Le Roux, A. and Schelpe, T. 1988. *Namaqualand: South African Wildflower Guide 1.* Revised edition. Cape Town: Botanical Society of South Africa.

Letty, C. 1962. *Wild Flowers of the Transvaal.* Johannesburg: Wild Flowers of the Transvaal Book Fund.

Mason, H. 1972. *Western Cape Sandveld Flowers.* Cape Town: Struik.

Moriarty, A. 1982. *Outeniqua, Tsitsikamma and Eastern Little Karoo: South African Wildflower Guide 2.* Cape Town: Botanical Society of South Africa.

Onderstall, J. 1996. *Sappi Wild Flower Guide: Mpumalanga and Northern Province.* Nelspruit: Dynamic Ad.

Onderstall, J. 1984. *Transvaal Lowveld and Escarpment Including Kruger National Park: South African Wildflower Guide 4.* Cape Town: Botanical Society of South Africa.

Plowes, D.C.H. and Drummond, R.B. 1976. *Wild Flowers of Rhodesia.* Rhodesia: Longman.

Reynolds, G.W. 1969. *The Aloes of South Africa.* Cape Town: A.A. Balkema.

Rourke, J.P. 1980. *The Proteas of Southern Africa.* Cape Town: Purnell & Sons.

Sheering, D. 1994. *Karoo: South African Wildflower Guide 6.* Cape Town: Botanical Society of South Africa.

Stewart, J., Linder, H.P., Schelpe, E.A. and Hall, A.V. 1982. *Wild Orchids of Southern Africa.* Johannesburg: Macmillan.

Trauseld, W.R. 1969. *Wild Flowers of the Natal Drakensberg.* Cape Town: Purnell.

Van Wyk, B. and Malan, S. 1988. *Field Guide to the Wild Flowers of the Witwatersrand and Pretoria Region.* Cape Town: Struik.

Van Wyk, B. and Smith, G. 1996. *Guide to the Aloes of South Africa.* Arcadia: Briza Publications.

Vogts, M. 1982. *South Africa's Proteaceae: Know them and Grow them.* Cape Town: Struik.

## Trees

Berry, C. n.d. *Trees and Shrubs of the Etosha National Park.* Windhoek: Multi Services.

Davidson, L. 1981. *Acacias: A Field Guide to the Acacias of Southern Africa.* Johannesburg: Centaur.

Giddy, C. 1984. *Cycads of South Africa.* 2nd edition. Cape Town: Struik.

Johnson, D. and S. 1993. *Gardening with Indigenous Trees and Shrubs.* Halfway House: Southern Book Publishers.

Palgrave, K.C. 1996. *Trees of Southern Africa.* 2nd revised edition. Cape Town: Struik.

Palmer, E. and Pitman, N. 1972. *Trees of Southern Africa.* 3 vols. Cape Town: A.A. Balkema.

Pooley, E. 1993. *The Complete Field Guide to Trees of Natal, Zululand and Transkei.* Durban: Natal Flora Publications Trust.

Van Wyk, P. 1984. *Piet van Wyk's Field Guide to the Trees of the Kruger National Park.* Cape Town: Struik.

Von Breitenbach, F. 1974. *Southern Cape Forests and Trees.* Pretoria: Department of Forestry.

Von Breitenbach, F. 1990. *National List of Indigenous Trees.* 2nd edition. Pretoria: Dendrological Foundation.

# INDEX

## LOWER INVERTEBRATES

## SPIDERS AND OTHER ARACHNIDS

## INSECTS

## FRESHWATER FISHES

## FROGS

## REPTILES

# BIRDS

## MAMMALS

## GRASSES, SEDGES, FERNS AND FUNGI

## WILD FLOWERS

### TREES